Faith, Tradition, and History

Faith, Tradition, and History

Old Testament Historiography
in
Its Near Eastern Context

edited by

A. R. Millard
James K. Hoffmeier
David W. Baker

EISENBRAUNS

Winona Lake, Indiana
1994

Library of Congress Cataloging in Publication Data

Faith, tradition, and history : Old Testament historiography in its Near Eastern
context / edited by A. R. Millard, James Hoffmeier, David W. Baker.
   p.   cm.
   Includes bibliographical references and index.
   ISBN 0-931464-82-X
   1. Bible. O.T.—Historiography—Congresses. 2. Middle Eastern
literature—Relation to the Old Testament—Congresses. 3. Middle East—
History—To 622—Historiography—Congresses. I. Millard, A. R. (Alan
Ralph) II. Hoffmeier, James Karl, 1951– .   III. Baker, David W. (David
Weston), 1950– .
BS1197.F34   1994
221.6′7—dc20   94-2529
                                          CIP

Contents

Preface

The commands "Keep this festival," for the Israelites at Passover and for Jesus' disciples at the Lord's Supper, mark Judaism and Christianity as historical religions. They proclaim the God who has revealed himself both through the thoughts of his messengers and through events and their consequences. His acts demonstrate his nature to those who believe and may guide others to belief.

The purpose of the papers collected here is to explore some of the ways the ancient Israelite writers and their contemporaries presented history and how their work should be understood today. Studies made over the past 200 years have treated the Bible largely in isolation or have used sociological or anthropological "models" that have little relevance to the ancient Near East. Now the wealth of documents available from the ancient world makes it possible to assess the biblical texts in comparison with other writings of their time to see what is similar and what is different. Among other things, this should provide some criteria for checking the appropriateness of current attitudes to the Hebrew books. Their contents, their form, and their style are, therefore, among the matters considered. Recent publications display a growing tendency to treat the Hebrew narratives as products of their authors' beliefs, molded by their theology, and in some sense created to suit it, rather than arising from actual events. The contributors to this volume favor a more positive view of the texts and their concerns and accordingly offer criticisms of such positions, while presenting positive approaches, drawing on both biblical and extrabiblical sources. The subject is a large one, and there is room (as well as need) for much more research and discussion about this aspect of Hebrew Scripture.

These papers were prepared for a symposium held at Wheaton College in November 1990, under the auspices of the McManis Lectureship, organized by James Hoffmeier in connection with the annual archeology conference. Our appreciation is extended to Dr. Ward Kriegbaum, Vice President for Academic Affairs, and Dr. Patricia Ward, Dean of Arts and Sciences, who administer the McManis Fund. A special thanks is due to the faculty of the Archaeology and Biblical Studies

Department for their assistance and advice in the planning and execution of the lectureship and symposium.

Alan Millard presented two keynote lectures, which are combined as a single article here, while Robert Gordon's two presentations, owing to the difference in topic, remain as separate articles.

It is our hope that the essays in this volume will make a positive contribution to the ongoing discussions on Old Testament historiography.

A. R. Millard
J. K. Hoffmeier
D. W. Baker

June, 1992

Abbreviations

Classical

Ag. Ap.	Josephus, *Against Apion*
Ant.	Josephus, *Jewish Antiquities*

General

Akk	Akkadian
AKL	Assyrian King List
BM	British Museum
DH	Deuternomistic History (Historian)
GHD	Genealogy of the Hammurapi Dynasty
HDR	History of David's Rise
Heb.	Hebrew
IM	Iraq Museum (Bagdad)
LKL	Larsa King List
NAKL	Neo-Assyrian King List
KHKL	Khorsobad King List
LXX	Septuagint
MT	Masoretic Text
NASB	New American Standard Bible
NEB	New English Bible
NIV	New International Version
NJPS	The New Jewish Publication Society Translation
NRSV	New Revised Standard Version
Pap.	Papyrus
RS	Ras Shamra texts
RSV	Revised Standard Version
Sir	Ben Sira, Sirach = Ecclesiasticus
SKL	Sumerian King List
SN	Succession narrative

Reference Works

AA	*American Anthropologist*
AAA	*University of Liverpool Annals of Archaeology and Anthropology*
AASOR	Annual of the American Schools of Oriental Research
AB	Anchor Bible
ADD	C. H. W. Johns, *Assyrian Deeds and Documents of the Seventh Century*
Aes	*Archives européens de sociologie*
AfO	*Archiv für Orientforschung*
AfO Beiheft	Archiv für Orientforschung Beiheft
Africa	*Africa: Journal of the International African Institute*
AHw	W. von Soden, *Akkadisches Handwörterbuch*
AJA	*American Journal of Archaeology*
AJSL	*American Journal of Semitic Languages and Literatures*
AKA	L. W. King, *Annals of the Kings of Assyria* (London: Harrison, 1902)
ANEP	J. B. Pritchard (ed.), *The Ancient Near East in Pictures Relating to the Old Testament*
ANESTP	J. B. Pritchard (ed.), *Ancient Near Eastern Supplementary Texts and Pictures*
ANET	J. B. Pritchard (ed.), *Ancient Near Eastern Texts Relating to the Old Testament* (3d ed.)
ANETS	Ancient Near Eastern Texts and Studies
AnOr	Analecta orientalia
AnSn	D. D. Luckenbill, *The Annals of Sennacherib* (Chicago: University of Chicago Press, 1924)
AOAT	Alter Orient und Altes Testament
AOSTS	American Oriental Society Translation Series
AR	D. D. Luckenbill, *Ancient Records of Assyria and Babylon*
ARI	A. K. Grayson, *Assyrian Royal Inscriptions*, 2 vols. (Wiesbaden: Harrassowitz, 1972).
ARM	Archives royales de Mari
ARTSM	A. K. Grayson, *Assyrian Rulers of the Third and Second Millennia to 1115 B.C.* (Toronto: University of Toronto Press, 1987)
AS	Assyriological Studies
ASOR	American Schools of Oriental Research
AsBi	*Assyriologische Bibliothek*
ATANT	Arbeiten zur Text und Sprache in Alten Testament
AUSS	*Andrews University Seminary Studies*
BA	*Biblical Archaeologist*
BaM	*Baghdader Mitteilungen*

BAR	*Biblical Archaeology Review*
BASOR	*Bulletin of the American Schools of Oriental Research*
BETL	Bibliotheca ephemeridum theologicarum lovaniensium
Bib	*Biblica*
BibOr	Biblica et Orientalia
BJRL	*Bulletin of the John Rylands Library*
BiOr	*Bibliotheca Orientalis*
BSac	*Bibliotheca Sacra*
BSO(A)S	*Bulletin of the School of Oriental (and African) Studies*
BTB	*Biblical Theology Bulletin*
BWANT	Beiträge zur Wissenschaft vom Alten und Neuen Testament
BZ	*Biblische Zeitschrift*
BZAW	Beiheften zur ZAW
CAD	*The Assyrian Dictionary of the Oriental Institute of the University of Chicago*
CAH	*Cambridge Ancient History*
CBC	Cambrdige Bible Commentary
CBQ	*Catholic Biblical Quarterly*
CH	Codex Hammurapi
ConBOT	Conciectanea Biblica, Old Testament
CT	Cuneiform Texts from the British Museum
CTA	A. Herdner, *Corpus des tablettes en cunéiformes alphbétiques*
CTH	*Catalogue des textes hittites*
CTM	*Concordia Theological Monthly*
CurTM	*Currents in Theology and Mission*
DJD	Discoveries in the Judaean Desert
EI	*Eretz Israel*
FAOS	Freiburger altorientalische Studien
FT	*Faith and Thought*
GAG	W. von Soden, *Grundriss der akkadischen Grammatik*
GKC	*Gesenius' Hebrew Grammar*, ed. E. Kautzsch, tr. A. E. Cowley
GTA	Göttinger theologische Arbeiten
HAT	Handbuch zum Alten Testament
HBT	*Horizons in Biblical Theology*
HCS	François Thureau-Dangin, *Une Relation de la huitième campagne de Sargon* (Paris: Geuthner, 1912)
HPIA	A. C. Piepkorn, *Historical Prism Inscriptions of Ashurbanipal* (Chicago: University of Chicago Press, 1933)
HSM	Harvard Semitic Monographs
HSS	Harvard Semitic Studies

HTR	*Harvard Theological Review*
HUCA	*Hebrew Union College Annual*
ICC	International Critical Commentary
IDB	G. A. Buttrick, ed., *Interpreters Dictionary of the Bible*
IDBSup	Supplement volume to *IDB*
IEJ	*Israel Exploration Journal*
Int	*Interpretation*
ISBE	G. W. Bromiley, ed., *International Standard Bible Encyclopedia*
ITC	International Theological Commentary
JAAR	*Journal of the American Academy of Religion*
JANES(CU)	*Journal of the Ancient Near Eastern Society (of Columbia University)*
JAOS	*Journal of the American Oriental Society*
JARCE	*Journal of the American Research Center in Egypt*
JASA	*Jounral of the American Scientific Affiliation*
JBL	*Journal of Biblical Literature*
JBTh	*Jahrbuch für Biblische Theologie*
JCS	*Journal of Cuneiform Studies*
JEA	*Journal of Egyptian Archaeology*
JETS	*Journal of the Evangelical Theological Society*
JNES	*Journal of Near Eastern Studies*
JNSL	*Journal of Northwest Semitic Languages*
JPOS	*Journal of the Palestine Oriental Society*
JR	*Journal of Religion*
JSNT	*Journal for the Study of the New Testament*
JSOT	*Journal for the Study of the Old Testament*
JSOTSup	Journal for the Study of the Old Testament Supplement Series
JSSEA	*Journal of the Society for the Study of Egyptian Antiquities*
JTS	*Journal of Theological Studies*
KAT	Kommentar zum Alten Testament
KAT	E. Schrader, ed., *Die Keilinschriften und das Alte Testament* (3d ed., 1903)
KBo 10–11	H. G. Güterbock and H. Otten, *Keilschrifttexte aus Boghazköi*, vols. 10–11: *Texte aus Gebäude K*, parts 1–2 (WVDOG 72–73; Berlin: Mann, 1960–61).
KTU	M. Dietrich, O. Loretz, and J. Sanmartín, *Die keilalphabetischen Texte aus Ugarit* (AOAT 24/1; Neukirchen-Vluyn: Neukirchener Verlag, 1976)
LAPO	Littératures anciennes du Proche-Orient
LCL	Loeb Classical Library

MAD	*Materials for the Assyrian Dictionary*
MC	Mesopotamian Civilizations
MDAIK	*Mitteilungen der deutschen archäologischen Instituts, Abteilungen Kairo*
MDOG	*Mitteilungen der deutschen Orient-Gesellschaft*
MKAW	*Mededelingen der Köninklijke Nederlandse Akademie van Wetenschappen*
MRS	Mission de Ras Shamra
MVAG	Mitteilungen der Vorderasiatisch-ägyptischen Gesellschaft
NICOT	New Internation Commentary on the Old Testament
NTS	*New Testament Studies*
OBO	Orbis biblicus et orientalis
OIP	Oriental Institute Publications
OLZ	*Orientalische Literaturzeitung (Berlin/Leipzig)*
Or	*Orientalia*
OrAnt	*Oriens antiquus*
OTL	Old Testament Library
OTWSA	*Ou Testamentiese Werkgemeenskap in Suider Afrika*
PAPS	*Proceedings of the American Philosophical Society*
PEA	J. C.Thompson, *The Prisms of Esarhaddon and Ashurbanipal* (London: Oxford University Press, 1931)
PEQ	*Palestine Exploration Quarterly*
PJ	*Palästina-Jahrbuch*
PRU	*Le Palais royale d'Ugarit*
RA	*Revue d'assyriologie et d'archéologie orientale*
RAI	Rencontre assyriologique internationale
RHR	*Revue de l'histoire des religions*
RlA	*Reallexikon der Assyriologie und vorderasiatischen Archäologie*
RMA	*Reports from the Magicians and Astrologers of Nineveh and Babylon*
Rost	P. Rost, *Die Keilschrifttexte Tiglat-Pilesers III* (Leipzig: Pfeiffer, 1893)
RSO	*Rivista degli studi orientali*
SAAB	*State Archives of Assyria Bulletin*
SANE	*Sources from the Ancient Near East*
SBL	Society of Biblical Literature
SBLDS	SBL Dissertation Series
SBTS	Sources for Biblical and Theological Study
ScrHier	Scripta hierosolymitana
Sem	*Semitica*
SJOT	*Scandanavian Journal of Old Testament*
SR	*Studies in Religion*

SS   *Studi Semitici*
SSEA Newsletter   *Society for the Study of Egyptian Antiquities Newsletter*
StBoT   Studien zu den Bogazköy-Texten
TAVO   Tübinger Atlas des vorderen Orients
TCS   Texts from Cuneiform Sources
TDOT   G. J. Botterweck and H. Ringgren, eds., *Theological*
                   Dictionary of the Old Testament
THAT   *Theologische Handwörterbuch zum Alten Testament*
                   (ed. E. Jenni and C. Westermann)
THeth   Texte der Hethiter
TOTC   Tyndale Old Testament Commentary
TLZ   *Theologische Literaturzeitung*
TynBul   *Tyndale Bulletin*
TZ   *Theologische Zeitschrift*
UF   *Ugarit-Forschungen*
Ug   *Ugaritica*
Urk IV.   K. Sethe, *Urkunden der 18. Dynastie*, pp. 1-1226.
                   W. Helck, *Urkunden der 18. Dynastie*, pp. 1227-1954.
USQR   *Union Seminary Quarterly Review*
UVB   Vorläufige Berichte . . . in Uruk/Warka unternommenen
                   Ausgrabungen
VAT   Vorderasiatische Abteilung Thontafeln
VO   *Vicino Oriente*
VT   *Vetus Testamentum*
VTSup   Vetus Testamentum Supplements
WBC   Word Biblical Commentary
WO   *Die Welt des Orients*
WTJ   *Westminster Theological Journal*
WVDOG   Wissenschaftliche Veröffentlichungen der deutschen
                   Orientgesellschaft
YNER   *Yale Near Eastern Researches*
YOS   *Yale Oriental Series*
ZA   *Zeitschrift für Assyriologie*
ZAW   *Zeitschrift für die Alttestamentliche Wissenschaft*
ZDMG   *Zeitschrift der deutschen morgenländischen Gesellschaft*
ZDPV   *Zeitschrift des deutschen Palästina-Vereins*
ZTK   *Zeitschrift für Theologie und Kirche*

The Current State of Old Testament Historiography

Edwin Yamauchi

Miami University
Oxford, Ohio

THE NATURE OF HISTORY

History is the study of what people have done and said and thought in the past. Historians attempt to reconstruct in a significant narrative the important events of the human past through a study of the relevant data. History involves primarily the interpretation of textual accounts supplemented by contemporary inscriptions and other materials recovered by archaeology.

While it may seem to most of us obvious that the textual accounts are primary, this is not the view of all. Fuelled by feminist concerns and interests in the underclass, some in the historical profession have looked askance at such reliance on accounts that admittedly came from the educated, upper-class, male scribes. This concern has spilled over into some critiques of biblical history. Keith Whitelam, for example, decries reliance upon texts, which he believes are not witnesses to historical reality but only to particular perceptions of reality. He avers:

> The standard treatments of the history of Israel, constrained as they are by the biblical texts, are set in the mould of political histories concerned with the unique event and unique individual. . . . However, the continued conviction that the biblical text remains the primary source for all periods of the history of Israel means that many historians perpetuate this unnecessary restriction in their consideration of other forms of potential evidence.[1]

1. Keith W. Whitelam, "Recreating the History of Israel," *JSOT* 35 (1986) 55.

1

Dorothy Irvin makes the astonishing declaration:

> Of these [David] narratives as well as all the narratives of the Pentateuch,
> the historical problem is not so much that they are historically unverifi-
> able, and especially not that they are untrue historically, but that they are
> radically irrelevant as sources of Israel's early history.[2]

History revolves around two poles, the past and the writer's present.
Earlier historians often were not self-conscious of the latter. According
to John Dewey, "All history is necessarily written from the standpoint
of the present, and is, in an inescapable sense, the history not only of the
present but of that which is contemporaneously judged to be important
in the present."[3] Unfortunately some scholars overemphasize the writer's
circumstances so as almost to eliminate the possibility of any meaningful
recovery of the past.

The definition that John Van Seters has utilized in his work on biblical historiography is J. Huizinga's statement, "History is the intellectual
form in which a civilization renders account to itself of its past."[4] Van
Seters, who uses this definition in a rather arbitrary and narrow way to
designate national history, does not believe that real historiography developed until the so-called Deuteronomist in the sixth century B.C. He
holds that history must be nonpragmatic and nondidactic, and therefore
eliminates much that others would recognize as historical.[5]

William Hallo, on the other hand, maintains that "history begins
where writing begins."[6] The earliest writing invented was the cuneiform script used by the Sumerians in southern Mesopotamia in the third
millennium B.C. Hallo's numerous studies have shown that men have
been interested in recording the past from the very beginning of literate
societies. "Together, they [letters] constitute impressive evidence that,
already in Sumerian-speaking times, the great political, military and cultic events of the court were chronicled as they happened."[7]

2. Dorothy Irvin, "The Joseph and Moses Narratives," in *Israelite and Judaean History*
(ed. John H. Hayes and J. Maxwell Miller; Philadelphia: Westminster, 1977) 212.

3. Cited by Jack Sasson, "On Choosing Models for Recreating Israelite Pre-Monarchic
History," *JSOT* 21 (1981) 8.

4. J. Van Seters, *In Search of History* (New Haven: Yale University Press, 1983) 1.

5. See the reviews of J. Van Seters, *In Search of History*, by Lawson Younger in *JSOT*
40 (1988) 111; by Josef Scharbert in *Biblische Zeitschrift* 30 (1986) 123: "Fragen wird
man müssen, ob nicht seine Definition von Geschichtsschreibung zu eng ist"; and by
Siegfried Herrmann in *TZ* 113 (1988) 180: "Ob diese Definition von 'Geschichtsschreibung' zutreffend ist, sei dahingestellt."

6. W. W. Hallo, "Biblical History in Its Near Eastern Setting: The Contextual Approach," in *Scripture in Context* (ed. C. D. Evans, W. W. Hallo, and J. B. White; Pittsburgh: Pickwick, 1980) 10.

7. W. W. Hallo, "Sumerian Historiography," in *History, Historiography and Interpretation*, (ed. H. Tadmor and M. Weinfeld; Jerusalem: Magnes, 1984) 20.

Kirk Grayson, in his survey of later Mesopotamian texts, points out that "the Assyrians and Babylonians were abundantly interested in the past and the reasons for this interest, which largely go back to Sumerian times, were multiple."[8] By the middle Assyrian period (twelfth–tenth centuries B.C.) Assyrian royal scribes were using chronicles and other sources in composing their texts. While not as extensive as the Mesopotamian texts, there are elements of a historical consciousness among the people of Ugarit and the Aramaeans.[9]

The Egyptians and the Hittites also had a keen interest in the past, but for the most part historical references are found only in royal texts. Sometimes, as in the later Persian inscriptions, successors simply copied the texts of their predecessors and claimed military victories where there were none. But in some cases, as in the inscriptions of Thutmose III, private texts of individuals who took part in a campaign can be used to corroborate such boasts.[10]

Harry Hoffner has shown the Hittites' interest in history in such texts as "Hattushili's Apology."[11] The Hittite texts admit that their kings have sometimes acted wrongly, as when they transgressed in attacking the Egyptians and were then punished by the ravages of a plague. Hans Güterbock responds:

> You will ask: does the objectivity go as far as admitting defeat? The answer is that I do not remember any mention of a defeat of one of the king's own campaigns. Advances of an enemy are frequently mentioned, but always as preceding the king's successful countermeasures. But Mursili says on some occasions . . . that he was unable to act, and why.[12]

BIBLICAL HISTORIOGRAPHY

Biblical historiography has some elements in common with other ancient historiographies (Mesopotamian, Egyptian, Hittite, and early Greek) in that it includes the intervention of supernatural powers in human affairs. Bertil Albrektson, in his famous study *History and the Gods*,[13]

---

8. A. K. Grayson, "Assyria and Babylonia," *Or* 49 (1980) 189.

9. N. Wyatt, "Some Observations on the Idea of History among the West Semitic Peoples," *UF* 11 (1979) 825–32.

10. See J. K. Hoffmeier, "Some Thoughts on William G. Dever's 'Hyksos,' Egyptian Destructions, and the End of the Palestinian Middle Bronze Age," *Levant* 22 (1990) 85.

11. H. A. Hoffner, "Histories and Historians of the Ancient Near East: The Hittites," *Or* 49 (1980) 283–332.

12. Hans G. Güterbock, "Hittite Historiography: A Survey," *History, Historiography and Interpretation* (ed. H. Tadmor and M. Weinfeld; Jerusalem: Magnes, 1983) 34.

13. Bertil Albrektson, *History and the Gods* (Lund: Gleerup, 1967).

stressed the striking parallels from other Near Eastern texts with other gods acting in history as in the biblical tradition. But W. G. Lambert, in reviewing Albrektson's work, notes:

> But when all these qualifications have been taken into account it remains a fact that considerable parts of the Old Testament do depict Yahweh as working in history to achieve a future goal which He had set. In ancient Mesopotamian texts there is nothing comparable.[14]

Daniel Block's *Gods of the Nations* also points out the numerous parallels between the Israelites' perception of the world and the views of her neighbors.[15] But he then notes their distinctives as well:

1. The Hebrews alone of all the peoples of the ancient Near East developed the concept of a monotheistic god. Malamat also stresses:

> Israel's *religious* distinctiveness, the divine revelation to the Patriarchs (with the attendant promise of land and progeny), and the later revelation through Moses of a revolutionary, monotheistic doctrine [had] no antecedents in the surrounding world.[16]

2. This god was not the projection of anthropomorphic features that one sees reflected in pagan gods.[17]
3. No other people claimed a divinely ordained history and revealed covenant, which enabled the Jews to sustain hope in an ultimate restoration in the face of periodic chastisement for their unfaithfulness.

Biblical historical texts contrast with the often chauvinistic, propagandistic royal annals and texts of Mesopotamian, Egyptian, and Hittite kings in that biblical writers were not reluctant to criticize the leaders and kings of their people.

Only a part of the Bible is ostensibly historical. That which is historical is selective and is based on a sacred perspective. For example, the royal achievements of Solomon's reign do not obscure disappointment in his backsliding.[18] The international reputation of Ahab and his major

---

14. W. G. Lambert, "History and the Gods: A Review Article," *Or* 39 (1970) 173.

15. D. I. Block, *The Gods of the Nations* (Jackson, Miss.: Evangelical Theological Society, 1988).

16. A. Malamat, "The Proto-History of Israel: A Study in Method," *The Word of the Lord Shall God Forth: Essays in Honor of David Noel Freedman in Celebration of His Sixtieth Birthday* (ed. C. L. Meyers and M. O'Connor; Winona Lake, Ind.: Eisenbrauns, 1983) 307. See E. Yamauchi, "Akhenaten, Moses, and Monotheism," *Tell el-Amarna in Retrospect: 100 Years of Amarna and Amarna Studies* (ed. G. D. Young and B. Beitzel; Winona Lake, Ind.: Eisenbrauns, forthcoming).

17. E. Yamauchi, "Anthropomorphism in Ancient Religions," *BSac* 125 (1968) 29–44.

18. E. Yamauchi, "Solomon," *The New International Dictionary of Biblical Archaeology* (ed. E. M. Blaiklock and R. K. Harrison; Grand Rapids: Zondervan, 1983) 419–22.

role at the battle of Qarqar (853 B.C.) are not noted in the biblical texts, but rather the iniquity of his queen, Jezebel, is highlighted.[19]

The reconstruction of biblical history by modern scholars depends, to a large degree, on their presuppositions about the nature of the biblical texts, which are our primary sources, and to the relative value of supplementary sources such as extrabiblical texts, inscriptions, and material evidences, or as William Hallo would designate these three sources, "Canons, Archives, and Monuments."[20] J. Maxwell Miller also suggests as the three sources "the biblical texts, other ancient Middle Eastern documents, and artifacts uncovered by archaeologists."[21]

A minimalist such as Van Seters believes that there were no earlier sources prior to the Deuteronomist; he invented all of his materials. A maximalist such as Hallo believes that biblical writers had earlier sources. Hallo remarks:

> And we may have to conclude that when the biblical authors appropriated Bronze Age sources for early Israelite history, they did so intelligently, purposefully and selectively. The surviving traditions were sifted and weighted. Their reflexes in biblical literature are neither free creations *de novo*, nor uncritical imitations of everything available.[22]

Orthodox Christians take history very seriously. As Mark Noll remarks:

> Christians . . . affirm that their very existence is defined by the meaning of purportedly historical events—an omnipotent deity who from nothing created the heavens and earth, the same God who called Abraham to be the father of many nations, who threw the Egyptian horse and rider in to the sea in order to preserve his purpose among a chosen people, and who sowed himself and his loving intentions for humanity supremely in becoming a person himself.[23]

Modern biblical criticism has been characterized by anti-supernaturalism. Literary criticism as influenced by Julius Wellhausen (1844–1918), Herman Gunkel (1862–1932), and Gerhard von Rad (1901–71) has sought the prehistory of the texts and concluded that though one may recover *Heilsgeschichte*, the expression of Israel's faith, her *Historie* can no longer be established. Thomas Thompson says flatly that one must discount the miraculous.[24]

19. E. Yamauchi, "Qarqar," *The New International Dictionary of Biblical Archaeology* (ed. E. M. Blaiklock and R. K. Harrison; Grand Rapids: Zondervan, 1983) 375–77.

20. Hallo, "Biblical History," 3.

21. J. Maxwell Miller, "Israelite History," in *The Hebrew Bible and Its Modern Interpreters* (ed. D. A. Knight and G. M. Tucker; Philadelphia: Fortress, 1985) 1.

22. Hallo, "Biblical History," 8.

23. Mark A. Noll, "Traditional Christianity and the Possibility of Historical Knowledge," *Christian Scholars Review* 19 (1990) 392.

24. T. L. Thompson, "History and Tradition," *JSOT* 15 (1980) 59.

Though presuppositions, such as a belief or disbelief in the supernatural, affect certain aspects of biblical history, it is possible, for the sake
of dialogue, to set this fact aside and concentrate on scholars' attitudes
toward the textual accounts. In this respect one finds that it is not only
in biblical studies that there is wide divergence in the spectrum between
credence and skepticism. Such disagreements occur among scholars in
the field of Near Eastern, Greek, and Roman history.

We may use Hallo's terms *maximalists* and *minimalists* to describe in a
nontheological manner attitudes toward the credibility of textual accounts.[25] Hallo reasonably maintains:

> The biblical record must be, for this purpose, scrutinized like other
> historiographical traditions of the ancient Near East, neither exempted
> from the standards demanded of those other traditions, nor subjected to
> severer ones than they are.[26]

In a similar fashion, Alan Millard, concludes a recent study by stating:

> Comparing the Aramaic monuments with the records of Israel's history
> seems to indicate that both describe the same sort of politics and similar
> attitudes to events. . . . With those, and other, ancient texts available, it
> is, surely, unscientific and very subjective to treat the Hebrew records
> from the start as if they are totally different creations.[27]

Among the public at large, the impression has been diffused that archaeology *proves* the Bible. That statement needs to be qualified. There
have indeed been striking cases in which passages that were questioned
by critics have been corroborated by excavations. But it is necessary to
recognize that there are also problems that have been presented by archaeology in regard to the interpretation of the biblical texts.[28]

William Dever has been so chagrined by unwarranted attempts to
correlate the Bible[29] and archaeology that he has urged the abandonment of the term *biblical archaeology* as unprofessional and proposes the
more secular term *Syro-Palestinian archaeology*. Dever was a student of
G. Ernest Wright, whom he admires for his expertise in archaeology,
but whom he criticizes for his attempt to combine theology and archaeology. Wright had declared, "In biblical faith, everything depends upon

---

25. W. W. Hallo, "The Limits of Skepticism," *JAOS* 110 (1990) 187.
26. Ibid., 193.
27. A. R. Millard, "Israelite and Aramean History in Light of Inscriptions," *TynBul*
41 (1990) 275.
28. See E. Yamauchi, *The Stones and the Scriptures* (Philadelphia: Lippincott, 1972);
idem, "The Proofs, Problems and Promises of Biblical Archaeology, " *JASA* 36 (1984)
129–38.
29. See M. Broshi, "Religion, Ideology, and Politics and Their Impact on Palestinian
Archaeology," *Israel Museum Journal* 6 (1987) 17–32.

whether the central events actually occurred."[30] Dever believes that the biblical theology movement, which emphasized the "God Who Acts," had its heyday in 1955–70 and is now passé.[31]

Literary approaches with their emphasis on the prehistory of the text, on contradictions, on alleged anachronisms and so forth, have generally yielded a negative evaluation of the biblical texts as historical records. As Miller observes:

> On the other hand, applying the critical procedures of biblical analysis— source criticism, tradition criticism, form criticism, etc.—also involves a high degree of subjectivity. Moreover, as indicated above, these procedures seem to be biased in that they are more effective for identifying characteristics and elements that reflect negatively on the historical reliability of an ancient document (a biblical narrative, for example) than they are for isolating historically reliable data that the same document may have preserved.[32]

The Documentary Hypothesis, most cogently summarized by Wellhausen, separates the Pentateuch, the first five books of the Old Testament, into four documents: J, E, D, and P. Wellhausen held that these documents came from long after Moses' day and were worthless historically.

Though the separation into these four documents is still widely accepted, some scholars see the preservation of authentic traditions by means of oral transmission. William F. Albright, who severely criticized Wellhausen's skepticism, placed J in the tenth century B.C., viewed E as a recension of J prepared for the northern kingdom in the ninth century B.C., and placed P in the mid–seventh century B.C. Gary Herion, recounting the view of the majority of scholars, observes:

> Note, for example, that most literary critics assign the J document to the Solomonic court, the D document to the Josianic court, and the P document to the (post-)exilic temple priesthood. Since these narratives subordinate past historical reality to the subjective concerns and theological values of the present, it is fair to say that these narratives display "mythic" characteristics.[33]

---

30. G. E. Wright, *God Who Acts* (London: SCM, 1952) 126–27.

31. W. G. Dever, "Biblical Theology and Biblical Archaeology," *HTR* 73 (1980) 1– 15; idem, "Archaeological Method in Israel: A Continuing Revolution," *BA* 43 (1980) 40–48.

32. Miller, "Israelite History," 20.

33. G. A. Herion, "The Role of Historical Narrative in Biblical Thought: The Tendencies Underlying Old Testament Historiography," *JSOT* 21 (1981) 31.

The disagreement even among scholars who accept the Documentary Hypothesis may be seen in the fact that Exod 33:7–11 is assigned to E by Walter Beyerlin, to J by Murray Newman, and to D by Martin Noth.[34] There has always been a minority of other scholars who have rejected the criteria used to establish the documentary hypothesis, for example, Umberto Cassuto, Cyrus Gordon, and Kenneth Kitchen.[35]

Wellhausen, Alt, Noth, and their modern day successors generally place very little credence in any of the books of the Bible as records of anything more than the later eras of their authors. In contrast to this skeptical viewpoint, archaeological discoveries in the 1950s and 1960s in Palestine and in surrounding lands led to a more positive evaluation of the biblical texts. This was particularly striking in respect to the biblical patriarchs Abraham, Isaac, and Jacob, whose stories had been questioned in the 1930s and 1940s. In particular, two sites in Mesopotamia, Mari and Nuzi, have produced thousands of tablets that seemed to confirm the authenticity of the patriarchal narratives.[36]

Mari provided us with names that are very similar to those in the genealogy of Abraham in the time and place, more or less, of Abraham and his family. Nuzi, although dating from the fifteenth century B.C., provided us with texts that seemed to illustrate vividly the social customs of the patriarchs. These discoveries were interpreted in a positive manner by Albright, Roland de Vaux, H. H. Rowley, E. A. Speiser, and Gordon.

There was also a general consensus that the patriarchs, in particular Abraham, should be placed in what is called the Middle Bronze I period, which is the early second millennium B.C. Now, the precise time span of the Middle Bronze I period is a matter of scholarly dispute.[37] The brief attempt by D. N. Freedman to raise the date of the patriarchal age to Early Bronze III, ca. 2800–2400 B.C., rested on his enthusiasm for G. Pettinato's translation of certain texts from Ebla, readings that more recently have been abandoned or challenged.[38]

34. W. Beyerlin, *Herkunft und Geschichte der ältesten Sinaitraditionen* (Tübingen: Mohr, 1961) 129–44; M. Newman, *The People of the Covenant* (Nashville: Abingdon, 1962) 8; M. Noth, *Exodus* (OTL; Philadelphia: Westminster, 1962) 252–57.

35. See my review of I. M. Kikawada and A. Quinn, *Before Abraham Was*, in *JAOS* 108 (1988) 310–11 for references.

36. E. Yamauchi, "Patriarchal Age," *Wycliffe Bible Encyclopedia* (ed. C. F. Pfeiffer et al.; Chicago: Moody, 1975) 1287–91.

37. E. Yamauchi, "A Decade and a Half of Archaeology in Israel and in Jordan," *JAAR* 42 (1974) 710–11.

38. D. N. Freedman, "The Real Story of the Ebla Tablets: Ebla and the Cities of the Plain," *BA* 41 (1978) 143–64; idem, "The Tell Mardikh Excavation, the Ebla Tablets, and Their Significance for Biblical Studies," *Near East Archaeological Society Bulletin* 13 (1979) 5–35; G. Pettinato, *The Archives of Ebla* (Garden City, N.Y.: Doubleday, 1981).

Since the 1970s, the positive assessments of the patriarchal narratives developed by such scholars on the basis of parallels with texts from Mari and Nuzi have been subjected to sharp criticisms by two scholars, Thomas Thompson in 1974[39] and John Van Seters in 1975.[40] Both studies contested the Abrightian synthesis and reverted essentially to the radical view of Wellhausen, who placed the origins of the Pentateuch not in the second millennium B.C. but in the first.

Thompson doubts whether there can be any correlation between Middle Bronze I archaeological artifacts and the patriarchs. He cites, for example, the excavations of Yohanan Aharoni at Beersheba. Aharoni found a well but did not find anything at Tell Beersheba prior to the early Iron Age or the twelfth century B.C.[41] But it may be recalled from the Old Testament that there is no indication that patriarchal Beersheba was a city. Abraham's Beersheba may have been simply a well with an associated cult place, quite possibly not the same well that Aharoni found.

Thompson asserts, "Not only has archaeology not proven a single event of the patriarchal traditions to be historical, it has not shown any of the traditions to be likely."[42] He argues that the story of Abraham's migration is not an originally independent tradition.

> Rather it is a historiographical reconstruction which is based on several originally independent and conflicting traditions. It not only must be understood as unhistorical, but any attempt to find movements analogous to Abraham's in the history of the Near East are [sic] essentially misdirected for the purposes of biblical interpretation.[43]

Furthermore, Thompson divorces Old Testament theology from history. He asserts:

> Salvation history is not an historical account of saving events open to the study of the historian. Salvation history did not happen; it is a literary form which has its own historical context. In fact, we can say that the faith of Israel is not an historical faith, in the sense of a faith based on historical events; it is rather a faith within history.[44]

Van Seters has likewise questioned many of the traditional interpretations of the patriarchal narratives and has suggested a radical dislocation.

---

39. T. L. Thompson, *The Historicity of the Patriarchal Narratives* (Berlin: de Gruyter, 1974).

40. John Van Seters, *Abraham in History and Tradition* (New Haven: Yale Univesity Press, 1975).

41. Y. Aharoni, "Nothing Early and Nothing Late," *BA* 39 (1976) 55–76.

42. Thompson, *Historicity*, 328.

43. Ibid., 315.

44. Ibid., 328–29.

He proposes that the idea of Abraham's migration from Ur to Haran should be placed in the Neo-Babylonian period, that is, the sixth century B.C., because at the time of Nabonidus there is evidence of a strong connection between Ur and Harran.[45] J. J. M. Roberts, in a review, comments, "Van Seters's positive arguments for dating the Abraham traditions to the Neo-Babylonian period are even less convincing."[46] Van Seters even suggests that the title "God Most High" mentioned in the patriarchal narratives must be placed in the Hellenistic period!

It should be conceded that Thompson and Van Seters have both raised some valid objections to some of the parallels from Nuzi that scholars like Speiser had adduced.[47] For example, Speiser had explained Abraham's marriage to Sarah on the basis of a wife-sister motif that he found in the texts of Nuzi.[48] Most scholars today feel that this parallel is not convincing.[49]

On the other hand, many of the critical judgments of Van Seters are not really justified. Where there are both second- and first-millennium B.C. parallels, Van Seters shows "a marked preference for first millennium sources and a cavalier dismissal of evidence from the second millennium texts," according to Martin Selman.[50] Commenting on the attempts of Van Seters and Morton Smith to postdate the Pentateuch, Hallo observes:

> In fact, some of their strongest arguments are based on the comparison of biblical data with neo-Assyrian and neo-Babylonian or even with classical Greek and Roman sources. What they rule out is only the comparison with older Near Eastern materials.[51]

For example, on the name *Abraham*, Van Seters correctly points out that in the first millennium there were names with the element *ab*, which

45. Van Seters, *Abraham*, 306–8.

46. J. J. M. Roberts, review of *Abraham in History and Tradition*, in *JBL* 96 (1977) 110.

47. E. A. Speiser, *Genesis* (Garden City, N.Y.: Doubleday, 1964) 91–93.

48. E. A. Speiser, "The Wife-Sister Motif in the Patriarchal Narratives," *Biblical and Other Studies* (ed. A. Altmann; Waltham, Mass.: Brandeis University Press, 1963).

49. S. Greengus, "Sisterhood Adoption at Nuzi and the 'Wife-Sister' in Genesis," *HUCA* 46 (1975) 5–31; idem, "The Patriarchs' Wives as Sisters: Is the Anchor Bible Wrong?" *BAR* 1/3 (1975) 22–26; M. J. Selman, "Comparative Methods and the Patriarchal Narratives," *Themelios* 3 (1977) 9–15; idem, "Comparative Customs and the Patriarchal Age," *Essays on the Patriarchal Narratives* (ed. A. R. Millard and D. J. Wiseman; Leicester: InterVarsity, 1980; repr., Winona Lake, Ind.: Eisenbrauns, 1983) 93–138; Thompson, *Historicity*, 328–29; S. M. Warner, "The Patriarchs and Extra-Biblical Sources," *JSOT* 2 (1977) 50–61. For a new interpretation of the wife-sister stories in Genesis, see J. K. Hoffmeier, "The Wives' Tales of Genesis 12, 20 and 26 and the Covenants at Beer-Sheba," *TynBul* 43 (1992) 81–99.

50. Selman, "Comparative Methods and the Patriarchal Narratives," 12; see also his "Social Environment of the Patriarchs," *TynBul* 27 (1976) 114–36.

51. Hallo, "Biblical History," 3.

means 'father' and names with the element *ram*, which means 'exalted'. But the closest parallels come from the second millennium. Nahum Sarna points out that 27 of the 38 names connected with the patriarchal families never recur later in the Bible, including Abraham, Isaac, and Jacob. To him this fact seems "to point more reasonably in the direction of authentic reflection of early historic tradition than to later inventiveness."[52] One of the objections that can be raised against the arguments of Van Seters is his refusal to acknowledge that many of the divine names in the patriarchal narratives, El Elyon, El Ro³i, El Olam, and El Bethel, were not current names of the first millennium B.C. but of the second millennium B.C., as pointed out by many scholars. The book *Essays on the Patriarchal Narratives*[53] has sought to demonstrate that the patriarchal histories are rooted in the second millennium.

The greatest problem for the revisionism of Thompson and Van Seters is that Hebrews in the first millennium B.C.—in the exilic, or even postexilic period—would not have invented the figure of Abraham and such offensive stories about him at that late date, stories such as his marriage to his half-sister and Jacob's marriages to two sisters. E. W. Nicholson comments:

> What is difficult about Van Seters' view is that we are required to believe that a narrative complex so very recently composed about an evidently hitherto unknown Israelite ancestor could have become virtually instantaneously so significant and so widespread during the exilic period, known not only among the exiles but also to those in Judah itself and to the Deuteronomic authors.[54]

In a more humorous vein, Dennis Pardee asks, "Where did this chap (Abraham) come from anyhow, who so dominates exilic and postexilic works which were written to restore the spirit of his putative descendants?"[55]

Donald B. Redford published an important book in 1970, *A Study of the Biblical Story of Joseph*.[56] On the observation that the Egyptian names given to Joseph and his wife are attested only in late Egyptological sources, he concludes that the story of Joseph was composed at a late date, between the seventh and fifth centuries B.C.[57] The names, however, may represent a modernization (cf. James for Jacob). Our lack of

---

52. N. Sarna, "Abraham in History," *BAR* 3 (1977) 9.

53. A. R. Millard and D. J. Wiseman (eds.), *Essays on the Patriarchal Narratives* (Leicester: InterVarsity, 1980; repr., Winona Lake, Ind.: Eisenbrauns, 1983).

54. Review of J. Van Seters, *Abraham in History and Tradition*, by E. W. Nicholson in *JTS* n.s. 30 (1979) 227.

55. Review of J. Van Seters, *Abraham in History and Tradition*, by D. Pardee in *JNES* 38 (1979) 147.

56. Donald B. Redford, *A Study of the Biblical Story of Joseph* (Leiden: Brill, 1970).

57. Ibid., 201, 228–31.

early attestation may be due to the fragmentary nature of the evidence, especially from the Delta.[58]

Redford discounts references to "camels" as anachronistic.[59] This is an old controversy because of the contention that camels were not certainly domesticated until after the Iron Age. But as Kitchen and others have pointed out, there is evidence, not necessarily literary but archaeological and artistic, of the use of camels that may indicate that they may have been sporadically domesticated before 1200 B.C.[60]

MOSES

Noth and Gerhard von Rad have denied that there is a trustworthy and unitary tradition about Moses.[61] They have argued that there exist only varying strands about Moses that were transmitted through separate tribal groups. They believe that they can discern four separate traditions: (1) the Exodus tradition, (2) the revelation at Sinai, (3) the wandering in the wilderness, and (4) the entrance into Transjordan. Scholars disagree about how many of these traditions they view as authentic. The most radical position is that of Noth, who believed that only the tradition about the burial of Moses in Transjordan is genuine. Noth believed that many of the narratives were etiologically based, that is, they were later stories devised to explain some visible phenomenon.[62]

In contrast to the views of scholars who wish to separate the Exodus tradition from the revelation of Yahweh at Sinai, Nicholson asserts after a thorough analysis:

> We may conclude therefore that Yahweh was associated with the Exodus tradition from the very beginning and that any suggestion that he was related to it only at a secondary stage in the development of the Exodus tradition is highly questionable.[63]

---

58. See K. A. Kitchen's review of D. B. Redford, *A Study of the Biblical Story of Joseph* in *OrAnt* 12 (1973) 233–42.

59. Redford, *Story of Joseph*, 195.

60. K. A. Kitchen, "Camel," in *New Bible Dictionary* (ed. J. D. Douglas; Grand Rapids: Eerdmans, 1962) 181–83; J. P. Free, "Abraham's Camels," *JNES* 3 (1944) 187–93; V. H. Matthews, *Pastoral Nomadism in the Mari Kingdom* (ASOR Dissertation Series 3; Missoula, Mont.: Scholars Press, 1978) 67–68; I. Finkelstein, *The Archaeology of the Israelite Settlement* (Jerusalem: Israel Exploration Society, 1988) 336–38.

61. M. Noth, *Überlieferungsgeschichte des Pentateuchs* (Stuttgart: Kohlhammer, 1948) 48–67, 172–91; idem, *The Deuteronomistic History* (JSOTSup 15; Sheffield: JSOT Press, 1981) chap. 5; G. von Rad, *The Problem of the Hexateuch and Other Essays* (Edinburgh: Oliver & Boyd, 1966) 14–20, 104–7, 114–17.

62. M. Noth, *Geschichte Israels* (Göttingen: Vandenhoeck & Ruprecht, 1950) 63–69.

63. E. W. Nicholson, *Exodus and Sinai in History and Tradition* (Oxford: Blackwell, 1973) 58.

The similarity of the Mosaic covenant to the Hittite suzerainty treaties, which date from the second millennium B.C., has convinced many
scholars of the antiquity of the Mosaic covenant. This led Edward Campbell to affirm the authenticity of the Exodus and Sinai traditions.[64]
Albright, in an essay published posthumously, affirmed:

> As founder, he [Moses] established Israel's religious and civil organization.
> This tradition is doubted even today, but it is strongly supported by his-
> torical analogy, and is now being confirmed by a rapidly increasing mass
> of evidence uncovered by archaeologists and philologians.[65]

Frank Cross, Freedman, and Campbell have dated the archaic poetic
passages of the Song of Moses in Exodus 15 and the Song of Deborah in
Judges 5 to the period prior to 1200 B.C., casting doubt on Noth's
theory of the origins of Israelite tradition cycles.[66] Nicholson has stated,
"No one today seriously questions that there was a bondage and Exodus."[67] Hallo has recently affirmed:

> Unless one rearranges the Biblical evidence completely, like Sean Warner,
> or utilizes it eclectically as Norman K. Gottwald has essentially done with
> his reinterpretation, one can hardly deny the reality of a conquest from
> abroad, implying a previous period of wanderings, a drastic escape from
> the prior place of residence and an oppression there that prompted the
> escape.[68]

In contrast to the maximalist opinions expressed by these scholars, there
are minimalist views on the plagues of Egypt. For example, according to
Van Seters's analysis,

> The Yahwist created it by expanding the very general statements in Deu-
> teronomy about God's judgments upon Egypt in order to construct a
> prophetic narrative in which the judgments were a series of curses sepa-
> rately invoked and enacted until the final judgment led to the people's re-
> lease. In other words, the plagues narrative is a literary creation by the
> Yahwist that made use of the various traditions of Hebrew prophecy,
> both the legends and the classical prophets, as well as the common Near
> Eastern and biblical curse tradition. There is no primary and secondary
> material, no ancient oral tradition behind the text. The plague narrative

---

64. E. F. Campbell, "Moses and the Foundations of Israel," *Int* 29 (1975) 145.
65. W. F. Albright, "Moses in Historical and Theological Perspective," *Magnalia Dei,
The Mighty Acts of God: Essays on the Bible and Archaeology in Memory of G. Ernest Wright*
(ed. F. M. Cross, W. E. Lemke, and P. D. Miller; Garden City, N.Y.: Doubleday, 1976) 120.
66. Ibid., 141–54; F. M. Cross and D. N. Freedman, *Studies in Ancient Yahwistic Poetry* (Missoula, Mont.: Scholars Press, 1975), chap. 2; D. N. Freedman, *Pottery, Poetry, and
Prophecy* (Winona Lake, Ind.: Eisenbrauns, 1980) 99–102, 147–66.
67. Nicholson, *Exodus and Sinai,* 53.
68. Hallo, "The Limits of Skepticism," 194.

did not exist as a specific tradition before the Yahwist's work and is, therefore, not older than the exilic period.[69]

Redford has also taken a very negative view toward the historicity of the Exodus account in a recent essay.[70] He believes that the Egyptian toponyms point to the Saite or Persian Period (ca. seventh–sixth centuries B.C.).[71] Again, this position disregards the lack of evidence from the northern area of the Delta and discounts the possibility of the modernization of names.

THE CONQUEST

John J. Bimson's major attempt to redate the Exodus and the Conquest to the mid–fifteenth century B.C. has aroused a great deal of interest.[72] Bimson associates Joshua's Conquest with Middle Bronze destruction levels at Jericho, Bethel, Hazor, Tell Beit Mirsim, Lachish, Hormah, and Dan by lowering their absolute chronological dates. In general, critics have responded favorably to his criticisms of the archaeological evidence used, for example, by Yigael Yadin to support the late date of the Exodus and the Conquest.[73] But they have also reacted unfavorably to Bimson's own attempt to correlate Middle Bronze sites with an early Conquest by Joshua.[74]

Three models of Israel's origins have been proposed: (1) The Conquest Model, (2) The Infiltration Model, and (3) The Peasant Revolt Model. The Conquest Model, which follows the biblical narrative of

69. J. Van Seters, "The Plagues of Egypt: Ancient Tradition or Literary Invention?" *ZAW* 98 (1986) 38.

70. D. B. Redford, "An Egyptological Perspective on the Exodus Narrative," *Egypt, Israel, Sinai* (ed. A. F. Rainey; Tel Aviv: Tel Aviv University Press, 1987) 137–61.

71. Ibid., 144.

72. John J. Bimson, *Redating the Exodus and the Conquest* (JSOTSup 5; Sheffield: JSOT Press, 1978).

73. Y. Yadin, *Hazor* (Schweich Lectures; London: Oxford Univesity Press, 1972) 126–32; idem, "The Transition from a Semi-Nomadic to a Sedentary Society in the Twelfth Century B.C." *Symposia Celebrating the Seventy-Fifth Anniversary of the Founding of the American Schools of Oriental Research (1900–1975)* (ed. F. M. Cross; Cambridge, Mass.: ASOR, 1979) 57–68.

74. See, for example, reviews by G. Bissoli in *Liber Annuus* 30 (1980) 419–23; H. Engel in *Bib* 61 (1980) 437–40; J. A Soggin in *VT* 31 (1981) 98–99; A. F. Rainey in *IEJ* 30 (1980) 249–51. Cf. J. J. Bimson, "A Reply to Baruch Halpern's 'Radical Exodus Redating Fatally Flawed'" *BAR* 14/4 (1988) 52–55; and M. Bietak, "Contra Bimson, Bietak Says Late Bronze Age Cannot Begin as Late as 1400 B.C.," *BAR* 14/4 (1988) 54–55, and the earlier articles cited there. A major conference on the "Pharaoh of the Exodus" was held in Memphis, Tenn. in 1987, dealing with issues relating to the Exodus. Unfortunately the papers have yet to be published.

Joshua's campaigns was favored by Albright, Paul Lapp, and Yadin.[75] Fitting into this framework is a series of Canaanite cities—Hazor, Bethel, and Lachish—destroyed by violence in the thirteenth century B.C. and reoccupied by a new group, presumably the Israelites.

Aharoni posited two waves of invading Israelite tribes. The first, appearing in the fourteenth century B.C., involved the House of Joseph. This group passed without opposition through Edom and Moab and captured Jericho and Bethel. The second wave of invaders, who were involved in the thirteenth-century B.C. Exodus, encountered opposition from the newly settled tribes in Edom and Moab. Because the excavations in the Negev at Arad, Malhata, and Masos have failed to yield Late Bronze remains that can be associated with the Canaanites, Aharoni concluded, "Therefore, the conquest tradition pertaining to it [the Negev] is not firmly anchored in history."[76]

In reexamining the pottery evidence, Bryant G. Wood now claims that, contrary to the views of Jericho's excavator, Kathleen Kenyon, that site can also be shown to have been captured in the Late Bronze Age by Joshua.[77] But this rather startling claim, which received considerable publicity in the *New York Times* and *Time* magazine,[78] has not gone uncontested.[79]

But there are problems with the Conquest Model. Excavations by Siegfried Horn at Tell Hesban, ancient Heshbon, failed to uncover a Late Bronze city.[80] There is also the lack of a Late Bronze settlement at Et-Tell, identified as Ai, excavated by Joseph Callaway.[81] J. B. Pritchard worked at Gibeon and found only Late Bronze tombs and no signs of a Late Bronze city.[82] It should be noted, however, that only small sections

---

75. W. F. Albright, "The Israelite Conquest of Canaan in the Light of Archaeology," *BASOR* 74 (1939) 11–23; P. Lapp, "The Conquest of Palestine in Light of Archaeology," *CTM* (1967) 283–300; Y. Yadin, *Hazor: The Rediscovery of a Great Citadel of the Bible* (New York: Random House, 1975); idem, "Is the Biblical Account of the Israelite Conquest of Canaan Historically Reliable?" *BAR* 8/2 (1982) 16–23. See also S. Yeivin, *The Israelite Conquest of Canaan* (Istanbul: Nederlands Historisch-Archaeologisch Instituut, 1971).

76. Y. Aharoni, *The Land of the Bible: A Historical Geography* (rev. ed.; Philadelphia: Westminster, 1979) 216.

77. Bryant Wood, "Did the Israelites Conquer Jericho? A New Look at the Evidence," *BAR* 16/5 (1990) 44–58.

78. *Time* (Mar. 5, 1990) 59; *New York Times* (Feb. 22, 1990) 1.

79. P. Bienkowski, "Jericho Was Destroyed in the Middle Bronze Age, Not the Late Bronze Age," *BAR* 17/5 (1990) 45. But see Wood's response, "Dating Jericho's Destruction: Bienkowski Is Wrong on All Counts," *BAR* 17/5 (1990) 45–49.

80. But see the recent article by David Merling ("Heshbon: A Lost City of the Bible," *Archaeology and the Biblical World* 1/2 [1992] 10–17), who suggests that Heshbon, like Bashan, which frequently occurs in parallel with it, is a region, not a city.

81. J. A. Callaway, "Excavating Ai (Et-Tell): 1964–1972," *BA* 39 (1976) 18–30.

82. J. B. Pritchard, *Gibeon, Where the Sun Stood Still: The Discovery of the Biblical City* (Princeton: Princeton University Press, 1962) 135–38.

of the mound were excavated because the modern village of El Jib still
sits on top of the site.[83]

Miller concludes concerning the Conquest Model:

> There are numerous issues involved—e.g., the complex matter of site
> identifications—and it perhaps would be an overstatement of the evi-
> dence to say that archaeology denies that a conquest of the sort described
> in the Bible occurred at the end of the Late Bronze Age. But it is cer-
> tainly no longer possible, in the light of recent developments, to say that
> archaeology confirms such a conquest.[84]

The Infiltration Model has been favored by scholars on the basis of
certain passages in Judges and in light of archaeological evidence.[85] Albrecht Alt and Noth had questioned the Conquest narratives on the basis
of literary analysis. In 1925, Alt suggested that the Israelites gradually
infiltrated into Canaan peacefully.[86] Manfred Weippert and Siegfried
Mittmann believe that the resettlement process in the region of Edom
did not begin as early as 1300 but only after 1200 b.c.[87]

Though Aharoni, as noted above, believed that some Canaanite cities
were captured in the initial waves, he also held that many others were not
won over until the period of the Judges. He suggested that the Israelites
peacefully penetrated sparsely settled areas in southern Upper Galilee,
the hill country of Ephraim and Judah, and the Negev.[88] In the latter
area, Aharoni has excavated at Beersheba, Tel Malhatah, and Tel Masos.
He did not find any Late Bronze settlements but recovered evidence of
early Iron Age occupation, which he would associate with the incoming
Israelites. Evidence from the northern Negev site of Tel Masos suggests
to Volkmar Fritz that the new settlers in the early Iron Age (twelfth century b.c.) were former seminomads who turned to agriculture.[89] Fritz,
however, wishes to qualify the Infiltration Model as follows:

---

83. On these problems see Yamauchi, *The Stones and the Scriptures*, 58–61; Finkelstein, *Archaeology of the Israelite Settlement*, 296–98.

84. Miller, "Israelite History," 4–5.

85. M. Noth, "Grundsätzliches zur geschichtlichen Deutung archäologischer Be-
funde auf dem Boden Palästinas," *Palästinajahrbuch* 34 (1938) 7–22.

86. A. Alt, The Settlement of the Israelites in Palestine," *Essays in Old Testament History and Religion* (Oxford: Blackwell, 1966, trans. of 1925 German edition).

87. M. Weippert, *The Settlement of the Israelite Tribes in Palestine* (London: SCM,
1971); idem, "Canaan, Conquests and Settlement of," in *IDBSup* (Nashville: Abingdon,
1976) 125–30; S. Mittmann, *Beiträge zur Siedlungs- und Territorialgeschichte des nördlichen
Ostjordanlandes* (Wiesbaden: Harrassowitz, 1970).

88. Aharoni, "The Israelite Occupation of Canaan," *BAR* 8/3 (1981) 14–23.

89. V. Fritz, "The Israelite 'Conquest' in the Light of Recent Excavations at Khirbet
el Meshâsh," *BASOR* 241 (1981) 61–73.

Our examination of the archaeological material has shown that the occupation of the land by the Israelite tribes probably occurred in a way similar to the so-called infiltration hypothesis—which must, however, be modified. The various groups that settled in the country cannot merely be regarded as former nomads. Periods of a partially sedentary life must have interspersed their nomadic existence; otherwise the wide-ranging adoption of Canaanite culture during the last phase of the Late Bronze Age cannot be explained. Therefore, I would like to call the new theory *the symbiosis hypothesis.*[90]

Recently Israel Finkelstein has criticized both the views of Aharoni and of Fritz. In the former case, recent Israeli surveys indicate that Israelite penetration into sparsely settled areas came after settlement closer to Canaanite centers. In the latter case, Finkelstein disputes the identification of Tel Masos as an Israelite site, which identification formed the basis of Fritz's hypothesis.[91] Finkelstein's own conclusions are as follows:

> During the 12th and 11th centuries, the hilly regions of the Land of Israel were the scene of the gradual transition by groups of pastoralists to a sedentary mode of existence. Although the cumulative results of archaeological field work all over the country support the view of the Alt school regarding the *manner* in which Israelite Settlement came about, the *origin* of the new settlers must be sought within the cultivated areas and the desert fringe, rather than in the adjacent deserts. The process itself was complex, variegated and complicated. Initially, the chief foes were natural obstacles; later, the Israelites came into conflict with the Canaanites living nearby and in the lowlands.[92]

In summary, I conclude that the archaeological evidence for the Conquest and the origins of the Israelite Settlement is at present mixed and inconclusive. As Miller has summarized the situation:

> It appears to the present writer that the archaeological evidence available at the moment neither supports, nor is easily accommodated with, any particular date for the Israelite conquest. In fact, the situation with regard to the conquest is not unlike that of the patriarchs. Were we dependent upon archaeological and other nonbiblical evidence alone, we would have no reason even to suppose that such a conquest ever occurred.[93]

The Peasant Revolt Model was first proposed by George Mendenhall and then developed by Norman Gottwald. In 1962, Mendenhall first proposed the idea that Israel came into existence as the result of sociopolitical upheaval and retribalization among the Canaanites at the end of

---

90. V. Fritz, "Conquest or Settlement? The Early Iron Age in Palestine," *BA* 50 (1987) 98.
91. Finkelstein, *Archaeology of the Israelite Settlement*, 45–46.
92. Ibid., 351.
93. Miller, "Israelite History," 11.

the Late Bronze age.[94] He furthered developed this thesis in his work, *The Tenth Generation: The Origins of the Biblical Tradition*.[95] According to this revisionist view, Israel was born as the result of an internal struggle rather than as the result of an invasion or migration.

Mendenhall's views have been severely criticized by Hauser, who comments:

> Mendenhall's reconstruction of "what actually happened" turns out, however, to be a reading into the past of *modern* socio-economic and religio-ethical perspectives, as I have shown. This is not surprising, since he *a priori* empties the biblical traditions of any meaningful historical content, and the vacuum needs to be filled.[96]

Though criticizing Mendenhall in some respects, Norman Gottwald built upon his proposal a thorough-going and massive sociological study over 900 pages long.[97] Gottwald's radical revision of Israelite history depends largely on his Marxist sociological perspectives.

Gottwald's thesis is that early Israel was a collection of oppressed Canaanite people including the *apiru*, pastoralists, nomads, and disaffected priests who prized the ideal of "egalitarianism," by which he means equal access to the means of production.[98] These banded together against their wealthy Canaanite oppressors.

In Gottwald's own summary his theses are:

1. In origin, the first Israelites were largely members of *lower or marginal classes* within powerful Canaanite states.
2. The Israelites emerged into history as a *revolutionary social* movement, struggling to break the iron grip of the state over the total life of the people.
3. These Israelites were a people of *mixed origins* in their ethnic and cultural identities. Socioeconomically, they were mostly peasants.
4. They were a people whose movement for liberation was made possible by large-scale *social combination and cooperation* among diverse oppressed groups.

94. G. E. Mendenhall, "The Hebrew Conquest of Palestine," *BA* 25 (1962) 66–87.

95. G. E. Mendenhall, *The Tenth Generation: The Origins of the Biblical Tradition* (Baltimore: Johns Hopkins University Press, 1973).

96. A. J. Hauser, "Israel's Conquest of Palestine: A Peasants' Rebellion?" *JSOT* 7 (1978) 9.

97. N. K. Gottwald, *The Tribes of Yahweh: A Sociology of the Religion of Liberated Israel, 1250–1050 B.C.E.* (Maryknoll, N.Y.: Orbis, 1979).

98. Note his word of regret at not more clearly defining this key concept: N. K. Gottwald, "Two Models for the Origins of Ancient Israel: Social Revolution or Frontier Society," *The Quest for the Kingdom of God: Studies in Honor of George E. Mendenhall* (ed. H. B. Huffmon, F. A. Spina, and A. R. W. Green; Winona Lake, Ind.: Eisenbrauns, 1983) 17.

5. They were a broadly *tribal people.*
6. They were a people of *approximate equality.* . . . In Marxist terms, they benefited from the use value of their own labor.
7. In order to break free from powerful states and overlords and to form a viable community of their own, these first Israelites had to conduct *a people's war* for freedom.
8. The strongest form of cultural self-expression among the Israelites was *a people's religion.*[99]

Gottwald uses a structural-functional, sociological model to describe ancient Israel, and also a Marxist, cultural-material model for analysis. He claims:

> Only a sociological approach to the notion of the chosen people can give it credibility and rescue it from absurdity. Other approaches, however ingenious, lose their way in mystifications, invoking idealist and supernatural notions of divine favoritism toward one people for no discoverable reason or else appealing to ethical or metaphysical attributes possessed by a superior gifted people. The end result of such non-sociological interpretations of "chosen people" is either irrelevant supernaturalism or exclusivist racism, or both together.[100]

In his concluding peroration, Gottwald declares:

> If my line of reasoning about the relation of biblical theology and biblical sociology is correct, the most important contribution of a social analysis of early Israel to contemporary religious thought and practice is to close the door firmly and irrevocably on the idealist and supernaturalist illusions still permeating and bedeviling our religious outlook. Yahweh and "his" people must be demystified, deromanticized, dedogmatized and de-idolized. . . . All such symbol systems, however venerable and psychically convenient, are bad dreams to be awakened from, cloying relics to be cast away, cruel fetters to be struck off. They are, in a word, the Canaanite idols that Israel smashed when it smashed the Canaanite kings.[101]

Many reviewers have found it difficult to see this vision in the biblical texts themselves. B. Beitzel objects:

> One searches vainly in these narratives for even the slightest hint of the supposed revolution; there one encounters instead the rather consistent notion of a group of Israelite forebears who entered Palestine from elsewhere and who were not at that time homogeneous with the people of Canaan.[102]

---

99. N. K. Gottwald, "The Impact of Ancient Israel on Our Social World," *Currents in Theology and Mission* 6 (April, 1979) 17.

100. N. K. Gottwald, "Biblical Theology or Sociology?" *Radical Religion* 2–3 (1975) 52.

101. Gottwald, *The Tribes of Yahweh,* 708.

102. Review of N. K. Gottwald, *The Tribes of Yahweh,* by B. Beitzel, *Trinity Journal* 1 (1980) 242.

The fact that the biblical texts themselves "lack revolutionary memory" does not trouble Gottwald. Because he finds that the biblical texts lack any single coherent perspective, he therefore feels compelled to supply it through his sociological model.[103]

Gottwald's tome has drawn lavish praise on the one hand and harsh criticism on the other. It has been ranked by one reviewer on the level of Wellhausen's *Prolegomena* and been compared to Albright's *From the Stone Age to Christianity*. The harshest criticism is leveled by Anson Rainey, who writes, "This book could safely and profitably be ignored. Unfortunately, it represents the most recent fad in Old Testament studies."[104] He further comments, "Gottwald himself has no real control over any of the relevant source material, linguistic, sociological or archaeological."[105]

Mendenhall, who supplied the original inspiration of Gottwald's Peasant Revolt Model, is no less scathing in his comments:

> What Gottwald has actually produced is a modern version of the ancient myth-making mentality. Utilizing both the terminology and the driving ideas of a nineteenth century political ideology, he proceeds blithely to read into biblical history whatever is called for in the program of that nineteenth century ideology.[106]

There is very little objective evidence for the Peasant Revolt Model, though Frank Yurco has recently claimed that figures he has identified as Israelites wearing Canaanite dress may lend some support to this view.[107] Thompson, after reviewing the evidence of the Late Bronze and Iron I settlements of those regions primarily associated with early Israel concludes, "The archaeological evidence from these central hills alone makes it categorically impossible to assert—as Mendenhall and Gottwald do—that the villages of Israel emerged out of an oppressed Late Bronze Age peasantry."[108] Finkelstein also concludes, "Both the settlement patterns arising from archaeological surveys and the material culture of Israelite Settlement sites refute any theory that the Israelites were malcontents fleeing from the Canaanite polity."[109]

103. N. K. Gottwald, "Religious Conversion and the Societal Origins of Ancient Israel," *JSOT* 15 (1988) 64.

104. Review of N. K. Gottwald, *The Tribes of Yahweh*, by Anson Rainey, *JAOS* 107 (1987) 541.

105. Ibid.

106. G. E. Mendenhall, "Ancient Israel's Hyphenated History," *Palestine in Transition: The Emergence of Ancient Israel* (ed. D. N. Freedman and D. F. Graf; Sheffield: Almond, 1983) 91.

107. F. J. Yurco, "3,200 Year-Old Picture of Israelites Found in Egypt," *BAR* 26/5 (1990) 20–44.

108. T. L. Thompson, "Historical Notes on Israel's Conquest of Palestine: A Peasants' Rebellion?" *JSOT* 7 (1978) 25.

109. Finkelstein, *Archaeology of the Israelite Settlement*, 352.

Though the new sociological and anthropological approaches, such as Gottwald's, can provide some helpful perspectives, their very nature often involves a highly reductionist attitude that sets aside religious elements for economic and social factors. Sociology concentrates on repeated patterns of behavior of groups of people, whereas history deals also with individuals. As I have pointed out elsewhere, there are some inherent problems with the application of sociological models to ancient historical texts.[110] C. S. Rodd concurs:

> My plea is that there is a world of difference between sociology applied to contemporary society, where the researcher can test his theories against evidence which he collects, and historical sociology where he has only fossilized evidence that has been preserved by chance or for purposes very different from that of the sociologist. It is a cardinal error to move promiscuously between the two. Indeed, the weaknesses of sociological studies of historical movements from Max Weber onwards suggests that historical sociology is impossible.[111]

OLD TESTAMENT HISTORIOGRAPHICAL STUDIES
IN THE 1980s

Building upon the trend begun by Thompson, Van Seters, and Gottwald in the 1970s, the 1980s have seen a veritable spate of works in the minimalist tradition. Authors of some of these include: Lemche, Ahlström, Coote, Whitelam, Thompson, Finkelstein, Garbini, and Ord.[112] Though each author has his distinctive contribution, the works in general share several tendencies. Ahlström supposes that the promise of the land to Abraham arose in the exilic period when the returnees were

---

110. E. Yamauchi, "Sociology, Scripture, and the Supernatural," *JETS* 27 (1984) 169–92.

111. C. S. Rodd, "On Applying a Sociological Theory to Biblical Studies," *JSOT* 19 (1981) 105. Gary A. Herion ("The Impact of Modern and Social Science Assumptions on the Reconstruction of Israelite History," *JSOT* 34 [1986] 3–33) notes that the leading assumptions associated with the social sciences include positivism, reductionism, relativism, and determinism.

112. Niels Peter Lemche, *Early Israel: Anthropological and Historical Studies on the Israelite Society before the Monarchy* (VTSup 37; Leiden: Brill, 1985); Gösta Ahlström, *Who Were the Israelites?* (Winona Lake, Ind.: Eisenbrauns, 1986); Robert B. Coote and K. W. Whitelam, *The Emergence of Early Israel in Historical Perspective* (Sheffield: Almond, 1987); Thomas L. Thompson, *The Origin Tradition of Ancient Israel, I: The Literary Formation of Genesis and Exodus 1–23* (JSOTSup 55; Sheffield: JSOT Press, 1987); Israel Finkelstein, *Archaeology of the Israelite Settlement*; Niels Peter Lemche, *Ancient Israel: A New History of Israelite Society* (Biblical Seminar 5; Sheffield: JSOT Press, 1988); Giovanni Garbini, *History and Ideology in Ancient Israel* (New York: Crossroad, 1988); Robert B. Coote and David Ord, *The Bible's First History* (Philadelphia: Fortress, 1989); and Robert B. Coote, *Early Israel: A New Horizon* (Minneapolis: Augsburg-Fortress, 1990).

confronted by the unavailability of land.[113] He rejects the conquest theme as a purely literary product that is not a reflection of actual history.[114] From an analysis of the Merneptah Stele as a ring composition, he infers that whereas *Canaan* represented the plains, *Israel* was the name of the hill country.[115] He then concludes that the people who moved up to the hills, who were not ethnically different from the Canaanites, were called "Israelites" after the name of the territory.

His arguments have not proved very persuasive to reviewers. A. J. Hauser, for example, comments:

> To argue primarily on the basis of the Mernepthah Stela that "Israel" is a geographical rather than an ethnic term, and to do so while dismissing rather quickly the significance of the determinative for a people before "Israel," is to impose on the reader's generosity.[116]

The most radical work is Garbini's. It is a collection of fourteen essays, eleven published previously. He rejects critical approaches such as Noth's Deuteronomistic History as "absurd hypotheses," and deems the synthesis of John Hayes and J. Maxwell Miller as lacking a "real historical approach."[117] In a highly idiosyncratic manner he dates Isaiah 40–48 to the reign of Darius, Joshua and Kings to the Hellenistic era (third century B.C.), and Ezra to the first century B.C.

After dismissing the narrative books of the Old Testament as ideology rather than history, Garbini informs us that the patriarchal narratives are "fictitious creations used to convey Israel's postexilic national ideology."[118] The motivation of the author was to represent the Israelites as compatriots of Nabonidus. The notion of the twelve tribes of Israel first arose in the Achaemenid era. David could not have known Hiram of Tyre nor defeated the Edomites, Ammonites, and Arameans. Solomon could not have married a daughter of a pharaoh. Ethical monotheism first developed in the exilic era. Ezra and his reforms are purely fictitious. Such opinionated declarations have only the author's thorough-going skepticism toward the biblical texts and his own fertile imagination for support. Garbini does show where a skeptical approach may lead if carried out to its logical end.

---

113. Ahlström, *Who Were the Israelites?*

114. Cf. G. W. Ahlström, "Another Moses Tradition," *JNES* 39 (1980) 67.

115. See G. W. Ahlström, "Where Did the Israelites Live?" *JNES* 41 (1982) 133–38; G. W. Ahlström and D. Edelman, "Merneptah's Israel," *JNES* 44 (1985) 59–61.

116. Review of Ahlström, *Who Were the Israelites?* by A. J. Hauser, *CBQ* 50 (1988) 486. See also reviews by J. A. Emerton in *VT* 38 (1988) 373 and H. M. Niermann in *TLZ* 113 (1988) 23.

117. Hayes and Miller, *Israelite and Judaean History.*

118. Garbini, *History and Ideology,* 81.

R. B. Coote and his coauthors, D. R. Ord and K. W. Whitelam, in their three books reject traditional concepts of the Patriarchs, the Exodus, the Conquest, and the Judges as anachronistic. They attempt to understand the emergence of Israel on purely geopolitical grounds, taking a cue from Braudel's emphasis on historical analysis over long periods of time.[119] Coote and Whitelam believe that the movement of populations from the coasts to the hill country may be explained as the result of fluctuating trade patterns, in particular the disruption in trade that occurred because of the population upheavals in the Eastern Mediterranean around 1200. They write, "This shift, we have suggested, occurred mainly in response to changes in the economy of the eastern Mediterranean area associated with a drop in trade during the thirteenth century."[120] There is nothing mysterious or unique about Israel at all. According to Coote:

> To locate the distinctiveness of the Scriptures and their theological revelation in the moment of Israel's origin takes both out of the realm of history. As such they become meaningless and susceptible to the manipulation of the self-justified.[121]

Other readers might conclude that the summary rejection of scriptural accounts prior to the reign of David by Coote, Whitelam, and Ord is itself the most brutal form of textual manipulation and that it is their economically determined origin of Israel that makes the Scriptures "meaningless."

W. H. Stiebing also looks at the dislocations of populations in the eastern Mediterranean in the thirteenth century B.C. and concludes that the primary factors were ecological—drought and famine. Such a set of circumstances might have been responsible

> . . . for the creation in Canaan of detached groups of semi-nomads, refugees, peasant farmers, and occasional bands of brigands who, together with a small contingent of escaped slaves from Egypt, would join to form the Israelite tribes.[122]

N. P. Lemche presents a mass of anthropological data in his first (1985) volume and then utilizes these data for his own theory of the origins of Israel in his second (1988) volume. Unwilling to grant the possibility of any historical traditions of the period before the monarchy, he

---

119. F. Braudel, *The Mediterranean and the Mediterranean World in the Age of Philip II* (2 vols.; New York: Harper & Row, 1972–1974); idem, *Afterthoughts on Material Civilization and Capitalism* (Baltimore: Johns Hopkins University Press, 1977).

120. Coote and Whitelam, *Emergence of Early Israel*, 116.

121. Coote, *Early Israel: A New Horizon*, 172.

122. W. H. Stiebing, Jr., *Out of the Desert? Archaeology and the Exodus/Conquest Narratives* (Buffalo: Prometheus, 1989) 187.

begins with a rejection of the Hebrew scriptural account: "It is accordingly methodologically wrong to base one's reconstruction of the emergence of Israel in the late second millennium B.C. on the Old Testament itself."[123] He then seeks an anthropological explanation:

> What follows is accordingly merely a suggested *model*, that is a *hypothesis*, which is based on experience of the relationships which have obtained in traditional peasant societies and pre-industrial urban societies in the Third World in recent times.[124]

Given the author's negative attitude to the historicity of the Hebrew Bible, it is not surprising that he comes to the conclusion that there was nothing distinctive about Yahwism:

> This quite negative final conclusion confirms the view that underlies this entire study, namely that the Old Testament is a very poor source if prenational Israelite society and its religion are the objects of enquiry. All that we can be sure of is that the Israelite conception of Yahweh during the period of the monarchy did not contain features that distinguished his worship from other types of religion in western Asia.[125]

Baruch Halpern declares, "Historical Israel is not the Israel of the Hebrew Bible."[126] He is of the opinion that

> . . . biblical scholarship is no more methodologically equipped to reconstruct the exodus than is America's National Aeronautics and Space Administration technologically equipped to send video probes to the Alpha Centauri system. The period of the judges, like Pluto or Uranus, presents a more realistic, if still elusive target.[127]

Halpern is selectively willing to believe some biblical traditions: "Simultaneously, it is unreasonable to gainsay traditions of an invasion into central Canaan under Joshua. That some group entered from Transjordan is, on the biblical testimony, impossible to deny."[128] But why he can believe some traditions and not others is not clear. According to Halpern's scenario Israel emerged from the Canaanite rural communities of the hill country. Israel's "growth and coalescence in the central hills must have occasioned the introduction of labor-intensive practices such as terracing."[129]

He supposes that the biblical texts have suppressed centrifugal forces such as shamans and mediums, which were overcome by the triumph of

---

123. Lemche, *Ancient Israel*, 7.
124. Ibid., 101.
125. Ibid., 256.
126. Baruch Halpern, *The Emergence of Israel in Canaan* (Chico, Cal.: Scholars Press, 1983) 239.
127. Ibid., 250.
128. Ibid., 239.
129. Ibid., 212.

Yahwism.[130] It is from Deborah's time "that real Israelite nationhood in the institutional and ideological senses can be traced."[131]

Israel Finkelstein, who believes that attempts to reconcile the biblical texts of the Conquest and archaeology have failed, looks primarily to the data of recent Israeli archaeological surveys in Galilee, Manasseh, Ephraim, and Judah. These show a striking decline in population from the Early Bronze to the Late Bronze, and then a remarkable proliferation of settlements in the hill country in Iron I. Since there is no later parallel for the biblical model of a conquest, Finkelstein rules this explanation out of court:

> Our present knowledge of the society of the ancient Near East, especially of the relations between sedentary people and pastoral nomads, does not permit the romantic reconstruction of hoards of desert nomads invading the settled lands and devastating their inhabitants. . . . Therefore, even if there were archaeological evidence for the contemporaneous destruction of many Canaanite cities at the end of the 13th century B.C., the identification of the agressors would have to be sought elsewhere than among obscure desert tribes.[132]

Finkelstein believes that "The most crucial factor in this process may have been the Egyptian economic exploration of the urban centers."[133] He cites the parallel development in Palestine in the Ottoman Empire[134] to argue that the new settlements were established by the resedentarization of local pastoralist groups from the fringe areas, some elements of which may have come from a desert background.[135] Regardless of what one may think of his explanatory theory, Finkelstein's summary of Israeli archaeological surveys is now indispensable data for further discussions.

CONCLUSIONS

What are some general observations one may make about these recent attempts to rewrite the history of Israel on the basis of sociological, geopolitical, and economic models based on analogies and on archaeological data rather than primarily on the Hebrew texts?

1. *The Hebrew Scriptures have been rejected as historical sources because their composition is later than the events they purport to describe.* Finkelstein believes that the failure of attempts to correlate the Conquest narratives

---

130. Ibid., 241.
131. Ibid., 241.
132. Finkelstein, *Archaeology of the Israelite Settlement*, 302.
133. Ibid., 346.
134. Ibid., 347
135. Ibid., 348.

with the archaeological data stems from the fact "that the biblical narratives were redacted centuries after the events they purport to describe
actually took place."[136] This assumption leads Miller and Hayes to begin
their reconstruction of Israel's history with the period of the Judges.
The same consideration leads Soggin, Whitelam, and others to begin
with David and Solomon, and Garbini to reject almost all of the Old
Testament as reflecting essentially developments from the Persian and
Hellenistic eras.

But the date of a text's composition is not necessarily a warrant
against the possibility that it preserves accurate memories, if it was able
to use earlier sources. The Homeric epics, composed five centuries after
the Mycenaean era they describe, can be shown to have preserved numerous memories of the Late Bronze age, in the personal and place
names and in artifacts mentioned.[137] Roman historians use Livy to reconstruct the history of the Roman Republic several centuries before his
lifetime. Classical historians use Plutarch (second century A.D.) for the
history of Themistocles (fifth century B.C.), and all historians of Alexander the Great (fourth century B.C.) acknowledge as their most accurate
source Arrian's *Anabasis* (second century A.D.)

2. *Hebrew Scriptures have been rejected where there is no external documentation or corroboration.* Some scholars have written off the patriarchal and
Exodus/Conquest eras, because they have no convincing corroborative
archaeological evidence or extrabiblical confirmation. Dever writes,
"After a century of modern research, neither biblical scholars nor archaeologists have been able to document as historical any of the events,
much less the personalities, of the patriarchal or Mosaic eras."[138] As
C. Westermann has pointed out, this suspicion of past texts springs out
of the enlightenment: "A further limitation of the Enlightenment's understanding of history follows from the reduction of events to that
which is verifiable through documentary evidence."[139]

It was not until 1932 that the exile in Babylon of Jehoiachin, the last
king of Judah, was attested in tablets published by E. Weidner. It was not
until 1961 that the first epigraphical attestation of Pontius Pilate was

136. Ibid., 302.
137. See E. Yamauchi, "Homer, History, and Archaeology," *Bulletin of the Near East
Archaeological Society* 3 (1973) 21–42.
138. W. G. Dever, "Recent Archaeological Discoveries and Biblical Research," *BAR*
16/3 (1990) 52.
139. C. Westermann, "The Old Testament's Understanding of History in Relation
to That of the Enlightenment," *Understanding the Word: Essays in Honor of Bernhard W.
Anderson* (JSOTSup 37; ed. J. T. Butler, E. W. Conrad, and B. C. Ollenburger; Sheffield:
JSOT Press, 1985) 208.

found, and only in 1966 was an inscription of Felix the procuator discovered.[140] As a matter of fact, there is still no contemporary attestation of Jesus or Paul.

If historians were to reject the account of Hannibal's fifteen-year campaign in Italy except where there was archaeological evidence, they would be confined to a few objects found at Lake Trasimene and a single inscription.[141] Roman historians do not reject Tacitus's account of Agricola's seven-year administration of Britain because only a single inscription of Agricola has been found there.[142]

3. *Hebrew Scriptures are rejected because they involve the intervention of a deity.* Critics reject the Hebrew Scriptures because biblical historiography invokes the intervention of Yahweh in working out his plans for his people. For example, Ahlström avers:

> Since the biblical text is concerned primarily with divine actions, which are not verifiable, it is impossible to use the exodus story as a source to reconstruct the history of the Late Bronze and Early Iron I periods. The text is concerned with mythology rather than with a detailed reporting of historical facts. As soon as someone "relates" a god's actions or words, mythology has been written.[143]

Yet Ahlström uses a double standard when he does not hesitate to use other ancient Near Eastern texts such as the Egyptian Merneptah inscription or the Moabite Mesha text that speak of divine action on behalf of the monarch.

Dever also comments, "The Bible contains no real historiography in the modern sense. . . . The modern notion of a disinterested secular history would have been inconceivable to Biblical writers."[144] Westermann notes that this view of history also arose from the Enlightenment: "The Old Testament has no concept of history, in the sense that history is only *history* that can be documented and that follows a verifiable course governed by causal laws."[145]

But the Old Testament's supernatural *Weltanschauung* is true of all ancient sources, some more than others, to be sure. Herodotus's belief in the Delphic Oracle does not disqualify him as an accurate source for Greek history.[146] Persian historians view Darius's Behistun inscription as

---

140. Yamauchi, *Stones and the Scriptures*, 159–60.
141. Gavin de Beer, *Hannibal* (New York: Viking, 1969) 141.
142. See W. S. Hanson, *Agricola and the Conquest of the North* (London: Batsford, 1987).
143. Ahlström, *Who Were the Israelites?* 46.
144. Dever, "Recent Archaeological Discoveries," 53.
145. Westermann, "The Old Testament's Understanding," 207.
146. E. Yamauchi, *Persia and the Bible* (Grand Rapids: Baker, 1990) 208–10.

the most informative Old Persian text.[147] They do not dismiss it because Darius invokes Ahura Mazda 69 times in the text. As A. Momigliano comments, "the basic elements of a sacred history are in Livy, as much as in the Pentateuch."[148]

4. *Hebrew Scriptures are rejected because they are viewed as ideologically conditioned.* Scholars like Thompson view Genesis and Exodus as "ideologically tendentious" and therefore completely irrelevant to the modern scholars' attempts to write a "scientific history" of early Israel.[149] But Roman historians do not reject Livy because his writings were ideologically slanted to promote the reign of Augustus, or Tacitus because of his senatorial prejudices against the emperors.[150] As A. N. Sherwin-White, a distinguished Roman historian, observes, "The refinement of source-criticism has not led to the notion that knowledge in ancient history is unattainable, or that the serious study of ancient politics is nothing but the history of rival propaganda."[151]

5. *Hebrew Scriptures that narrate stories about individuals rather than nations are judged unhistorical.* Van Seters's use of Huizinga's definition of *history* is an arbitrarily restrictive one that concentrates on the nation to the exclusion of the histories of individuals, families, clans, and tribes, which constitute much of the early materials of the Old Testament before the establishment of the monarchy under Saul. His view is a notion born of the Enlightenment. But as Westermann notes, "At the basis of this critique is the assumption that familial affairs have no place in *historical-political* events, which have to do instead with the nation, not with the family."[152]

6. *Hebrew Scriptures are rejected as historical when they betray literary traits.* Some critics have assumed that literary traits in the biblical narrative inevitably betray the fictional nature of the texts. In the eyes of some, anything that makes a story interesting or entertaining renders it suspect. Van Seters, who hails the Deuteronomist, regards his work primarily as literature.[153]

---

147. A number of scholars have suspected the Behistun Inscription for ideological rather than religious reasons, but wrongly so, in my opinion. See ibid., 143–45.

148. A. Momigliano, "Biblical Studies and Classical Studies: Simple Reflections upon Historical Method," *Annali della Scuola Normale Superiore* 11 (1981) 25.

149. Thompson, *Origin Tradition,* 1.39.

150. See M. L. W. Laistner, *The Greater Roman Historians* (Berkeley: University of California Press, 1963), chaps. 4 and 7.

151. A. N. Sherwin-White, *Roman Society and Roman Law in the New Testament* (Oxford: Clarendon, 1963) 186.

152. Westermann, "The Old Testament's Understanding," 211.

153. Van Seters, *In Search of History,* chap. 10.

But as Zevit reminds us, though history is indeed a genre of literature it should not be regarded as fiction: "The presence of literary patterns in such a composition does not necessarily invalidate its representation of events."[154] Halpern notes, "Historical narrative, the form in which history is presented, employs literary tropes; it is often highly stylized (as are the annals of the Assyrian kings, which by and large are fairly reliable)."[155]

Nor can literary analyses by themselves determine the date or historicity of biblical sources. In reviewing a work by Thompson, B. O. Long writes:

> Literary analyses, whether in the form of "source" or "redaction" criticism, composition theory as Thompson presents it, or modern structuralist analysis, are theoretical explanations for discontinuities which we observe in our reading of the canonical text. I am not sure that they contribute much, if anything, to the question of what in the utterance of an author, redactor, or implied author might be directly historical. That judgment must rest on other grounds.[156]

7. *The rejection of Hebrew Scriptures inevitably leads to historiographical suicide.* In a highly perceptive work the sociologist Peter Berger noted that the *a priori* rejection of the supernatural elements in the New Testament by Rudolf Bultmann inevitably led to theological suicide.[157] I would suggest that the rejection of the Old Testament texts inevitably leads to historiographical suicide either by degrees or at the outset.

Some scholars, such as Mendenhall and Gottwald, use the Scriptures in a highly selective manner to support their hypotheses. When one wonders why their theories are not better reflected in the biblical texts, the response is that such memories were suppressed! Others such as Lemche are more consistent in rejecting the Scriptures altogether.

Coote and Whitelam note the problem of setting aside the Old Testament, though they avoid its full implications:

> It might be thought that this debate strips the historian of the ability to write any kind of history of early Israel by removing the greatest body of information about its emergence and development that we have at hand. . . . The result has been for many a retreat into historiographic skepticism.[158]

---

154. Z. Zevit, "Clio, I Presume," *BASOR* 260 (1985) 78.
155. B. Halpern, "Biblical or Israelite History?" *The Future of Biblical Studies: The Hebrew Scriptures* (ed. R. E. Friedman and H. G. M. Williamson; Atlanta: Scholars Press, 1987) 111. D. C. Hopkins, in reviewing N. P. Lemche, *Ancient Israel*, in *JBL* 109 (1990) 319, comments: "The presence of ideology or fictional style offers no blanket criterion for rendering judgments about the historical intentions of a particular text."
156. B. O. Long, reviewing T. L. Thompson, *Origin Traditions of Israel*, in *JBL* 108 (1989) 330.
157. P. L. Berger, *A Rumor of Angels* (Garden City, N.Y.: Doubleday, 1970).
158. Coote and Whitelam, *Emergence of Early Israel*, 18.

As A. J. Hauser notes, "Lemche's discounting of the biblical traditions leaves no means of testing new hypotheses against the only major direct body of materials we possess relating to Israel's origin."[159]

Of such revisionists' rejection of texts like Herodotus, a Greek historian, Charles Hignett, writes that such scholars "remain undaunted by the results of their speculations, and after destroying the available ancient evidence settle down happily amid the ruins to write what can only be called historical fiction."[160]

8. *The rejection of the Hebrew Scriptures leaves us at the mercy of the hypotheses of scholars.* We are then left to the hypotheses of scholars who are quite assured that they know when and why scriptural texts were written and what is the best "scientific" explanation of the archaeological data. Such explanations still require faith, not in the Bible, but faith in the insight of a given scholar's reconstruction. As Hauser observes:

> Lemche *assumes* that the social, economic, cultural, and political analysis he presents concerning Palestine after 1500 B.C. relates directly to the origin of Israel, but that certainly is not a given, and constitutes no less a leap of faith than the assumption that certain core elements in the biblical traditions, such as Israel's coming to the land from outside, may be true.[161]

There often seems to be an inverse relationship between the lack of confidence in the historicity of texts and the scholar's self-confidence in his ability to analyze and date them. As R. E. Clements observes of Van Seters:

> Where other scholars have sought to trace datable connections with the Abraham tradition, Van Seters is uniformly critical. On the other hand, he is himself remarkably dogmatic about his ability to date features which few scholars would venture such confidence about.[162]

Coote, who rejects the patriarchal narratives as historical, has a better idea of why we have the story of Abraham. According to his interpretation,

> Abram was portrayed, moreover, as migrating from the far east solely because David's historian, as an urban cleric, employed cuneiform sources originating in Mesopotamia rather than Palestinian folk traditions for his history of early humanity, and thus at the appearance of Abraham had to shift the scene from Mesopotamia to Palestine.[163]

159. A. J. Hauser, review of Lemche, *Early Israel*, in *CBQ* 51 (1989) 526.

160. C. Hignett, *Xerxes' Invasion of Greece* (Oxford: Clarendon, 1963) 4.

161. Hauser, review of Lemche, *Early Israel*, 527.

162. R. E. Clements, review of J. Van Seters, *Abraham in History and Tradition*, in *JSS* 22 (1977) 92.

163. Coote, *Early Israel*, 157.

Readers may judge whether this is a more convincing explanation than the belief that the patriarchal narratives contained ancient traditions of an actual migration from Mesopotamia.

9. *These theories seek the explanation for the phenomenon of Israel in recurring geopolitical, ecological, or economic factors, using a reductionist methodology.* Whitelam claims, "It is now widely conceded that the study of history should not be restricted to the analysis of differences, the novel or the unique." It is inevitable that historical models influenced by the social sciences, such as anthropology, sociology, and economics, will conclude that Israel and its faith were not unique; these disciplines are inherently structured to recognize patterns, and are basically uninterested in the unique.[164]

This indeed is the programmatic task that Coote sets forth:

> To understand early Israel, one must once and for all leave behind the idea of an ideal community. One must set aside notions of the unique or social character of Israel, early or otherwise, and instead examine the sparse evidence with an eye for what is usual, normal, and expected in the history of Palestine.[165]

Having set out on such a quest, it is not surprising that Coote finds what he is looking for. Such scholars are confident that the material evidence is proof that Israelite religion cannot have been different from Canaanite religion.[166]

10. *Though scholars are united in their lack of confidence in Scripture and supremely confident in their own theories, they are highly critical of each other's views.* Mendenhall is rebuked by Ahlström and Lemche for overgeneralization. Gottwald, who acknowledges that he derived the original inspiration for his "revolt" model from Mendenhall, is nonetheless scathingly attacked by Mendenhall. Gottwald is criticized by Lemche for having assumed a tripartite system for ancient Near Eastern society, rather than a socio-economic continuum. Regarding Gottwald's favorite concept, Lemche declares:

> Whether these sorts of conditions have ever existed anywhere or are merely a *fata morgana* of the academic imagination, it is at least possible to say that no egalitarian socio-economic structure has characterized Palestine within the last 5,000 years or so.[167]

---

164. K. W. Whitelam, "Recreating The History of Israel," *JSOT* 35 (1986) 55.
165. Coote, *Early Israel*, viii.
166. Ahlström, *Who Were the Israelites?* 35; cf. W. G. Dever, "Material Remains and the Cult in Ancient Israel: An Essay in archaeological Systematics," in *The Word of the Lord Shall Go Forth: Essays in Honor of David Noel Freedman in Celebration of His Sixtieth Birthday* (ed. C. L. Meyers and M. O'Connor; Winona Lake, Ind.: Eisenbrauns, 1983) 578ff.
167. Lemche, *Ancient Israel*, 22.

Finkelstein is fairly scornful of the Revolt Models of both Mendenhall and Gottwald:

> While examples of this superficiality abound in fairly current publications, they are especially blatant in the works of members of the "sociological" school of Settlement study, since they, even more than others, are in need of a direct familiarity with environmental opinions. Gottwald, for example, resorted to distant parallels to shore up his opinions. . . , totally ignoring relevant population groups still living in traditional ways in the region under study.[168]

Finkelstein concludes his lengthy critique of the sociological models by observing:

> Finally, another crucial point that is usually forgotten in the heat of the debate is the simple fact that no process of the type hypothesized by Mendenhall and Gottwald can be traced in any ancient Near Eastern source.[169]

Lemche criticizes Coote and Whitelam for using rigid economic models:

> From the first to the last page of their book the two authors work with a consistent model for the emergence of ancient Israel in Palestine, and they never question their methodological basis. Nowhere are arguments tolerated which are not in accordance with the premises of the model.[170]

Finkelstein faults Coote and Whitelam for failing to utilize the archaeological data sufficiently.[171] He deems Lemche's "treatment of the archaeological materials" as "artificial and insufficient."[172] He also believes that archaeology refutes Halpern's theses.[173] In turn, Finkelstein's hypothesis is set aside as "improbable" by Coote.[174]

11. *Archaeology does not simply provide "objective" evidence, but rather data that must then be analyzed by "subjective" interpretation.* Some critics seem to oppose the "unhistorical" biblical stories to the "truly historical" methods of Syro-Palestinian archaeology, thereby understating the high degree of subjectivity that is involved in the interpretation of archaeological data.[175] One can see why this generation of scholars has ques-

---

168. Finkelstein, *Archaeology of the Israelite Settlement*, 21.

169. Ibid., 314.

170. Niels Peter Lemche, review of R. B. Coote and K. W. Whitelam, *The Emergence of Early Israel in Historical Perspective*, in *Bib* 69 (1988) 581.

171. I. Finkelstein, "The Emergence of Early Israel: Anthropology, Environment, and Archaeology," *JAOS* 110 (1990) 677–86.

172. Finkelstein, *Archaeology of the Israelite Settlement*, 21.

173. Ibid., 311.

174. Coote, *Early Israel*, 120.

175. See Long, review of Thompson, *The Origin Traditions of Israel*, in *JBL* 108 (1989) 329.

tioned early opinions of such giants in the field as Albright, Glueck, Kenyon, and Yadin, and why archaeologists have disagreed among themselves, most notoriously in the case of Yadin versus Aharoni. Questions of interpretation are especially acute in matters of dating and the identification of the agents involved in historical processes. One wonders how scholars such as Ahlström and Lemche are certain that sites were destroyed by the Egyptians and Sea Peoples rather than by the Israelites.

Dates are still difficult to assign to various strata, especially if one rejects the aid of Scripture as a historical background. Finkelstein states that it is impossible to say whether Bethel was destroyed in 1250 or in 1175, or whether the village at Ai was established in 1210 or 1125.[176] He himself seems consistently to prefer the later dates. Finkelstein observes:

> Another point to be emphasized is that trade, even when crucially important, can be archaeologically mute. The rise and fall of the Nabatean kingdom, for example, would not have been ascribed to the Arabian trade were it not for historical documentation.[177]

Tel Masos, a site seven mile east of Beersheba, was interpreted as an Israelite site by its excavator, Volkmar Fritz,[178] but this has been contested by Finkelstein and others.[179] A structure at Mt. Ebal discovered by Adam Zertal has been interpreted by him as an altar,[180] whereas Ahron Kempinski has interpreted it as a watchtower.[181]

12. *Archaeological continuity may not necessarily rule out the influx of newcomers.* Numerous scholars have pointed to the continuity of cultural artifacts between the Canaanite Late Bronze period and Iron I assemblages to rule out the idea of an incursion of a new ethnic element.[182] The presumed continuity has been stressed so much that differences in local traits and in quantitative distribution have been overlooked, according to Finkelstein:

> On the other hand, the pottery of Israelite Settlement sites in the hill country is completely different form that of the Canaanite centers, whereas the repertoire of Late Bronze types found at Israelite Settlement sites in the hill country was comparatively small. But while Late Bronze

---

176. Finkelstein, *Archaeology of the Israelite Settlement*, 315.

177. Finkelstein, "Emergence of Early Israel," 682.

178. Fritz, "The Israelite 'Conquest' in the Light of Recent Excavations"; idem, "Conquest or Settlement?"

179. Finkelstein, *Archaeology of the Israelite Settlement*, 45.

180. A. Zertal, "Has Joshua's Altar Been Found?" *BAR* 11/1 (1985) 26–43.

181. A. Kempinski, "Joshua's Altar: An Iron Age I Watchtower," *BAR* 12/1 (1986) 42, 44–49.

182. Ahlström, *Who Were the Israelites?* 3, 26; Whitelam, "Recreating the History," 60; Coote and Whitelam, *Emergence of Early Israel*, 126.

pottery was uniform in appearance throughout the country, Israelite Settlement pottery was characterized by locally divergent subtypes.[183]

In commenting on the conclusions drawn from this continuity in culture by other scholars, Finkelstein comments:

> Nor is it surprising to find points of similarity to Canaanite pottery, for groups lacking an established ceramic culture would, when undergoing the process of sedentarization, be likely to absorb traditions from the well-developed cultures in their vicinity, especially if they had contacts with the settled people before their sedentarization.[184]

Elsewhere he declares, "Even when new groups of people enter a given area, their material culture is soon influenced by the material culture prevailing in that area, and thus a seeming link to the previous period is forged."[185]

While Finkelstein's explanation is designed to suggest that the "Israelites" were not necessarily derived from the Canaanite settlements on the plains but from the pastoralists on the fringes, it could equally be suited to the phenomenon of a newer group immigrating from outside. This was what happened, for example, when the Kassites came down from the Zagros Mountains and settled in Mesopotamia.[186]

As an objection to the biblical view of the Conquest, Finkelstein presupposes that the archaeological data should show immediate evidence of occupation rather than a gap after Canaanite cities such as Hazor were destroyed.[187] But if one supposes that the Israelites were more accustomed to a pastoral way of life than to urban life, why should this be so? In the Aegean world, after the destruction of numerous Mycenaean settlements ascribed by Greek traditions to the Dorians, who were pastoralist Greeks from the north, there is also a considerable gap in reoccupied settlements.[188]

13. *The absence of archaeological evidence is not evidence of absence.* The positive evidence of new archaeological surveys in various districts of Israel is of the greatest significance and must be considered in all future discussions. On the other hand, the alleged absence of Late Bronze sites as evidence against the biblical Conquest is of another character.

183. Finkelstein, *Archaeology of the Israelite Settlement*, 313.
184. Ibid., 274.
185. Ibid., 338.
186. E. Yamauchi, "Kassites," *The New International Dictionary of Biblical Archaeology* (ed. E. M. Blaiklock and R. K. Harrison; Grand Rapids: Zondervan, 1983) 276–78.
187. Finkelstein, *Archaeology of the Israelite Settlement*, 299.
188. See V. R. d'A. Desborough, *The Last Mycenaeans and Their Successors* (Oxford: Clarendon, 1964).

Numerous scholars have pointed to the evidence of such sites as Jericho, Ai, and Gibeon as providing negative evidence against the biblical Model of a Conquest by Joshua. Finkelstein, for example, writes, "Late Bronze material was found in the cemetery at Gibeon. . . . But because no remains of the period have been found on the tell itself . . . , it is hard to envision an important city there at the time."[189] But such a conclusion fails to take into account the fact that a modern village, El-Jib, rests on the mound. As Pritchard himself wrote:

> Much of the evidence has been irretrievably denuded from the top of the wind-swept hill on which the city stood, and much of it remains to be uncovered in land that, for the present at least, is under cultivation in the olive orchards and vineyards of the peasants who eke out a livelihood in the village of El-Jib.[190]

Such apparent lack of archaeological evidence is not necessarily evidence of absence. First, numerous sites have not been excavated; second, in many cases no definitive final reports of excavated sites (Shechem, Dothan, etc.) have appeared; third, earlier reports have been questioned (e.g., Jericho), and some negative conclusions have been overturned by later excavations.

Outside of Israel this latter development has been illustrated on numerous occasions. Early British excavators dug at Zakro in Crete but missed a Minoan palace that was found later.[191] Austrian excavators dug at Ephesus after 1894 without finding any Late Bronze or Mycenaean materials; these were found only in 1963 by accident under a parking lot.[192] French excavators dug at Susa on the Apadana mound from 1851 to 1967; it was only in the 1970s that a monumental gate house was uncovered.[193]

In Jerusalem Kathleen Kenyon excavated the Ophel area from 1961 to 1967. At one site where her probes showed no evidence of walls, she concluded that no structures were present.[194] Later excavations by Meir Ben-Dov revealed a mammoth building with ten rooms, five cisterns, and three ritual baths.[195] The Danish excavator H. Kjaer worked in five

---

189. Finkelstein, *Archaeology of the Israelite Settlement*, 297.

190. J. B. Pritchard, "Gibeon: Where the Sun Stood Still," in *Archaeological Discoveries in the Holy Land* (New York: Crowell, 1967) 146.

191. *Archaeological Discoveries in the Holy Land*, 146.

192. E. Yamauchi, "The Archaeological Confirmation of Suspect Elements in the Classical and the Biblical Tradition," in *The Law and the Prophets: Essays in Honor of O. T. Allis* (ed. J. H. Skilton; Nutley, N.J.: Presbyterian and Reformed, 1974) 66.

193. Yamauchi, *Persia and the Bible*, 298–300.

194. K. Kenyon, *Digging up Jerusalem* (London: Benn, 1974).

195. M. Ben-Dov, *In the Shadow of the Temple* (New York: Harper & Row, 1985) 34, 150–53.

areas at Shiloh from 1926 to 1929. Only a few Late Bronze objects, which were not found *in situ*, turned up.[196] But then the site was re-excavated by Finkelstein in 1981–84. He reports, "During our excavations, it became clear that there was a genuine Late Bronze stratum at Shiloh, directly beneath the Iron I level."[197]

Isserlin has compared the evidence in Canaan for the Israelite Conquest with other invasions and conquests in later history that are well documented.[198] He used three examples: (1) the Arab invasion of Palestine in the seventh century, (2) the invasion of Britain by the Anglo-Saxons in the fifth century, and (3) the invasion of England by the Normans in 1066. In each case the textual evidence, like the Bible, spoke of numerous destructions, whereas the archaeological evidence was extremely scanty, if not nonexistent. Does this mean that one cannot believe that those invasions took place? I think not. In these cases, as in the biblical example, I would argue that the textual evidence must be primary even where the archaeological evidence is lacking.

196. H. Kjaer, "A Summary Report of the Second Danish Expedition, 1929," *Palestine Exploration Fund Quarterly Statement* (1931) 71–88.

197. Finkelstein, *Archaeology of the Israelite Settlement*, 218; cf. 319. Finkelstein does not believe that there was a settlement but rather a cultic center there in the Late Bronze era.

198. B. S. J. Isserlin, "The Israelite Conquest of Canaan," *PEQ* 115 (1983) 85–94. A very important survey, which appeared after I had written this essay, is: Richard S. Hess, "Early Israel in Canaan: A Survey of Recent Evidence and Interpretations," *PEQ* 125 (1993) 125–42.

Story, History, and Theology

A. R. Millard

Liverpool University

There are a variety of ways of studying the Old Testament, and there are various levels of study. Although the title of the present study concerns questions of history and literature, the focus here is primarily on the ancient Near East. It needs to be made clear at the outset that comparing biblical texts with those from other regions and cultures of the ancient world cannot prove the Hebrew material is true in any way, but comparisons can help in understanding and evaluating it, especially when it stands alone, as it usually does.[1] The Bible is "a holy book that tells stories," according to a recent analysis of Kings,[2] raising the question: What is a story? The Oxford English Dictionary sets out several definitions of *story*, the English word having the same origin as *history*. Its first meaning, now obsolete, is "a narrative, true or presumed to be true," another meaning is "history . . . as opposed to fiction," another, "a recital of events that have or are alleged to have happened," and then "a narrative of real or, more usually, fictitious events, designed for the entertainment of the hearer or reader." The last is probably the most widely accepted use of the word today.

Some stories are acceptable simply as entertainment, however unlikely their plot or circumstances (e.g., "Jack and the Beanstalk" or space stories); others are acceptable because they present situations that the audience perceives to be realistic, even though they may be exaggerated, or

---

1. M. Malul does not seem to have understood my position on the purpose of comparative studies in *The Comparative Method in Ancient Near Eastern and Biblical Legal Studies* (AOAT 227; Kevelaer: Butzon & Bercker/Neukirchen-Vluyn: Neukirchener Verlag, 1990) 58.

2. B. O. Long, *1 Kings, with an Introduction to Historical Literature* (FOTL 9; Grand Rapids: Eerdmans, 1984).

to be morally correct (i.e., the "good" win). In some cases the veracity of the story affects the audience directly. News stories demonstrate this point: announcements of disaster prompt the desire to help, and reports of an attack on strongly-held beliefs provoke riots, as the Salman Rushdie affair shows. The supposed truth of a story asserting that a present state results from certain events in the past can mold a nation's history. Thus, the hostility between Israelis and Arabs stems from the Jewish conviction that the land of Canaan was given to their ancestors by God and therefore still belongs to them, while the Arabs assert that it is theirs through Ishmael, Abraham's eldest son. Neither claim can be proved. For many stories, the real value does lie in the claims they make to be true: the events told and the views expressed did occur in that way and were spoken in that sense. If, for example, no Israelites escaped from Egypt and made their way to the Promised Land, the Exodus story becomes a pious fiction and its portrayal of a redeeming God is no more than a dream. Any other ancient theologian could concoct a different story with an utterly amoral deity at its center and demand that his concept be treated as equally valid. Of course, that is what did happen and still continues. The biblical challenge is to a faith in a God who has actually revealed himself by words and deeds that men have heard and experienced in the past and not, therefore, to a totally subjective faith that may build on other people's opinions but is ultimately a matter of what one chooses to believe. Its challenge is to a faith that has as part of its evidence objective, historical episodes that display consistency with recorded statements. This is far from being "a faith based on works," a mechanical system into which one fits, for the major tenets the biblical faith demands are inevitably beyond proof (the existence of God, the resurrection of Jesus); otherwise faith would not be required. The biblical stories give grounds for the validity of these beliefs, and if they are largely fictional, then their value is no greater than the value of the Greek myths or the stories of King Arthur; they give no aid to faith.

Story, Not History?

Biblical scholars today offer various criteria for arguing that narratives in the Old Testament are story rather than history. Although already more than fifteen years old, James Barr's paper "Story and History in Biblical Theology" is a useful starting point because he set out the case with his usual clarity.[3] Barr stated his view, "The long, narrative corpus

---

3. J. Barr, "Story and History in Biblical Theology," *Journal of Religion* 56 (1976) 1–17; repr. in *The Scope and Authority of the Bible* (London: SCM, 1980) 1–17.

of the Old Testament seems to me, as a body of literature, to merit the title of story rather than that of history. Or, to put it in another way, it seems to merit entirely the title of story, but only in part the title of history." He listed certain ways in which the narrative material of the Old Testament differs from history:[4]

1. Elements belonging to the area of myth and legend are present in "material running all through the patriarchal period and indeed right down through the later story to the end of the kingdom."
2. The mixing of human and divine actions as the cause of events and "the statement of events utilizing express and large-scale divine intervention are also present."
3. Motives appear that are not "historical" but "aetiological," explaining "how something came to be as it now is," and "paradigms" that provide "analogies in which experience, past or future, can be understood and expressed."
4. There is a notable absence of "some critical evaluation of sources and reports."

These factors, Barr argued, mean that the term *history* is unsuitable for the compositions containing them; *story* is more appropriate. Using the term *story* raises questions about the material that require further investigation, for the answers commonly given rest on assumptions that can be disputed.

The Authors as Critics

Each of the factors listed deserves consideration, and for the purpose of this paper they are best taken in reverse order. Critical questioning of sources is present, Barr asserted, in the work of Herodotus at the beginning of Greek history writing, in contrast to the Bible. In Herodotus, this attitude is most obvious when the author reports what he has heard and then adds a skeptical or negative comment of his own. For example, he repeats a Scythian tale that once a year every member of a neighboring tribe turns into a wolf for a day or two, and comments, "For myself, I cannot believe this tale."[5] On the other hand, there are many instances where the historian is convinced of the truth of what he records but realizes that his readers may not credit it, the case of Babylonia's astonishing fertility being one.[6] Herodotus' critical attitude is apparent through

---

4. Barr, "Story and History," 7.
5. Herodotus 4.105 (9 books; LCL 117–20; Cambridge: Harvard University Press, 1922–28).
6. Herodotus 1.193.

his own comments. Even so, he reports without comment many things that are recognized today as untrue (e.g., that the semen of Indians and Ethiopians is black, like their skins)[7] and takes some incidents as "clear evidence of divine intervention."[8]

Yet it is surely possible that a critical attitude did lie behind the selection the compilers of Kings made from more extensive records. The Israelite presentation of history did involve critical judgment, inasmuch as it claims to be true, thereby making others' claims false, to a greater or lesser degree. Moabite or Assyrian viewpoints were denied: the God of Israel raised Assyria and cast her down, not the god Aššur. Israelite history writers had little interest in telling their readers what they did not believe to be true (unless it was vital to their narrative, such as the Assyrian claims in the messages to Jerusalem). These writers were not jackdaw historians, like Herodotus who relayed any piece of information brought to his attention, whether he believed it or not, as a means of preserving the memory of the past.[9] The Israelite historians had definite purpose in their writing and rejected the irrelevant, informing the inquisitive that there were sources containing other material that they could consult if they wished (e.g., "the book of the annals of the kings of Israel," 2 Kgs 1:18). Where Herodotus might have included the story of Balaam, now partly known from the inscribed plaster fragments from Tell Deir ᶜAlla, the Israelite historians would not have, because they would have recognized it as untrue.

Etiology and History

Neither etiological nor paradigmatic narratives can have a place in historical writing, according to Barr. These are "two modes in which the 'mythical' thinking of Israel flows into the 'historical' writing."[10] On a larger scale, it may be noted, all history writing is a specie of etiology, and analogy is basic to the work of modern historians. Within the context of ancient recording, there is an assumption shared by many that has to be contested, namely, that an etiological narrative is by nature unhistorical. This is not so; it is an example of the adage, "Give a dog a bad name. . . ." The term *etiological* is purely descriptive. An etiological narrative is one that gives the past reason for a present circumstance. Etiologi-

---

7. Herodotus 3.101.
8. Herodotus 7.138.
9. Herodotus, Prologue.
10. Following R. Smend, *Elemente alttestamentlichen Geschichtsdenkens* (Theologische Studien 95; Zürich: EVZ, 1968).

cal narratives are found worldwide, many involving gods or goddesses, the devil, or legendary beings, to give the reason for certain customs or features[11] (e.g., unexpected natural or man-made features of the landscape given names like "the Devil's Punchbowl" and "Devil's Dyke"). The etiologies identified in biblical writings tend to have putatively historical figures or moments as their focus (such as the stones set up at Gilgal in Joshua 4). Etiologies of this kind may be the inventions of folklore or propaganda to enhance a pilgrim site. Attention has been drawn to the "ability of striking phenomena to form traditions,"[12] but it is as illogical to argue for imaginary stories underlying every tradition on the basis of that observation as it is to argue in favor of a historical basis for every tradition from the ascertainable authenticity of traditional explanations given to some striking phenomena.

A particular event can give a name to a place and through that name have its memory preserved. In the south of England stand the ruins of a medieval abbey named Battle Abbey. Visitors who ask the reason for the name are told how William of Normandy defeated and killed Harold II, the Saxon king of England, there in October 1066 and won the country for himself. In thanksgiving to God he founded the abbey two years later. This is an etiological story that need not be doubted, one that is accepted as accurate in modern historical writing. It is accepted because there is good evidence for it from more than one source. The impossibility of demonstrating the accuracy of a biblical etiology such as that of the twelve stones at Gilgal does not require it to be rejected as devoid of factual basis. Each etiology has to be examined from both points of view before any verdict is passed; the name alone can neither validate nor invalidate the information carried with it.

There is, equally, reason to contest the claim that the paradigmatic form of reporting events is "not really historical in original basis and motivation." Ancient writers deliberately set out the reports of military campaigns in paradigmatic form, demonstrating sequences of events, actions, and their consequences, which they saw repeated and accepted as conforming to certain patterns.[13] Rebellion against the suzerain brought his forces to the vassal's territory in punishment, just as Israel's apostasy brought her enemies to humiliate her. These extrabiblical accounts are

---

11. G. S. Kirk, *The Nature of Greek Myths* (Harmondsworth: Penguin, 1974) 53ff.

12. M. Weippert, *The Settlement of the Israelite Tribes in Palestine* (London: SCM, 1971) 139.

13. For some discussion, see M. Liverani, "Memorandum on the Approach to Historiographic Texts," *Or* n.s. 42 (1973) 178–94, especially 182–83; and essays in *Assyrian Royal Inscriptions: New Horizons in Literary, Ideological, and Historical Analysis* (ed. F. M. Fales; Orientis antiqui Collectio 17; Rome: Istituto per l'Oriente, 1981).

really historical in their basis, and their motivation follows their authors'
philosophies of history clearly, leading the audience to expect recurrence
of the sequence on the one hand and to recognize that departure from
the pattern would point to a basic difference in the events.

Divine Intervention and History

Divine intervention in human affairs was the second of Barr's points
of difference between history and the Old Testament texts:

> The story moves back and forward, quite without embarrassment, be-
> tween human causation and divine causation, between the statement of
> events in entirely human terms . . . and the statement of events in a fash-
> ion utilizing express and large-scale divine intervention. The ability to
> mingle these styles is a mark of the genius of the literature, but it is also a
> sign that history is not a governing factor in the selection and presentation
> of material.

The matter of divine intervention in events will receive attention later
(pp. 63–64); here the pervasive biblical belief that God spoke directly to
individuals calls for attention. Communication between God and man is
integral to the biblical writings yet is a feature beyond historical verification. Naturally, a twentieth-century writer is tempted to discount these
records as fantasy or as the inventions of ancient authors, and, in biblical
studies, they may be treated as a means of giving authority to particular
opinions. However, it is beyond doubt that major events in the history of
the world have resulted from the conviction of one person or another
who believed he had heard heavenly voices giving instructions. Muham-
mad is the outstanding example since the rise of Christianity, but, as for
biblical history, there are no contemporary documents available to assess.
In another case there are directly relevant contemporary texts, the case of
the Maid of Orleans, Joan of Arc. In 1429, this seventeen-year-old girl
roused her countrymen to face English forces and drive them out of part
of France. Her charismatic leadership was produced by voices she heard,
celestial voices, she claimed, a claim that ultimately led to her being
burned as a witch. Her achievement is a matter of history, its causes open
to various analyses. Narrating both the girl's claims and their effects in
the language of the time is a form of history writing that many find satisfactory. Extracts from Sir Winston Churchill's account of Joan illustrate
that. He recounted her visions and their impact on her:

> In the fields where she tended her sheep the saints of God, who grieved
> for France, rose before her in visions. St. Michael himself appointed her,
> by divine right, to command the armies of liberation. . . . There welled in

the heart of the Maid a pity for the realm of France, sublime, perhaps miraculous, certainly invincible.

The consequence was not limited to Joan's family or village or compatriots:

> The report of a supernatural visitant sent by God to save France, which inspired the French, clouded the minds and froze the energies of the English. The sense of awe, and even of fear, robbed them of their assurance.[14]

Historians may explain the voices in the context of hallucinations not uncommon among adolescents, girls in particular, and give weight to political machinations and shifting alliances to present the episode in a more prosaic way, yet they cannot deny that Joan's convictions carried her countrymen to victory and herself to the stake (May 29, 1431).[15] Older descriptions incorporating similar events may warrant equal confidence. How Moses, David, or Isaiah, for example, were aware God spoke to them is an unanswerable question, yet they were certain and acted accordingly. The presence of a report of a divine communication does not invalidate the accompanying episodes in biblical or other ancient texts any more than it does in the story of Joan of Arc. Whether scholars today share the belief that these figures were in communication with a supernatural power, or not, has no effect on the fact that these people possessed such beliefs or on the fact of their ensuing actions. Those actions and their results may be open to the historian's scrutiny.

Legend, Folklore, and History

Barr's initial objection to classing the biblical narrative as history is the presence of legendary elements. To a great extent, the arguments already given about reports of heavenly voices apply here. When the compiler(s) of Kings included the incident of the iron axhead that floated, they were plainly not interested in the mechanism that brought about the unexpected, only in recording the event (2 Kgs 6:1–7). If their record reads like a legend today, that may be due in part to the brevity of the account and in part to the conditioning of the modern reader. Neither is sufficient ground for demoting it from "history" to "legend" without more ado. Other reasons may be adduced from the position of the pericope in a series of stories about Elisha for suggesting that this is one of a cluster of popular tales, but there is nothing in it itself to mark

14. Winston S. Churchill, *A History of the English-Speaking Peoples* (London: Cassell, 1956) 1:328, 330.

15. See W. S. Scott, *Jeanne d'Arc* (London: Harrap, 1974) 131–45; and E. Lucie-Smith, *Joan of Arc* (London: Lane, 1976) 14ff.

it as a composition of different nature from the accounts of David's wars
or Merodach-Baladan's embassy to Hezekiah. The inability of modern
man to do as Elisha did is no basis for denying the ancient report, any
more than the inability of most people today to divine for water proves
that it is impossible.

Interwoven with the terms *legend* and *etiology* is another concept often
used in describing biblical narratives: *folktale.* Folktales arise all over the
world and may contain myths, legends, and etiologies. They may be etiological in purpose, or they may be hero tales. Analysis of folktales has
revealed recurrent motifs, which have been catalogued and indexed.
These motifs may be universal, or common to many similar communities, and disclose some of the hopes and fears, the values and taboos of
the societies where they were known. In the Bible the most famous example is the story of Moses in the Bullrushes (Exod 1:8–2:10), which is
a case of "the common motif of the exposed child, who is rescued to become king," according to many commentators.[16]

A century ago, the discovery of a Babylonian story about the birth
and exposure in a basket on a river of a baby who was rescued and became Sargon, founder of the Dynasty of Akkad (ca. 2300 B.C.), encour-
aged scholars to suppose a Hebrew writer adopted a current motif to his
hero Moses.[17] Examining the Sargon legend, Brian Lewis collected
seventy-one other specimens of the tale of the hero cast away at birth,
ranging from a Hittite text of the sixteenth century B.C. to East-Asian
versions of recent times—and Superman![18] In some the motif is clear; in
others alterations are assumed, as when a flight through the desert re-
places abandonment in the case of the birth of Jesus.[19] Behind them all is
deduced a hypothetical archetype arising in the Near East well before the
date of the Hittite representative. Another common motif is the poor
boy who rises to wealth and fame, or its fellow, the youngest son who
outstrips his brothers. Joseph and David exemplify the latter.

It is logical to see the common motifs and label the biblical narratives
"folktales" like all the others. This is a suitable classification, yet in its
common use it carries a connotation that is not always justifiable, in the
same way that the term *etiology* does: a folktale is thought to be a fictional

16. B. S. Childs, *Exodus* (OTL; London: SCM/Philadelphia: Westminster, 1974) 12.
17. The Assyriologist W. W. Hallo, noting the seventh-century B.C. date of the
manuscripts of the Sargon Legend, raised the possibility of Babylonian borrowing from
the Moses story in "The Birth of Kings," *Love and Death in the Ancient Near East: Essays
in Honor of Marvin H. Pope* (ed. J. H. Marks and R. M. Good; Guilford, Conn.: Four
Quarters, 1987) 45–52, esp. p. 47.
18. B. Lewis, *The Sargon Legend* (ASOR Dissertations Series 4; Cambridge, Mass.:
American Schools of Oriental Research, 1980).
19. Ibid., 164, 201 n. 41.

or imaginary story with little likelihood of any foundation in historical events. Yet there are folktales that have their origins in real events, even though they conform to common patterns. The poor boy rising against the odds to fame and fortune is the theme of the story of Dick Whittington, who became Lord Mayor of London, a theme illustrated many times over in the history of the United States.

From this observation a very significant factor in the recurrence of folktale themes appears: those themes will be common that societies will readily accept, that is, themes that reflect the experiences of the societies or kinds of events that they can envisage. These experiences may be real, therefore, or exaggerations of reality, or imaginary. My purpose here is to stress that they may be real. Mankind worldwide shares obvious basic features and functions and reacts in the same way to certain situations. Thus, the mother who cannot keep her baby, yet tries to save its life at the same time as she abandons it, is a figure of our society today. Newspapers report such occurrences from time to time, and were one of those babies to become prominent in later years, the unusual circumstances of the first days of its life could well be made known. The unexpected is the more memorable when it is associated with a famous person. In pre-Christian societies, unwanted babies were often discarded on town rubbish dumps, so a child more carefully left and then rescued could gain attention. That the Sargon and Moses stories both have the baby placed in a basket on the river need not demonstrate a link between them; that feature may be no more than the inevitable result of the setting for each story.

In Babylonia, the waters of the river supplied a natural means of waste disposal: dead bodies and other unwanted things could be carried out of sight. The presence of a "folklore" motif need not count against the actuality of a particular case. Sargon's birth story is beyond verification; however, a number of other texts that tell of his triumphs when he had risen to rule Babylonia can be investigated historically. All the available manuscripts originated later than 1800 B.C., that is, at least five hundred years after Sargon's death. Some are literary compositions, "legends" of campaigns against enemies at home and far away, in Syria, Anatolia, and even Crete.[20] Another group is a series of scribal exercises done between 1800 and 1600 B.C., copies of ancient royal monuments. Everything indicates that these are accurate, reliable reproductions of texts carved in stone or engraved on metal, available to the scribes at the

20. A new edition of the texts by J. Goodnick Westenholz will be published soon, *Legends of the Kings of Akkade* (Mesopotamian Civilizations 7; Winona Lake, Ind.: Eisenbrauns, forthcoming).

time they were made. At Sargon's table, according to one of these, 5400 soldiers took their meals.[21] Reluctance to place any historical value on these records has been giving place in recent years to recognition that they preserve credible and valuable information from Sargon's reign.[22] Gaston Maspero's negative verdict on the Sargon Legend a century ago[23] is being replaced by more positive evaluations, such as "there is nothing incredible in the statements attributed by this 'legend' to Sargon,"[24] even though the words themselves are unlikely to be "an authentic utterance of the great king." The far-reaching expeditions have gained some credibility as knowledge of the third millennium B.C. has increased. Historians are prepared to treat the legions of men eating at the king's table as fact.[25] Now, both journeys to exotic places and extravagant displays of hospitality are natural themes of folklore, yet here they are treated as events of history, although in the first case related in a story "applying . . . romantic color to facts which might seem exciting enough in themselves."[26]

Faced with examples like these from the ancient Near East, it is hard to accept the wholesale judgment of a modern historian on the accounts of Solomon's reign. Thus "close parallels in stories associated with other kings of the ancient world" allegedly cast doubt on "the report of Yahweh's appearance to Solomon in a dream while he slept in the Gibeon sanctuary."[27] A passage from Herodotus is the sole example offered,[28] despite the existence of numerous instances of first-hand report in cuneiform and Egyptian royal inscriptions of royal experiences, real or claimed, more like Solomon's (e.g., Gudea, Thutmosis IV).[29] Again, the historicity of the "pharaoh's daughter," mentioned four different times (1 Kgs 3:1–2; 9:16, 24; 11:1), is doubted on similar grounds. She also turns up

21. E. Sollberger and J.-R. Kupper, *Inscriptions royales sumériennes et akkadiennes* (LAPO 3; Paris: Du Cerf, 1971) 99.

22. C. J. Gadd, "The Dynasty of Agade and the Gutian Invasion," in *Early History of the Middle East* (CAH 1/2; 3d ed.; Cambridge: Cambridge University Press, 1971) 417–63.

23. Gaston Maspero (*The Dawn of Civilization* [London: SPCK, 1885] 599) argued that the Sargon Legend projected into a remote past the deeds of Sargon II of Assyria, ca. 721–705 B.C., telling nothing of an earlier period.

24. Gadd, "The Dynasty of Agade," 418.

25. See B. R. Foster's review of Aage Westenholz, *Old Sumerian and Old Akkadian Texts in Philadelphia*, Part 2, in *BiOr* 46 (1989) 358; Foster comments on the organization of the court.

26. Gadd, "The Dynasty of Agade," 429.

27. J. M. Miller, *A History of Ancient Israel and Judah* (ed. J. M. Miller and J. H. Hayes; London: SCM/Philadelphia: Westminster, 1986) 195.

28. Herodotus 2.141.

29. A. L. Oppenheim, *The Interpretation of Dreams in the Ancient Near East* (Transactions of the American Philosophical Society 46/3; Philadelphia: American Philosophical Society, 1986).

fairly regularly in Arabic lore.[30] This is no reason for doubting the biblical text; Solomon and other figures from the Bible also frequent Arabic lore simply because the Bible was a major source of Islam. Parallel stories of diplomatic marriages are no basis for discounting this one as "fanciful." The expression is also applied to "the sweeping editorial claims regarding Solomon's daily food supply (ten oxen, twenty cattle, a hundred sheep, and on and on)." A host of ancient records document the food supplies of courts in Babylonia, Egypt, and elsewhere, from the menu of the celebratory banquet at the inauguration of Ashurnasirpal's palace at Calah (Nimrud) for 69,574 people in 879 B.C.,[31] to the daily barley supplies for the palace at Mari a millennium earlier.[32] Where quantities can be compared, Solomon's are not extraordinary. As with Sargon, so with Solomon, the sources can be treated soberly as the basis for satisfactory historical reconstructions. Modern readers are not forced to conclude that the texts portray an "idealized Solomon of legend."

The purpose of the stories is also important. Folktales entertain, hence the frequent appearance of the fantastic or the farcical. Biblical stories rarely have that aim; rather, they make a point connected to a larger narrative, or they give information pertinent to the narrative. They may, like the Sargon Legend, enhance the picture of a hero. Unlike sagas and epics, which are designed to entertain, biblical stories are not burdened with or extended by circumstantial detail or descriptions that add nothing to the story line.

Storytelling and History

The biblical stories possess a continuing appeal that is a tribute to the skill of the narrators. The setting of scenes, delineation of character and development of plot is usually done with great economy. Recent decades have seen the art of the storytellers become a major topic of research, approached along several avenues. Beside continuing search for sources and traces of redactional activity, concern has grown for the books or narrative blocks as wholes. This falls into two categories. One is the approach to the texts as artistic creations, advocated in the writings of Robert Alter and others. The other is the structural analysis that tries to uncover universal concepts at the roots of the stories, either in function, as pioneered

---

30. Miller, *History of Ancient Israel*, 195.
31. A. Leo Oppenheim, "Babylonian and Assyrian Historical Texts," in *ANET*, 558–60.
32. ARM 9:246–47; S. Dalley, *Mari and Karana* (London: Longman, 1984) 78–96; K. A. Kitchen, "Food," in *The New Bible Dictionary* (2d ed.; ed. J. D. Douglas and N. Hillyer; Leicester: InterVarsity, 1982) 386–87.

by the Russian folklorist Vladimir Propp, or in "binary discriminations," like good and bad, as developed by the French ethnologist Claude Levi-Strauss.[33] Fascinating and instructive insights come out of all these approaches, enhancing appreciation of the stories in many ways. Before a full assessment of their value for *biblical* studies can be made, comparative studies are needed. Does structural analysis give the same results when it is applied to Assyrian royal "annals" or other ancient Near Eastern narratives? Can comparable skills of storytelling be found in those texts, even if at a lower level? Certainly they have plots, characterizations, and clear goals.[34] The reasons for asking these questions about *extrabiblical* sources are, first, the various similarities between them and the biblical texts and, second, a strong suspicion that many of the features and dimensions literary and structural studies have brought to light are not peculiar to storytelling but are inherent in much of human narration of all kinds.

"In a real sense, the writing of history is creative activity, though what it creates is something which has really gone on."[35] This creative activity can involve many of the ingredients of the storyteller's art. Unless the storyteller is composing the first narrative his language or culture has ever known, orally or in writing, he is likely to employ inherited words and phrases, figures, and patterns. Not all of these need to be borrowed from compositions in the same genre as the teller's. Some will be shared with many societies, such as a "bad" king becoming "good" as a result of a religious conversion or a political *volte-face*, depending on the stance and purpose of the narrator. Some genres arise from the customs of the storyteller's society. Messengers, for example, may bring a token of the truth of their words, whether the words are divine or human: in Babylonian myth, the winds carry the feathers of the defeated Anzu-bird to the gods; in an Assyrian royal inscription and on its sculptured counterpart soldiers bear the head of a conquered king to the emperor.[36] Where writing was entirely in the hands of professional scribes for whom the works of earlier generations were schoolbooks, echoes of one piece of literature in another or direct quotations and stock phrases are to be expected.[37] The history writer is only as limited to the repertoire of his

33. For a summary see M. W. G. Stibbe, "Structuralism," in *A Dictionary of Biblical Interpretation* (ed. R. J. Coggins and J. L. Houlden; London: SCM, 1990) 650–55.

34. Cf. H. G. Güterbock's remarks on the Hittite "Proclamation of Telepinu," in *History, Historiography and Interpretation* (ed. H. Tadmor and M. Weinfeld; Jerusalem: Magnes, 1983) 28–29.

35. J. Marsh, *Saint John* (Harmondsworth: Penguin, 1968) 18.

36. E. Reiner, *Your Thwarts in Pieces, Your Mooring Rope Cut: Poetry from Babylonia and Assyria* (Ann Arbor: Dept. of Slavic Studies, University of Michigan, 1985) 65–66.

37. Ibid., chap. 2; cf. W. W. Hallo, "The Limits of Skepticism," *JAOS* 110 (1990) 187–99, esp. 190–91.

genre as any other artist is, namely, by the constraints of the primary materials. The writer's store of language, experience, and imagination can all contribute to enriching the narrative without smothering the reality of the events he describes or detracting from it. To speak of Solomon's wealth as so great that silver had no value, "as common in Jerusalem as stones" (1 Kgs 10:27), is oriental hyperbole of exactly the same sort as the assertions by indigent Mesopotamian kings who wrote to the Pharaoh, "Gold is like dust in your land, one simply scoops it up" (El Amarna Letters 16, 19, 20, 29).[38] The writers were describing unusual riches in phrases that convey the thought clearly enough, without demanding a literal interpretation.

Now such expressions approach the legendary portrayals of a garden of gem-fruited trees in the "Epic of Gilgamesh" (Tablet IX, end), in Jewish traditions about Solomon, and elsewhere.[39] The Gilgamesh passage may reflect a traveler's tale of a luxuriant orchard in distant Anatolia, embellished so that it no longer describes a specific place. Can a difference between metaphor and fiction be established? Distinguishing *story*, as a narrative that may or may not report real events, from *history*, which is required to be factual narrative, is made more difficult since both may use the same language and relate comparable episodes. Egyptologists face this problem with the text called "The Taking of Joppa." A general, Djehuty, captured Joppa by gaining the confidence of the local ruler, then introducing his soldiers into the city hidden in baskets, a stratagem recalling the Trojan Horse.[40] Djehuty is known to have served Thutmosis III (ca. 1479–1425 B.C.), who rewarded him with a golden dish now in the Louvre. Is the story history, legend, or a mixture? Egyptologists are ambivalent, the authors of a standard handbook saying, "it is not entirely unlikely. . . . it may seem dangerous to count as historical an event, however likely, which is attested by a single story which has clear legendary inspiration."[41] Another author remarks, "Although the details of the story . . . may be of the stuff of folklore rather than history, the central fact that the city was besieged and taken may well be true."[42] Terms like *legendary inspiration* and *folkloristic features* flow as easily from the pen as *etiology*, and the same dangers accompany them. Skeptical or negative

---

38. W. L. Moran, *Les Lettres d'El Amarna* (LAPO 13; Paris: Du Cerf, 1987).

39. P. Soucek, "The Temple of Solomon in Legend and Art," *The Temple of Solomon* (ed. J. Gutmann; Missoula, Mont.: Scholars Press, 1976) 73–123, especially 86–87.

40. J. A. Wilson, "Egyptian Myths, Tales, and Mortuary Texts," *ANET,* 22–23.

41. E. Drioton and J. Vandier, *L'Égypte* (Paris: Presses Universitaires, 1952) 496–97.

42. M. S. Drower, "Syria *c.* 1550–1400 B.C.," in *The Middle East and the Aegean Region c. 1800–1380 B.C.* (*CAH* 2/1; 3d ed.; Cambridge: Cambridge University Press, 1973) 447.

attitudes are adopted toward the whole of a narrative containing these elements, often without the caution just quoted, because discarding what seems less than likely can, superficially, be presented as the "scientific" way. However, discarding should be the last resort, for it risks rejecting evidence that may be the only source for an episode of history.

For the most part, biblical stories are uncorroborated, like the "Taking of Joppa." There is no way, therefore, to prove the nature of them as either historical or fictional. What can be done is to establish some criteria that may guide in evaluating their role for a modern re-creation of the history of Israel.[43]

1. Anachronisms may indicate that the story comes from a period long after the events it describes, if they are true anachronisms. Anachronisms may appear in language, the attitudes or behavior of the characters, the context of the story, or the material equipment (*Realien*).
2. Imaginary or fantastic elements will prove that the story stands some distance from reality, but these should be truly imaginary, such as gem-bearing trees or flying horses, not phenomena that are explicable, like the voices Joan of Arc heard or divine interventions (a topic discussed below).
3. There should be no irreconcilable contradiction with other, connected biblical texts.

Beyond these, all judgments are subjective (they cannot be otherwise), and each passage should be given an equal and equitable judgment. Literary, folkloristic, etiological, paradigmatic, and all other ways of studying the narratives are to be welcomed, but no one of them can take priority over any other except for the assessment of them for what they claim to be on their own terms.

THEOLOGY AND HISTORY

Without the Bible and books based on it, we would not even have an outline of Israel's history.[44] Inscriptions from other nations (Egypt,

43. For a more detailed series of criteria proposed for the evaluation of partially comparable material preserved in Greek tradition see J. K. Davies, "The Reliability of the Oral Tradition," *The Trojan War: Its Historicity and Context* (ed. L. Foxhall and J. K. Davies; Bristol: Bristol Classical Press, 1984) 87–119, esp. 98–101. For a discussion of similar issues in gospel criticism, see S. C. Goetz and C. L. Blomberg, "The Burden of Proof," *JSNT* 11 (1981) 39–63.

44. The second part of this paper includes some material taken from two of my earlier studies, "The Old Testament and History: Some Considerations," *FT* 110 (1983) 34–53; and "Sennacherib's Attack on Hezekiah," *TynBul* 36 (1985) 61–77.

Assyria, Babylonia, Moab) mention the names of various kings in Samaria or Jerusalem, or report a few military events. Archaeological discoveries disclose the cultures of Palestine in the Bronze and Iron ages without presenting any features that mark parts of them as Israelite rather than Ammonite, Edomite, or Phoenician, except for documents written in Hebrew. The Bible, therefore, is the only extensive source for writing a history of Israel. Questions arise, however, about interpreting what it says, even in the "historical" books, because of its nature: it is a religious book, the product of the growth of Israelite faith over several centuries. The books of the Old Testament were brought together by Jews who believed they contained divine revelation, although the date and circumstances of that collection are obscure. Many of the books themselves were clearly written to present and explain Israel's history from a particular point of view; they are, therefore, forms of propaganda. It follows that the statements and opinions in them reflect that point of view. This situation is common; historians recognize that preconceptions and bias of some sort exist in every writer's work, consciously acknowledged or not.

From this point, biblical scholars step into paths of assumption and speculation that lead to increasingly subjective hypotheses. The religious outlook of biblical authors is not only traced in the selection of the events they narrate (events that supported their point of view), their religious interests are held to have led the writers to distort and even invent episodes in order to produce "history" to suit their purposes. If the information given by the sources the writers had at hand was unacceptable, then, some scholars conjecture, it could have been tailored to fit the pattern. Here is an example of the way such a transformation is envisaged, as expressed more than a century ago by Julius Wellhausen with reference to an episode in Chronicles that is absent from Kings.

> The Book of Kings knows no worse ruler than Manasseh was; yet he reigned undisturbed for fifty-five years—a longer period than was enjoyed by any other king (2 Kings xxi.1–18). This is a stone of stumbling that Chronicles must remove. It tells that Manasseh was carried in chains by the Assyrians to Babylon, but there prayed to Jehovah who restored him to his kingdom; he then abolished idolatry in Judah ([2 Chr] xxxiii. 11–20). Thus on the one hand he does not escape punishment, while on the other hand the length of his reign is nevertheless explained. Recently indeed it has been sought to support the credibility of these statements by means of an Assyrian inscription from which it appears that Manasseh did pay tribute to Esarhaddon. That is to say, he had been overpowered by the Assyrians; that is again to say, that he had been thrown into chains and carried off by them. Not so rapid, but perhaps quite as accurate, would be the inference that as a tributary prince he must have kept his seat on the throne of Judah, and not have exchanged it for the prison of Babylon.

In truth, Manasseh's temporary deposition is entirely on the same plane with Nebuchadnezzar's temporary grass-eating. The unhistorical character of the intermezzo (the motives of which are perfectly transparent) follows not only from the silence of the Book of Kings (a circumstance of no small importance indeed), but also, for example, from Jer. xv.4; for when it is said there that all Judah and Jerusalem are to be given up to destruction because of Manasseh, it is not presupposed that his guilt has already been borne and atoned for by himself.[45]

Whatever one may think about the peculiar and complex problems of Chronicles, this passage reveals plainly the attitude I have described: if a narrative explains an event in terms of religious interest, any question of a factual element may be dismissed or ignored, all the more if there appears to be lack of harmony or contradiction with another passage or with modern thought.

Much Old Testament scholarship today follows the line that Wellhausen laid down. In reviewing a historical study entitled *The Royal Dynasties of Israel and Judah*, a prominent professor commented, "Biblical texts are handled as if they provided rather more of historical information than is likely to be the case."[46] At greater length, another eminent writer has issued a volume devoted to arguing that the account of the deliverance of Jerusalem from the Assyrian army of Sennacherib in 701 B.C. "is a product of a distinctive royal Zion theology, which emerged during the reign of Josiah in the seventh century."[47] For this writer, there was no deliverance; Hezekiah submitted to the Assyrian and retained his throne and the enemy army then presumably continued on its way unhindered by any "angel of the Lord." A combination of literary criticism, form criticism, and historical criticism helped to produce this conclusion. According to this study, the sense of the story in 2 Kgs 18:17–19:37 is the result of shaping by a school of religious propagandists; it does not relate the actual events of 701 B.C.

If one account or another may be reinterpreted in these ways, then all such accounts may be. In fact, a great many parts of the Old Testament are treated in this way, as those acquainted with current work are aware. Followed consistently, this approach to the text could result in its being emptied of any significance for history apart from its testimony to a religious faith. Extrabiblical documents prevent anyone from going to

45. J. Wellhausen, *Prolegomena to the History of Israel* (Edinburgh: Black, 1885) 206–7.
46. P. R. Ackroyd, *The Expository Times* 91 (1979) 23, referring to T. Ishida, *The Royal Dynasties in Ancient Israel: A Study on the Formation and Development of Royal-Dynastic Ideology* (BZAW 142; Berlin: de Gruyter, 1977).
47. R. E. Clements, *Isaiah and the Deliverance of Jerusalem: A Study of the Interpretation of Prophecy in the Old Testament* (JSOTSup 13; Sheffield: JSOT Press, 1980) 95.

this extreme by corroborating a few of the Old Testament's historical statements. At least the existence of a Judean king named Hezekiah and an attack on him by Sennacherib are beyond dispute. Where there are no sources apart from the Old Testament, the protagonists of such attitudes may be free to treat those passages as totally fictional, the products of religious fantasy. King David can be turned into an entirely imaginary figure on these lines of argument, a necessary ancestor for the dynasty of Judah, credited with a powerful kingdom to make him glorious, with heroic acts to exalt the figure of the king, and with moral failings balanced by a religious conscience to encourage orthodoxy. Here the question imposes itself: Is this a proper way to treat the biblical writings? Is one confined to a state in which accepting the Bible as a religious composition compels him to doubt, or even to discount, any and every apparent statement of fact?

Ancient Records and Religious Beliefs

Although all the records that survive from the Old Testament world were written by people for whom religious beliefs were an integral part of their lives, it is not normal to treat them in this way, whether or not other sources support their claims. Thus the Assyrian kings, who can be characterized as excessively vainglorious, frequently took care to acknowledge that their campaigns were undertaken at the behest of their gods and that their victories and booty were the gifts of the same gods. They had the reports of their achievements written so that future generations would learn from them, remember the prowess of their predecessors, and honor the gods of Assyria. Tiglath-pileser I, for example, about 1100 B.C. began the account of a successful campaign with this assertion:

> At that time, with the exalted might of the god Ashur, my lord, with the firm approval (through divination) of the god Shamash, the warrior, with the support of the great gods with which I have ruled properly in the four quarters and have no rival in battle nor equal in conflict, at the command of the god Ashur, (my) lord, I marched to the lands of distant kings, on the shore of the Upper Sea.[48]

These kings, or their historians, naturally wrote the records in the framework of their own beliefs. They believed that their gods and others were at work in the events they observed, much as the Israelite writers did, and sometimes they asserted that there was divine intervention (see below, p. 64). Additional texts from different sources complement only a few of

48. A. K. Grayson, *ARI*, 2.12.

the narratives, either in other cuneiform tablets (e.g., letters) or the records of other nations (e.g., Aramean states, Urartu). Nevertheless, the Assyrian kings' inscriptions are basic to modern histories of the ancient Near East. Overt theological intent and the authors' clearly held beliefs that the gods did involve themselves directly in human affairs have not brought rejection of the "historical" narratives, nor cast much doubt on them.

Bias and Historicity

Occasionally allegations are made that an ancient document is historically unreliable because of its bias. One case is a well-known Assyrian text called the Synchronistic History. It purports to relate victorious Assyrian campaigns against Babylonia over a period of 700 years, approximately 1500–780 B.C. Peace treaties terminated many of the campaigns, with boundary demarcations usually in Assyria's favor. The introduction to the text is lost. An epilogue implies that the text was engraved on a stele to display the glory of Assyria and the wickedness of the treaty-breaking Babylonians. In editing the tablet, an Assyriologist speaks of its blatant pro-Assyrian prejudice and arbitrary selection of facts, claiming that one victory ascribed to the Assyrians was really won by the Babylonians. He concludes that the composition was intended to be a historical justification of a particular boundary line: "the line existed of course only in the author's imagination, but this did not prevent him from regarding any Babylonian violation of this boundary as a crime."[49] Here, according to the editor, is a piece of ancient "history writing" that shows a heavy bias, totally in Assyria's favor, producing distortion of facts and invention. At the same time, several lines are demonstrably quoted from the inscriptions of earlier kings, up to four centuries older than the text.

Upon further investigation, so negative an evaluation of the document is seen to be ill-founded. Part of the editor's mistaken conclusion arises from treating this Synchronistic History alongside another series of records, the Babylonian Chronicles. The latter win the editor's approval as reliable and sober accounts of affairs, for the most part, and thus precipitate a contrast with the former, as if it is pretending to be a text of a comparable type. Yet it is not. It claims to be a copy of an inscription on a boundary marker, dealing principally with changes in the boundary over previous generations. There is nothing unlikely in this. Stone pillars or blocks marking the extent of an estate were customary in Babylonia.

---

49. A. K. Grayson, *Assyrian and Babylonian Chronicles* (TCS 5; New York: Augustin, 1975) 53.

Special ones had details of the terrain inscribed on them, occasionally with a plan and measurements, sometimes with the history of the ownership of the property and details of litigation in the past. The Synchronistic History is more like the Babylonian Boundary Stones than it is like the Babylonian Chronicles, and that is what it claims to be.

Since that evaluation of the Synchronistic History, further discoveries have given additional reason for accepting it at face value. Two stelae erected by Assyrian kings to signal the boundaries they had set between warring subject rulers have been found.[50] On one of them the arrangements made by one Assyrian king were reinforced by his son, who added his inscription on the other side of the stone. These two monuments delineated territories in the north of the Levant, but their discovery (no others are known) makes it likely that similar stelae stood to mark the disputed and often shifting line between Assyria and Babylonia. If one allows this, then the Synchronistic History may be interpreted as a copy of the Assyrian inscriptions on a series of such stelae. It contains precisely what might be expected on those monuments: Assyrian reverses have no place but can be seen to be tacitly accepted when the boundary appears to have been redrawn in Babylonia's favor. Read thus, the major objections raised against the Synchronistic History disappear, and it can be treated positively by historians.[51]

Undoubted bias, therefore, need not carry a totally adverse attitude to a document or give rise to allegations that the accounts are untrue or imaginary. Recognition of the unconcealed standpoints of many ancient documents has resulted in fuller understanding of their contents, without any recourse to a devaluation or discrediting of them. The fact that the modern interpreter does not share the beliefs and aims of the writers does not prevent him from respecting them and giving them their due weight. When Pharaoh Ramesses II returned from the Syrian expedition culminating in the Battle of Qadesh (ca. 1274 B.C.), he had carvings of the battle and inscriptions put on the walls of temples in Egypt, describing how by his prowess he snatched victory from defeat. Their *raison d'être* was clearly the glorification of the king; his exploits are plainly exaggerated, as is the magnitude of the victory.[52] In the "poem" about the battle, the king attributes his heroism to his god's aid:

50. V. Donbaz, "Two Neo-Assyrian Stelae in the Antakya and Kahramanmaraç Museums," *Annual Review of the Royal Inscriptions of Mesopotamia Project* 8 (1990) 5–24.

51. See my review of Grayson, *Assyrian and Babylonian Chronicles*, in *JAOS* 100 (1980) 366–67.

52. Alan Gardiner, *The Kadesh Inscriptions of Ramesses II* (Oxford: Griffith Institute, 1960); K. A. Kitchen, *Pharaoh Triumphant: The Life and Times of Ramesses II* (Warminster: Aris and Phillips, 1983) chap. 4.

I called to you, my father Amun, when I was among multitudes of strangers. All foreign countries were combined against me, I was alone by myself, no-one else was with me, my numerous infantry had abandoned me, none of my chariotry attended me. I kept on shouting to them, but not one of them listened to me as I called. I found Amun more useful than millions of infantry, than hundreds of thousands of chariotry. . . . I found Amun came when I called him; he gave me his hand and I rejoiced. He called from behind me as if face to face, "Forward! I am with you. I am your father."[53]

Notwithstanding this open reliance on divine help and the obvious propaganda purpose of the whole series of sculptures, Egyptologists accept Ramesses' records as primary documents in reconstructing a major episode in Egyptian military history. They find no grounds for doubting that the Egyptian forces did defeat the Hittites at that moment, nor that the Pharaoh had a key role in the battle, even though the Hittites won the war.[54]

Turning back to the biblical narrative about Manasseh in 2 Chronicles 33, it is easy to see how presuppositions about the Chronicler colored the comment quoted earlier (see pp. 51–52). Within the Old Testament itself the grounds for certain of the observations are hard to find; there is no evidence that the long reign of a wicked king was a stumbling block to the Israelite historian, nor is it stated that Manasseh's imprisonment atoned for his idolatry. The text observes explicitly that people continued to worship at Manasseh's high places, albeit worshiping the Lord (2 Chr 33:17). Even if a sin is forgiven, the Old Testament consistently explains that its consequences cannot be avoided. Assyrian records name Manasseh as a vassal of Esarhaddon and of Ashurbanipal.[55] Nothing is said of an imprisonment in Babylon, but that is no basis for denying that it happened. Both Assyrian kings were concerned with affairs at Babylon, rebuilding what Sennacherib had destroyed, and in each reign an unsuccessful revolt took place in which the king of Judah could have shared, just as his father Hezekiah had.[56] To deport a rebel king, hold him awhile, and then return him to his throne would have been no novelty in Assyrian imperial politics. That

---

53. Adapted from Gardiner, *Kadesh Inscriptions*, 9, 10.

54. R. O. Faulkner, "Egypt: From the Inception of the Nineteenth Dynasty to the Death of Ramesses III," *The Middle East and the Aegean Region c. 1380–1000 B.C.* (*CAH* 2/2; 3d ed.; Cambridge: Cambridge University Press, 1975) chap. xxiii, section VI.

55. See R. Borger, *Die Inschriften Asarhaddons, Königs von Assyrian* (Graz: E. F. Weidner, 1956) 60, line 55; cf. A. Leo Oppenheim, "Babylonian and Assyrian Historical Texts," *ANET*, 291; M. Streck, *Assurbanipal* (Leipzig: Hinrichs, 1916) 138; cf. Oppenheim, *ANET*, 294.

56. B. Landsberger, *Brief des Bischofs von Esagila an König Asarhaddon* (Mededelingen der Köninklijke Nederlandse Akademie van Wetenschappen, Afd. Letterkunde Niewe Reeks, Ded 28/6; Amsterdam: Noord-Hollandsche Uitgeuers Maatschappij, 1965).

is not to say it did happen, simply that it could have. Surviving Assyrian records are far too meager to allow anyone to suppose that their lack of reference to an imprisonment of Manasseh is evidence that he was not held captive in Babylon.

On the basis of the treatment normally accorded to ancient writing, the absence of the story from 2 Kings is equally unsatisfactory evidence for its fabrication by the Chronicler. Instead of discarding the Chronicler's account from Judean history, we may see it as preserving a piece of information that otherwise would have been lost. The information was useful to him, not to explain Manasseh's long reign, but to demonstrate that even determinedly wicked men could repent and could still obtain God's mercy.

Opposing Biased Views

The case of Sennacherib's invasion of Judah deserves further examination, for both Hebrew and Assyrian accounts of the affair survive. They come from the opposing parties, so bias is plain in each! Both agree on the principal points: Hezekiah rebelled against Assyria, allying himself with Egypt, so Sennacherib advanced against Judah, overrunning the whole of the kingdom, isolating Hezekiah in Jerusalem, and extracting a heavy tribute from him. The Hebrew historian is emphatic: Sennacherib did not capture Jerusalem, and, on the contrary, the Assyrians withdrew, leaving the city inviolate. The Assyrian texts do not mention capturing Hezekiah's capital. A modern scholar, analyzing the records and reconstructing developments in Judean theology, concludes that Hezekiah surrendered

> . . . to the Assyrians before any attack on Jerusalem was pressed home. Virtually alone, among the cities of Judah, therefore, Jerusalem escaped a battle, the horrors of a prolonged siege, or any serious destruction. Hezekiah had submitted in time to avert a holocaust. The terms that were imposed upon the king of Judah have often been interpreted as surprisingly lenient, since he retained his throne and his status as a client vassal.[57]

The texts of Sennacherib and of 2 Kgs 18:13–16 give the historical basis for this case, he claims. As for the longer biblical narrative of 2 Kgs 18:17–19:36, culminating in the decimation of the Assyrian army, it "is a piece of 'narrative theology,' rather than a historical narrative proper. . . . Its explanation for the event that forms its climax is dramatically theological in character."[58] In the light of the prophet Isaiah's assurance that God would deliver Jerusalem,

57. Clements, *Isaiah and the Deliverance of Jerusalem*, 19.
58. Ibid., 21.

. . . then it is not too difficult to believe that the inference should have been drawn even if mistakenly, that such a deliverance had taken place. The belief that a prophecy would be fulfilled could so easily have been turned into a belief that it had been fulfilled.[59]

Two questions demand inquiry: Does the Assyrian record bear such an interpretation? Are the arguments adequate for claiming that the longer Hebrew account is a historical narrative proper?

Sennacherib, according to his report, followed the normal course for dealing with a rebel subject king: he invaded his land, conquered large parts, and gave some of the territory to submissive neighboring rulers. He invested the capital with its king inside, "like a bird in a cage," setting a string of watchtowers around it to prevent any escape. He mentions no other action against the city. Instead, the dread majesty of the Assyrian king overwhelmed Hezekiah, the special troops he had brought for his defence deserted, and he paid tribute, sending it after Sennacherib to Nineveh. At first glance this seems straightforward. Yet in the context of Assyrian royal inscriptions it has several unusual features. Rebels had to be punished, and punishment was the purpose of Sennacherib's campaign. Assyrian kings told of rebels' fate, and for the majority, their fate was disgrace and captivity or death, as it was for Sidqa of Ashkelon and the leaders of the revolt in Ekron who were in league with Hezekiah. If they tried to resist, their cities were besieged, captured, and despoiled (Sennacherib lists some of them), the booty being carried off to Nineveh. In some cases the dread majesty of Assyria's king or gods overwhelmed the rebel, causing him to flee and die far from home, or to approach the emperor seeking his clemency. There were exceptions. One was the city of Tyre, a particular nuisance to would-be conquerors, as Nebuchadnezzar and Alexander were to discover. Its king, Ba^cali "threw off the yoke of Assyria," so Esarhaddon, Sennacherib's son, invested it when on his way to Egypt in 671 B.C., denying food and water to its inhabitants. Esarhaddon's inscriptions do not report the submission or capture of Tyre.[60] It was his son, Ashurbanipal, who surrounded the city by land and sea, bringing Ba^cali to surrender. When the Tyrian came out of his city he presented his daughters and his son to the conqueror, and Ashurbanipal was magnanimous: "I had pity on him and gave back his son to him." The watchtowers were removed, Ba^cali was left on his throne, subject to a heavy tribute, and the Assyrian returned to Nineveh.[61]

---

59. Ibid., 23.
60. Borger, *Inschriften Asarhaddons*, 112, lines 12–14.
61. A. C. Piepkorn, *Historical Prism Inscriptions of Ashurbanipal I* (AS 5; Chicago: University of Chicago Press, 1933) 40–45.

In the Hezekiah episode, some of these elements are present, but they are oddly incomplete. Sennacherib encircled Jerusalem with watchtowers, yet did not press a siege. This contrasts with his action against the other towns of Judah, which he attacked with all the military skills at his command, with "stamped earth ramps, bringing battering rams, infantry assault, tunneling, breaches, and siege-tools." These activities are brought to life when the results of excavations at Lachish are set beside the reliefs from Sennacherib's palace representing the attack, the siege, the surrender, and the spoilation in a single panorama. A "stamped earth ramp" has been uncovered heaped against the city wall at one point, while iron arrowheads, fragments of armor, and what may be part of a grappling chain have come to light. Apparently these belong to the time of the Assyrian siege.[62] Jerusalem did not suffer such a fate. Yet Sennacherib's sparing of the city is not expressed in his campaign records. There is no statement like Ashurbanipal's concerning the king of Tyre, there is no announcement: "Hezekiah the Judean came out of Jerusalem and brought his daughters to be my servants, together with his son. I had mercy on him and replaced him on his throne. A tribute heavier than before I imposed upon him." Nothing hints at the Assyrians entering the city. According to the record, Hezekiah did pay tribute, but that was because the dread majesty of Sennacherib overcame him. The expression *dread majesty* often implies that the threat of an Assyrian onslaught was sufficient to produce surrender or flight.[63] (Earlier in the third campaign, the dread majesty of the Assyrian emperor sent Luli, King of Sidon, to seek refuge overseas.) Faced with the devastation of his small state, with the possibility of a siege looming, the Judean submitted. That is the implication. Notice, nevertheless, how the tribute was paid, not to Sennacherib at Lachish or at Libnah or outside Jerusalem, but later. "After me," says Sennacherib, "he sent to Nineveh my royal city." The rebel ruler, who had held captive the pro-Assyrian king of Ekron delivered to him by the rebels there, and who was obviously enmeshed in the intrigue that brought the Egyptian army to face the Assyrians, was left on his throne, left in his intact city, and required only to pay tribute. Hezekiah was treated lightly in comparison with many. Loyal vassal kings were normally allowed to retain their thrones under Assyrian suzerainty, with considerable independence, but Hezekiah had not been loyal.

According to Clements the Assyrian wanted to "retain some degree of political stability without the cost of maintaining a substantial Assyrian force in Judah."[64] If this were so, the absence of any hint in the Assyrian

---

62. D. Ussishkin, *The Conquest of Lachish by Sennacherib* (Tel Aviv: Tel Aviv University Press, 1982) 49–58.

63. See E. Cassin, *La Splendeur divine* (Paris: Mouton, 1968).

64. Clements, *Isaiah and the Deliverance of Jerusalem*, 62 n. 4.

text is surprising, given the detailed accounts of the way other rulers were treated. Sennacherib replaced Sidqa of Ashkelon, who was unsubmissive, and deported him to Assyria, slaughtered the revolutionary leaders of Ekron who had called for Egyptian aid, and in other expeditions he or his troops pursued rebel rulers into Anatolian fastnesses, besieged and captured their towns, and returned to Nineveh with them and their treasures. Furthermore, the note of triumph with which the reports of Assyrian campaigns normally end is absent from this one. True, the listing of Hezekiah's tribute contains a note of success, yet it is muted in comparison with the ending of every one of Sennacherib's campaigns in which he proclaims what he had done. In the seventh year he even admits a reverse: the weather was too much for him, so he turned back from the mountains of Elam. In the light of these observations, the narrative of Sennacherib's campaign against Hezekiah seems to be less straightforward than it may appear when read in isolation.

The testimony of the sculptures is relevant to this point. In Sennacherib's palace in Nineveh, in a central place, reliefs announced the capture and submission not of Jerusalem and Hezekiah, but of Lachish, one of Hezekiah's "strong-walled cities," but none of this is named in the narrative, in contrast with places on the coastal road belonging to Ashkelon.[65] Admittedly, Hezekiah may have had a place on another wall in reliefs lining a room no longer preserved, yet the emphasis is definitely on Lachish in the surviving materials. Perhaps the siege was unusually long or difficult, or perhaps Sennacherib supervised it personally and ordered its commemoration. For whatever reason the reliefs about the siege of Lachish were carved, the fact remains that they were the ones to be set prominently in a room by themselves, rather than reliefs portraying the surrender of the capital, Jerusalem, or the tribute of its king, Hezekiah.

"Narrative Theology" versus "Historical Narrative Proper"

Turning to the biblical narratives, a distinction appears at once between the initial, brief notice of Sennacherib's attack and Hezekiah's submission (2 Kgs 18:13–16) and the lengthy account of the Rabshakeh's embassy (2 Kgs 18:17–19:36). The king of Assyria's account and Sennacherib's "annals" are taken as the evidence for a reconstruction of events by some scholars. The longer account "does not appear to fit within this framework of events"[66] and so causes embarrassment and de-

---

65. See Ussishkin, *Conquest of Lachish*, for the sculptures.
66. Clements, *Isaiah and the Deliverance of Jerusalem*, 21 n. 4.

mands explanation. Clements's monograph sets out to answer the problem with an argument erected on a hypothesis about the development of theology among some Judean thinkers in the seventh century B.C. Suggestions that the longer account describes an action carried out later in 701 B.C., after the completion of the shorter account, or that it refers to a second invasion later in Sennacherib's reign, are dismissed and so are not discussed here. That the final verse mentions the death of Sennacherib, Clements asserts, proves that the narrative is "not from a time closely contemporaneous with the events it describes."[67] Rather, this account was "written up after a considerable interval of time had elapsed, and is intended to draw the maximum in the way of theological significance out of the fact that Jerusalem was not subjected to any military attack."[68] The account is "a piece of 'narrative theology,' rather than a historical narrative proper"[69] and "is a product of a distinctive royal Zion theology, which emerged during the reign of Josiah in the seventh century."[70] What one reads in 2 Kgs 18:17–19:37 is in effect no more than a theologian's fairy-tale, an interweaving of an old story with theological theory to produce a narrative that is unhistorical.

The need to examine the Assyrian record carefully has already been explained. By reading the Hebrew text against its contemporary background the way may be opened to a very different conclusion. A variety of fascinating studies result from placing this passage and contemporary documents side by side. There is the course of the campaign, the strategy, and the aim of the Egyptians.[71] The contents of the Rabshakeh's speech before the walls of Jerusalem and the circumstances of its delivery gain in credibility the more carefully they are examined.[72] The Rabshakeh himself arouses interest. Was he a captive Israelite or the descendant of one, who spoke in the dialect of Judah? Men of foreign stock filled many high positions in the Assyrian administration, as their names reveal, so this one could have had a western background. Equally, the Assyrians employed interpreters and could have done so to speak to the people of Jerusalem.[73]

67. Ibid.

68. Ibid., 59.

69. Ibid., 21.

70. Ibid., 95.

71. See K. A. Kitchen's studies, *The Third Intermediate Period in Egypt* (2d ed.; Warminster: Aris and Phillips, 1986) 158–61, 383–86, 552–54, 584–86, with references.

72. See C. Cohen, "Neo-Assyrian Elements in the First Speech of the Biblical Rabšaqe," *Israel Oriental Studies* 9 (1979) 32–48.

73. H. Tadmor has argued that the Rabshakeh was of western origin, "The Aramaization of Assyria: Aspects of Western Impact," in *Mesopotamien und seine Nachbarn* (ed. H. J. Nissen and J. Renger; Berlin: Reimer, 1982) 2.464 n. 45; for the possible use of an interpreter outside Jerusalem, see A. R. Millard, "Israelite and Aramean History in the Light of Inscriptions," *TynBul* 41 (1990) 269 n.12.

Sennacherib's military reports were reproduced largely unaltered over many years and similar reports survive from his grandson, Ashurbanipal. During his reign, a change of editorial policy took place. Some reports stood, repeated from one edition of the "annals" to the next; others were altered, a phrase or two here, a sentence or two there, and on occasion they were augmented with later information. A well-known example is the account of Ashurbanipal's relations with the kingdom of Lydia. Clay prisms inscribed with the Assyrian emperor's "annals" about 643 b.c. describe the episode.[74] An emissary reached Nineveh from distant Lydia bringing Gyges' plea for help against invading Cimmerians. Gyges had been inspired by a dream that directed him to Ashurbanipal. The Cimmerians were conquered and two of their chieftains sent in fetters to Assyria. Presently Gyges changed his policy, giving military aid to an Egyptian ruler in rebellion against Ashurbanipal. The Assyrian prayed for Gyges' downfall, and the Cimmerians overwhelmed him. Gyges' son atoned for his father's folly by seeking Ashurbanipal's protection again. This account reads as a whole, with a natural break before the change in Gyges' stance is announced. However, the prisms written in approximately 643 b.c. are among the latest of Ashurbanipal's reign. Gyges' embassy to Nineveh was already noted in the earliest prisms, written over twenty years before,[75] and the account was repeated in an abbreviated form in prisms of later years (ca. 648, 646, 645 b.c.). Only in the latest, from about 643 b.c., are the disloyalty and fate of Gyges recounted. One can assume that his death took place shortly before. Assyrian annalists clearly were interested in keeping their records up to date, particularly when recent events improved Assyria's standing. If Assyrian scribes worked in this way, may not Hebrew scribes have done so, too? In 2 Kgs 19:37, the report of Sennacherib's assassination, I do not see a sign that "[t]he narrative (of 2 Kgs 19:17–19:37) is self-evidently not from a time closely contemporaneous with the events it describes, since it concludes with a mention of the circumstances of Sennacherib's death, which did not take place until 681 b.c."[76] The verse can be well explained as an addition made to an existing history by a scribe who heard the news of the emperor's death and felt that a note about it would round off the story that ended quite naturally with v. 36. (The attribution of the title *king* to Tirhakah in 2 Kgs 19:19 could also come from this time, since he acceded to the throne in 690 b.c.) There is no compelling reason to make this verse date the whole of the preceding narrative any more than the introduction of the account of Gyges' fate in the latest of Ashurbanipal's prisms

74. D. D. Luckenbill, *ARAB*, §§ 784–85.

75. M. Cogan and H. Tadmor, "Gyges and Ashurbanipal: A Study in Literary Transmission," *Or* n.s. 46 (1977) 65–85.

76. Clements, *Isaiah and the Deliverance of Jerusalem*, 21 n. 4.

indicates that the account of the whole Gyges episode was composed at that time. In neither case does the interval of twenty years between first and last events recorded affect the content of the reports. The first argument against the longer Hebrew narrative's being properly historical loses its force, therefore, when examined in the ancient Near Eastern context.

Divine Intervention in Human Affairs

The second argument against the historical nature of 2 Kgs 18:17–19:37 involves a more far-reaching issue. Sennacherib's army suffered at the hand of "the angel of the Lord"; in other words, a miracle occurred. At once the modern historian looks askance at the text: miracles do not happen, he reasons, so writings that report or accept the miraculous are classed as unhistorical. Either they are products of fantasy and wishful thinking, or they are inventions for a propagandist purpose, confirming a prophecy in the case of Sennacherib and his army. Yet before ancient texts are written off in this way, they should be examined more extensively as relics of ways of thought that are different from those of twentieth-century historians. Since this is a matter explored in previous studies,[77] only certain aspects and consequences demand attention here.

First, the term *miracle* is best avoided because of the negative reaction it provokes. Frequently, the ancient records state what the event was, so that modern writers can speak in terms of an unusually heavy hailstorm (Josh 10:11) or a very strong wind (Exod 14:21). It is when the texts make no indication of this sort that modern writers become most negative, and so the expression *the angel of the Lord* is not considered to have any reality behind it. Yet the angel of the Lord was as much a reality to the ancient authors as the meteorological phenomena they mention, a reality that they could only express in this way, for they perceived none of the natural forces in action that were known to them. This does not allow twentieth-century historians to discount it. Rather, they should accept the fact that something did happen, with remarkable results (such as the decimation of Sennacherib's army in 2 Kgs 19:35). The processes at work in such events remain subject to speculation; they should not be treated automatically as divine suspension of natural law, as the word *miracle* might be thought to imply.

Second, the similarity between Israelite and other ancient Near Eastern reports has to be recognized. A collection of comparable records was made recently,[78] and my previous essays describe some of them. There is

77. See n. 1.
78. M. Weinfield, "Divine Intervention in War in Ancient Israel and the Ancient Near East," *History, Historiography and Interpretation* (ed. H. Tadmor and M. Weinfield; Jerusalem: Magnes, 1983) 121–47.

no difference in the type or result in these episodes: divine intervention brings success to the narrator's side in an unexpected way. Each nation believed her own deity or deities acted on her behalf. Just as the Lord sent the hailstones on the Amorites, so that more died from them than from Israelite swords, so Adad finished off the enemy of Sargon of Assyria with thunder and hailstones.[79] There need be no doubt that the Assyrian enemy's experience was as real as the Amorites', both being beaten down by heavy hail. Again, the historian and commentator is obliged to treat the reports as factual evidence of ancient events. At this point the secular historian may halt, however, and view the Hebrew histories as no different from the Assyrian or Hittite or Egyptian.

The third point, consequently, concerns the distinction between Israelite writers and other writers on this score. Both saw divine intervention as a historical reality. They believed their god(s) had acted. Both recorded occasions when they believed divine intervention had taken place and included them in continuous chronicles (such as Kings or the Weidner Chronicle). Often in the case of the Israelite reports, rarely with the others, come accounts of divinely-given forecasts of the events. These may be treated by modern scholars as realizations created afterward or as theological reflections on Israel's history by one or more schools of thought; there is much debate on the possibilities. Alternatively, the words may be accepted as forms of prophecy that were fulfilled. With hindsight we today may find a consistency in the Old Testament's correlation of divine words and divine deeds with historical crises that leads them to conclude that there is more than coincidence in them. The Israelites in Moses' day needed the power of God to free them from servitude, and their children needed that power to gain a foothold in the Promised Land; they were privileged to see and believe, whereas several of the following generations were called to hear and believe. Yet had nothing occurred to display the power of their God memorably, there would have been little impetus to believe in him when Canaanite and other gods were so much more attractive and so much less demanding. The continuity of that belief through the Exile and other adversities, a continuity that contrasts with the extinction of all the contemporary religions, is a noteworthy testimony to faith firmly founded in history. Israel's history cannot be fully comprehended without knowledge of her faith, nor can her faith be understood without a realistic portrayal of her history.

79. F. Thureau-Dangin, *Une relation de la huitième campagne de Sargon* (Paris: Geuthner, 1912) line 147.

Scribes as Transmitters of Tradition

David W. Baker

Ashland Theological Seminary

From the perspective of the contemporary layperson, scribes have earned their bad name due to their repeated appearance with Pharisees in New Testament passages that do not reflect positively on either group. The word for scribes and Pharisees that comes to mind most readily is *hypocrites* (Matt 23:13, 14, 15, 23, 25, 27, 29; Luke 11:44). How is it that a group described as scribes, writers (from the Latin *scribere* 'to write'), or even counters and enumerators (from the Hebrew *sōfēr*) have received such bad press? This essay provides some background concerning the training and functions of this group of people in their early history in the ancient Near East and shows that their role, transmitting and preserving tradition, had further developed into interpreting the tradition by the time of the New Testament. In the process I hope to show them to be worthy of praise rather than vilification in their role as transmitters and preservers of tradition.

It is a truism that every written text must have a writer who is technically a scribe, a truism that does not really penetrate until one considers that even in the United States approximately two million adults do not read and write (more than one percent of the population). How much more seriously is literacy to be considered in a society that does not have the interest or the wherewithal to make education generally available? In the ancient Near East, this situation was exacerbated by the problem of the writing systems, such as cuneiform Sumerian, Akkadian, and Hittite, or hieroglyphic Egyptian, which possess far greater complexity than the alphabet. In such societies, writing becomes much more of a technical skill and its practitioners become far fewer. The relative scarcity of scribes adds to their importance, the respect in which they are held, and their power and standing in the community. This social stature affords opportunities beyond the simple recording of texts, a subject to which I shall return.

In Mesopotamia, from the ninth millennium B.C. onward, small, shaped clay tokens were used to symbolize various agricultural products being tallied. These appear to have evolved into an early sign system of cuneiform pictograms.[1]

By the fourth millennium B.C., the early sign system in Mesopotamia became too complex and extensive for any but a trained practitioner to master.[2] Therefore there arose the é.dub.ba ('tablet house' or school) as an institution dedicated to preparing trained scribes. Evidence of the nature and even the curriculum of these schools is provided by texts describing schools and life in them, published and studied by Kramer, Falkenstein, Gadd, and others.[3]

1. D. Schmandt-Besserat, "An Archaic Recording System and the Origin of Writing," *Syro-Mesopotamian Studies* 1/2 (1977) 1–32; "The Earliest Precursor of Writing," *Scientific American* 238 (June, 1978) 50–59; "An Archaic Recording System in the Uruk-Jemdet Nasr Period," *AJA* 83 (1979) 19–48; "The Envelopes that Bear the First Writing," *Technology and Culture* 21 (1980) 371–74; "From Tokens to Tablets: A Re-Evaluation of the So-Called 'Numerical Tablets,'" *Visible Language* 15 (1981) 321–44.

2. See I. M. Diakonoff, "Ancient Writing and Ancient Written Language: Pitfalls and Peculiarities in the Study of Sumerian," *Sumerological Studies in Honor of Thorkild Jacobsen on His Seventieth Birthday, June 7, 1974* (AS 20; Chicago: Oriental Institute, 1976) 99–121; M. W. Green, "The Construction and Implementation of the Cuneiform Writing System," *Visible Language* 15 (1981) 345–72. M. T. Larsen points out the interesting and temporary phenomenon that took place during the Old Babylonian and Old Assyrian periods (2300–1600 B.C.), in which the number and form of signs necessary for basic communication was greatly reduced and simplified, allowing for a wider access to writing ("The Mesopotamian Lukewarm Mind: Reflections on Science, Divination and Literacy," *Language, Literature, and History: Philological and Historical Studies Presented to Erica Reiner* [ed. F. Rochberg-Halton; New Haven, Conn.: American Oriental Society, 1987] 219–220). This was reversed by the mid-second millennium B.C. (ibid., 210).

3. S. N. Kramer, "Schooldays: A Sumerian Composition Relating to the Education of a Scribe," *JAOS* 69 (1949) 199–215 (cf. *Schooldays* [Philadelphia: University Museum, 1949]); A. Falkenstein, "Der Sohn des Tafelhauses," *WO* 1 (1948) 172–86; "Die babylonische Schule," *Saeculum* 4 (1954) 125–37; C. J. Gadd, "Fragments of Assyrian Scholastic Literature," *BSO(A)S* 20 (1956) 255–65; *Teachers and Students in the Oldest Schools* (London: University of London, 1956).

Other studies: L. Dürr, *Das Erziehungswesen im Alten Testament und in antiken Orient* (Mitteilungen der Vorderasiatisch-Ägyptischen Gesellschaft 36/2; Leipzig: Heinrich, 1932); J. J. A. van Dijk, "L'Édubba et son esprit," *La sagesse suméro-accadienne* (Leiden: Brill, 1953) 21–27; A. L. Oppenheim, "Note on the Scribes in Mesopotamia," *Studies in Honor of Benno Landsberger on His Seventy-Fifth Birthday, April 21, 1965* (AS 16; Chicago: Oriental Institute, 1965) 253–56; idem, *Ancient Mesopotamia* (Chicago: University of Chicago Press, 1964) 228–87; B. Landsberger, "Babylonian Scribal Craft and Its Terminology," *Proceedings of the 23rd International Congress of Orientalists* (1954) 123–26; idem, "Scribal Concepts of Education," *City Invincible: A Symposium on Urbanization and Cultural Development* (ed. C. H. Kraeling and R. M. Adams; Chicago: University of Chicago Press, 1960) 94–102; Å. W. Sjöberg, "Der Vater und sein missratenen Sohn," *JCS* 25 (1973) 105–69; idem, "The Old Babylonian Eduba," *Sumerological Studies in Honor of Thorkild Jacobsen on His Seventieth Birthday, June 7, 1974* (AS 20; Chicago: Oriental Institute, 1976) 159–79; W. H. Ph. Römer, *Iets over school en schoolonderricht in het Oude Mesopotamie* (Assen/Amsterdam: Van Gorcum, 1977); H. L. J. Vanstiphout, "How Did They Learn

There also exist a large number of "exercise" tablets in which one can not only discern the sure hand of the trained scribe, but also the rudimentary efforts of the beginning student as he practiced the most basic of the Sumerian or Akkadian signs, or, in the case of the Ugaritic scribe, as he learned his "A B C's."[4] As the apprentice scribe progressed beyond the basic forms of the signs, he learned Sumerian and, later, Akkadian, as well as the technical terminology of a variety of different fields using a number of different literary genres, including, as one bilingual text states, how "to write a stele [royal inscriptions], to draw a field [surveying, geometry, and cartography], and to settle accounts [mathematics]."[5] One of the evidences that some of the tablets are school exercises is the juxtaposition of diverse genres on the same tablet.[6]

Part of the learning process involved not only exercise tablets but also "model" tablets,[7] tablets of different genres that the scribe had to learn to copy accurately. This allowed him not only to learn the technical vocabulary for the different kinds of texts, but also to become familiar with important representatives of the various literary genres. Since the curriculum was by its very nature relatively conservative and slow to change, it aided the preservation of important texts over an extended period of time with a high degree of accuracy, for faithful copying of the original was part of the purpose of the exercise. As Rochberg-Halton stated, "the scribal curriculum can therefore be seen in the service of cultural continuity."[8]

This copying was no mean feat, as is evidenced by spelling errors, omissions and wrong sign forms not only in the novices' exercise tablets,

---

Sumerian?" *JCS* 31 (1979) 118–26; M. Civil, "Sur les 'livres d'écolier' à l'époque paléo-babylonienne," *Miscellanea babylonica: Mélanges offerts à Maurice Birot* (ed. J.-M. Durand and J.-R. Kupper; Paris: Éditions Recherche sur les Civilisations, 1985) 67–78.

4. See the discussions in M. Haran, "On the Diffusion of Literacy and Schools in Ancient Israel," *Congress Volume, Jerusalem 1986* (VTSup 40; Leiden: Brill, 1988) 85–91; E. Puech, "Les Écoles dans l'Israel préexilique: Données épigraphiques," *Congress Volume, Jerusalem 1986* (VTSup 40: Leiden: Brill, 1988) 189–203.

5. Å. Sjöberg, "In Praise of the Scribal Art," *JCS* 24 (1971–1972) 127; see Larsen, "Mesopotamian Lukewarm Mind," 208–10, concerning the place of lists in scribal education and society at large.

6. H. W. F. Saggs, *The Greatness that Was Babylon* (New York: Hawthorn, 1962) 187.

7. E.g., W. G. Lambert, *Babylonian Wisdom Literature* (Oxford: Clarendon, 1960) pl. 73, VAT 10071 with VAT 10756 (see pp. 356–57); W. W. Hallo, "New Viewpoints on Cuneiform Literature," *IEJ* 12 (1962) 22; S. N. Kramer, *The Sumerians* (Chicago: University of Chicago Press, 1963) 237; A. Westenholz, "Old Akkadian School Texts: Some Goals of Sargonic Scribal Education," *AfO* 25 (1974) 95–110; A. Al-Fouadi, *Lenticular Exercise School Texts* (Texts in the Iraq Museum 10; Baghdad: State Organization of Antiquities, 1979); H. Sauren, "E₂-*dub-ba* Literatur: Lehrbuch des Sumerischen," *Orientalia lovaniensia periodica* 10 (1979) 97–107; A. Cavigneaux, *Textes scolaires de temple de Nabu sha ḫārê* (Baghdad: State Organization of Antiquities and Heritage, 1981); R. S. Falkowitz, "Round Old Babylonian School Tablets from Nippur," *AfO* 29/30 (1982) 18–45.

8. F. Rochberg-Halton, "Canonicity in Cuneiform Texts," *JCS* 36 (1984) 133.

but also in the products of the fully trained professional scribes, a feature of hand-copying worldwide.[9]

As an incentive to master all aspects of the scribal craft, corporal punishment was not uncommon at the *é.dub.ba*. One unfortunate, who fell short in a number of areas, was caned so many times that he states, "(And so) I (began) to hate the scribal art."[10]

The educational process was long and arduous, but it usually proved profitable if pursued to its end. One text states that "(1) the scribal art is the mother of orators, the father of masters, (2) The scribal art is delightful, it never satiates a person, (3) The scribal art is not (easily) learned, (but) he who has learned it need no longer be anxious about it. (4) Strive to (master) the scribal art and it will enrich you, (5) Be industrious in the scribal art and it will provide you with wealth and abundance."[11]

It is not absolutely clear from what source potential scribes were recruited, but most likely they were the sons of the upper class. Schneider made a preliminary study of a number of scribes named on seals from the Ur III period (late 3d millennium B.C.) and he came to this conclusion, based on a study of the position in society of the fathers of the scribes.[12] Green posits that scribes in early Uruk, even though none bears the specific title *dub.sar* 'scribe', "like those of Fara and Abu-Salabikh later were members of the *SANGA*-college of temple priest-administrators. . . . In that case, they were selected from an already hierarchically ordered, exclusive class."[13] Green also goes on to note that, even if scribes did not

---

9. F. Delitzsch, *Die Lese- und Schreibfehler im Alten Testament* (Berlin/Leipzig: de Gruyter, 1920); W. W. Hallo, "Haplographic Marginalia," *Essays on the Ancient Near East in Memory of Jacob Joel Finkelstein* (ed. M. deJong Ellis; Memoirs of the Connecticut Academy of Arts and Sciences 19; Hamden: Archon, 1977) 101–3; B. Kienast, *Die altbabylonische Briefe und Urkunden aus Kisurra* (FAOS 2/2; Wiesbaden: Steiner, 1978) 1.75; R. Frankena, *Kommentar zu den altbabylonischen Briefen aus Lagaba und anderes Orten* (Tabulae cuneiformes a F. M. Th. de Liagre Böhl collectae 4; Leiden: Nederlands Instituut voor het Nabije Oosten, 1978) 56; and many others. See for Ugaritic: S. Segert, "Die Schreibfehler in den ugaritischen literarischen Keilschrifttexten," *Von Ugarit nach Qumran* (ed. J. Hempel; BZAW 77; Berlin: Töpelmann, 1958) 193–212; idem, "Die Schreibfehler in den ugaritischen nichtliterarischen Keilschrifttexten," *ZAW* 30 (1959) 23–32; idem, "The Ugaritic Texts and the Textual Criticism of the Hebrew Bible," *Near Eastern Studies in Honor of William Foxwell Albright* (ed. H. Goedicke; Baltimore: Johns Hopkins University Press, 1971) 413–20; M. E. J. Richardson, "Ugaritic Spelling Errors," *TynBul* 24 (1973) 3–20; A. F. Rainey, "The Scatterbrained Scribe," *Studies in the Bible and the Ancient Near East Presented to Samuel E. Loewenstamm on His Seventieth Birthday* I (ed. Y. Avishur and J. Blau; Jerusalem: Rubinstein, 1978) 141–50; W. J. Horwitz, "The Ugaritic Scribes," *UF* 11 (1979) 391 n. 12.

10. Kramer, *Sumerians*, 239.

11. Sjöberg, "In Praise of Scribal Art," 127; cf. Hallo, "New Viewpoints," 25.

12. N. Schneider, "Der *dub.sar* als Verwaltungsbeamter im Reiche von Sumer und Akkad zur Zeit der 3. Dynastie von Ur," *Or* 15 (1946) 64, 86–87.

13. Green, "Construction," 367.

come from an upper-class family background, the very nature of the profession as an esoteric skill not readily available to the masses would confer status on its members.[14]

There is also some indication that in a few cases the office of scribe was, if not hereditary, at least followed by members of the same family over several generations.[15]

The use of masculine nouns and pronouns in reference to scribes in the discussion to this point is not just a vestige of male chauvinism, but rather a reflection of the historical situation in the ancient Near East. Schneider, based on his analysis of 464 Ur III scribes, states that "among the *dub.sar* names is not found one single woman's name, so therefore this occupation was reserved for men alone."[16] My own preliminary research in collecting the names and backgrounds of scribes from a range of periods upholds Schneider's conclusion to a large extent, though there are a few women who held the position and are called scribes at various times. For example, in addition to the famous Enheduanna, the daughter of Sargon of Akkad and earliest known author in world literature,[17] there are over a dozen female scribes from Old Babylonian Sippar[18] and several at Mari.[19]

Scribal education played a role not only in the accurate preservation of textual material through time by the use of the "model" tablets, but also served to disseminate the material geographically. When Akkadian

14. Ibid.

15. Schneider ("Der *dub.sar*," 86) cites three texts where the father was also a *dub.sar*; cf. J. N. Postgate, "Assyrian Texts and Fragments" *Iraq* 35 (1973) 1, 17:rev. 9′; cf. F. W. Golka, "Die Israelitische Weisheitsschule oder 'des Kaisers neue Kleider,'" *VT* 33 (1983) 263; E. Lipiński, "Royal and State Scribes in Ancient Jerusalem," *Congress Volume, Jerusalem 1986* (VTSup 40; Leiden: Brill, 1988) 162–63.

16. Schneider, "Der *dub.sar*," 84.

17. W. W. Hallo and W. K. Simpson, *The Ancient Near East: A History* (New York: Harcourt, Brace, Jovanovich, 1971) 59; W. W. Hallo and J. J. A. van Dijk, *The Exaltation of Inanna* (Yale Near Eastern Researches 3; New Haven: Yale University Press, 1968); cf. R. Harris, "The Female 'Sage' in Mesopotamian Literature (with an Appendix on Egypt)," *The Sage in Israel and the Ancient Near East* (ed. J. G. Gammie and L. G. Perdue; Winona Lake, Ind.: Eisenbrauns, 1990) 8.

18. See CT 48, 30:rev. 9; 52:rev. 10; cf. CT 6, 40c: 16, discussed by M. Stol, "On Ancient Sippar," *BiOr* 33 (1976) 152; cf. R. Harris, *Ancient Sippar: A Demographic Study of an Old-Babylonian City (1894–1595 B.C.)* (Uitgaven van het Nederlands historisch-archaeologisch instituut te Istanbul 36; Istanbul: Nederlands historisch-archaeologisch instituut, 1975) 197; idem, "Female 'Sage,'" 6.

19. M. Birot, "Textes économiques de Mari," *RA* 50 (1956) 5–6; B. Batto, *Studies on Women at Mari* (Baltimore: Johns Hopkins University Press, 1974) 5; S. Dalley, *Mari and Karana: Two Old Babylonian Cities* (White Plains, N. Y.: Longman, 1984); J.-M. Durand, "Trois études sur Mari," *Mari: Annales de recherches interdisciplinaires* 3 (1984) 167 n. 41; idem, "Les Dames du palais de Mari à l'époque du royaume de haute-Mésopotamie," *Mari: Annales de recherches interdisciplinaires* 4 (1985) 419; Harris, "Female 'Sage,'" 7.

with its cuneiform script became the *lingua franca* of the ancient Near East and continued in this capacity for many centuries before it was replaced by the less cumbersome Aramaic alphabet,[20] expert scribes were needed to write and read this medium of international exchange. As is well known, the Amarna tablets from fourteenth-century B.C. Egypt were written in Akkadian, even though these tablets contain correspondence between parties, namely Egypt and the rulers of various city-states in the western Levant, that did not use Akkadian as their native language.[21] The same is true of the treaties between Egyptian and Hittite and other rulers that also were written in Akkadian.[22] Akkadian and Sumerian texts have been found at numerous sites in Asia Minor,[23] owing to the international nature of Akkadian literacy, as well as in Syria–Palestine, especially at Ebla and Ugarit.[24]

Scribal schools were established in Babylonia and Assyria to provide trained personnel for domestic needs.[25] Scribes may have moved on from

20. See Saggs, *The Greatness That Was Babylon*, 153; A. L. Oppenheim, *Ancient Mesopotamia* (Chicago: University of Chicago Press, 1964) 48–63.

21. E. A. Knudtzon, *Die El-Amarna Tafeln* (Vorderasiatische Bibliothek 2; Leipzig: Hinrichs, 1915; repr. Aalen: Zeller, 1964); A. F. Rainey, *El-Amarna Tablets 359–379* (AOAT 8; Neukirchen-Vluyn: Neukirchener Verlag, 1970). For the most recent translation of the tablets, see W. L. Moran, *Les Lettres d'El-Amarna: Correspondance diplomatique du pharaon* (LAPO 13; Paris: Du Cerf, 1987; Eng. tr.: *The Amarna Letters*; Baltimore: Johns Hopkins University Press, 1992).

22. See J. H. Walton, *Ancient Israelite Literature in Its Cultural Environment* (Grand Rapids: Zondervan, 1989) 95–100, for the most recent listing of the relevant covenants with bibliography.

23. Sultantepe (eighth–seventh centuries B.C.): see O. R. Gurney and J. J. Finkelstein, *The Sultantepe Tablets*, vol. 1 (London: British Institute of Archaeology in Ankara, 1957); O. R. Gurney and P. Hulin, *The Sultantepe Tablets*, vol. 2 (London: British Institute of Archaeology in Ankara, 1964).

24. Ebla (ca. 2300 B.C.): 6 volumes by G. Pettinato in the series Materiali epigrafici di Ebla (Naples: Istituto universitario orientali di Napoli, 1979–1982); the ongoing series Archivi reali di Ebla, Testi, of which nine volumes have appeared to date (Rome: Missione archeologica italiana in Siria, 1981–1990); Ugarit (thirteenth century B.C.): J. Nougayrol, *Le palais royal d'Ugarit* (hereinafter *PRU*), vol. 3: *Textes accadiens et hourrites des archives est, ouest et centrales* (Mission de Ras Shamra [MRS] 6; Paris: Imprimerie nationale/Klincksieck, 1955); *PRU* 4: *Textes accadiens des archives sud (archives internationales)* (MRS 9; Paris: Imprimerie nationale/Klincksieck, 1956); *PRU* 6: *Textes en cunéiformes babyloniens des archives du grand palais et du palais sud d'Ugarit* (MRS 12; Paris: Imprimerie nationale/Klincksieck, 1970); see W. J. Horowitz, "The Ugaritic Scribe," *UF* 11 (1979) 389–94.

25. See n. 3 above; also D. Charpin, *Le Clergé d'Ur au siècle d'Hammurabi: (XIXe–XVIIIe siècles av. J.-C.)* (Hautes études orientales 22; Geneva: Droz, 1986) 459–85, concerning a possible school at Ur; at Uruk: M. Hoh, "Die Grabung in Ue XVIII 1," *Vorläufige Berichte über die . . . Ausgrabungen in Uruk-Warka* (Berlin: Mann, 1979) 29/30: 28, 33–34; at Nippur: see the debate in D. E. McCown, *Nippur I: Temple of Enlil, Scribal Quarter, and Soundings* (OIP 78; Chicago: University of Chicago Press) 178–79; Sjöberg, "Old Babylonian Edubba," 176; M. Civil, *Ea A = nâqu, Aa A = nâqu: With Their Forerunners and Related Texts* (Materials for the Sumerian Lexicon 14; Rome: Pontifical Bibilical Institute, 1979) 8; E. C. Stone, *Nippur Neighborhoods* (SAOC 44; Chicago: Oriental Institute, 1987)

these for further training in religious institutions or to meet the needs of international diplomacy. Scribes trained in one center might move abroad, from Babylonia to Syria, for example. The presence at a site of bi- or multilingual lexical texts could indicate the existence of a scribal training establishment, though this is not direct proof.[26] The so-called "excercise tablets," which contain lists of signs and words repeated for practice, are the best evidence. Schools are known to exist elsewhere, outside of the central area of Mesopotamia itself.[27] Some evidence of this is direct: archaeological remains of classrooms have been discovered at Mari and Terqa, though the former is now disputed.[28] That non-native scribes rather than expatriate Mesopotamians were writing the Akkadian is shown by the occurrence of explanatory glosses on some Akkadian words in texts from some of the peripheral areas.[29] Since scribes needed to be trained to a level commensurate to that of the Mesopotamian scribes, and also in the same literary conventions and techniques, the curriculum of the schools in the peripheral areas closely paralleled that in Mesopotamia, thus leading to a geographical dispersion of the texts used as models. For example, copies of the Gilgamesh epic have been found not only in Assyria and Babylonia, but also in Asia Minor (with translations into Hittite and Hurrian) and at Megiddo in Israel itself.[30] This international network of educational institutions thus led to both the temporal and geographical spread of some Akkadian literature.

56–59; D. Charpin, "Un Quartier de Nippur et le problème des écoles à l'époque paléo-babylonienne (suite)," *RA* 84 (1990) 1–16; see Römer, *Iets over school.*

26. See D. O. Edzard, "Amarna und die Archive seiner Korrespondenten zwischen Ugarit und Gaza," *Biblical Archaeology Today: Proceedings of the International Congress on Biblical Archaeology, Jerusalem, April 1984* (ed. J. Amitai; Jerusalem: Israel Exploration Society, 1985) 248–59, and bibliography therein concerning scribes and Akkadian texts, including bilinguals, from a number of peripheral sites.

27. See A. F. Rainey, "The Scribe at Ugarit: His Position and Influence," *Proceedings of the Israel Academy of Science and Humanities* 3 (1969) 126–47.

28. A. Parrot, "Les Fouilles de Mari: Deuxième campagne (hiver 1934–35)," *Syria* 17 (1936) 21; idem, *Mission archéologique de Mari II: Le palais, architecture* (Paris: Geuthner, 1958) 186–91, pls. XLI–XLII; G. E. Mendenhall, "Mari," *BA* 11 (1948) 8; A. Malamat, "Mari," *Encyclopedia Judaica* 11 (1971) col. 972–89. The identification is apparently not now accepted, since there is no mention of a scribal school per se by A. Spycket, "Mari B. 3.2.1. Palais royal," *Reallexikon der Assyriologie* 7:399–401. The existence of exercise tablets at the site indicates some kind of scribal training, however. Mark Chavalas provided information concerning Terqa (oral communication).

29. See P. Artzi, "The Glosses in the El-Amarna Documents," *Bar Ilan* 1 (1963) 24–57 (Hebrew); D. Sivan, *Grammatical Analysis and Glossary of the Northwest-Semitic Vocables in Akkadian Texts of the 15th–13th C[enturies] B.C. from Canaan and Syria* (AOAT 214; Neukirchen-Vluyn: Neukirchener Verlag, 1984); J. Huehnergard, *Ugaritic Vocabulary in Syllabic Transcription* (HSS 32; Atlanta: Scholars Press, 1987).

30. See J. H. Tigay, *The Evolution of the Gilgamesh Epic* (Philadelphia: University of Pennsylvania Press, 1982) 11.

The existence, or not, of scribal schools for Hebrew writers in Israel during the Old Testament period is a topic in itself.[31] Since they are later in date than the majority of the cuneiform evidence cited, and since the writing system was different, I will not discuss them here. Hebrew, which was written with pen and ink on papyrus rather than clay, is perhaps more similar to Egyptian.[32]

Scribal concern for accuracy in transmitting tradition was inculcated as part of the educational system, and it is also clearly evident in the professional output after training was complete. One source of information are colophons; a colophon is, according to Hunger's definition, "a note by the scribe, separated from the text, which is at the end of a tablet of literary content, containing statements concerning the tablet and the people who had something to do with the tablet."[33] These are found not only in Akkadian texts, but also in Ugaritic documents, and similar elements have been noted in Aramaic and Hebrew.[34]

Among other things recorded by the scribe were the source text from which he was copying and some of the scribal procedures he employed. The latter at times include mention of whether the scribe collated (Akk. *barû*) the original text, that is, if he carefully compared the copy in detail

31. A. Klostermann, "Schulwesen im alten Israel," *Theologische Studien: Theodor Zahn* (ed. N. Bonwetsch et al.; Leipzig: Deichert [Böhme], 1908) 193–232; A. Demsky, "Education (Jewish)," *Encyclopaedia Judaica* 6 (Jerusalem: Keter, 1971) 381–98; idem, "Scribes," ibid., 14, 1041–43; A. Millard, "The Practice of Writing in Ancient Israel," *BA* 35 (1972) 98–111; M. Haran, *Temples and Temple Service in Ancient Israel: An Inquiry into Biblical Cult Phenomena and the Historical Setting of the Priestly School* (Oxford: Oxford University Press, 1978; repr. Winona Lake, Ind.: Eisenbrauns, 1985); B. Lang, "Schule und Unterricht in alten Israel," *La Sagesse de l'Ancien Testament* (ed. M. Gilbert; Bibliotheca ephemeridum theologicarum lovaniensium 51; Gembloux: Duculot/Louvain: Louvain University Press, 1979) 186–201; A. Lemaire, *Les Écoles et la formation de la Bible dans l'ancien Israel* (OBO 39; Fribourg: Éditions universitaires/Göttingen: Vandenhoeck & Ruprecht, 1981); Golka, "Weisheitschule," 257–70; A. Lemaire, "Sagesse et écoles," *VT* 34 (1984) 270–81; A. Millard, "An Assessment of the Evidence for Writing in Ancient Israel," *Biblical Archaeology Today: Proceedings of the International Congress on Biblical Archaeology, Jerusalem, April 1984* (ed. J. Amitai; Jerusalem: Israel Exploration Society, 1985) 301–12; J. L. Crenshaw, "Education in Ancient Israel," *JBL* 104 (1985) 601–15; Haran, "Diffusion of Literacy," 81–95; Puech, "Les Écoles," 189–203; Lipiński, "Royal and State Scribes," 164.

32. Concerning Egyptian scribes and education see: H. Brunner, *Altägyptische Erziehung* (Wiesbaden: Harrassowitz, 1957); R. J. Williams, "Scribal Training in Ancient Egypt," *JAOS* 92 (1972) 214–21; T. G. H. James, *Pharaoh's People* (London: Bodley Head, 1984) 132–80; H. te Velde, "Scribes and Literacy in Ancient Egypt," *Scripta signa vocis* (ed. H. L. J. Vanstiphout et al.; Groningen: Forsten, 1986) 253–64; A. Schlott-Schwab, *Schrift und Schreiber in Alten Ägypten* (Munich: Beck, 1989).

33. H. Hunger, *Babylonische und assyrische Kolophone* (AOAT 2; Neukirchen-Vluyn: Neukirchener Verlag, 1968) 1.

34. D. W. Baker, "Biblical Colophons: Gevaryahu and Beyond," *Studies in the Succession Narrative: OTWSA 27 (1984) and OTWSA 28 (1985): Old Testament Essays* (ed. W. C. van Wyk; Pretoria: OTWSA, 1986) 29–61.

with the original and if he proofed (Akk. *sanāqu*) the text. These factors all indicate that scribes were concerned with accuracy.

Most colophons also report the name of the scribe himself, which indicates that he was interested in making the best possible copy. A scribe was not likely to want to present shoddy workmanship for scrutiny, since the presence of his name in the colophon proclaimed the responsible party; identifying himself with poor copying would tend to prevent obtaining further livelihood in the scribal profession.

The respect with which scribes seemed to view their source documents is also clear from an examination of the copies they made. Some scribes, at least, considered it important not only to copy the content but also the form of the source document accurately. In some cases even the division into lines within the text is preserved in the copy. For example, in a copy of the tenth tablet of the Gilgamesh Epic a scribe several times marks places where two lines from the source document were apparently copied by him onto one line. He separates the two originally separate lines by a *Glossenkeil*, two small wedges.[35] There are also several cases in which the scribe wanted to present as accurately as he could his copy of a damaged text. Here, in the position on the line corresponding to the break in the original, the scribe wrote, usually in letters smaller than those in the surrounding text, *ḫipi* 'broken'.[36] He no more felt able to hypothesize what might have been originally in the break and restore it than did the Masoretic scribes in the case of the missing numbers in the description of Saul's life and reign in 1 Sam 13:1. In both of these instances, a Mesopotamian text and a biblical text, accuracy in copying the original was a primary concern.

The existence of these accurately copied texts shows the care of the scribes in presenting their exemplar, but does not prove that this was a universal practice. If a scribe correctly filled in a lacuna in his exemplar, there is no way a reader could know that he did so. Most interesting are the instances in which the scribe chose not to supply information that was obvious for a lacuna.

In the Old Testament, the accuracy of the text is at times called into question concerning relatively minor details such as census figures or battle casualties. Mesopotamian scribal practice can also be brought to bear on this issue. Reliefs of battle scenes or royal expeditions commonly portray scribes tallying the booty or casualties.[37] Quite often there are

35. See D. W. Baker, "Reverse Archaeology, Disconstruction of Texts: A Critique of Jeffrey Tigay," *Proceedings: Eastern Great Lakes and Midwest Biblical Societies* 9 (1989) 40 nn. 22–27.

36. See *AHw*, s.v. *ḫīpu(m)*; CAD, s.v. *ḫīpu* 1b.

37. See A. R. Millard, "Large Numbers in the Assyrian Royal Inscriptions," *Ah, Assyria . . . : Studies in Assyrian History and Ancient Near Eastern Historiography Presented to Hayim Tadmor* (ScrHier 33; Jerusalem: Magnes, 1991) 215.

two scribes depicted side by side,[38] one apparently using a scroll of some kind to record his observations, most likely in Aramaic, and the other using another medium, probably a writing board.[39] The latter was covered with wax, into which the scribe incised his cuneiform text with a stylus. He could later transcribe it on some more permanent medium such as a clay tablet, cylinder, or even onto one of the wall reliefs themselves, if the events were of sufficient import to merit a permanent public record. Both the papyrus and writing board were light and relatively easy to transport, allowing the leader of the campaign to keep a running account of his observations. This simultaneous record-keeping explains how such precise figures could be accurately preserved.

The scribal accuracy that I have attempted to document in several different ways is significant when considering the transmission of tradition. One must distinguish, however, between the accurate rendition of a traditional text and the accurate transmission of historical data. The former falls into the area of technical expertise, which has been the subject of this essay, while the latter involves questions of historiography. In other words, a scribe could be meticulous in copying a text, making it a faithful replica of the original, but if the original was a nonhistorical myth, so would be the copy.

It is debatable whether writers in the Old Testament period were interested in writing history per se, a topic addressed in a number of ways in this volume. Even in recording historical events, the scribe's presuppositions and goals in producing the document can skew the "objective" presentation. As A. R. Millard stated,

> At first glance, the contemporaneity of the Aramaic monuments might appear to ensure their accuracy as records of their times and the events that took place in them. Consideration of their nature may throw some doubt on that impression. . . . These inscriptions are bombastic public declarations designed to ensure continued respect for the kings and veneration of their names by subsequent generations. Now the names of several of the kings and their realms are attested independently, so they cannot be dismissed as inventions, nor is there any reason to suppose they did not build the defences or palaces or shrines they boast about. Yet several of them

---

38. L. Messerschmidt, "Zur Technik des Tontafel-Schreibens," *OLZ* 9 (1906) 187; A. Paterson, *Assyrian Sculptures: Palace of Sinacherib* (The Hague: Nihoff, 1915) pls. LII, LV–LVI, LXXXVIII–LXXXIX; J. H. Breasted, "The Physical Processes of Writing in the Early Orient and Their Relation to the Origin of the Alphabet," *AJSL* 32 (1915–1916) 344–46; D. J. Wiseman, "Assyrian Writing Boards," *Iraq* 17 (1955) 12, pl. 3.2; *ANEP* 236; R. D. Barnett and M. Falkner, *The Sculptures of Tiglath-Pileser III* (London: British Museum, 1962) pl. 6; R. D. Barnett, *Assyrian Sculpture in the British Museum* (Toronto: McClelland and Stewart, 1975) 54.

39. Wiseman, "Assyrian Writing Boards," 3–13; cf. also Hallo, "New Viewpoints," 18.

happily speak of their gods placing them on their thrones, saving them, and giving them success . . . Such an inscription is religious propaganda.[40]

Nonhistorical or suprahistorical motives behind the composition of a number of seemingly historical texts is discernible, ranging (in Akkadian) from the Code of Hammurabi, which seeks to bolster the reputation of the king before the gods,[41] through the autobiographies in Assyrian royal inscriptions treated briefly by Tadmor in 1983,[42] with a much fuller treatment by Longman,[43] to the more mundane royal inscriptions such as Esarhaddon's "Babylon Inscription," in which Cogan, through the occurrence of relatively minor textual variants, has identified the presence of political and ideological agendas.[44] This type of deliberate "airbrushing" is also clearly discernible in the Hebrew Scriptures, for example, in the Chronicler's portrayal of the life of King David.[45]

While scribes were not primarily interested in producing what modern writers might designate history, through their close ties with temple and palace they worked almost daily with texts on which modern scholars base a reconstruction of history, namely legal and economic texts. My preliminary observations would lead to the suggestion that more scribal names are affixed to this genre of texts than to any other. A number of these texts simply indicate the scribe as writer,[46] but a number give him an additional role, that of witness or notary to the transaction recorded in the document.[47] It is clear that in the Old Babylonian period (2000–1600 B.C.) the

40. A. R. Millard, "Israelite and Aramean History in the Light of Inscriptions," *TynBul* 41 (1990) 267.

41. See the epilogue in particular (*ANET* 177–80), especially xxiv:1–xxv:58.

42. H. Tadmor, "Autobiographical Apology in the Royal Assyrian Literature," *History, Historiography and Interpretation: Studies in Biblical and Cuneiform Literature* (ed. H. Tadmor and M. Weinfeld; Jerusalem: Magnes, 1983) 36–57.

43. T. Longman III, *Fictional Akkadian Autobiography: A Generic and Comparative Study* (Winona Lake, Ind.: Eisenbrauns, 1990).

44. M. Cogan, "Omens and Ideology in the Babylon Inscription of Esarhaddon," *History, Historiography and Interpretation*, 76–87.

45. See, for example, the absence in the Chronicler of aspects of David's life that are recorded in Samuel, but probably omitted so as not to reflect negatively upon David as a king, e.g., his gathering a band of renegades (1 Sam 22:1–2) who, with him, involved themselves in extortion (25:2–42, especially 6–8), his treasonous alliance with Judah's enemies the Philistines (27–29), and his ignominious ouster by his son Absalom (2 Samuel 15–18).

46. E.g., PRU 3.16.178:21; 4.31:27; 6.18:1; 45:34; see n. 24; E. Chiera, *Exchange and Security Documents: Joint Expedition with the Iraq Museum at Nuzi* (henceforth JEN) (Paris: Guethner, 1931) 3:276; R. H. Pfeiffer, *Excavations at Nuzi*, vol. 2: *The Archives of Shilwateshub, Son of the King* (HSS 9; Cambridge: Harvard University Press, 1932) 27 (Middle Assyrian); J. S. Cooper, "A Sumerian šu-íl-la from Nimrud with a Prayer for Sin-šar-iškun," *Iraq* 32 (1970) 63, col. E:1 (Neo Assyrian); *ANET* 644–45.

47. This being the most frequent function of the scribe, texts are numerous, see, e.g., J. J. Finkelstein, *Late Old Babylonian Documents and Letters* (YOS 13; New Haven: Yale University Press, 1972) 89:30 (Ammisaduqa 6); ADD 120:8; 162:8; 318:32; 472:38 (Neo-Assyrian).

scribe was viewed not only as simple penman (stylusman?) but as a reputable member of society who can be relied upon to validate a decision recorded on a document. In all probability, this is undoubtedly the case earlier as well. This practice seems to indicate that the visibility and role of the scribe in society stood at a higher level than that of simply a copier of texts. This is also indicated in the body of some texts, where the benefits of a scribal education alluded to earlier seem, in a few cases at least, to come to fruition. Scribes not only witness transactions, but they are also at times owners or buyers of land[48] or recipients of royal grants.[49]

The literacy of scribes, their standing in society, and the recognition of their integrity also led to their functioning as supervisors not only in aspects of commerce,[50] but also in the Old Testament of military projects, including conscription[51] and even of Temple finances.[52]

As scribes gained prestige and position in the community, they not only produced written material, with the concomitant task of orally delivering written messages to their intended recipients, who could not usually read; they also came to be responsible for the next logical step: the interpretation of texts. At least some of them became wise men or sages. This would be a natural advance particularly where the scribe was associated with the religious shrine, as was the case with the previously mentioned priest-scribes. Thus the scribe gained even greater power, not only having his hand in matters of business and politics, but now also in religion. Scribes not only mediated king to vassal or fellow king, merchant to buyer, or contractor to employer, but now also god to man. It seems to be only at this last stage that the Gospel writers had the problems mentioned at the beginning of this essay. They were not frowned

---

48. CT 51,23:7 (Kurigalzu); JEN 416; (Nuzi; see A. Fadhil, *Studien zur Topographie und Prosopographie der Provinzstädte des Königreichs Arrapḫe* [Baghdader Forschungen 6; Mainz am Rhein: von Zabern, 1983] 40); ADD 324:11 (see T. Kwasman, *Neo-Assyrian Legal Documents in the Kouyunjik Collection of the British Museum* [henceforth *NALD*] [Studia Pohl: Series Maior 14; Rome: Pontifical Biblical Institute, 1988] 333); 335:9 (*NALD* 93); 359:1 (*NALD* 153); 470:2 (*NALD* 256; all Neo-Assyrian).

49. PRU 3.16.209:9, 11.

50. A. Alberti and F. Pomponio, *Pre-Sargonic and Sargonic Texts from Ur Edited in UET 2, Supplement* (Studia Pohl: Series Maior 13; Rome: Pontifical Biblical Institute, 1986; henceforth *PSST*) 16 rev. II 1′–2′ (deliverer of bitumen, see p. 56); *PSST* 44: rev. II 4–5 (cf. *PSST* 42: 4, rev. 1); I. Sparr, *Tablets, Cones, and Bricks of the Third and Second Millennium B.C.* (Cuneiform Texts in the Metropolitan Museum of Art 1; New York: Metropolitan Museum of Art, 1988) 33:8 (foreman [*ugulla*]); see M. Dandamayev, *Babylonian Scribes* (Moscow: Nauka, 1983; Russian, English summary, 235–42).

51. Judg 5:14; 2 Chr 26:11.

52. 2 Kgs 12:11; 22:3 and further in the passage; Neh 13:13. For a more thorough study of other duties and functions of a scribe, see T. N. D. Mettinger, *Solomonic State Officials* (Lund: Gleerup, 1971) 25–51; cf. M. Weinfeld, *Deuteronomy and the Deuteronomic School* (Oxford: Clarendon, 1972; repr. Winona Lake, Ind.: Eisenbrauns, 1992) 158–71.

upon as relayers of tradition, but for their interpretation of that tradition. In their earlier role as writers and transmitters they played a vital function in ancient Near Eastern society, a role which has ultimately opened for us windows into their society through the texts that they so carefully preserved and passed on.

The Sumerian Historiographic Tradition and Its Implications for Genesis 1–11

Richard E. Averbeck

Dallas Theological Seminary

Although there were some differences between the earlier and later cultures as a result of ethnic and linguistic change, in many respects Assyrian and Babylonian ideas and institutions are Sumerian ideas and institutions in new garb, the new garb being a different language, Akkadian. Ideas about the past in Assyria and Babylonia were inherited from the Sumerians and, despite some alteration, their essential Sumerian character continued to be recognizable. In the discussion of historiographical genres we shall find only a few innovations in Assyrian and Babylonian times.[1]

So wrote A. Kirk Grayson in 1980 in his introduction to a major study of Assyrian and Babylonian historiography. However, if, as Grayson goes on to say, the study of historiography in ancient Mesopotamian sources in general is in its "infancy,"[2] then the scholarly study of Sumerian historiography in particular is barely "kicking in the womb." The reasons for this are not difficult to understand. The conditions under which one studies Sumerian texts are not yet conducive to authoritative synthesis. For example, although progress is being made, we are still awaiting the appearance of good critical editions of some of the important compositions. Moreover, while the *Chicago Assyrian Dictionary* is

---

A special note of thanks is due to Alan Millard, who took the time to read this paper carefully and make valuable suggestions, David Baker, who helped with bibliographic information, and James Hoffmeier, who invited me to participate in the conference. Of course, I alone am responsible for the ideas and quality of the essay as it stands.

1. A. Kirk Grayson, "Histories and Historians of the Ancient Near East: Assyria and Babylonia," *Or* 49 (1980) 142.

2. Ibid., 143. See also the remarks in Omar Carena, *History of the Near Eastern Historiography and Its Problems, 1852–1985, Part One: 1852–1945* (AOAT 218/1; Neukirchen-Vluyn: Neukirchener Verlag, 1989) 1–14.

nearing completion, only the A part 1 and B volumes of the *Pennsylvania Sumerian Dictionary* have appeared.

In the light of the current state of scholarly research, it is premature to attempt an overall synthesis of "the Sumerian view of history." To be sure, it may not be legitimate to speak of one homogeneous Sumerian view of history because there are simply too many Sumerian city-states or regions with different economic, social, religious, political, and historical experiences for their textually discernible historiographic points of view to be all of one piece. Nevertheless, the Sumerians did leave behind some significant textual traces of their own ideas about their past and, as Grayson has observed, their historiographic genres and ideas had longstanding impact in Babylonia and Assyria even after the Sumerians themselves had disappeared.

SUMERIAN HISTORIOGRAPHY:
DEFINITION, THEORY, AND METHOD

Recently, O. Carena has pointed out that within the field of Mesopotamian (not to mention Sumerian) historiography there is a lack of "methodological reflection about the nature of historiography,"[3] so the first task is to lay a methodological and programmatic foundation for the study of Sumerian historiography. On the front end of the tradition, because of the intermixture of Sumerians and Semites in Mesopotamia from before the advent of history writing, it is not possible to be sure that even the earliest Sumerian historiographical documents reflect a purely "Sumerian" tradition. On the back end of the tradition, it is true that Sumerian continued as a literary language long after it was dead as a spoken everyday tongue, and the historiographic tradition of the Sumerians seems to have had a longstanding impact on the later Akkadian historiographic tradition, as already noted. But one cannot simply ignore the linguistic shift from Sumerian to Akkadian and refer generally to "Mesopotamian historiography."

Therefore, strictly speaking, it might be better to speak of the "Sumero-Mesopotamian" tradition found in texts written in Sumerian, especially those composed before 2000 B.C. (i.e., about the end of the Third Dynasty of Ur). This makes it possible to focus on the point of view of the particular documents under study as opposed to the origin of the ideas that make up that point of view. Accordingly, the Sumerian inscriptions and other types of compositions with historiographic dimensions from the periods after 2000 B.C.—the Isin-Larsa, Old Babylonian, and later dynasties—should be taken as complementary to the earlier

---

3. Ibid., 4–5.

materials,[4] even though all the extant copies of some of the premier historiographic texts (e.g., the Sumerian King List) are dated to these later periods.[5] Taken together, all of these are sources for "Sumerian historiography," but priority and control should be given to those Sumerian compositions that clearly have their origin before 2000 B.C.

There are two main periods of Sumerian historiographic writing prior to 2000 B.C.[6] They are: (1) the pre-Sargonic or Old Sumerian period from about 2500 to 2350 B.C., especially the inscriptions from the Lagash I dynasty,[7] and (2) the post-Sargonic or Neo-Sumerian period from about

4. For the presumed Sumerian origin of the cuneiform writing system, the very early mixture of Sumerians and Semites in Sumer, and the debate over when Sumerian died out as a living language to become a literary language only, see the summary and literature cited in John L. Hayes, *A Manual of Sumerian Grammar and Texts* (Aids and Research Tools in Ancient Near Eastern Studies 5; Malibu: Undena, 1990) 265–72. Regarding the latter point, it seems to me that since administrative and economic tablets were still being written in Sumerian by the thousands during the Ur III period, the language was most likely still very much alive and in everyday use. The prior question of the origin of the Sumerians themselves is another matter altogether. The standard treatment is Tom Jones, *The Sumerian Problem* (New York: Wiley, 1969).

5. For some of these later texts there have been proposals that, even though all the extant copies were made after 2000 B.C., there is good reason to believe that there were earlier versions; see the discussion of the Sumerian King List in Claus Wilcke, "Genealogical and Geographical Thought in the Sumerian King List," *DUMU-E₂-DUB-BA: Studies in Honor of Åke W. Sjöberg* (ed. Hermann Behrens, Darlene Loding, and Martha T. Roth; Occasional Publications of the Samuel Noah Kramer Fund 1; Philadelphia: Babylonian Section, University Museum, 1989) 557–71, and the literature cited there.

6. The inscriptions are surely one of the best places to start in the study of Sumerian historiography. William W. Hallo writes, "The literary tradition can be used to fill the lacunae of Sumerian history, but only where the contemporary monuments and archives have provided the framework" ("The Coronation of Ur-Nammu," *JCS* 20 [1966] 139). Hallo's concern here is in clearly establishing the historicity of events rather than the historical mentality of the Sumerians.

My concern is more with their view of their own past and their manner of writing about it. But the inscriptions also provide the best starting point for this sort of investigation. In fact, this essay focuses on some "historical narratives" (see the discussion below, pp. 93–98) embedded within or making up certain pre-Sargonic Sumerian inscriptions. They are arguably the "cleanest" texts that we have for the foundations of Mesopotamian historiography because: (1) this is the earliest corpus of texts containing whole historiographic texts or passages within texts, and (2) in general, "inscriptions" as a genre are less complicated in their textual and literary development than other genres with historiographic dimensions.

The "literary tradition" is made up of sources for which it is often difficult to establish a certain date of origin. Moreover, such texts are often more "creative" in their view of the past than is desirable for the present stage of the investigation. They can eventually be brought into consideration, but this should probably wait until the framework has been laid by the inscriptional evidence (cf. Hallo's statement, cited above).

7. See the chart in Jerrold Cooper, *Sumerian and Akkadian Royal Inscriptions*, vol. 1: *Presargonic Inscriptions* (AOSTS 1; New Haven, Conn.: American Oriental Society, 1986) 14. The recent scholarly treatments are the work of Cooper, cited here, and H. Steible and H. Behrens, *Die Altsumerischen Bau- und Weihinschriften* (Freiburger Altorientalische Studien 5–6; 3 vols.; Wiesbaden: Steiner, 1982), where one can find a transliteration as well as a German translation, commentary, and a separate glossary volume (vol. 6) by

2200 to 2000 B.C., especially the inscriptions of the Lagash II dynasty (to which Gudea belonged),[8] Utuhegal of Uruk,[9] and the kings of the Third Dynasty of Ur.[10] These were productive periods in the writing of Sumerian texts (some of which have historiographic dimensions) by writers who were essentially, at least according to the estimation of some scholars, also *speakers* of Sumerian.

History, Historicity, and Historiography

Defining *Sumerian* is simple compared to the difficulties with the term *historiography*. Many have lamented the problem. So, instead of adding to debates over words, I will simply take as my point of departure Johan Huizinga's well-known and resilient definition of history: "History is the intellectual form in which a civilization renders account to itself of its past."[11] Thus, *history* is the general term used for what is happening

---

Hermann Behrens. For a thorough discussion of the historical situation lying behind many of these compositions see Jerrold Cooper, *Reconstructing History from Ancient Inscriptions: The Lagash-Umma Border Conflict* (Sources from the Ancient Near East 2/1; Malibu: Undena, 1983).

8. See especially Horst Steible and Hermann Behrens, *Die Neusumerischen Bau- und Weihinschriften* (Freiburger Altorientalische Studien 9/1; Stuttgart: Steiner, 1991). The chronology and dating of the Lagash II dynasty is confused. The majority opinion has been that "nearly all the rulers of this dynasty, including the famous Gudea, are to be dated prior to the establishment of the Ur III empire by Urnammu"; Jacob Klein, "From Gudea to Shulgi: Continuity and Change in Sumerian Literary Tradition," *DUMU-E$_2$-DUB-BA: Studies in Honor of Åke W. Sjöberg* (ed. Hermann Behrens, Darlene Loding, and Martha T. Roth; Occasional Publications of the Samuel Noah Kramer Fund 11; Philadelphia: Babylonian Section, The University Museum, 1989) 289; and the summary of the scholarly discussion leading to this opinion in Richard E. Averbeck, *A Preliminary Study of Ritual and Structure in the Cylinders of Gudea* (Ph.D. diss., Dropsie College, 1987) 8–17. The minority opinion that Gudea was in fact a contemporary of Urnammu has received new support from Piotr Steinkeller's prosopographic study of the administrative tablets from Lagash ("The Date of Gudea and His Dynasty," *JCS* 40 [1988] 47–53), but not all scholars are convinced (see, e.g., Klein, "From Gudea to Shulgi," 289).

9. See the discussion and references in William W. Hallo, "The Coronation of Ur-Nammu," *JCS* 20 (1966) 135–39.

10. See the discussion and references in William W. Hallo, "The Royal Inscriptions of Ur: A Typology," *HUCA* 33 (1962) 1–43. These texts provide the working foundation for Hayes, *A Manual of Sumerian Grammar.*

11. Johan Huizinga, "A Definition of the Concept of History," *Philosophy and History: Essays Presented to Ernst Cassirer* (ed. R. Klibansky and H. J. Paton; New York: Harper & Row, 1963) 9. His definition continues to be highly regarded and widely used in modern theoretical discussions as well as in the scholarly discussions of both Mesopotamian and biblical historiography. See, for example, Perez Zagorin, "Historiography and Postmodernism: Reconsiderations," *History and Theory* 29 (1990) 273–74; William W. Hallo, "Biblical History in Its Near Eastern Setting: The Contextual Approach," *Scripture in Context: Essays on the Comparative Method* (ed. Carl D. Evans et al.; Pittsburgh: Pickwick, 1980) 6; K. Lawson Younger, Jr., *Ancient Conquest Accounts: A Study in Ancient Near Eastern and*

when a civilization takes account of its own past from its own point of view. Other terms (see below) fit under its umbrella.

Historiography may be distinguished from *history* by taking the former to refer to "the principles, theory, and history of historical writing."[12] Thus, in his definition Huizinga is both defining history and doing historiography. Similarly, this essay looks at history from a historiographic point of view by seeking to understand the principles and practices of history writing in ancient Sumer.

Biblical History Writing (JSOTSup 98; Sheffield: JSOT Press, 1990) 26–27; John Van Seters, *In Search of History: Historiography in the Ancient World and the Origins of Biblical History* (New Haven: Yale University Press, 1983) 1, although Van Seters seems to have misused Huizinga's definition (see the remarks in Younger, *Ancient Conquest Accounts*, 26–27, and Baruch Halpern, *The First Historians: The Hebrew Bible in History* [San Francisco: Harper & Row, 1988] 14 n. 10).

12. Younger, *Ancient Conquest Accounts,* 46 (citing *Webster's Third New International Dictionary* 1.1073). It is essential that we be clear what exactly we are talking about. White has written, "The historical discourse should be viewed as a sign-system which points in two directions simultaneously: first, toward the set of events it purports to describe and, second, toward the generic story form, to which it tacitly likens the set in order to disclose its formal coherence considered as either a structure or a process" (Hayden V. White, "Historicism, History, and the Figurative Imagination," *Essays on Historicism* [History and Theory: Studies in the Philosophy of History 14/4, supplement 14; Hanover, N.H.: Wesleyan University Press, 1975] 54). Elsewhere White says it this way: "The historical text thus *mediates* between the events reported in it on the one side and pregeneric plot structures conventionally used in our culture to endow unfamiliar events and situation[s] with meanings, on the other" (emphasis mine). He goes on to argue that one can distinguish between science and history by the "want of conceptual rigor and failure to produce the kinds of universal laws that the sciences characteristically seek to produce." Similarly, we can distinguish between literature and history by means of the latter's "interest in the 'actual' rather than the 'possible,' which is supposedly the object of representation of 'literary' works" ("The Historical Text as Literary Artifact," *Tropics of Discourse: Essays in Cultural Criticism* [Baltimore: Johns Hopkins University Press, 1978]; originally published in *Clio* 3/3 [1974] 88–89).

One might put it this way. In the study of a historical text there are really four distinct foci that are possible: (1) the events and circumstances of the past with which the author of the document has concerned himself, (2) the account that the author has produced and that is now the immediate object of investigation, (3) the scholar's understanding of the account itself, and (4) the scholar's reconstruction of the events and circumstances that were past from the point of view of the author of the document. The first is actually inaccessible. The original events and the context in which they occurred are past and cannot be directly observed. Number four is a substitute for it, albeit necessarily incomplete and, by virtue of that fact, if not for other reasons as well, imperfect. (Actually, the original author's account is similarly incomplete and imperfect, so this should not bother us. The difference is that the original author was ostensibly a relatively good representative of his civilization.) Numbers two and three are the crux, making the philological, literary, cultural, and historiographical finesse of the scholar the heart of the process of doing history today. Actually, from this one can see how history gets "swallowed-up" in historiography when one studies ancient historical documents. Our analysis of the account and reconstruction of the past events and circumstances becomes, in turn, an object of study by other scholars either in the present or perhaps even centuries from now.

Historicity is different from both *history* and *historiography* in that it looks primarily at the actual events or circumstances supposedly witnessed to by the text(s) under study. Huizinga himself breaks his definition of history into four parts. Accordingly, *history* is: (1) an intellectual form, (2) the product of a civilization, (3) a rendering of account to oneself, and (4) about the past. *Historicity* focuses on the last point, "about the past." Because of the strong positivist tradition in Assyriological scholarship, most of the limited amount of historiographic work has been concentrated here.

A good example in the field of Sumerian historiography in particular is some of the work of William W. Hallo and several of his students at Yale (e.g., Piotr Michalowski and Douglas Frayne). One of his stated purposes is to draw on the various categories and genres of Sumerian texts "in order to reconstruct the historical reality lying behind them."[13] This has given rise to a rather lively and not always cordial debate over the historical reliability of at least some of the documents and the feasibility of reconstructing ancient Mesopotamian history from them. One can see this in somewhat stark form in Hallo's 1989 presidential address to the American Oriental Society entitled: "The Limits of Skepticism."[14]

---

13. W. W. Hallo, "Sumerian Historiography," *History, Historiography and Interpretation: Studies in Biblical and Cuneiform Literatures* (ed. H. Tadmor and M. Weinfeld; Jerusalem: Magnes, 1983) 11. In the context, Hallo assures us that "historicity" has not always nor does it continue to be his only preoccupation, as his many contributions to the study of genre and other literary features of Sumerian literary texts prove. Nevertheless, in the essay cited here, his concern is with using the various genres together in reconstructing historical reality. Van Seters (*In Search of History*, 55) cites previous writers who have contributed to the study of ancient Mesopotamian historiography from the point of view of "historical reliability" and summarizes their views.

14. W. W. Hallo, "The Limits of Skepticism," later published in *JAOS* 110 (1990) 187–99. Here he decries the skepticism of such scholars as Leo Oppenheim, Miguel Civil, and Jerrold Cooper (see references there). This debate is not limited, of course, to the study of ancient Mesopotamia. "Historical narrative" has been a subject of much discussion in modern historiography and related disciplines. A good recent summary with bibliography and analysis of the issues is provided by Andrew P. Norman, "Telling it Like It Was: Historical Narratives on Their Own Terms," *History and Theory* 30 (1991) 119–35. Norman has observed that the "epistemic legitimacy of the historical narrative has been denied on philosophical, scientific, and literary grounds" (ibid., 119–20). Philosophically, some have doubted the adequacy of the narrative form to represent historical realities, since in narrative authors necessarily select, omit, alter, or embroider in order to tell the story. Scientifically, historical narratives are questionable because they do not lend themselves to explanatory completeness and distort the subject matter. Literarily, the narrative form necessarily imposes narrative structure on a prenarrativized past so that interpretive violence takes place.

All of these criticisms hold in common the opinion that, since narratives are "constructed," they are necessarily falsifications of the past reality. Norman's response is that "construction does not entail falsification." Historical narrative can be both "figural" and "literal" at the same time: "there is nothing contradictory in this" (ibid., 133–34). Again,

Hallo has not approached this effort at historical reconstruction naively. On the contrary, he has continually given attention to delineating the various "categories of cuneiform writing," which he describes as "canonical, monumental, and archival."[15] From a position of literary categorization and sensitivity to genre characteristics he thinks it possible, in many cases, to discern what is historically reliable and what is literary license or religious or political bias within the literary tradition. Whether or not he has always been successful is another matter.[16]

The social science approach to the ancient Near East offers another angle from which to look at historicity. The economic and administrative texts have come under serious scrutiny for the reconstruction of material and cultural history.[17] Though these texts cannot be considered "historical narrative" and they thereby escape the criticisms of those who denigrate the epistemological reliability of such narratives, at the same time, they are not very helpful in reconstructing historical mentality. In fact, these texts often have nothing to do with the Sumerians' writing of history per se but focus rather on the recording of transactions, whether religious, political, administrative, or economic. From them one can begin to reconstruct some aspects of historical reality contemporary with the writers of the texts, but not the historical mentality of the writers. They were not writing history. This essay concentrates on texts where the Sumerians were writing their own history and therefore focuses on "historical narratives" found in the extant sources.

---

he writes: "A good historian will interact dialogically with the historical record, recognizing the limits it places on possible construals of the past" (ibid., 132).

This is all written from the perspective of modern historiography. What about ancient historiography? Here the reliability of the sources depends to some extent on the purpose behind the writing of the particular historical narrative. And this is reflected, at least to some degree, by the genre in which or within which the narrative account of the past is written or embedded, as the case may be. Certainly, to take the genre on which this study is based (see below, pp. 93–98), royal inscriptions will tend to take a point of view favoring the ruler and the gods for whom the author writes. But this does not necessarily mean that there is no truth to the account. The veracity of the account needs to be openly investigated. In the meantime, the native accounts about the author's and, therefore, presumably the civilization's view of their own past reveal a great deal. And that is precisely the focus of the term *historiography* (see above, pp. 83–84, and below, pp. 86–93).

15. Hallo, "Sumerian Historiography," 10–11.

16. For example, his evaluation of the flood tradition as deriving from the "flood" of Amorites into southern Mesopotamia is certainly debatable (see Hallo, "The Limits of Skepticism," 194–99).

17. The best-known proponent of this approach from within the ranks of cuneiformists was I. J. Gelb. See, for example, his "Approaches to the Study of Ancient Society," *JAOS* 87 (1967) 1–8.

The primary difficulty with approaching the texts initially from the point of view of historicity is that the Sumerian concept of the past extends back beyond the bounds of what is normally thought of as the "historical" past. To some extent, therefore, this approach can tend to use the text for its own purposes rather than engage the text on its own terms.

The search for verifiable historical facts is of course valid and a worthy pursuit. There is, however, another way of looking at the texts, namely, from the point of view of the situation in which the composers themselves lived. The focus here is upon the way the ancient Sumerians wrote about their past and, therefore, the mentality of the ancients about their past and its implications for their present and future as reflected in the extant sources.[18] This is "historiography" and is, to some extent at least, distinct from "historicity."

Among Mesopotamian scholars, Mario Liverani is a proponent of this approach:

> The thing to do should be to view the document not as a "source of information," but as information in itself; not as an opening on a reality laying [sic] beyond, but as an element which makes up that reality. . . . not as an informer, but as a member of the community under study.[19]

This is of course another worthy goal in the study of ancient documents. The idea is to study a text on its own terms rather than to use the text for the reconstruction of past events or material culture. In this way the reader can more effectively engage in understanding the world view and mentality of ancient writers.

Almost 40 years ago Samuel Noah Kramer wrote of the need to understand the mythical/cosmological thought of the Sumerians in order to grasp their view of history and history writing. As far as he was concerned the main points are:

1. The cosmos was created, guided, and controlled by the Pantheon.
2. Man was created to serve the gods. This is often conceived of in a rather mundane way.

---

18. The "history-of-ideas" approach to ancient Mesopotamian historiography fits generally into this category; see Van Seters, *In Search of History*, 56–59, and the literature cited there. More basic work needs to be done before generalizations of the sort offered in, for example, Speiser's work (referred to by Van Seters) can be justified. It seems to me that even Liverani enters into a premature discussion of notions of time (e.g., "cyclic" versus "linear" versus "arrested" time) when he discusses the reforms of Uruinimgina (not Urukagina) in his rightly celebrated article on historiographic texts (see Mario Liverani, "Memorandum on the Approach to Historiographic Texts," *Or* 42 [1973] 178–94; quotation from p. 179).

19. Ibid., 179.

3. To make the created order work well for their purposes, the gods established a set of rules for culture, the *mes*. These *mes* provided a foundation for human civilization.[20]

One might ask which methodological approach should take priority. Should the priority be given to the etic task of reconstructing past events from the texts (referred to here as "historicity"), or should the focus be

---

20. See S. N. Kramer, "Sumerian Historiography," *IEJ* 3 (1953) 217–32 and compare P. Charvat, "A Note on Sumerian Historiography," *Aspects of Ancient Oriental Historiography* (ed. V. Souček; Prague: Charles University Press, 1975) 75–77. It is true that the *mes* were also, in a sense, conceived of as bringing order to the world of the gods. This can be detected from several points made in Sumerian literary compositions. For example, one of the *mes* is in fact "godship" itself (Kramer, "Sumerian Historiography," 219–20 n. 3). Also, the myth of Inanna and Enki shows how important the possession of and control over the *mes* was for a deity's status among the gods. And in Gudea's Cylinder B, at the dedication of Ningirsu and Baba's new temple household, the various minor deities involved in establishing the household and court of the divine couple entered one by one "with his *mes*" (Sumerian *me-ni-da*). The entry of the first of the fifteen deities in the list is described as follows:

> To put righteous deeds in order, to subjugate evil deeds, to make the temple firm, to make the temple good, to purify his city—the sanctuary, Girsu—to set up the throne of destiny, to put the scepter of the long day in the hand, to lift the head of the shepherd, Ningirsu, toward heaven like a beautiful crown for Gudea, to show (ritually correct) places in the court of the Eninnu to the leather-clad, linen-clad, (and) those with covered head, the great door, the fortress of the princely way, the great galla-spirit(?) of Girsu, Igalim, his [i.e., Ningirsu's] beloved son, passed in review 'with his *me*(s)' [Sumerian: *me-ni-da*] before the lord Ningirsu (Gudea Cylinder B vi 11–23).

The deity Igalim was the keeper of the door to the temple. He needed to bring his *me*(s) with him in order to fulfill his appointed duties. For this translation see R. E. Averbeck, *Ritual and Structure in the Cylinders of Gudea*, 688–89. T. Jacobsen (*The Harps That Once . . . : Sumerian Poetry in Translation* [New Haven: Yale University Press, 1987] 430–31) translates *me-ni-da* plus the verb *dib* as '(was) going about his duties'.

There are, in addition to *me*, other important terms such as *nam(-tar)* meaning 'destiny, fate, prospect' or something of the sort, and *giš-ḫur* meaning 'plan' or 'design'. For these see the discussion and literature cited in D. O. Edzard, "Deep-Rooted Skyscrapers and Bricks: Ancient Mesopotamian Architecture and Its Imagery," *Figurative Language in the Ancient Near East* (ed. M. Mindlin et al; London: School of Oriental and African Studies, 1987) 18–21, and G. Farber-Flügge, *Der Mythos "Inanna und Enki" unter besonderer Berücksichtigung der Liste der me* (Studia Pohl Series Maior 10; Rome: Pontifical Biblical Institute, 1973) 181–90, respectively.

None of these subjects can be treated here. But we cannot afford to ignore these overriding concerns lest we essentially denude the texts and the ancients themselves of their point of view. The ancients, it seems, did "speculative thought" largely through "mythography." They understood cause and effect and were fully capable of logical induction and deduction, but their application of these human capacities toward understanding and handling their world on a speculative level took mythological and ritual form. This had a decided impact on the way they conceived of and wrote about their own past, present, and future. For more on the relation between myth and history, see the discussion below (pp. 92–93, 97–98).

upon the emic understanding of the individual documents, categories of documents, and genres on their own terms (referred to here as "histori-ography")? The answer, it seems to me, is obvious: it is the latter.[21]

It is easy to see that Huizinga's first three points come into their own here. That is, history is not just about the past but also (1) an intellectual form (2) by which a civilization (3) renders account of its past to itself. Each of these three points affects the study of Sumerian historiography and requires some amplification. These three points will be treated here in reverse order.

Literature, Civilization, and Speculation in Historiography

First, the fact that historical narratives work partly by rendering an account of the past raises the issues of literary genres and preformed lit-erary patterns. *Genre* is difficult to define, and it will be used here simply to refer to a distinct kind of literature within the collection of literature produced by a civilization.[22] For the time being I will refer primarily to Sumerian "royal inscriptions." A full study of the structure of these in-scriptions remains a desideratum,[23] but in general, they were written to honor and show the ruler's devotion to the god(s).[24] This is the bias. It

---

21. This does not mean that we cannot consider factual accuracy along the way. But we should be most concerned at this point with the mentality of the ancients regarding their past, not the question of the factual accuracy of their record of the events of the past. Taking this approach we will be more likely to enter into their historical records from their point of view rather than our own. This turns out to be especially important when we consider their view of pre- or protohistory, that is, their disposition toward the kind of subjects dealt with in Genesis 1–11. And this, in turn, is basic to looking at Gene-sis 1–11 from the ancient Near Eastern and therefore ancient Israelite point of view. It is certainly true that the divine revelatory claims of the biblical text must also be taken into consideration and, for some of us, this is the ultimate concern. Yet, it is patently obvious to anyone who has studied the subject that the ancient Near Eastern cultural context of ancient Israel cannot be taken lightly.

22. On *genre* in relation to Mesopotamian and biblical literature, see the discussion and literature cited in William W. Hallo, "Compare and Contrast: The Contextual Ap-proach to Biblical Literature," *The Bible in the Light of Cuneiform Literature: Scripture in Context III* (ed. W. W. Hallo et al.; Ancient Near Eastern Texts and Studies 8; Lewiston, N.Y.: Mellen, 1990) 1–30; Younger, *Ancient Conquest Accounts*, 27–31, and the literature cited there. In my opinion, the combination of treating *genre* as a function of discourse grammar and relating it to historical cultural institutions shows the most promise of the methods of handling the concept. But this treatment will have to wait for another occa-sion. For now, see Robert E. Longacre, *The Grammar of Discourse* (New York: Plenum, 1983) chap. 1; and Ralph Cohen, "History and Genre," *New Literary Theory* 17 (1985–86) 203–18 (with LaCapra's response, 219–21).

23. Cooper, *Presargonic Inscriptions*, 7 n. 27.

24. See G. van Driel, "On 'Standard' and 'Triumphal' Inscriptions," *Symbolae Biblicae et Mesopotamicae Francisco Mario Theodoro de Liagre Böhl Dedicatae* (ed. M. A. Beek et al.; Leiden: Brill, 1973) 99–106, and his review of R. S. Ellis, *Foundation Deposits in Ancient*

naturally follows that in the texts where a historical narrative is present, the historical situation will be viewed from the vantage point most complimentary and beneficial to the local ruler before the god(s).

The term *preformed literary pattern* refers to the plot or narrative story line used to make the historical narrative (i.e., the account of previous history) embedded in the royal inscription recognizable and acceptable within the context of the author's community.[25] The earliest "historical narratives" known from Mesopotamia are several passages found in certain pre-Sargonic Lagash inscriptions, from Urnanshe (ca. 2600 B.C.) to Uruinimgina (ca. 2350 B.C.).[26] This is one reason for taking this corpus of texts as the foundation for an initial essay on the subject of Sumerian historiography.[27]

Obviously, not only the genre of the composition as a whole but also the subject of the historical narrative embedded within or making up the document has an effect on the "preformed literary pattern" chosen to tell the story. In the case of Enmetena's summary of the Umma-Lagash border dispute, the literary pattern is something akin to "the good guys (the rulers of Lagash) versus bad guys (the rulers of Umma)" motif of modern war movies.[28] The literary level of the composition is, on the one hand, one step back from the more advanced royal hymns, for example, of the Ur III kings and, on the other hand, one step forward from the more mundane archival texts. The plot is made up more or less of religio-political ideology that is of the utmost importance to the intended effect of the composition on the god(s).[29]

Mesopotamia, in *JAOS* 93 (1973) 67–74. His conclusion is that "royal (and private) inscriptions of the earliest periods are without exception dedicatory inscriptions," and there is no need to distinguish, for example, between dedicatory, standard, and triumphal inscriptions; van Driel, "On 'Standard' and 'Triumphal' Inscriptions," 105.

25. See Liverani, "Historiographic Texts," 182, and n. 14 above on the problem of historical narratives as literary "constructs" in contrast to supposed philosophically or scientifically sound accounts of ideas or phenomena.

26. See Cooper, *Presargonic Inscriptions*, 3, 10–14.

27. This is only a start at a program very similar to that suggested by Jerrold Cooper (*Reconstructing History*, 43): "The uses of language and interpretation of history in our earliest corpus of historical inscriptions deserve more detailed and comprehensive treatment than the tentative discussion offered here. A rigorous, synchronic literary and historical analysis of the Presargonic material should be followed by diachronic studies in which the historical inscriptions of much later times will be related back to their Early Dynastic precursors. In observing the unfolding of this genre through time, we have much to learn about the ancient attitudes toward language, writing, and history, and perhaps, also, something about our own."

28. Cooper, *Presargonic Inscriptions*, 11, 54–57. In choosing this Enmetena text (and the Uruinimgina Reforms, see below, pp. 90–98) I have ended up following the precedent of Kramer in his still-useful essay (cited above, n. 20) "Sumerian Historiography."

29. It is important to remember that these inscriptions are dedicated to the god(s).

The Uruinimgina Reforms use the plot or preformed literary pattern described by Liverani as "the restorer of order."[30] One might view it partly as a literarily more advanced and ancient look at what the modern social science approach views as the way to look at history. The primary concern is domestic cultural ethics and economics, but the ancients would never leave the god(s) out of even this sort of account. The text makes this self-evident. The so-called Lagash Lament, which recounts the atrocities of Lugalzagesi of Umma against the temples and crops of Lagash, may rightly be categorized as a literary composition rather than a royal inscription. Nevertheless, it gives account of a historical situation in terms of a literary pattern that might be referred to as "the enemy (namely, Lugalzagesi, the ruler of Umma) of the gods" and has dedicatory or at least petitionary purposes toward the god(s), as the final lines cursing Lugalzagesi show.[31]

Second, the "rendering of an account of the past" that constitutes history writing is the product of a civilization. Civilizations are naturally delimited by time and space. In the case of pre-Sargonic Sumer (the temporal factor) I am speaking of a "sectional civilization,"[32] a segment of which is the Lagash city-state (the geographical factor) from which our texts derive.

Temporally, the texts themselves reflect the progress of time from the viewpoint of the authors and the sectional civilization as a whole. One point that stands out, for example, is the beginning of the Enmetena Cone where the demarcation of the boundary between Lagash and Umma is attributed originally to the god Enlil in the ancient past (whether before or at the time of Mesalim, see presently). The implications of this will be discussed below. From there the text progresses to the time of Mesalim (king of Kish, ca. 2550 B.C.), and then to the border conflicts in the times of Ush (ruler of Umma), Eanatum (ruler of Lagash), and, finally, Enmetena himself (ca. 2400 B.C.). The historical continuity of human rulers is explicit and stretches over several generations.

Geographically, the historically documented dispute between Lagash and Umma seems to reflect a conflict that not only spanned essentially the entire time of the Lagash I dynasty (see above), but endured far be-

30. Liverani, "Memorandum on the Approach to Historiographic Texts," 186–88.

31. For these two documents, see Cooper, *Presargonic Inscriptions*, 70–79, esp. the texts labeled La 9.1 and 9.5. Regarding the status of the latter as a literary text rather than a royal inscription see Cooper, *Reconstructing History*, 13.

32. See Huizinga, "History," 5–7, and Younger, *Ancient Conquest Accounts*, 26–27. The point of the term *sectional* is that ancient Sumer was in one sense a unified civilization but in another sense divided into relatively distinct "city-states." The latter were often in competition with one another, as in the case of Lagash versus Umma. And competing viewpoints result in competing histories, at least to some degree.

yond the limits of the pre-Sargonic period and extended geographically to include a Lagashite conflict with Uruk, Ur, and Umma combined.[33] The implications of this are significant enough to warrant some preliminary remarks on the evidence of the Sumerian King List (SKL).

Piotr Michalowski has shown that, in its final form, the SKL is an apology for the post–Ur III Isin dynasty.[34] The rulers of the Isin dynasty saw themselves as continuing the tradition of kingship at Ur. Furthermore, Claus Wilcke has proposed that the original form of the SKL goes back to the Ur III period. Neither the antediluvian nor the post–Ur III Isin rulers were included in the original composition. Instead, the pattern of several successions of the kingship of Sumer from Kish to Uruk to Ur dominates the list.[35]

It is well known that the very important Lagash dynasties of the pre-Sargonic period were not included in this list. In fact, there is a Lagash King List published by Edmond Sollberger that he considers to be a satirical parody of the SKL.[36] And, in fact, it seems that the isolation of Lagash from the Umma-Uruk-Ur coalition has a history that is reflected even in the pre-Sargonic inscriptions.[37] Moreover, Wolfgang Heimpel has recently suggested that the Sumerian myth of Lugale, which may well have an originally Lagashite provenience, reflects a Tigris-influenced history as opposed to a Euphrates history.[38] He notes that Gudea Cylinder A i 3–9 mentions only the importance of the Tigris for the prosperity of Lagash.

---

33. See Cooper, *Reconstructing History*, 9 and 36–37, and the discussion below. Cf. the remarks in Hallo, "The Coronation of Ur-Nammu," 137–38.

34. Piotr Michalowski, "History as Charter: Some Observations on the Sumerian King List," *JAOS* 103 (1983) 237–48. Even the textual history of this composition is fraught with complications, and since this is a literary text rather than a dedicatory inscription, it cannot be treated in the same manner.

35. Claus Wilcke, "Genealogical and Geographical Thought in the Sumerian King List," *DUMU-E₂-DUB-BA-A: Studies in Honor of Åke W. Sjöberg* (ed. Hermann Behrens, Darlene Loding, and Martha T. Roth; Occasional Publications of the Samuel Noah Kramer Fund 11; Philadelphia: University Museum, 1989) 557–71.

36. Edmond Sollberger, "The Rulers of Lagash," *JCS* 21 (1967) 279–91. In the light of the scholarly discussion summarized here, Jacobsen's suggestion that the reason there are no Lagashite rulers mentioned in the SKL is that "the author had no list from Lagash among his sources" is unlikely; see also his *Sumerian King List* (AS 11; Chicago: University of Chicago Press, 1939) 181.

37. See the suggestive remark in Cooper, *Reconstructing History*, 9 n. 11.

38. Wolfgang Heimpel, "The Natural History of the Tigris according to the Sumerian Literary Composition Lugal," *JNES* 46 (1987) 309–17. See also William Hallo's similar suggestion of a Lagashite and, in fact, Gudean background for this and other major Sumerian compositions known mainly from later Old Babylonian copies: "Toward a History of Sumerian Literature," *Sumerological Studies in Honor of Thorkild Jacobsen on His Seventieth Birthday, June 7, 1974* (AS 20; Chicago: University of Chicago Press, 1976) 183–85.

Although this is not the place to develop the full potential of the observations just summarized, a few remarks are justifiable. Is it possible
that one should consider broadening the geographical discussion? That is,
the pre-Sargonic inscriptions, SKL, and other associated traditions may
reflect a longstanding rivalry not only between Lagash and Ur–Uruk–
Umma but also between competing Tigris and Euphrates city-state coali-
tions, or something of that sort. Thus, the Euphrates tradition (including
Ur) would naturally exclude the Lagashite kings from its list.

This distinction between the Lagash and Ur historical-geographical
milieus is even perpetuated into the Isin-Larsa period. The Isin kings link
themselves with the Ur III kings while the Larsa tradition is peculiarly
Lagashite. The opposition, therefore, continued in another form. In all
these traditions the unity of the pantheon was assumed and the original
source of human kingship was Kish. This they held in common even
early in the pre-Sargonic period. Thus, the border conflict between Lagash and Umma may be connected to large-scale formative and enduring
geographical factors. These geographical factors are, in turn, reflected in
a longstanding and qualitatively varied historiographic tradition.

Third, a civilization renders account of its own past in intellectual
form. It is well known that historical narrative is shaped by the narrator
(see, for example, the discussion of genre and literary patterns above). In
the case of the Sumerians, their tendency to do speculative thought in
terms of "myth" results in the fact that it was not characteristic of them
to separate myth from history. This is reflected in their historiography.

Myth has been defined in two contrasting ways.[39] From the point of
view of content a myth could be defined as a "purely fictitious narrative
usually involving supernatural persons, actions, or events, and embodying
some popular idea concerning natural or historical phenomena."[40] But
from the viewpoint of its function in society, myth "by narrating a 'sacred history,' stabilizes and orders, or regenerates and gives meaning to,
what is seen as the chaos of human, or secular and profane, existence."[41]
When the element of time is considered, the same term is again used in
two different ways. Paul Ricoeur writes:

> Myth is a narrative of origins, taking place in a primordial time, a time
> other than that of everyday reality; history is a narrative of recent events,

---

39. Cf. the distinction made in Richard H. Moye, "In the Beginning: Myth and History in Genesis and Exodus," *JBL* 109 (1990) 578–79.

40. "Myth," *The Oxford English Dictionary* 10.177.

41. Moye, "In the Beginning," 578–79. See also the extensive discussion of the problem of defining *myth* in William G. Doty, *Mythography: The Study of Myths and Rituals*
(University of Alabama Press, 1986) chap. 1.

extending progressively to include events that are further in the past but that are nonetheless, situated in human time.[42]

But the term is now used to refer to any context where divine intervention is found, or as Ricoeur calls it, *salvation history.* When a narrative of origins is being referred to, it may be called a *founding myth.* But when referring to "human time," the phrase *permeating myth* might be applied. These definitions will be used in this essay.

Legend is another important term.[43] Like *history* it is often found with a significant intermixture of *permeating myth,* but *legend* refers to another mode within narrative writing. As Otto Eissfeldt put it: "If the men or places or occasions which are central to the narrative are of religious significance . . . then we call such a narrative a legend."[44] Both myth and legend will become important considerations in the following discussion of pre-Sargonic Sumerian historiography.

THE PRE–SARGONIC INSCRIPTIONS AND THE SUMERIAN HISTORIOGRAPHIC CORE

Since the core of the Sumerian historiographic tradition is probably best discerned through its earliest textual attestation, it makes good sense to look first at the pre-Sargonic dedicatory inscriptions (cf. the remarks above, p. 89, n. 28). These texts consist largely of Royal Inscriptions, especially from Lagash, and include several compositions (or major portions thereof) that can and should be classified as *historical narratives.*[45] Fortunately, within this corpus of texts one finds reflections on and even accounts of history long antedating the composition and its composer(s). This provides a good starting point for investigating the Sumerian and especially Lagashite view of history and their way of writing it (i.e., "historiography"). The text of the Enmetena cone begins as follows:

---

42. Paul Ricoeur, "Myth and History," *The Encyclopedia of Religion* (vol. 10; ed. Mircea Eliade; New York: Macmillan, 1987) 273.

43. I use the term *legend* instead of *epic* because, in the case of the Sumerian materials considered here, the term *epic* is certainly inappropriate, and in the case of the biblical materials *epic* has come under heavy attack when applied to the narratives found in Genesis. See the response of Frank Moore Cross to critics of his proposal that there was an extensive epic tradition in early Israel ("The Epic Traditions of Early Israel: Epic Narrative and the Reconstruction of Early Israelite Institutions," *The Poet and the Historian: Essays in Literary and Historical Biblical Criticism* [ed. R. E. Friedman; Chico, Cal.: Scholars Press, 1983] 13–19); and the noncommittal remarks of W. Hallo ("Compare and Contrast," 15).

44. Otto Eissfeldt, *The Old Testament: An Introduction* (New York: Harper & Row, 1965) 34.

45. See Cooper, *Presargonic Inscriptions,* 9–13; and idem, "Medium and Message: Inscribed Clay Cones and Vessels from Presargonic Sumer," *RA* 79 (1985) 105, 110.

Enlil, king of all lands, father of all the gods, by his authoritative command, demarcated the border between Ningirsu and Shara. Mesalim, king
of Kish, at the command of Ishtaran, measured it off and erected a monument there.[46]

Thus, the text begins by focusing on the god Enlil as the "king" (*lugal*)
of all the lands, who originally established the boundary between Lagash
and Umma. It then moves to Mesalim "king" (*lugal*) of Kish, who had in
the distant past actually measured it all off and erected a monument as a
marker.[47]

The next step is to recount the previous history of the border
conflict. Interestingly, it begins with an incident describing the treachery
of a ruler of Umma, but no corresponding ruler of Lagash is mentioned:

Ush, ruler of Umma, acted arrogantly: he smashed that monument and
marched on the plain of Lagash. Ningirsu, warrior of Enlil, at his (Enlil's)
just command, did battle with Umma. At Enlil's command, he cast the
great battle-net upon it, and set up burial mounds for it on the plain.[48]

The defeat of Ush is accomplished, according to the text, by the direct
intervention of the god Ningirsu under the authority of Enlil. Although
the ancient writer(s) and his audience may well have assumed that one did
exist, no human agent is mentioned. Both this and the previous section of
the composition are a mix of myth and history, a fact that cannot be ignored when seeking to understand the Sumerian *view* of history. Further
discussion of this factor in Sumerian history writing follows below.

The large middle section of the composition describes the border
conflicts between the rulers of Lagash and Umma from Eanatum of
Lagash and Enakale of Umma down to Enmetena of Lagash and Il of
Umma. It begins:

Eanatum, ruler of Lagash, uncle of Enmetena ruler of Lagash, demarcated
the border with Enkale, ruler of Umma. . . . He inscribed (and erected)
monuments at that (boundary-) channel and restored the monument of
Mesalim. . . .[49]

---

46. Cooper, *Presargonic Inscriptions*, 54–55. All the following quotations from the pre-
Sargonic Inscriptions are from Cooper's translation. There is no space here to deal with
philological problems, and in any case, the points made in this discussion do not require
technical treatment of the minor points of the text.

47. See the discussion above (pp. 91–92) concerning Kish as the source of human
kingship even in the Sumerian King List. This is an example of a point in Sumerian historical ideology that seems to have endured through virtually all ancient Mesopotamian
chronological, geographical, and genre boundaries; see the pertinent remarks and literature cited in Cooper, *Reconstructing History*, 7, especially regarding the use of the title
"King of Kish."

48. Ibid., 54–55.

49. Ibid., 55.

There are several points of interest here. First, Eanatum is described not only as the "ruler of Lagash" but also as the "uncle of Enmetena." This shows that, although there was a long early history to the boundary dispute,[50] this composition focuses on the immediate history of about a generation and a half. To put it another way, the history of the dispute is written primarily in terms of its peculiar relationship to Enmetena.

Second, the term *demarcated* (*ki-sur*) is used only twice in all of the pre-Sargonic inscriptions, here and earlier in this same inscription where Enlil is said to "demarcate the border between Ningirsu and Shara" (i.e., the gods of Lagash and Umma, respectively; see the first excerpt above). The literary linkage to the distant past is obvious. The third point, the reference to restoring "the monument of Mesalim," has essentially the same effect (again, see the first excerpt above). So, the introductory lines involving Enlil, Mesalim, and Ush constitute something of a prologue. The end of the composition therefore stands as an epilogue, but one that carries very important historiographical implications in the way that it parallels the prologue (see the excerpt and remarks below).

In the meantime, toward the end of the recounting of historical events, when the composition comes to what appears to be the immediate conflict between Enmetena and Il, divine intervention again enters the picture:

> When, because of those (boundary-) channels, Enmetena ruler of Lagash, sent envoys to Il, Il ruler of Umma, the field thief, speaking hostiley, said: "The boundary-channel of Ningirsu and the boundary-channel of Nanshe are mine! I will shift the boundary-levee from Antasura to Edimgal-abzu," he said. But Enlil and Ninhursag did not allow him (to do) this.[51]

Essentially, from the Lagashite point of view, the "ruler(s)" (*ensi*) of Umma acted arrogantly against the gods, especially Ningirsu the patron deity of Lagash, while the "ruler(s)" (*ensi*) of Lagash sought to protect their divinely bestowed rights. Of course, Enlil the divine king of all the lands supported Ningirsu and therefore Lagash.

It is important to recognize that the text is saturated with such "mythical" (or "theological") statements. In fact, very near its end the composition comes back to its beginning by focusing again upon Enlil and Ningirsu, but this time with a look toward the future (precative verbs):

> If the leader of Umma transgresses the boundary-channel of Ningirsu and the boundary channel of Nanshe, to take away fields by force—whether

---

50. See the remarks on Ush above (p. 94) and the analysis in Cooper, *Reconstructing History*.

51. Cooper, *Presargonic Inscriptions*, 55.

he be the leader of Umma or an(y) other leader—may Enlil destroy him! May Ningirsu, after casting his great battle-net upon him, bring down upon him his giant hands and feet! May the people of his own city, after rising up against him, kill him there within his city.[52]

Therefore, not only is divine intervention part of what has happened in their *past* and what is happening in their *present*, but also something that the gods are called upon for in their *future*.

Interestingly, I have not detected that the Lagashite writers viewed the battles as battles between the gods of Umma and Lagash. The problem is with an arrogant *man*! This is significant because it reveals to us that, in their ideology, a man could create history even if in a negative way. The same point is found in Uruinimgina's reforms, which he enacted because men (i.e., Lagashite rulers and bureaucrats) had offended the gods.[53]

Again, in the Lagash lament the composer looks forward into the future and sees the same thing.[54] Moreover, as noted above, even here it is not that the gods of the corresponding cities do battle. Rather, all the gods, including the god of the antagonist, are called to avenge the atrocities perpetuated against Lagash by Lugalzagesi. It is readily understandable that the rulers of Lagash would see themselves as having Enlil and Ningirsu on their side. What is especially significant is that they did not, in their own understanding of things, pit themselves or their gods against other gods even of rival rulers or city-states.

I have not yet determined whether this all-inclusive mentality toward the gods continues without exception throughout the history of Sumerian historiography as delimited in this essay. My suspicion is that it may and that its influence is felt in the continuity of the religious hegemony of Nippur (the home of Enlil) in Sargonic and Ur III times and even beyond the end of the Ur III period.[55] Even the city laments reflect this mentality in their theodicy about why the cities fell. The enemies are not gods, but the very men who failed to see to the will of the gods.

---

52. Ibid., 56.

53. "The bureaucracy was operating from the boundary of Ningirsu to the sea. . . . These were the conventions of former times. . . . When Ningirsu, warrior of Enlil, granted the kingship of Lagash to Uruinimgina, selecting him from among the myriad people, he replaced the customs of former times, carrying out the command that Ningirsu, his master, had given him" (quoted from Cooper, *Presargonic Inscriptions*, 71).

54. "The leader of Umma, hav[ing] sacked L[ag]ash, has committed a sin against Ningirsu. The hand which he has raised against him will be cut off! It is not a sin of Uruinimgina, king of Girsu! May Nisaba, the god of Lugalzagesi, ruler of Umma, make him (Lugalzagesi) bear the sin!" (ibid., 79).

55. See the evidence for this, e.g., in W. W. Hallo, "A Sumerian Amphictyony," *JCS* 14 (1960) 88–114.

With this analysis as a foundation, I would like to propose that there is depth of reasoning behind the Sumerian historiographic mentality, some of it conventionally called historical and some mythical. The two are mingled in a seemingly inextricable way in the texts, but one may schematize it into four levels. The scheme is not only temporal (i.e., the progress of events through time) but also involves what might be called "modes" of historical thought where levels of reality are mixed.

First, explicit attention is paid to *contemporary history*, the events or circumstances most recent or currently active. The current politics or other circumstances of a society are naturally implicit in its history writing.[56]

Second, there is *previous history* in contemporary history writing. The recital of the history of the Lagash/Umma border conflict in the middle of the Enmetena Cone is an example of this.

Third, the traces (sometimes *only* traces) of *legendary history* may be discerned in the gap between "previous history" and the fourth phase, namely, *mythic history*. The line between the latter two phases is not clear and one cannot always be certain when myth is of the founding kind and when it is of the permeating kind.[57] It has already been observed that, for example, in the Enmetena Cone the story line begins with Enlil and then moves to Mesalim, who was by this time a legendary king of Kish.[58] Moreover, in the case of Ush (the first ruler of Umma in the Cone), no corresponding ruler of Lagash is mentioned, and the defeat of Ush comes directly from the hand of Ningirsu. Apparently, from the

---

56. For example, it has been argued that when these documents refer to the Gu'edena land as belonging in its entirety to Ningirsu and Lagash, they are reflecting a theoretical construct. The reality is that the Gu'edena was most probably always divided between Lagash and Umma. See the references and discussion in Cooper, *Reconstructing History*, 23. Of course, the theoretical construct may have a longstanding history of its own and not be limited to the contemporary scene reflected in any one document.

57. See p. 93 above. For example, it is hard to tell if the reference to Enlil's demarcation of the border between Lagash and Umma at the beginning of the Enmetena Cone referred in the mind of the author to something that happened in the divine court long before the time of Mesalim or in close temporal proximity to him. Eighty years ago, Hugo Gressmann proposed a "tripartite division of history" similar to, although not exactly the same as, what I am suggesting here. Ricoeur summarizes Gressmann's view in this way: "First there is the history that concerns recent events. . . . Then come legends, concerning distant events, and, finally, myths, relating to primordial times" (Ricoeur, "Myth and History," 278 and bibliography on 282).

58. On the importance of the title "King of Kish" as well as thorough discussions of the Kish civilization, see now I. J. Gelb, "Ebla and the Kish Civilization," *La Lingua di Ebla: Atti del convegno internazionale (Napoli, 21–23 Aprile 1980)* (ed. L. Cagni; Napoli Seminario di Studi Asiatici Series Minor 14; Naples: Istituto Universitario Orientale, 1981) 52–73; idem, "Mari and the Kish Civilization," in *Mari in Retrospect: Fifty Years of Mari and Mari Studies* (ed. Gordon D. Young; Winona Lake, Ind.: Eisenbrauns, 1992) 121–202. On its relationship to Ebla, however, see the doubts expressed by J. G. Dercksen, "Ebla," *BiOr* 47 (1990) 438.

perspective of this later time (i.e., the time of Enmetena), both Mesalim and Ush were viewed as men from the distant past. They can be called legendary figures if one is willing to grant that legends have historical plausibility or at least that they often contain a historical kernel.

The fourth phase, *mythic history*, has characteristics of both time and mode. That is, the composition begins with Enlil and the gods, (nearly) ends with them, and involves them in the intervening events (see the quotations and discussion earlier).[59] In other words, mythic history goes back to the time or focuses on a dimension of supposed reality where gods are the actors. What is essential for us to take into account is that the ancient historiographers saw a mythic unity and continuity running all the way from ancient times to the recent past and into the present. Furthermore, it is not so much that there is an "eternal return" to the mythic beginning but a mythic continuity to the present and on into the future.[60]

In order to read the Sumerian "historiographic" texts sympathetically, one must be willing to take all four parts of the scheme seriously. The ancient Sumerians did, and it is their view of history, just as much as the actual facts of history, that is being discerned from the sources.

GENESIS 1–11 AND SUMERIAN HISTORIOGRAPHY

The possible avenues of comparison between the results of the above (admittedly preliminary) analysis of Sumerian historiography and Genesis 1–11 and the implications this could carry for such matters as literary genre, the growth of the biblical text, and biblical canonicity go beyond the scope of this essay. Here the comparison will be limited to the four-fold pattern of myth and history just delineated.

From the perspective of Israelites in the process of forming their nation in Canaan, the account of the Conquest and Settlement is the contemporary history, the history of Israel in Egypt and the Exodus

---

59. On Enlil and his importance in both "founding" and "permeating" myth for the Sumerians, see Thorkild Jacobsen, *The Treasures of Darkness: A History of Mesopotamian Religion* (New Haven: Yale University Press, 1976) 86–104. See also the discussions in Hallo, "A Sumerian Amphictyony," 88–96; W. G. Lambert, "The Historical Development of the Mesopotamian Pantheon: A Study in Sophisticated Polytheism," *Unity and Diversity: Essays in the History, Literature, and Religion of the Ancient Near East* (ed. Hans Goedicke; Baltimore: Johns Hopkins University Press, 1975) 191–200; and his recent summary, "Ancient Mesopotamian Gods: Superstition, Philosophy, Theology," *RHR* 207 (1990) 115–30.

60. Regarding the future focus, compare the previous remarks on the end of the Enmetena Cone and the Lagash Lament (pp. 95–96).

would be the previous history, the legendary history would be that of the patriarchs, and Genesis 1–11 would be the mythic history.

Of course, the biblical text is well developed, whereas the Enmetena Cone is relatively spare in detail. Moreover, one can hardly compare Genesis–Exodus on the level of genre: "It is the conflation and transformation of different genres through their interrelations that mark the distinctive character of the Bible."[61] All of this and more is readily admitted. But, at least in terms of the connection between myth and history, there certainly seems to be something worth considering here. Moye has recently argued pursuasively that the mixture of genres had the very purpose of "merging myth and history."[62] He concludes his essay with the following summary sentence:

> That is, the incorporation of independent mythical narratives into a forward-moving, linear narrative through a complex thematic and structural interrelation of mythical form and the historicizing form of genealogy makes "history" of "myth," while the subsequent narration of the Patriarchal "history" and of the exodus through the interpretive patterns of the original myths makes "myth" of "history."[63]

But this merging of myth and history is nothing new in the ancient Near East. On the contrary, it extends all the way back to pre-Sargonic times. It is characteristic of Mesopotamian "historiography."

Although the biblical canon has developed in such a way that it looks, and is, much more complicated, the pattern is nonetheless quite similar. That the Sumerian historiographic mentality, as proposed here, possessed a sort of depth perception is useful in this regard, because it shows that the major point(s) made by Moye about the nature of the Genesis–Exodus narratives is (are) not really anomalous in ancient Near Eastern historiography. Quite the opposite is true; one should expect these patterns in the biblical material. And if the ancient Sumerians had possessed the necessary physical materials and communal opportunity to develop a canon like that of Israel, there would have undoubtedly been some interesting comparisons to make between the two.[64] From the reverse point of

---

61. Moye, "In the Beginning," 579.

62. Ibid., 580.

63. Ibid., 598.

64. Here I am in sympathy with J. J. M. Roberts. "Myth versus History," *CBQ* 38 (1976) 1–13. Superficial contrasts have often been drawn between the Bible and its ancient Near East context. However, there are indeed contrasts; see the methodological discussions in Hallo, "Biblical History"; and idem, "Compare and Contrast." On the issue of canon in Mesopotamian literature, see Hallo, "Limits of Skepticism," 190, and the literature cited there. Hallo has proposed that we view the Mesopotamian canon as "approximately the equivalent of the offical school curriculum of the scribal schools at any given time." Robert Vasholz has recently proposed a view of Old Testament canonicity that

view, one might speculate about the kinds of sources used in the writing of Genesis. Could some of them have been similar to what one finds even in the pre-Sargonic inscriptions?

If detailed comparisons of the Bible with ancient Near Eastern literature are to be made, they must be framed with more fully developed understandings of the framework of thought within the ancient Near East and the Bible. It seems that myth was at least one of the main ways in which the Sumerian historiographers and probably virtually all ancient Mesopotamian historiographers framed their view of the world, how they fitted into it, and the circumstances of life. Myth was mixed with legend and history writing precisely because, on one level, the ancient historiographers viewed events from this perspective.

The material found in Genesis 1–11 did the same for the ancient Israelites. These chapters were intended to "level the ground" in the sense that they provided the ancient Israelites with Yahweh's explanation of the world, its origin, how humans fit into it, and the nature of their circumstances in life. Moreover, they provide the foundation for understanding God's redemptive program, beginning with the Abrahamic relationship and covenant with God in Genesis 12. The textual link between the primeval narratives and the redemptive program is made explicit in the relationship between Gen 12:3, "in you all the families [*mišpĕḥōt*] of the earth shall be blessed" and Gen 10:32, "these are the families [*mišpĕḥōt*] of the sons of Noah, according to their genealogies, by their nations; and out of these the nations were separated on the earth after the flood."

CONCLUSIONS

Today it is difficult to separate "myth" from "religion," so anything that is "religious" tends to be viewed as "myth" rather than "history."[65] If the reality of God is allowed, and if the concept of His intrusion into history (if one can call it that) is permitted,[66] then there is still the prob-

---

accords well with the scribal school model of Hallo. He writes, "There is absolutely no reason why the writings of the Old Testament authors from the start could not have been carefully maintained just as Israel's neighbors maintained works which they deemed sacred": Robert I. Vasholz, *The Old Testament Canon in the Old Testament Church: The Internal Rationale for Old Testament Canonicity* (Ancient Near Eastern Texts and Studies 7; Lewiston, N.Y.: Mellen, 1990) 82.

65. For a broad perspective on this subject see Ernst Breisach, "Historiography," *The Encyclopedia of Religion* (vol. 6; ed. Mircea Eliade; New York: Macmillan, 1987) 370–83. Cf. also the remarks and references in Younger, *Ancient Conquest Accounts*, 31.

66. This is an element of the Bible that is not at all strange in its ancient Near Eastern milieu as the above discussion has shown, even if it is a problem in the modern world of empirical science and secular humanism.

lem of the Bible as the word of that God. The question could be put this way: How much of the Bible is still myth in contrast to history inasmuch as it is a product of human reflection?

Karl Barth sought to make a place for scripture in a modern world where historical criticism had greatly reduced confidence in the Bible as the divinely inspired and scientifically and historically accurate word of God. He did this by separating the Bible from the Word of God but, at the same time, retaining it as the primary witness to the Word of God. Brevard Childs's canonical approach to the Old Testament, for example, is implicitly Barthian.

The ancient Near Eastern parallels to the creation, flood, and other narratives in Genesis 1–11 as well as the empirical hard and soft sciences raise a formidable challenge to those who live in this modern world and yet hold to the veracity of the biblical text. This essay is a preliminary attempt to read the ancient Near Eastern, specifically Sumerian, historiographic tradition on its own terms and to suggest briefly some implications for viewing Genesis 1–11 as history. The problems are many, but it is clear that what we moderns call myth and history were not easily distinguishable in either the Sumerian or the biblical tradition.

The Genesis 1 creation account is an example. Our universe is an amazing complex of physical elements in relation to one another; it seems to require something truly amazing, even supernatural, to bring it into being. But we were not there when the world began, whether we are scientists, historians, or biblical scholars. This leaves us with unproven theories or beliefs—unproven in that they are not scientifically verifiable to everyone's satisfaction.

Among those evangelicals who deal with the empirical sciences there are two polarized views today. First, there are the "recent creationists" who take the seven-day creation pattern to be historically factual and argue for a young earth on both textual and scientific grounds. Second, there are those who consider recent creationism and its related flood geology to be "bad science." More and more these thinkers are moving toward a hypothesis that explains the early chapters of Genesis as literarily and theologically shaped rather than reporting historical events. There are various ongoing debates and currently there is no full-fledged alternative model of historical creation events.[67]

Another approach that may not satisfy anybody, but is a possible alternative, could be based upon the example of the variations between the

---

67. See the summary in P. P. T. Pun, "Evolution," *Evangelical Dictionary of Theology* (ed. Walter A. Elwell; Grand Rapids, Mich.: Baker, 1984) 388–92. For more developed discussions of the textual issues, see the essays in Ronald Youngblood (ed.), *The Genesis Debates: Persistent Questions about Creation and the Flood* (Nashville: Thomas Nelson, 1986).

gospel accounts in the New Testament or the Old Testament synoptic problem of the text of Samuel–Kings compared with the text of Chronicles. In scripture, history can be presented according to literary patterns that suit the varied ideological-theological tendencies of the authors. Is it possible that, for example, the seven-day pattern in Genesis 1 is a literary device? Would the ancient Israelites have understood it that way and therefore believed God to be the creator by fiat, and so on, without clinging to the seven-day cycle? Or would they have even raised the question if they had a view of the past similar to the Sumerians, who saw and wrote history from a viewpoint that we today might describe as a mixture of historiography and nonfictional mythography? In this third view the Genesis accounts may be seen as reshaped history.

The dialectic between the biblical text, other ancient Near Eastern literature, and modern empirical hard and soft sciences cannot be ignored. I only hope that the tension over such matters can be *con*structive rather than *de*structive. In the meantime, we need to engage seriously and objectively in the quest for data from the world of the Old Testament, and interpretations of the data that will stand the test of time.

Genealogical History as "Charter": A Study of Old Babylonian Period Historiography and the Old Testament

Mark Chavalas

University of Wisconsin, LaCrosse

INTRODUCTION

My first thought is one of intense astonishment at the current opinion that, in the study of primeval history, the Greeks alone deserve serious attention, that the truth should be sought from them, and that neither we nor any others in the world are to be trusted. In my view the very reverse of this is the case. For in the Greek world everything will be found to be modern. On the contrary, the Egyptians, Chaldaeans, and the Phoenicians possess a very ancient and permanent record of the past.[1]

Most modern historians, of course, do not share this opinion, given by Josephus, about the relative worth of Greek and ancient Near Eastern historiographic documents.[2] My purpose in this paper is to study some

---

I would like to acknowledge support from the University of Wisconsin, La Crosse, which provided a small research grant to pursue this work, as well as A. R. Millard and M. Zanger, who gave valuable suggestions leading to the completion of this manuscript. Any errors are my own responsibility.

1. Josephus, *Ag. Ap.* 1.6–8; cf. Herodotus 2.77; and B. Brundage, "The Birth of Clio," in *Teachers of History: Essays in Honor of Lawrence Bradford Packard* (ed. H. Hughes et al.; Ithaca: Cornell University Press, 1954) 199.

2. The term *historiography* has been ambiguous since it was reintroduced in Europe in the middle of the last century; cf. O. Carena, *History of Near Eastern Historiography and Its Problems, Part One: 1852–1945* (AOAT 218/1; Neukirchen-Vluyn: Neukirchener Verlag, 1989) 1; P. Michalowski, "History as Charter: Some Observations on the Sumerian King List," *Studies in Literature from the Ancient Near East Dedicated to Samuel Noah Kramer* (ed. J. Sasson; AOS 65; New Haven: American Oriental Society, 1984) 237. Historiography has only recently become an issue in Assyriology, since the heritage of Assyriology has been to discourage debate on theoretical issues. It can, for example, mean the study of Assyrian annals, the annals themselves, or general histories (see Carena, *History*, 1; and

103

ancient Near Eastern historiographic documents, specifically those concerning propaganda, such as the royal king lists and genealogies of the early second millennium B.C. These include the Sumerian King List (SKL), Larsa King List (LKL), the early portions of the Assyrian King List (AKL), the Genealogy of the Hammurapi Dynasty (GHD), and later historical narratives (Apology of Hatusilis, Telepinu, Idrimi, and the Davidic succession narratives).[3] Three of the documents (the AKL, LKL, and GHD) do not have propaganda as a primary purpose in their present form but instead exhibit subtle evidences of propagandistic origins.

Modern scholars have described historiographic texts as those that are "scientific" in nature, or those that set out to answer a set of questions about the past for self-realization or self-knowledge.[4] This is a limited definition that catgorizes all preclassical "historical" writing as of dubious historical worth. A more appropriate perspective on the subject is the Dutch historian Johan Huizinga's statement that "history is the intellectual form in which a civilization renders account of itself."[5] This definition has been modified by William Hallo, who has said that history is "a subjective enterprise in which each culture ultimately defines the ethnic parameters of its own past for itself."[6] Civilizations, it is clear, use a

---

W. W. Hallo, "Sumerian Historiography," *History, Historiography, and Interpretation: Studies in Biblical and Cuneiform Literature* [ed. H. Tadmor and M. Weinfeld; Jerusalem: Magnes, 1986] 9). These categories were first introduced by A. Olmstead, *Assyrian Historiography* (Columbia: University of Missouri Press, 1916). In fact, no text can be excluded on principle from the category of historiographic raw material because much apparently incidental information from other contexts provides significant data about the community in which the texts originate (N. Wyatt, "Some Observations on the Idea of History among the West Semitic Peoples," *UF* 11 [1979] 831; and J. J. M. Roberts, "Myth vs. History," *CBQ* 38 [1976] 3). Also, see the important recent work by K. L. Younger (*Ancient Conquest Accounts: A Study in Ancient Near Eastern History Writing* [JSOTSup 98; Sheffield: JSOT Press, 1990] 25–58), who discusses the nature of preclassical history-writing. He concludes that there are no literary rules for ascertaining which ancient texts are more "historical" than others. He defines ancient history-writing as that which claims to be a true account and imposes form on the actions of men (pp. 43–46). But this still seems to impose modern writers' ideas on the ancients. The ancients did not have definable categories that separated "truth" from fiction and may not have made a conscious effort to create a "true account." Modern historians, in fact, impose their own form upon the past and thus in part are creating representational fiction.

3. The use of the term *propaganda* is discussed in "The Use of Propaganda in Ancient Texts," below, p. 106.

4. R. Collingwood, *The Idea of History* (Oxford: Clarendon, 1946) 11.

5. J. Huizinga, "A Definition of the Concept of History," *Philosophy and History* (ed. R. Klibansky and H. Paton; Oxford: Clarendon, 1936) 9.

6. W. W. Hallo, "Biblical History in Its Near Eastern Setting: The Contextual Approach," *Scripture in Context: Essays on the Comparative Method* (ed. C. Evans et al.; Pittsburgh: Pickwick, 1980) 6. Also see J. Sasson, who has modified Huizinga's definition in a similar manner: "History is an intellectual form in which civilizations render account to themselves of the past" ("Mari Historiography and the Yakhdun-Lim Inscription," *Lingering*

plurality of modes to define history. It is not necessary to restrict one's attention only to those genres that most resemble one's own.[7] But including unfamiliar genres from other cultures exposes the contemporary historian to the hazard of applying western categories to unfamiliar phenomena. This danger is unavoidable to a degree, even though historians strive to be objective and to divest themselves of their inherent ethnocentric tendencies.[8] All civilizations are aware of their past, but not all react in the way that we do in the contemporary West.[9]

Ancient Texts as Information

Historians must also be aware of their approach to historiographic texts. Mario Liverani has suggested that we need a "comprehensive reading" of these texts.[10] Previously, in dealing with written documents of "dead" societies, scholars have expected texts to play the role of "informer," their expectations being similar to the nineteenth-century ethnologists' expectations. They assumed that facts of interest lay beyond the texts and when questioned, these texts could give the needed information.[11] But this type

---

over Words: Studies in Ancient Near Eastern Literature in Honor of William L. Moran [ed. T. Abusch et al.; HSS 37; Atlanta: Scholars Press, 1990] 439).

7. See J. Finkelstein, "Mesopotamian Historiography," *PAPS* 107 (1963) 462. However, cf. J. Van Seters (*In Search of History: Historiography in the Ancient World and the Origins of Biblical History* [New Haven: Yale University Press, 1983] 1), who does not accept the theory that all civilizations developed a literary form that could be called "history." Sasson more correctly realizes that "In this undertaking, it will be necessary to consider even the most tendentious letter, the most bombastic ultimatum, the most apocalyptic vision, the most terrorizing dream, and the most self-conscious counsel" ("Mari Historiography," 449). Sasson concludes that all related documents are not to be viewed just as sources for political and biographical information, but as historiographic products. This is echoed by M. Liverani, "Memorandum on the Approach to Historiographic Texts," *Or* 42 (1973) 178–94; see n. 10 below.

8. Finkelstein, "Mesopotamian Historiography," 461.

9. Finkelstein believes that the most reliable historiographic texts in ancient Mesopotamia were omina, texts which have no counterpart in our culture ("Mesopotamian Historiography," 461–72). See A. K. Grayson, "Divination and the Babylonian Chronicles" (*La Divination en Mésopotamie ancienne et dans les régions voisines* [ed. J. Nougayrol; Paris: Presses Universitaires, 1966]) 69–76 for a dissenting view. Also, see H. Güterbock, "Die historische Tradition und ihre literarische Gestaltung bei Babyloniern und Hethitern bis 1200," *ZA* 42 (1934) 8, 16, and 47–61; and A. Goetze, "Historical Allusions in Old Babylonian Omen Texts," *JCS* 1 (1947) 253–65. S. Kramer, although believing that the Sumerians did not write historiography in the modern sense of the word, feels that Sumerian votive inscriptions are the closest to the modern idea of historical texts ("Sumerian Historiography," *IEJ* 3 [1953] 218). For Egyptian historiographic material, see D. B. Redford, *Pharaonic King-Lists, Annals, and Day-Books* (Mississauga, Ontario: Benben, 1986) xiii–xxi.

10. Liverani, "Memorandum."

11. Ibid., 179.

of information is foreign to the texts themselves due to the cultural gap between the historian and the text, a gap not filled by the "informer" text. The documents must not be viewed only as a "source of information," but as information themselves; not as an opening into another reality beyond, but as an element that makes up that reality.[12] If one simply extracts information from the text, she must be aware that the text often may be "wrong" and that the error could be passed on to the historical reconstruction.[13] A more critical study of the text is needed. The type of information in the text may not always satisfy the scholar, who has different interests. The scholar should try to view a document as a source of knowledge of itself.[14] What is important is not the event or "fact" mentioned in the text, but the narration itself, and the scholar should attempt to understand the author's intentions and his/her historical environment. Irregularities, inconsistencies, and reticent elements in the document will then cease to be an obstacle.[15] To use a document simply as a source of information is to excerpt information out of context. One needs to set in historical perspective the relationship between the scholar and the environment under study. Every historical society has its own way of conceiving and forging reality. The document in question must be read in its entirety for a complete understanding, to ascertain why the text was written and to read it from all points of view.

The Use of Propaganda in Ancient Texts

I now turn to the subject of propaganda in various texts, keeping Liverani's suggestions in mind. Propaganda has been defined as a deliberately manipulated communication, closely related to other modes of communication.[16] It is not just an act of premeditation but is connected with the social setting in which there is controversy, embodying a deliberate attempt to influence favorably the outcome of controversy. This

12. Ibid.
13. H. Hoffner, "Histories and Historians of the Ancient Near East: The Hittites," *Or* 49 (1980) 289. He adds, "We only have the artist's impression and not the photograph. We must attempt to figure what he saw."
14. Liverani, "Memorandum," 179.
15. Ibid., 180. The contributions of Younger (*Ancient Conquest Accounts*, 25–56) about the factual worth of ancient history writing become less relevant in light of Liverani's concept of viewing the document itself as a source of knowledge.
16. H. Lasswell, *Propaganda and Communication in World History* (Honolulu: University of Hawaii Press, 1979) 4–5. Also, see the discussion of ancient "ideology" in Younger, *Ancient Conquest Accounts*, 47–52.

does not mean that propagandistic texts necessarily alter "facts" as they are known. They may be factual or even illuminating for study.[17] The fact that a work is propagandistic does not preclude it from having historical value.[18] The unique feature of a propagandistic work is its polemical nature.[19] From this perspective, much of the Old Testament can be considered propagandistic.

Often an authority in power uses historical data,[20] including genealogies, to achieve a propagandistic goal of social control.[21] Propaganda actually played a minor role in the manipulation of classes and the enhancement of the authority of rulers in the ancient Near East.[22] Many ancient texts were composed to persuade members of the audience to whom they were addressed of the legitimacy of the authority on whose behalf they were issued and of the unique truth of the ideology or principle set forth. This was especially the case when ruling authorities recognized the existence of alternative or competing ideologies whose authority they denied. There must have been a segment of the population that was considered a threat by the ruling class.

The Value of Genealogies in Historiography

Propagandistic texts often contain genealogies, and they are found in king lists, court "apologies," and other miscellaneous narratives. Therefore, ancient genealogical tables, especially those of the Old Testament, have

17. See Liverani, "Memorandum," 180; and R. Wilson, *Genealogy and History in the Biblical World* (YNES 7; New Haven: Yale University Press, 1977) 200, for genealogical data.

18. Hoffner, "Histories: Hittites," 331.

19. Often a ruler's purpose in propagandistic literature is not to relate what the king did, but why he aspired to the throne and to portray him in a favorable light, creating a certain image; H. Tadmor, "History and Ideology in the Assyrian Royal Inscriptions," *Assyrian Royal Inscriptions: New Horizons in Literary, Ideological, and Historical Analysis* (ed. F. M. Fales; Rome: Istituto per L'Oriente, 1981) 15; A. Oppenheim, *Ancient Mesopotamia: Portrait of a Dead Civilization* (Chicago: University of Chicago Press, 1964) 149–50.

20. A. K Grayson ("Histories and Historians of the Ancient Near East: Assyrian and Babylonian," *Or* 49 [1980] 149–94) considers propaganda to be one of the most important motives for ancient historical writing, exhibiting national pride (or, more accurately, corporate identity). See J. Van Seters, "Histories and Historians of the Ancient Near East: The Israelites," *Or* 50 (1981) 137; for chronological aids, for omina, and fostering the cult of dead kings, see Grayson, "Histories: Assyrian, Babylonian," 189–91.

21. This is noted by J. Plumb: "Where the service of the past has been urgently needed, truth has ever been at a disadvantage" (*The Death of the Past* [London: Macmillan, 1969] 2).

22. See J. J. Finkelstein, "Early Mesopotamia 2500–1000 B.C.," in Lasswell, *Propaganda*, 50–110.

come under scrutiny.[23] Before nineteenth-century biblical criticism, genealogies were considered by biblical historians to be valuable in reconstructing history, and thus scholars took them at face value.[24] The traditional
view has been shattered by the existence of "apparent contradictions" in
the genealogical records. They consider these records to be artificial creations, having little or no historical value.[25] However, based on the previously described approach to historiographic texts, it can be shown that
these texts do have value, mainly as explanations of the milieu in which
they were created. The modern western researcher has a problem in dealing with the lineage systems reflected in these texts, since societies in western Asia, Africa, and America (native Americans) still maintain and use
complex, oral lineage systems in a variety of ways, while western societies
tend to view genealogies as historical documents to be preserved in archives.[26] Imposing modern views about genealogy on such texts results in
a narrow and erroneous understanding of oral, biblical, and ancient Near
Eastern lineage systems. Puzzled western observers cannot determine
which lineage system is "correct" when two or more "contradict" each
other, since the functions of the systems may not be clear.[27] Lineage ties
usually have little to do with ethnic identity (no such concept existed in
the ancient world) but rather were often concerned with political unity.[28]

A genealogy can be defined as a written or oral expression of the descent of a person or persons from a common ancestor or ancestors.[29] It
functions as an important medium of expression and interaction.[30] When
a genealogy expresses more than one line of descent from a given ancestor, it exhibits a segmented or branching structure. If it exhibits one line
of descent, it is described as linear.

---

23. See R. R. Wilson, "The Old Testament Genealogies in Recent Research," *JBL* 94
(1975) 169–89; idem, "Between Azel and Azel: Interpreting the Biblical Genealogies," *BA*
42 (1979) 11–21; and idem, *Genealogy*. Also see M. Johnson, *The Purpose of the Biblical
Genealogies* (SNTS 9; Cambridge: Cambridge University Press, 1969; 2d ed., 1988).

24. Wilson, "Old Testament Genealogies," 169.

25. See Wilson, *Genealogy*, 200; genealogies may be historically accurate according to
western standards in one sphere but not in others.

26. Wilson, "Azel," 11.

27. Ibid., 12. The question of the accuracy of the genealogies is more complex than
supposed. They express a reality that is often unknown to the scholar. They are, however, accurate perceptions of the authors, even if they do not correspond to western ideas
of "objective data" (ibid. 21; L. Bohanon, "A Genealogical Charter," *Africa* 22 [1952]
314).

28. G. Mendenhall, *The Tenth Generation: The Origins of the Biblical Tradition* (Baltimore: Johns Hopkins University Press, 1973) 178–79; acknowledgment of blood ties is
not always the most important function of a genealogy.

29. Wilson, *Genealogy*, 9.

30. K. Andriolo, "A Structural Analysis of Genealogy and World View in the Old
Testament," *AA* 75 (1973) 1663.

In the nineteenth century, scholars noticed connections between the written genealogies in the Old Testament and oral genealogies encountered in anthropological research.[31] However, these connections have only recently been taken seriously by biblical scholars. Oral genealogies contain a number of characteristics particularly relevant to this study:[32]

1. *Segmentation:* A person receives status by virtue of his kinship ties;[33]
2. *Depth:* This feature is found in linear lists, functioning to relate living lineage members to ancestors; and,
3. *Fluidity:* Segmented societies in particular, must change in order to mirror alterations in lineage.[34] They also change when the function of the genealogy changes. Some names of ancestors disappear (when they no longer have any relevant function), while other names are added.[35]

Genealogical function varies according to circumstances and can be categorized in domestic, political, and religious terms.[36] The genealogy of a society may exhibit any or all of these functions synchronically, causing the apparent "contradictions."[37] (My interest in this research is in the political function of genealogies.)[38] It seems to me that anthropological study of lineage systems among modern tribal societies helps to illuminate the ancient systems, even though they are from different historical and sociological contexts.[39] The surviving ancient systems were written, while most of the modern systems are orally transmitted.[40] For this reason,

31. Wilson, *Genealogy,* 13–17; A. Malamat, "Tribal Societies, Biblical Genealogies, and African Lineage Systems," *Aes* 14 (1973) 126–36.

32. See Wilson, *Genealogy,* 18–30.

33. Bohanon, "Genealogical Charter," 312.

34. I. Cunnison, "History and Genealogy in a Conquest State," *AA* 59 (1957) 21.

35. Wilson, "Old Testament Genealogies," 181.

36. *Domestic:* to justify contemporary lineage configurations or to be used in domestic disputes and property claims (Wilson, "Azel," 13; Malamat, "Tribal Societies," 127); *political:* to validate the incumbents in the existing government, to justify the right of a usurper, especially where the authority of an office holder is in question, in order to link him with the ancestors who reigned before him; *religious:* to be associated with the ancestor cult, cultic offices, or divine kingship (Johnson, *Purpose,* 79).

37. Wilson, "Old Testament Genealogies," 182.

38. As exhibited in the king lists, which do not fit well as genealogies, but do exhibit partial lineage lists (Wilson, *Genealogy,* 72).

39. A. Malamat, "King Lists of the Old Babylonian Period and Biblical Genealogies," *JAOS* 88 (1968) 163. One must proceed with caution with this analogy. Whether modern anthropological studies can in fact shed light on the third and second millennia B.C. is problematic (Johnson, *Purpose,* xi–xii; Malamat, "Tribal Societies," 126).

40. I.e., "frozen" in time. Putting the lineages in writing seems to inhibit genealogical change (Wilson, "Old Testament Genealogies," 13). Thus, the biblical genealogies are also literary creations (Johnson, *Purpose,* xii).

historians must also be concerned with determining when oral lineages became written texts.

OLD BABYLONIAN GENEALOGIES

The Sumerian King List

The Sumerians had no historiographic texts in the modern sense but were the first to gather information from available sources.[41] The first extant documents that reveal any historiographic detail with a propagandistic purpose concerns the Lagash–Umma border conflict.[42] The rulers of Lagash created these documents in order to justify their city's actions. Another document is the Sumerian King List (SKL) The text deals relatively little with genealogies but is concerned with the succession of cities possessing kingship in Sumer.[43] While reflecting the political tensions of different and conflicting governments, it attempts to maintain the ideal that one city and its king were ranked as first among equals.[44] There has been little critical study of its nonphilological aspects.[45] It has been described as having a "tendentious" historical nature.[46] It is hard to define the nature of this text, because it is similar to annals, chronicles, and genealogical tables. There is disagreement concerning the original date of

41. See P. Charvat, "Aspects of Sumerian Historiography," in *Aspects of Oriental Historiography* (ed. V. Souček; Prague: Academy Press, 1975) 77; Kramer, "Sumerian Historiography," 217.

42. Kramer, "Sumerian Historiography," 217–32; and J. Cooper, *Reconstructing History from Ancient Inscriptions: The Lagash-Umma Border Conflict* (SANE 2; Malibu: Undena, 1983).

43. The succession lists are linear, although T. Jacobsen has shown a number of the kings to be contemporary (*The Sumerian King List* [AS 11; Chicago: University of Chicago Press, 1939] 208). C. Wilcke ("Genealogical and Geographical Thought in the Sumerian King List," in *Dumu-E₂-Dub-Ba-A: Studies in Honor of Åke W. Sjöberg* [ed. H. Behrens et al.; Philadelphia: Babylonian Section, The University Museum, 1989] 557–71) has argued that before its final form during the Isin dynasty, the SKL was used for genealogical and geographical purposes as an argument for positional succession.

44. W. W. Hallo and W. K. Simpson, *The Ancient Near East: A History* (New York: Harcourt Brace Jovanovich, 1971) 39.

45. The classic work on the SKL is by Jacobsen (*Sumerian King List*). Michalowski ("History as Charter," 237–48) has attempted to understand the political nature of the text.

46. Jacobsen (*Sumerian King List*, 165–67) felt that although the arrangement of the list was of negligible historical value, since the order of dynasties varies depending on the provenience of the text, much of the actual material from the list was reliable, even though exaggerated (see Hallo and Simpson, *The Ancient Near East*, 48). However, few of the kings mentioned in the SKL are attested in other contexts with their own inscriptions, a point which needs some further study. Also, see E. Sollberger "The Tummal Inscription" (*JCS* 16 [1962] 40–47), for kings who are mentioned in an important historiographic source, the Tummal inscription. Michalowski sees little reason to trust the data in the text of the SKL and believes it impossible to produce a composite text that reflects any historical "reality" ("History as Charter," 240, 243).

composition,[47] and the place of its origin is also uncertain. The document provides greatest detail for the cities of Kish, Uruk, and Ur,[48] although most manuscripts are from the Isin dynasty. Of the more than one dozen manuscripts and fragments of this text, nine come from Nippur, but most seem to derive from a single original;[49] the variants are due to errors in copying.[50]

The SKL contains a fiction that power was located in Sumer in the hands of one dynasty in any given period.[51] Piotr Michalowski believes that this idea had its origin in the period after the Guti, but ultimately people realized the legitimacy of the Isin dynasty.[52] After the fall of the Ur III dynasty (ca. 2000 B.C.) many Amorite dynasties who ruled in Sumer exhibited traditions different from the SKL. They were interested in connecting themselves with the Amorite chieftains.[53] Legitimacy in

47. D. Edzard, "Königslisten und Chroniken, A: Sumerisch," *RlA* 6.80–81; Jacobsen, *Sumerian King List*, 137–41. Edzard and Jacobsen contend that there is philological evidence of versions from the reign of Utu-Hegal of Uruk (ca. 2100 B.C., just before the Ur III dynasty). M. Rowton prefers a date during the Ur III period ("The Date of the Sumerian King List," *JCS* 19 [1960] 158–62), while F. R. Kraus accepts a date at least two hundred years later ("Zur Liste der ältern Könige von Babylonien," *ZA* 50 [1952] 46–51). Michalowski believes that the most likely sources for the SKL are from the Old Akkadian period, possibly derived from the date lists ("History as Charter," 239). There is a tablet from Khafajah showing an antediluvian tradition independent from the SKL in its final form (J. J. Finkelstein, "The Antediluvian Kings: A University of California Tablet," *JCS* 17 [1963] 39–51). Others who have dealt with the problem include W. W. Hallo, "Beginning and End of the Sumerian King List in the Nippur Recension," *JCS* 17 (1963) 55; idem, "The Last Years of the Kings of Isin," *JNES* 18 (1964) 66; idem, "Antediluvian Cities," *JCS* 23 (1970) 66; Hallo and Simpson, *Ancient Near East*, 88; E. Sollberger, "New Lists of the Kings of Ur and Isin," *JCS* 8 (1954) 135–36; M. Civil, "Texts and Fragments," *JCS* 15 (1961) 79–80; A. Westenholz, "Early Nippur Year Dates and the Sumerian King List," *JCS* 26 (1974) 154–56 (who has studied a connection between the Nippur year dates and the SKL); D. Edzard, *Die "zweite Zwischenzeit" Babyloniens* (Wiesbaden: Harrassowitz, 1957) 15; and H. Nissen, "Eine neue Version der sumerischen Königsliste," *ZA* 57 (1965) 1–5 (who discusses a new version of the SKL). The excavators at Isin have recently uncovered another text of the SKL; see C. Wilcke, "Die Inschriftenfunde der 7. und 8. Kampagnen (1983 und 1984)," *Isin-Išān Baḥrīyāt III: Die Ergebnisse der Ausgrabungen 1983–85* (ed. B. Hrouda; Bayerischen Akademie der Wissenschaft, Phil.-Hist. Klasse, 94; Munich: Beck, 1987) 89–93.

48. Jacobsen, *Sumerian King List*, 141; Lagash and Umma are missing.

49. See Michalowski, "History as Charter," 238.

50. Jacobsen, *Sumerian King List*, 128–29; Michalowski sees the variations in entries as being connected with different ideologies that have not yet been recovered ("History as Charter," 240).

51. Finkelstein, "Early Mesopotamia," 60-63.

52. Michalowski, "History as Charter," 240; also, Finkelstein, "Mesopotamian Historiography," 459.

53. See GHD, AKL, LKL, and some of the inscriptions of Sin-Kashid at Uruk, who uses an Amorite title (Edzard, *"Zweite Zwischenzeit"*, 106). Curiously, Sin-Kashid has an Akkadian name, evidence of an interest in continuing the Sumero-Akkadian tradition (see A. Falkenstein, "Zu den Inschriften der Grabung in Uruk-Warka 1960–1961," *Baghdader Mitteilungen* 2 [1963] 35 n. 155).

this period was not only a function of traditional Mesopotamian kingship, but the status of a given ruler was determined within the kinship
structure of the Amorite tribes.[54] These ties formed a genealogical charter for the legitimacy of kingship; it was not enough just to be king, but
one had to claim descent (and thereby legitimacy) from the proper lineage within a tribe.[55]

These Amorite titles are absent at Isin, the city which is connected
with dynastic legitimacy in the SKL. The founder of the Isin dynasty,
Ishbi-Irra, was either not an Amorite or not from a recognized lineage.
He did attain a high status—like that of the Ur III kings—but not because of any tribal status.[56] He thus had no right to claim Amorite heritage, but probably felt threatened by the political moves of Larsa, Uruk,
and other city-states. Thus his different basis for a claim on kingship
would have been a central issue of the SKL. The fiction that each city in
Mesopotamia had a "turn of office" provided an alternative to the requirement for legitimate descent. It served to bolster the claims to legitimacy of all the territory of the Ur III kings by providing evidence that
the Ur and Isin kings had one unbroken line.[57]

This ideology can also be seen in the Lamentation over the Destruction of Sumer and Ur.[58] One city that was omitted from the SKL was
Larsa, a rival of the Isin dynasty, that claimed tribal connections with the
Amorite Yamutbal tribe living in the area of Lagash, another city omitted
from the SKL.[59] The text BM 23103 is a fanciful list of rulers of Lagash
from postdiluvian times to Gudea. Only seven of the thirty names in the
text are known from outside sources. Edmond Sollberger contends that
the text is a politico-satirical work written by a Lagash scribe in answer
to the author of the SKL, who ignored the Lagash rulers. He wanted to
show that Lagash could also trace its lineage back a great distance. It is a
parody on SKL phraseology, with imaginary names and biographical
notes compared to the terse notes in the SKL. Although the text is from
the Old Babylonian period, the author left out the post-Gudean Lagash

---

54. Michalowski, "History as Charter," 241.

55. On this note, see Bohanon, "Genealogical Charter," 301–15.

56. Michalowski, "History as Charter," 242.

57. See Sollberger ("New Lists," 135–36), commenting on an Ur-Isin king list written
in the fourth year of the Isin king Damiq-Ilushu (ca. 1813 b.c.), who traces his lineage
back to Ur-Nammu, founder of the Ur III dynasty, thereby justifying any connections Isin
had with Ur. Also, see A. K. Grayson, "Königslisten und Chroniken B. Akkadisch," *RlA*
6.90; and Hallo, "Last Years," 57.

58. *ANET,* 611–19.

59. M. Stol, *Studies in Old Babylonian History* (Leiden: Brill, 1976) 63–72; also see
E. Sollberger, "The Rulers of Lagaš," *JCS* 21 (1967) 279–92.

kings, because Lagash was no longer a proud independent state, but an Ur III province.[60] Thus, there were two means of establishing political legitimacy in Old Babylonian Mesopotamia: presence in the SKL and belonging to one of the Amorite lineages.

The Larsa King List

Another Old Babylonian period document is the Larsa King List (LKL), found at Senkereh (ancient Larsa).[61] The text, which is in poor condition, is a practice tablet with the same list on both the obverse and reverse. Although its primary purpose was not propaganda, the document lists the names and regnal years from the founder of the dynasty, Naplanum, to Hammurapi and Samsu-Iluna of Babylon. Similar lists, such as those containing Assyrian eponym names, may have served the practical purpose of determining the date of a particular document, which was of great importance to scribes working under the new rulership.

Larsa was conquered by Hammurapi of Babylon in his thirtieth regnal year (ca. 1762 B.C.). The text ascribes twelve years to the reign of his son Samsu-Iluna, which means that it was written in that year or in the following year.[62] The first seven names on the list are reputedly Amorite in nature.[63] However, it is not until Gungunum, the fifth king named in the LKL, that the title "king" is used in the date formulae.[64] The early kings were thus his ancestors.[65] Although not explicitly stated, it is possible that the Hammurapi dynasty composed the genealogy to support the argument that the Babylonian kings were the legitimate heirs of Larsa, presumably because of their Amorite connections (GHD). It can be compared to the Ur-Isin king list, which has a different tradition of royal legitimacy.[66]

---

60. Ibid., 280.

61. E. Grice, *Chronology of the Larsa Dynasty* (YOS 4/1; New Haven, Conn.: Yale University Press, 1919) 1–43; A. Ungnad, "Datenlisten," *RlA* 2.149–59; and Grayson, "Königslisten," *RlA* 6.89.

62. 1738–1737 B.C.; see Grayson, "Königslisten."

63. See Stol, *Studies*, 87–88; and Michalowski, "History as Charter," 240–41. Abi-Sare is called a *rabian amurrum* (Amorite chieftain), as is Zabaya. See n. 64.

64. Hallo, "Last Years," 57; and Grice, *Chronology*, 13–20. Also see the recent article on Zabaya (the fourth name mentioned in the LKL) by D. B. Weisberg ("Zabaya, an Early King of the Larsa Dynasty," *JCS* 41 [1989] 194–97). Weisberg thinks that Zabaya was not merely an ancestor in the list, but an individual who actually ruled Larsa.

65. See G. Roux, "Le Père de Gungunum," *RA* 52 (1958) 233–35, and G. Buccellati, *The Amorites of the Ur III Period* (Naples: Istituto orientale, 1966) 56–59.

66. See n. 54 above.

The Assyrian King List

The Assyrian King List (AKL; see the appendix) has long been considered an important source for early Assyrian history.[67] Because the AKL preserves a detailed list of Assyrian rulers and their general length of reign for a span of about one thousand years, and because it provides material unavailable to scholars in other sources, modern historians have accepted the document with little critical examination.[68] By applying Liverani's model, one can find historical "worth" in this text, but it, like the SKL, may not provide the historical accuracy desired by modern historians. It has been categorized as a "chronographic text" by A. Kirk Grayson.[69] The oldest extant version of the AKL is a tenth-century B.C. manuscript published in 1927.[70] Later, other versions from the eighth century B.C. were encountered in the 1932–33 excavations at Khorsabad.[71] Another

67. However, see Finkelstein ("Mesopotamian Historiography," 469), who has dismissed the AKL as not directly relevant to the subject of historiography in Mesopotamia. H. Lewy is not sure that the Assyrians have helped modern historians by having produced this list ("Assyria 2600–1816 BC," *CAH* 1/2, 740). Also, see W. W. Hallo, "Assyrian Historiography Revisited," *EI* 14 (1978) 3*.

68. F. R. Kraus, "Könige in die Zelten wohnten Betrachtungen über den Kern der assyrischen Königsliste," *MKAW* 28 (1965) 125; J. A. Brinkman, "Comments on the Nassouhi King List and the Assyrian King List Tradition," *Or* 42 (1972) 310. M. B. Rowton, ("Mesopotamian Chronology and the Era of Menophres," *Iraq* 8 [1946] 97) believes the chronological figures in the AKL to be highly reliable.

69. Grayson, "Histories: Assyrian, Babylonian," 171; also see A. Poebel ("The Assyrian King List from Khorsabad," *JNES* 1 [1942] 281) and B. Landsberger ("Assyrische Königsliste und 'dunkles Zeitalter,'" *JCS* 8 [1954] 34 n. 23), who both classify the document among the chronicles. Comparatively, the Turin Canon, a document written on the back of an old papyrus, is the sole survivor of this type of list from Egypt (Redford, *Pharaonic King-Lists*, 5).

70. That it is the oldest does not mean that it is the best; Brinkman, "Comments," 313; cf. A. Ungnad, "Die synchronistischen Königslisten aus Assur," *ZDMG* 72 (1918) 313–16; W. Baumgartner, "Zur Form der assyrischen Königsinschriften," *OLZ* 27 (1924) 133–54; and E. Nassouhi, "Grand liste des rois d'Assyrie," *AfO* 4 (1927) 1–11; Neo-Assyrian King List = (NAKL); E. F. Weidner also published comments on the text ("Die grosse Königsliste aus Assur," *AfO* 3 [1926] 66–77; "Die neue Königsliste aus Assur," *AfO* 4 [1927] 11–17; "Die Königsliste aus Chorsabad," *AfO* 13–14 [1939–44] 85–102; and "Bemerkungen zur Königsliste aus Chorsabad," *AfO* 15–16 [1945–51] 364–69). The text was edited in the Middle Assyrian period (Landsberger, "Assyrische Königsliste," 33–34, 109–10; A. K. Grayson, "The Early Development of the Assyrian Monarchy," *UF* 3 [1971] 314 n. 27; and Hallo, "Assyrian Historiography," 6*. The AKL may not have taken its final form until the thirteenth century B.C. because of Babylonian influence in Assyria (cf. P. Machinist, "Literature as Politics: The Tukulti-Ninurta Epic and the Bible," *CBQ* 38 [1976] 455–82).

71. Named the Khorsabad King List (KHKL); Poebel, "Assyrian King List," 247–306, 460–91; idem, "The Assyrian King List from Khorsobad Concluded," *JNES* 2 (1943) 53–90; cf. the commentary by Landsberger, "Assyrische Königsliste," 31–45, 47–73, 103–33; and Kraus, "Könige," 123–42.

was found under strange circumstances,[72] while other fragments have also been discovered.[73] There are thus five versions of the text,[74] most of which are connected with the city of Assur.[75]

The AKL at first lists one ruler after another, but later in the list there are narrative sections which are in fact short chronicles, listing regnal years and filiation, and these sections sometimes include prose narration. The material may have been extracted from the summary formulas of the date lists.[76] Again, in its final form it is not primarily a propagandistic document, but the AKL does display some minor features relevant to the subject. The list contains a series of kings from the earliest times of Assyria to Shalmaneser V (726–722 B.C.). It probably later functioned as a chronological aid and as support for the belief that kingship in Assyria descended in a continuous line, with few interruptions, as though every king officially belonged to the same dynasty.[77]

The composite version of the AKL is divided into a number of sections. The first seventeen names are listed without filiation, tribal relationship, or length of reign. At the end of this section there is a statement, "These are kings who dwelt in tents." This may imply, though it is hardly certain, that these rulers did not rule from Assur. But one is reminded of the Mari texts, in which the "nomads" are described as partly urbanized or seminomadic. Thus the "kings who dwelt in tents" may very well have been based at Assur.[78] The phrase, Akkadian *ašibūt kultāri*, occurs elsewhere only in Neo-Assyrian texts, while the Mari texts, the most important for Old-Babylonian nomadic activities, mention nothing about nomads who "live in tents." Some scholars have viewed this phrase as an anachronistic insertion from a later date and thus

---

72. See I. J. Gelb, "Two Assyrian King Lists," *JNES* 13 (1954) 209–30. This is the Seventh Day Adventist Theological Seminary version (SDAS) from the eighth century B.C.

73. O. Schroeder, *Keilschrifttexte aus Assur verscheidenen Inhalts* (WVDOG 35; Leipzig: Hinrichs, 1920); A. R. Millard, "Fragments of Historical Texts from Nineveh: Middle Assyrian and Later Kings," *Iraq* 32 (1970) 167–76; cf. W. Lambert, "Tukulti-Ninurta and the Assyrian King List" (*Iraq* 38 [1976] 85–94), for a possible early allusion to the AKL.

74. See the discussion by Grayson, "Königslisten," *RlA* 6.101.

75. The SDAS text has a colophon from Assur, while the KHKL, which is partly damaged, was copied from an original from Assur. The provenience of the NAKL is unknown, while the fragment published by Millard ("Fragments of Historical Texts," 94 n. 76) came from Nineveh.

76. Grayson, "Histories: Assyrian, Babylonian," 172, although Brinkman is skeptical of this idea: "Comments," 317.

77. Grayson, "Histories: Assyrian, Babylonian," 179; Tadmor, "History and Ideology," 25. Tukulti-Ninurta II and Sargon II, both usurpers, omitted their parental ancestry and thereby any connection with the earlier kings (J. Pečirkova, "Form and Functions of Handing Down Historical Events in Babylonia and Assyria," in Souček, *Aspects*, 27).

78. See Wilson, *Genealogy*, 11–55, for a discussion of this tendency in the Arab tribes of modern North Africa.

of no particular significance, but the evidence does not seem sufficient to warrant this view.[79] The source material for the list of these early "kings" is unknown. The names, which will be described in more detail with the GHD, are considered western Semitic in nature,[80] possibly remnants of an Amorite genealogical list.[81] Some of the names are found as toponyms.[82] Personal names were not always derived from the toponyms; many places were named after a person, a custom that may have a Hurrian origin.[83]

The second group of kings is evidently in reverse order, because each king is mentioned as the son of the following king. Thus, the last king listed, Apiashal, is the earliest and is also the last king mentioned in the first section. Correspondingly, Aminu, the first name listed in the second section, is the father of Sulili, the first name of the third section. The second section is considered a linear genealogical list, probably of the latest ruler mentioned, Aminu. It appears that the compiler has not given the results of his research but the source itself.[84] The second section implies that the kings are now at Assur (at least since Apiashal). Some of these names can be found in contemporary inscriptions at Assur.[85] The section ends with the statement, "These are ten kings who are ancestors." But whose ancestors? The names in this section are also West Semitic, apparently not Akkadian.[86] Only one of the names, Ilu-kabkabu, was known before Arno Poebel's article of 1942. It is he who was listed as the father of Shamshi-Adad.[87] The third section is a list of just six names that gives the filiation only of the first name, Sulilu. It ends with the statement, "Six kings mentioned on brick inscriptions; their eponyms

---

79. Hallo, "Assyrian Historiography," 5*; J.-R. Kupper, *Les Nomades en Mésopotamie au temps des rois de Mari* (Paris: Société d'édition "Les belles lettres", 1957) 14. *Ašibūt kultāri* may be a translation of a Sumerian phrase, za-lam-gar-ti-(la) (Buccellati, *Amorites*, 92, 330).

80. Poebel, "Assyrian King List," 253.

81. Landsberger, "Assyrische Königsliste," 35–37.

82. *Khanu*, the area surrounding Terqa and a tribal name in the Mari archives; *Ḫarḫaru*, a province of Media in the Neo-Assyrian annals; *Imṣu* or *Iamṣum*, in the Mari texts and also the second name in the LKL (cf. Poebel, "Assyrian King List," 252; and Lewy, "Assyria," 744–45). Ushpia, the penultimate king in the first list, is the first Assyrian king attested from sources outside the AKL; E. F. Weidner, *Studien zur assyrisch-babylonischen Chronologie und Geschichte auf Grunde neuer Funde* (MVAG 20/4; Leipzig: Hinrichs [1917] 29).

83. See Lewy, "Assyria," 734.

84. Poebel, "Assyrian King List," 269.

85. Grayson, "Histories: Assyrian, Babylonian," 179; Landsberger, "Assyrische Königsliste," 35–37; Ushpia is known from two building inscriptions of the later kings, Shalmaneser I and Esarhaddon (see H. Lewy, "Assyria," 744). Many of the other names are found in inscriptions of the early Assyrian kings (Poebel, "Assyrian King List," 268).

86. Ibid., 273.

87. J. Lewy, "Le Nom du père de Shamshi-Adad Ier," *RA* 31 (1934) 170.

are missing," the scribe thus providing information about his source. The author of the text is ignorant of the relationships of the individuals named in this group. The last three names, Puzur-Ashur, Shallim-ahhe, and Ilu-shuma, are Akkadian in character and may be a new line of rulers.[88] This group is also attested in later inscriptions, showing that later writers either knew of the AKL or of a similar source.[89]

The remainder of the text is a long list of Assyrian kings with complete information, including the relation of each to his predecessor and the length of his reign. The text can almost be considered a chronicle, since a number of different verbal forms are used. The first part of this section ends with a fairly lengthy narrative concerning Shamshi-Adad and his dynasty, showing his relative importance.[90] He is a pivotal figure in Assyrian history, as reflected in the fact that the term *king* (Akkadian: *šarrum*) is not used in Assyrian inscriptions until his reign.[91] He modified the internal structure of Assyrian society, and it was during his reign that Assyria became a leading power in the ancient Near East. The origins of the Assyrian monarchy may be tied to him. The scribe admits that he was a usurper who "removed Erishum II from the throne."[92] His father was Ilu-kabkabu, presumably the same individual listed in the second section, although about ten generations are listed between the two.[93] Shamshi-Adad is thus connected with the second list of ten kings, implying that they are his ancestors.[94] These predecessors, who are not attested at Assur, may have ruled from Terqa, the supposed ancestral home of Shamshi-Adad.[95] The earliest version of the AKL may have been created in this period, although this has been debated.[96]

Later scribes began to make regular entries at the death of each king, evidently motivated by a sense of history. Thus, the document seems to have been intended to justify Shamshi-Adad's claim to the throne[97] and

88. Poebel, "Assyrian King List," 277.

89. Ibid., 278.

90. His son Ishme-Dagan is also listed, although the regnal years in the AKL are different from those in the inscriptions.

91. Grayson, "Early Development," 317.

92. See Gelb ("Assyrian King List," 212), who has been able to reconstruct the broken portions of the section.

93. See Poebel, "Assyrian Ling List," 286 for a dissenting view.

94. First noticed by Landsberger, "Assyrische Königsliste," 33.

95. Ibid., 35 n. 26.

96. Tadmor believes that it would have been possible to list the events and dates in this period ("Observations of Assyrian Historiography," *Essays on the Ancient Near East in Memory of Jacob Joel Finkelstein* [ed. M. deJ. Ellis; Hamden: Archon, 1977] 212); also see Landsberger, "Assyrische Königsliste," 109. Hallo disputes this ("Assyrian Historiography," 5*–6*).

97. Grayson, *ARI* 1.1, 2.179; D. Oates, *Studies in the Ancient History of Northern Iraq* (London: British Academy, 1968) 24 n. 2; and Landsberger, "Assyrische Königsliste," 33.

to incorporate his non-Assyrian antecedents or possibly even to obscure his non-Assyrian origins.[98] Hallo has serious reservations that this is the case, however, since Shamshi-Adad ruled from Shubat-Enlil, while Assur in this period was not even a provincial capital.[99] Furthermore, in his inscriptions he mentions only his father, Ilu-kabkabu, claims no succession from the Old Assyrian kings, and in fact seems to derive his legitimacy from the kings of Akkad.[100] After the Shamshi-Adad dynasty, seven kings are listed as the "son of a nobody," indicating a troubled period.[101] But what appears at first to be surprising is that the AKL also contains the ancestors of Erishum II, the king who was overthrown by Shamshi-Adad. This lineage is listed immediately after the lineage of Shamshi-Adad, since the compiler felt it necessary to place Shamshi-Adad in a position of legitimacy before Erishum II.[102] When one realizes that the writer was attempting to list as much information as possible about each monarch, the inclusion of his ancestry is not unusual. Since Shamshi-Adad was successful, his claim of legitimacy gained acceptance, and four later kings adopted his throne name. What began as propaganda was later accepted as orthodoxy. Erishum's lineage, however, cannot be connected with the earliest kings mentioned in the extant versions of the AKL.[103]

Shamshi-Adad is linked with earlier kings and also to "those who dwelt in tents," the kings from the Amorite tradition. The scribes of Shamshi-Adad have fabricated his associations with the earlier kings, notably showing a connection with the last of the "kings who dwelt in tents," Ushpia and Apiashal.[104] Hallo, however, believes that the AKL did not originate during this period, but later. Its purpose was to conceal

98. Hallo and Simpson, *Ancient Near East*, 97.

99. Hallo, "Assyrian Historiography," 5*–6*; his son Ishme-Dagan, ruled from Ekal-latum, a day's journey from Assur.

100. Ibid., 7* n. 5 in the addenda; also, see Grayson, *ARI* 1.18–28. The Sargonic overlords would be considered the predecessors of the kings of Assur.

101. Most versions list only the son of Shamshi-Adad, but see Schroeder (*Keilschrift-texte*, 35), who lists at least three of his descendants. Also see Grayson, *ARI* 1.29, and *Assyrian and Babylonian Chronicles* (Texts from Cuneiform Sources 6; Locust Valley, N.Y.: Augustin, 1975) 270. Two of the "sons of nobody," Adashi and Belu-bani, are mentioned in later Neo-Assyrian inscriptions of Esarhaddon. Adashi is called one of the founders of Assyrian kingship of the land of Assur (W. Röllig, "Zur Typologie und Entstehung der babylonischen und assyrischen Königslisten," *Lišān mithurti: Festschrift Wolfram Freiherr von Soden* [ed. M. Dietrich and W. Röllig; AOAT 1; Neukirchen-Vluyn: Neukirchener Verlag, 1969] 276).

102. See Kraus, "Könige," 131–40; and Finkelstein, "Early Mesopotamia," 63. He also may have been interested in increasing the number of the list to show the great antiquity of Assyrian kingship (Wilson, "Azel," 16).

103. His lineage is probably parallel in time to Shamshi-Adad's; Wilson, "Old Testament Genealogies," 94 n. 112.

104. Kraus, "Könige," 124; Landsberger, "Assyrische Königsliste," 109–10; and Kupper, *Les Nomades*, 208–11.

the subservience of Assur to both the Sargonic and Ur III periods by featuring their nomadic ancestors and inserting foreign overlords, whose memory could not be suppressed (e.g., Shamshi-Adad) and who were known to have ruled in Assyria. The date of this propaganda (according to Hallo) must be contemporary with the resurrection of the royal names of Shamshi-Adad and his son, Ishme-Dagan, during the sixteenth century B.C.[105]

The AKL can also be shown to have been used partly for propagandistic purposes, since it deliberately censors a number of names of Assyrian rulers that are attested or corroborated elsewhere.[106] Many of the rulers whose names were censored were subordinate to other rulers from the Ur III to the Mitanni periods. The implication is that some rulers were not acceptable, either because they were usurpers or not genuinely kings.[107] There is a relatively high number of variants in the lineages of different versions of the AKL.[108] Different versions omit some rulers, cite a different lineage for Shamshi-Adad, and give varying lengths of reign for some kings.[109] Based on royal inscriptions, Benno Landsberger concluded that many "sons" of kings were most likely brothers instead.[110] It is thus unsafe to accept the general statements in the list from a historical point of view without other supporting evidence.[111]

The two most notable omissions from the AKL are Zāriqum and Puzur-Sin. Zāriqum is possibly the oldest attested chief magistrate at Assur in the Ur III period. His name is not only omitted from the AKL, but it also is not mentioned in any of the inscriptions of later kings.[112] He is, however, listed in contemporary economic documents.[113] But there is not sufficient evidence to show that he was considered a "king" at Assur. A mere governor may not have been important enough to be

---

105. Hallo, "Assyrian Historiography," 5*–6*.

106. See Grayson (*ARI* 1.1–4), who lists the inscriptions of Assyrian "rulers" in the Old Akkadian period who are not mentioned in the AKL; it is not certain that these rulers were actually kings of Assur (also see Finkelstein, "Mesopotamian Historiography," 469). Those who accept the document as historically accurate must take this into account.

107. Lambert, "Tukulti-Ninurta," 89–91.

108. This can also be seen in the Babylonian King List (J. A. Brinkman, *A Political History of Post-Kassite Babylonia* [AnOr 43; Rome: Pontifical Biblical Institute, 1968] 27 n. 39).

109. See Brinkman, "Comments," 310–11; Grayson, *ARI* 1.1.

110. Landsberger, "Assyrische Königsliste," 142–43. It is possible that the throne passed from older to younger brothers in the Old Assyrian period and did not pass to the next generation until all brothers were dead.

111. The AKL appropriated the concept of royalty from the Sumerians and also claimed ethnic affiliation with the Amorites; Hallo, "Biblical History," 5*.

112. Hallo, "Zāriqum," *JCS* 5 (1961) 220. Zāriqum also became a governor at Assur (see Grayson, *ARI* 1.3).

113. This has led Hallo to consider the AKL to be of little historical value in the Ur III period ("Zāriqum," 221).

included in the list. A more blatant omission is Puzur-Sin, mentioned in a unique inscription found at Assur.[114] He evidently deposed Asinu, grandson of Shamshi-Adad, and also destroyed one of his palaces, justifying this by stating the Shamshi-Adad line was begun by one with "alien" seed.[115] Ironically, along with his presumed successors, his name was not included in the Assyrian canon by later editors of the AKL, who must have seen him as a usurper who deserved to be forgotten.

The Genealogy of the Hammurapi Dynasty

The text known as the "Genealogy of the Hammurapi Dynasty" (GHD: BM 80328; see appendix, p. 128) was in the British Museum (Budge) collection for quite some time before Jacob Finkelstein recognized its importance.[116] The provenience of the text is not known, but it is presumed to have been from Sippar. The obverse has a roster of personal names that are unfamiliar.[117] The reverse contains the names of the first dynasty of Babylon, from Sumuabum to Ammiditana (1646–1626 B.C.). The text was composed for the successor of Ammiditana, his son Ammi-saduqa. The first nineteen names placed before Sumuabum are considered a consecutive series of earlier kings and/or ancestors, comparable to the early names in the AKL. In fact, a number of the names can be equated with the names in the AKL. After the list of names there is a list of dynasties (Akkadian *palû*), the meaning of which is not entirely understood.[118] In other words, the first six names in the list are associated with the Guti dynasty (only because they are contemporary), the next five with the Ḫana dynasty (beginning with the eponymous ancestor Ḫeana), and the last are affiliated with the Amorite dynasty.[119] Finkelstein has interpreted the unnamed dynasty as representing the Akkadian period.[120] He considers the dynasties to be a "history" of the Western Semitic tribes, coordinated with the historical traditions of Sumer and Akkad. W. G. Lambert has criticized this viewpoint, since the text makes no attempt to explain the connection between personal names and dynasties.[121] Rather,

114. See Grayson, *ARI* 1.29–30.
115. Finkelstein, "Early Mesopotamia," 63; Landsberger, "Assyrische Königsliste," 32–33, 37.
116. Jacob Finkelstein, "The Genealogy of the Hammurapi Dynasty," *JCS* 20 (1966) 95–118.
117. This explains why the text was ignored for so long (ibid., 95).
118. Finkelstein believes that the dynasties correspond to the preceding genealogy in reverse order.
119. Including the nine Babylonian kings (ibid., 106–14).
120. Ibid., 106.
121. W. G. Lambert, "Another Look at Hammurabi's Ancestors," *JCS* 22 (1968–69) 1–2.

he sees the list of ancestors as summed up by the "dynasty of the Amorites," the first dynasty mentioned, while the next three are intended to cover all other contemporary dynasties. So the list is comprehensive.[122]

The remainder of the text betrays its purpose. It is not a king list or a dynastic ancestry[123] but a text for a memorial service to the spirits of the dead for use in the *kispu* rites of food and drink, providing evidence for a previously unknown function of genealogies.[124] The dynasties and soldiers who fell in battle are spirits who may be considered a threat to the present king unless appeased.[125] Ammisaduqa demonstrated concern for his people's welfare by distributing food to both the dead and the living. This "cult of the dead" has also been found at Ugarit in a list of retrograde kings.[126] Two of the kings come under the "assembly of Didanu," a name mentioned in both the AKL and GHD, as well as the Krt Epic from Ugarit and the biblical book of Genesis.[127]

The text, then, in its context does not have a propagandistic purpose, but instead presents a common lineage tradition for the Western Semitic tribes of the Euphrates region. The GHD and the first section of the AKL show common recognition of tribal origins. The names in the first three lines of the GHD are abnormally long and cannot be understood until divided in half. They then show a decided resemblance to some of the early names in the AKL.[128] Other names show more obvious connections: GHD *Ḫeana* = AKL *Ḫanu*, GHD *Ditānu* = AKL *Didanu*, GHD *Zummabu*

---

122. Ibid., 2. There is no indication of any formal division in the GHD. Also, see Röllig ("Typologie," 273), who considers the dynasties to be contemporary.

123. It is not a true genealogy but does exhibit fluidity; Wilson, "Old Testament Genealogies," 185.

124. Finkelstein, "Genealogy of Hammurapi," 115–17.

125. The *kispu* rites are well known at contemporary Mari; cf. ARM 7.199, 9.283, 11.139, 12.23 and 25; and recently, A. Tsukimoto, *Untersuchungen zur Totenplege (Kispum) im alten Mesopotamien* (AOAT 216; Neukirchen-Vluyn: Neukirchener Verlag, 1985). These ceremonies are also known at nearby Terqa (Finkelstein, "Genealogy of Hammurapi," 117). The possibility that the AKL was composed partly with this intention cannot be entirely discounted.

126. A. Rainey, "The Kingdom of Ugarit," *BA* 28 (1965) 107; K. Kitchen, "The King List at Ugarit," *UF* 9 (1977) 131–42; D. Pardee, *Les Textes paramythologiques de la 24ᵉ campagne (1961)* (Ras Shamra–Ougarit 4; Paris: Éditions recherche sur les civilisations, 1988) 165–78. See also the recent work on the cults of the dead in ancient Israel and Ugarit by T. Lewis (*Cults of the Dead in Ancient Ugarit and Israel* [HSM 39; Atlanta: Scholars Press, 1989] 47–52), who discusses the Ugaritic King List.

127. Kitchen, "King List," 141–42 and Gen 25:3 (see n. 130, below).

128. (a) *ya-am-qú-us-su-ḫa-lam-ma* is similar to AKL *ya-an-qi-*KIT/ [or *saḫ*]*-la-mu*; Finkelstein, "Genealogy of Hammurapi," 98; (b) *a-ra-am-ma-da-ra* is similar to Harharu/ Madaru in the AKL; Kraus, "Könige," 123ff.; (c) *tu-ub-ti-ya-mu-ta* is similar to Tudiya/ Adamu in the AKL; Finkelstein, "Genealogy of Hammurapi," 99. For Adamu, see A. Poebel, "The Assyrian King List from Khorsabad (Concluded)," *JNES* 20 (1943) 253; I. J. Gelb, *Glossary of Old Akkadian* (Materials for the Assyrian Dictionary 3; Chicago: University of Chicago Press, 1957) 19.

= AKL *Zuᵓabu.*[129] A number of the names have been found in texts as geographic toponyms or tribal names,[130] similar to the list of ancestors of Abraham.[131]

129. Sumuabum?; Poebel, "Assyrian King List," 252.

130. These names are:

Harharu/Mandaru: Kraus, "Könige," 130.

Yamuta = the tribe of Yamutbal: see the personal name Sumu-Yamutbal; Goetze, "Allusions," 65.

Amnanu, a tribe in the Mari region: see Kupper, *Les Nomades,* 49; Edzard, "*Zweite Zwischenzeit,*" 126; Sin-Kashid of Uruk is known as "King of the Amnanum": Falkenstein, "Zu den Inschriften," 22, 56.

Hana: see Edzard, "*Zweite Zwischenzeit,*" 37.

Didanu = Tidnum: I. J. Gelb, "The Early History of the West Semitic Peoples," *JCS* 5 (1961) 30; Buccellati, *Amorites,* 243; J. de Moor, "Rapiᵓuma–Rephaim," *ZAW* 88 (1976) 324; M. Heltzer, *The Suteans* (Naples: Istituto universitario orientale, 1981) 4–6; and Pardee, *Les Textes,* 179–88; also see Gen. 25:3. Dedan, an ancestor of Assur, is also mentioned in a Shu-Sin year date.

Both the Sethite line and the line of Shem have some connections with the early part of the AKL and GHD; see J. Sasson, "A Genealogical 'Convention' in Biblical Chronography?" *ZAW* 90 (1978) 174; and T. Hartman, "Some Thoughts on the Sumerian King List and Genesis 5 and 11b," *JBL* 91 (1972) 29. The vertical genealogies in the Bible recall West Semitic archetypes (Malamat, "Tribal Societies," 134). On the Amorites, see R. O'Callaghan, *Aram Naharaim: A Contribution to the History of Upper Mesopotamia in the Second Millennium BC* (AnOr 26; Rome: Pontifical Biblical Institute, 1948); J. T. Luke, *Pastoralism and Politics in the Mari Period* (dissertation, University of Michigan, 1965); and H. Huffmon, *Amorite Personal Names in the Mari Texts* (Baltimore: Johns Hopkins University Press, 1965).

131. Malamat, "King Lists," 166; these include:

Haran (*Harran*) was a well-known city.

Serug, Nahor, and Terah have also been attested as topographic entries:

(a) Serug: N. Schneider ("Patriarchennamen in zeitgenossischen Keilschrifturkunden," *Bib* 33 [1952] 521–22) has cited one example of Serug (*Sa-ru-gi*) used as a personal name in the Ur III period, probably from Tello (G. Barton, *Documents from the Temple Archives of Tello, Vol. III* [Philadelphia: University Museum, University of Pennsylvania, 1914] no. 51). Sarugi is also attested as a city 60 km. northwest of Harran in the Neo-Assyrian period (C. H. W. Johns, *An Assyrian Doomsday Book* [Assyriologische Bibliothek 17; Leipzig: Hinrichs, 1901] 29); K. Kessler, *Untersuchungen zur historischen Topographie Nordmesopotamiens des 1. Jahrtausends v. Chr. nach Keilschriften Quellen* [TAVO 26; Wiesbaden: Ludwig Reichert, 1980] 197–200; and S. Parpola, *Neo-Assyrian Toponyms* [AOAT 6; Neukirchen-Vluyn: Neukirchener Verlag, 1974] 306).

(b) Nahor has been found as a personal name in the Ur III period in four documents coming from Nippur (Na-ha-rum: A. L. Oppenheim, *Catalogue of the Cuneiform Tablets of the Wilberforce Eames Babylonian Collection* [New Haven: Yale University Press, 1948] no. 197) and as a town near Harran (Nahur/Til Nahiri) in the Old Assyrian texts from Cappadocia (Nahuru: see E. Bilgič, "Die Ortsnamen der 'Kappadokischen' Urkunden," *AfO* 15–16 [1945–51] 22–23), and in the Mari texts (see ARM 15.130; Kupper, *Les Nomades,* index; ARM 9, nos. 124 and 128).

(c) Terah was the name of the Israelite encampment in the wilderness (Num 33:27–28), as well as a town in Neo-Assyrian texts (*Til ša turaḫi*) on the Balikh river south of Harran (D. Luckenbill, *ARAB* 1, nos. 563, 610, and 646; the inscriptions of Shalmaneser III). The place-names are located in the district of Harran, precisely where the biblical tradition placed them.

The AKL and GHD thus seem to have a common genealogical tradition that begins with many of the same putative eponyms.[132] The fluid usage of personal names, tribal names, and geographic toponyms is typical of the Western Semites,[133] providing an authentic ring to the list.[134] One might conclude that these lineages (including the Genesis lists) are all manifestations of an Amorite custom, namely, the use of genealogies for political purposes.[135] Shamshi-Adad and Hammurapi were contemporaries, and each was engaged in a struggle for political dominance. Both kings may have attempted to justify their right to rule by appealing to a common genealogical tradition of nomadic "kings." The original political sphere of these lists was shadowed by other considerations (cultic, in the case of the GHD). Change in the function of the lists may explain the disappearance of kinship terms and the variation in order of names in the AKL and GHD, since the precise order was probably no longer important in the new setting of these documents.[136] It is therefore problematic to attempt to use either list to reconstruct a history of Amorite lineages. The sudden genealogical interest seems to be connected with the arrival of the Amorites into Mesopotamia.[137]

Other Second-Millennium B.C. Historiographic Texts

Later in the second millennium B.C., evidence of more sophisticated historical traditions composed for political purposes appeared in Anatolia (Boghazköy) and at Alalakh.[138] These are departures from the annalistic documents of Mesopotamia. The "Proclamation of Telepinu" is an edict from the fourteenth century B.C. with an unusually long historical prologue justifying a specific cause.[139] Telepinu, a usurper, attempted to justify his

---

132. See Ezek 16:3 for the Amorite heritage of Israel.

133. Kupper, *Les nomades*, 215.

134. The AKL begins with three names from the Old Akkadian period, then six rhyming pairs of names, probably created for mnemonic purposes; Hallo, "Zāriqum," 221.

135. Wilson, "Old Testament Genealogies," 175, 185.

136. Ibid., 186; idem, *Genealogies*, 17.

137. Hallo, "Antediluvian Cities," 62–63.

138. We can also include the Tukulti-Ninurta epic (Machinist, "Literature as Politics," 455–82; Finkelstein, "Early Mesopotamia," 69–71), propagandistic literature in poetic form that purports to demonstrate that the reign of Tukulti-Ninurta I (1244–1208 B.C.) was a continuation of, rather than in violation of, the tradition, while the contemporary Babylonian monarchy was in breach of certain oaths.

139. E. Sturtevant and G. Bechtel, *A Hittite Chrestomathy* (Philadelphia: Linguistic Society, 1935) 182–200; H. A. Hoffner, "Propaganda and Political Justification in Hittite Historiography," *Unity and Diversity: Essays in the History, Literature, and Religion of the Ancient Near East* (ed. H. Goedicke and J. J. M. Roberts; Baltimore: Johns Hopkins University Press, 1975) 49–62; idem, "Histories: Hittites," 306ff.; H. Güterbock, "Historische

accession to the throne by recalling events that actually occurred generations before the reign of the king he overthrew. Although he could not claim hereditary legitimacy,[140] he showed that he belonged to a line of lawful predecessors, whose principles were betrayed by the king whom he removed.[141]

The "Apology of Hatusilis" was written later but has much in common with the Proclamation of Telepinu.[142] Hatusilis III also usurped the throne and the "Apology" was composed in order to justify his assumption of the throne by force. The document begins with a genealogy descending from the royal line of Suppiluilumas. All but the last two paragraphs contain the historical introduction. He, like Telepinu, usurped the throne because of an unworthy predecessor, who happened, in the case of Hatusilis, to be a nephew. Wolf has pointed out similarities between the "apology" of David in 2 Samuel 9–20 and this Hittite document.[143]

The autobiographical Story of Idrimi of Alalakh (fifteenth century B.C.) was composed to legitimize yet another usurper to the throne.[144] His predecessor, however, is never named. The text in its present form may not have been composed shortly after his death, but two centuries later as a memorial or pseudoautobiography to remember the activities of a past leader.[145] All three of the above-mentioned documents display the

Tradition," 138–39; idem, "Hittite Historiography," in *History, Historiography, and Interpretation: Studies in Biblical and Cuneiform Literature* [ed. H. Tadmor and M. Weinfeld; Jerusalem: Magnes, 1986] 21–35; and M. Liverani, "Storiographia politica hittita II: Telepino, ovvero; della solidarieta," *OA* 16 (1977) 105–31.

140. Hoffner, "Propaganda," 51; he shows no pretense of an actual blood descent.

141. Hoffner, "Histories: Hittites," 307.

142. See H. Wolf, *The Apology of Hatusilis Compared with Other Political Self-Justifications of the Ancient Near East* (dissertation, Brandeis University, 1967); Hoffner, "Propaganda," 49–62; idem, "Histories," 306–8; Sturtevant and Bechtel, *A Hittite Chrestomathy*, 64–99; H. Cančik, *Grundzüge der hethitischen alttestamentlichen Geschichtsschreibung* (Wiesbaden: Harrassowitz, 1976) 41ff.; and A. Kammenhuber, "Die hethitische Geschichtsschreibung," *Saeculum* 9 (1958) 136–55.

143. Wolf, *Apology of Hatusilis*.

144. S. Smith, *The Statue of Idri-mi* (London: The British Institute of Archaeology in Ankara, 1949); *ANET* 557–58; J. Sasson, "On Idrimi and Sarruwa, the Scribe," *In Honor of Ernest R. Lacheman on His Seventy-Fifth Birthday, April 29, 1981* (Studies on the Civilization and Culture of Nuzi and the Hurrians 1; ed. M. A. Morrison and D. I. Owen; Winona Lake, Ind.: Eisenbrauns, 1981) 309–24; M. Dietrich and O. Loretz, "Die Inschriften der Statue des Königs Idrimi von Alalah," *UF* 13 (1981) 201–68; H. Klengel, "Historischer Kommentar zur Inschrift des Idrimi von Alalah," *UF* 13 (1981) 269–78; and R. Mayer-Opificius, "Archäologischer Kommentar zur Statue des Idrimi von Alalah," *UF* 13 (1981) 279–90.

145. Sasson, "On Idrimi," 311. This has been criticized by G. Oller, "The Inscription of Idrimi: A Pseudo-Autobiography?" in *Dumu-E₂-Dub-Ba-A: Studies in Honor of Åke W. Sjöberg*, (ed. H. Behrens et al; Philadelphia: Babylonian Section, University Museum, 1989) 411–17.

common theme of a usurper who recalls a positive past and a negative present, depicting the usurper himself as a "restorer of order."[146]

The Narratives of David's Rise to Kingship

The narratives in 1 and 2 Samuel concerning David's rise to kingship may be related to the above texts.[147] These narratives can be considered political propaganda in the previously accepted sense of the word.[148] The intent of the author of the narratives was to answer the charge of wrong-doing, with an attempt to demonstrate David's innocence in the series of events that led to his succession.[149] The narrative of David's rise promulgates a political point of view supported by a theological interpretation of events.[150] David's accession to the throne is portrayed as lawful because he was loyal to Saul's line and because Yahweh supported him; he also had hereditary legitimacy, which is relevant to this discussion. By virtue of the fact that he married Saul's daughter Michal,[151] he could claim the throne through the right of Michal's inheritance (matrilineal descent).[152] Thus it was important for David to demand her return after their separation.[153] David also brought Saul's relatives to his palace for political reasons.[154]

146. It may also be compared with the later Behistun Inscription of Darius I: G. Cameron, "Ancient Persia," in *The Idea of History in the Ancient Near East* (ed. R. Dentan; AOS 38; New Haven, Conn.: AOS, 1983) 86–94; W. Benedict and E. von Voigtlander, " 'Darius' Behistun Inscription: Babylonian Version, Lines 1–29," *JCS* 10 (1956) 1–10.

147. G. Buccellati, "Da Saul a David: Le origini della monarchia alla luce della storiografia contemporanea," *BiOr* 1 (1959) 99–128; idem, *Cities and Nations of Ancient Syria* (SS 26; Rome: Università di Roma) 209–12; L. Rost, *The Succession to the Throne of David* (Historic Texts and Interpreters in Biblical Scholarship 1; Sheffield: Almond Press, 1982); and A. Weiser, "Die Legitimation der Königs David zur Eigenart und Entstehung der sogennanten Geschichte von Davids Aufsteig," *VT* 16 (1966) 325–54.

148. R. Whybray, *The Succession Narrative: A Study of II Samuel 9–20; I Kings 1 and 2* (Studies in Biblical Theology 9; Naperville: Allenson, 1968) 50–55; P. K. McCarter, *I Samuel* (AB 10; Garden City: Doubleday, 1979); idem, "Plots, True or False: The Succession Narrative as Court Apologetic," *Int* 35 (1981) 357.

149. See H. Tadmor, "Autobiographical Apology," in Tadmor and Weinfeld, *History, Historiography, and Interpretation*, 56.

150. P. K. McCarter, "The Apology of David," *JBL* 99 (1980) 494.

151. 1 Sam 18:20–27; see McCarter, "Apology of David," 494.

152. P. K. McCarter, "The Historical David," *Int* 40 (1986) 120; J. Flanagan, "Chiefs in Israel," *JSOT* 20 (1981) 61; idem, "Succession and Genealogy in the Davidic Dynasty," *The Quest for the Kingdom of God: Studies in Honor of George E. Mendenhall* (ed. H. B. Huffmon, F. A. Spina, and A. R. W. Green; Winona Lake, Ind.: Eisenbrauns, 1983) 51; see Num 27:1–11.

153. 2 Sam 3:13; see McCarter, "Historical David," 124; and Flanagan, "Succession and Genealogy," 52.

154. 2 Sam 9:1–13; G. von Rad, "The Beginnings of Historical Writing in Ancient Israel," *The Problem of the Hexateuch and Other Essays* (New York: McGraw-Hill, 1966) 178.

When David initiated a relationship with Saul's son Jonathan, it may also have been for political expediency.[155]

Although it has been considered an unimportant appendix, the Davidic linear genealogy in both Ruth 4:18–22[156] and 1 Chr 2:3–17 betrays a political function. In the book of Ruth, the author wants the audience to associate the story's events with David's ancestors. The same divine guidance that led his ancestors also brought David to the forefront.[157] His kingdom was in agreement with Yahweh's divine plan. Thus, the book of Ruth was intended to bolster his claim to the throne and addressed a historical context in which David's claim to the throne and his ancestry were a matter of discussion, if not controversy.[158] The book showed that his dynasty had continuity with the past.[159] What is puzzling is that Perez, not Judah, heads the genealogy in Ruth, allowing Boaz to be seventh and David tenth in the list.[160] The initial generations of the Davidic ancestors, like those of the GHD and the AKL, reflect intratribal names and geographic toponyms.[161]

The linear genealogy (vv. 13–17 are segmented) in 1 Chr 2:3–17 also may have a political purpose.[162] Here, as in Ruth, David was connected to an ancestor who already was accepted and established in order to legitimize his position.[163] The employment of linear genealogies to support royal claims in Israel was evidently discontinued after Solomon, although later kings in Judah were concerned to show a connection with the Davidic line.[164]

---

155. Flanagan, "Chiefs in Israel," 57.

156. E. F. Campbell, *Ruth: A New Translation with Introduction, Notes, and Commentary* (AB 7; Garden City, N.Y.: Doubleday, 1975) 172; also see R. Witzenrath, *Das Buch Rut: Eine literaturwissenschaftliche Untersuchung* (Munich: Kösel, 1975) 26–36.

157. See R. Hubbard, *The Book of Ruth* (NICOT; Grand Rapids: Eerdmans, 1988) 41–42.

158. J. Sasson, *Ruth: A New Translation with a Philological Commentary and Formalist-Folklorist Interpretation* (Baltimore: Johns Hopkins University Press, 1979) 232.

159. Hubbard, *Ruth*, 43.

160. Sasson, "Genealogical 'Convention,'" 184; idem, *Ruth*, 184. Malamat ("King Lists," 171) thinks that this was done purposely, to conform to a traditional model befitting a royal lineage. The genealogy is incomplete and the purpose of these ten names is unclear.

161. See Malamat, "Tribal Societies," 136.

162. H. G. M. Williamson, "Sources and Redaction in the Chronicler's Genealogy of Judah," *JBL* 98 (1979) 358–59; the purpose would be to advance the position of David within the tribe of Judah.

163. R. Braun, *1 Chronicles* (WBC 14; Waco, Tex.: Word, 1986) 2.

164. See Wilson, "Old Testament Genealogies," 18.

SUMMARY

The Old Testament shows evidence that its cultural and political context was the ancient Near East. Historians should realize the historiographic nature and worth of the ancient Near Eastern documents and be able to recognize their "limitations" (*à la* Liverani). Second-millennium B.C. documents on propaganda and royal genealogies have an importance unique to themselves, and the modern historian must encounter each text in its own environment to interpret it for those of us in the present.

APPENDIX I

The AKL (to Shamshi-Adad I: cf. *ANET*: 564)

Tudiya, Adamu, Yangi, Kitlamu, Harharu, Mandaru, Imsu, Harsu, Didanu, Hanu, Zuabu, Nuabu, Abazu, Belu, Azarah, Ushpiya, Apiashal: 17 kings who lived in tents.

Aminu s. of Ilu-Kabkabu, Ilu-Kabkabu s. of Yazkur-ilu, Yaskur-ilu s. of Yakmeni, Yakmeni s. of Yakmesi, Yakmesi s. of Ilu-Mer, Ilu-Mer s. of Hayani, Hayani s. of Samanu, Samanu s. of Hale, Hale s. of Apiashal, Apiashal s. of Ushpiya.

Sulilu s. of Amini, Kikkiya, Ahiya, Puzur-Ashur, Shallim-ahhe, Ilu-shuma: 6 kings whose eponyms are missing.

Erishu s. of Ilu-shuma (40 yrs), Ikinu s. of Erishu (x yrs), Sharru-kin s. of Ikinu (x yrs), Puzur-Ashur (II) s. of Sharru-kin (x yrs), Naram-Sin s. of Puzur-Ashur (x yrs), Erishu (II) s. of Naram-Sin (x yrs).

Shamshi-Adad, s. of Ilu-Kabkabi (33 yrs).

APPENDIX II

The GHD
(First part of the list only; cf. Finkelstein, *JCS* 20 [1966] 95–118)

1. A-ra-am-ma-da-ra
2. Tu-ub-ti-ya-mu-ta
3. Ya-am-qú-uz-zu-ha-lam-ma
4. Ḫe-an-na
5. Nam-zu-ú
6. Di-ta-nu
7. Zu-um-ma-bu
8. Nam-hu-ú
9. Am-na-nu
10. Ya-aḫ-ru-rum
11. Ip-ti-ya-mu-ta
12. Bu-ḫa-zu-um
13. Su-ma-li-ka
14. Aš-ma-du
15. A-bi-ya-mu-ta
16. A-bi-di-ta-an
17. Ma-am?-x-[x-x?]
18. Su-x-ni?-x-[x?]
19. Da-a[d?]-x-[x-x?]
20. Su-m[u-a-bu-um]

The Weidner Chronicle and the Idea of History in Israel and Mesopotamia

Bill T. Arnold

Ashland Theological Seminary

In the nineteenth century, during the early days of Assyriology, the rush to find parallels was often accompanied by the conviction that original ideas were born in Mesopotamia and transported to the West. This sentiment climaxed in the pan-babylonianism of Friedrich Delitzsch.[1] Though Delitzsch's theories were never widely accepted, Old Testament studies have been plagued by similar attempts to prove parallels with ancient Near Eastern culture and religion ever since.[2]

As Assyriology came of age, specialists began to warn of the dangers of the earlier comparative approach. One of the most revered of Assyriologists, Benno Landsberger, published an influential article calling for the study of Mesopotamian culture for its own sake.[3] Landsberger insisted that any culture is "conceptually autonomous" and will be misunderstood when approached through the concepts of another culture. Few

My work on this chronicle was undertaken at the Oriental Institute of the University of Chicago during the summer of 1988. Many thanks are due the National Endowment for the Humanities for a summer stipend during that year. I am also indebted to John N. Oswalt for his helpful comments on the manuscript, and to John A. Brinkman for reading and commenting on an early translation of the chronicle.

1. Friedrich Delitzsch, *Babel und Bibel* (Leipzig: Hinrichs, 1902) [English translation: *Babel and Bible* (Chicago: Open Court, 1902).] For convenient summary, see Herbert B. Huffmon, "*Babel und Bibel*: the Encounter between Babylon and the Bible," *Michigan Quarterly Review* 22 (1983) 309–20; reprinted in *Backgrounds for the Bible* (ed. M. P. O'Connor and D. N. Freedman; Winona Lake, Ind.: Eisenbrauns, 1987) 125–36.

2. Indeed, each major archaeological find seems to create a new wave of parallels: Ugaritic and Dahood's rewrite of the psalter, Nuzi and Speiser's patriarchal parallels, etc. One wonders if the coming decades will not witness a "pan-eblaism."

3. Benno Landsberger, *The Conceptual Autonomy of the Babylonian World* (Sources and Monographs on the Ancient Near East 1/4; Malibu: Undena, 1976), originally published as "Die Eigenbegrifflichkeit der babylonischen Welt," *Islamica* 2 (1926) 355–72.

Assyriologists today question this assertion, and it has become something akin to an unwritten credo. Without question, scholars have had difficulty steering safely between a mania for parallels on the one hand and isolated specialization on the other. When reading the Old Testament in its Near Eastern context, the extremes of parallelomania and specialization loom on either side as Scylla and Charybdis, and conformity to contemporary trends is a deadly siren song.

Among the few scholars who have objected to the lack of a balanced comparative approach, William W. Hallo has been most effective in forging a new path. Hallo's method is not simply *comparative*; he prefers a *contextual* method in which similarities as well as differences are examined. Thus the pitfalls of superficiality may be avoided. The terms *context* and *comparative* are meant to define this method not as a new strain of parallelomania, but as an attempt to "weigh similarities and differences so as to be able to chart diachronic and synchronic variation within and across cultures."[4]

In this paper I am using the contextual approach to reexamine the Weidner Chronicle in light of important recent discoveries in Iraq. The chronicle belongs to a genre that is often identified as historiographic and that is a primary source for the Mesopotamian view of the past. I have chosen a specific example of this literary type that comes early in the tradition. The Weidner Chronicle has been considered by some to be "the first Mesopotamian textbook on the idea of history."[5] After offering a new translation of the chronicle, in which the text has been significantly expanded by museum finds and copies discovered recently in excavations, both comparisons and contrasts between this text and the historiography of the Old Testament are drawn. Several specifics are outlined, but I am also using this opportunity to draw general conclusions on the differences between historiography in ancient Israel and Mesopotamia.

---

4. William W. Hallo, "Biblical History in its Near Eastern Setting: The Contextual Approach," in *Scripture in Context: Essays on the Comparative Method* (ed. by C. D. Evans, W. W. Hallo, and J. B. White; Pittsburgh Theological Monograph Series 34; Pittsburgh: Pickwick, 1980) 1–26. And see now also the excellent discussion in K. van der Toorn, *Sin and Sanction in Israel and Mesopotamia: A Comparative Study* (Studia Semitica Neerlandica 22; Assen: Van Gorcum, 1985) 1–7.

5. E. A. Speiser, "Ancient Mesopotamia," in *The Idea of History in the Ancient Near East* (ed. R. C. Dentan; New Haven: Yale University Press, 1955) 59. Note also the comment of Hartmut Gese, who calls this Chronicle "a classic textbook for the conception of history as the consequence of human action" ("The Idea of History in the Ancient Near East and the Old Testament," in *The Bultmann School of Biblical Interpretation: New Directions?* [ed. R. W. Funk; New York: Harper, 1965] 57). Grayson divides Mesopotamian historiography into royal inscriptions, chronographic texts, and historical-literary texts ("Assyria and Babylonia," *Or* n.s. 49 [1980] 149).

NEW TRANSLATION OF THE WEIDNER CHRONICLE

It is impossible to date the composition of this chronicle with precision. The kings listed are from the earliest stages of recorded history, but the only copies of the text available are from the first millennium B.C. Until recently, the best copy was from Ashur and dated to the Neo-Assyrian Period. This was supplemented by four Neo-Babylonian fragments (from Uruk and Babylon and two of unknown provenance).[6] Just recently excavations have unearthed a nearly complete copy from Neo-Babylonian Sippar.[7] The events described in the chronicle range from the Early Dynastic Period of Sumerian history to the reign of Sumulael, near the beginning of the first dynasty of Babylon (1880–1845 B.C.). The chronicle may be dated to the late second millennium B.C. on the basis of internal content and ideological perspective.[8]

One of the Weidner Chronicle's most distinctive features is the narrowly focused nature of the content. The author was concerned exclusively with the city of Babylon and its patron god, Marduk. More specifically, the author was interested in the supply of fish offerings for Esagil, Marduk's temple in Babylon. The recent discoveries made available by Farouk Al-Rawi require a reinterpretation of what has long been taken as a mythological preamble to the chronicle proper. The total document now appears to be a literary letter written by one Old Babylonian king to another (probably Damiq-ilišu of Isin to either Apil-Sin of Babylon or Rim-Sin of Larsa). Since the letter was probably composed several hundred years after the Old Babylonian Period, Al-Rawi has correctly labeled the document a "supposititious royal letter."[9]

---

6. For the last decade, the most widely used translation available has been that of A. Kirk Grayson, *Assyrian and Babylonian Chronicles* (Texts from Cuneiform Sources 5; Locust Valley, N.Y.: Augustin, 1975) 145–51. His sources were the Neo-Assyrian copy supplemented by the fragment from Uruk and another of unknown provenance. Since Grayson's volume appeared, the other two fragments have been made available in Irving L. Finkel, "Bilingual Chronicle Fragments, " *JCS* 32 (1980) 65–80.

7. The discovery of a Neo-Babylonian temple library at Sippar included a copy that contributes significant new material (Farouk N. H. Al-Rawi, "Tablets from the Sippar Library, I: The 'Weidner Chronicle': A Supposititious Royal Letter Concerning a Vision," *Iraq* 52 [1990] 1–14. I am indebted to A. R. Millard for calling this material to my attention prior to publication and providing an early copy of Al-Rawi's presentation.

8. Specifically the "latter Kassite and early Isin II period" (Grayson, *Assyrian and Babylonian Chronicles*, 278–79). The new copy from Sippar is in the Standard Babylonian dialect and Marduk is called "King of the Gods." When viewed in light of additional orthographic and linguistic evidence, there is no reason to jettison the Kassite/Isin II date for the chronicle (Al-Rawi, "Tablets from the Sippar Library," 2).

9. Al-Rawi, "Tablets from the Sippar Library," 1. The idea of one Old Babylonian ruler advising another to support the Marduk ideology of Babylon also seems to reflect the Kassite/Isin II Period (see n. 8).

In the first section of the letter, the author imparts advice to his reader concerning religious devotion. He describes a night vision in which the goddess Gula appeared to him (lines 14–32). In the vision, Gula explains that Marduk, in divine council, has requested a supreme position for his city, Babylon. This was granted, first by Ea (lines 25–26) and then by Anu and Enlil (lines 27–31). In concluding the vision, Gula appears to warn the letter-writer that no one can compete with Marduk of Babylon for supremacy, and any king who chooses to rebel will certainly lose his position (lines 34–38). The author closes the first part of the letter with a reference to "the conduct of each former king," which is a transition to the chronicle itself (line 40). The text then systematically lists thirteen kings in chronicle fashion and provides a critique of each reign in light of the care with which that king tended to the sacrifices at Esagil (lines 41–rev. 38).

It is impossible to know whether the chronicle itself had an independent existence, especially since only later copies, several centuries removed from the original, are extant. However, it is possible that the chronicle proper was primary and that its use in this literary letter is secondary. The author thus used the former kings in the chronicle section as illustrations of rulers who failed to heed the advice proffered in the opening section.

The historical implications of this document were investigated by Hans Gustav Güterbock sixty years ago, and Assyriologists have long been aware of its significance for the study of Mesopotamian historiography.[10] John Van Seters has recently assessed the historical worth of this document.[11] He agrees with earlier scholars that the chronicle is of little value for reconstructing the events of early Mesopotamian history because of its tendentious agenda and mythological prologue (now known to be the content of Gula's night vision). But these features may be indicative of its earlier composition *vis-à-vis* the objectivity of the later Babylonian Chronicle series. Moreover, my interest in the chronicle is not in its historical reliability so much as its ideological perspective. As one of the earliest examples of this genre from Mesopotamia, it presents an excellent opportunity to compare and contrast the idea of history in Israel and Mesopotamia.

---

10. Güterbock presented the *editio princeps* of this chronicle in his seminal work on Babylonian and Hittite historical traditions ("Die historische Tradition und ihre literarische Gestaltung bei Babyloniern und Hethitern bis 1200," *ZA* 42 [1934] 1–91, see especially pp. 47–57).

11. John Van Seters, *In Search of History: Historiography in the Ancient World and the Origins of Biblical History* (New Haven: Yale University Press, 1983) 88.

1. Say to King [Apil(?)]-Sin, ki[ng of Baby]lon(?), thus speaks Damiq-
   ilišu(?—or Enlil-bani), King of Isin:[12]
2. . . . like . . . his reign.
3. I wrote to you words of wisdom, words. . . . You did not take them
   to heart.
4. You did not listen or bend your ear to the instruction I gave you.
5. You did not heed the choice advice that . . . , and you are pursuing
   other purposes.
6. To do you a favor . . . , but it is not in your heart.
7. For your own benefit, I advised(?) you to strengthen the discipline
   of your army(?) till distant days, but you did not consolidate(?) it
   in your hands.
8. . . . shrines where I sought advice. . .
9. Now I will tell you my experience(s) . . . acquaint yourself quickly
   with this!
10. I offered an offering to my lady Ninkarrak, mistress of E-gal-mah.
11. I prayed to her, I took prayers to her, I spoke to her the thoughts
    that I desired in my heart. Thus I said:
12. "Deliver into [my] hand the people of Sumer and Akkad . . . all the
    lands. . . .
13. Let them bring . . . the heavy tribute of the Upper and Lower Lands
    into E-gal-mah."
14. At dead of night, holy Gula, the exalted lady, stood before me,
    [heard] my words and spoke to me truthfully.
15. She blessed me: "In the *apsû* you will establish a base, in the subter-
    ranean ocean . . .
16. You will lift your head to the distant heavens, . . . protection on
    high."
17. Afterwards(?), Marduk, King of the Gods, who . . . all of heaven
    and earth,
18. [Will . . .] the peoples of Sumer and Akkad . . . to the dominion(?)
    of his city Babylon.
19. He has hurried to the *bit apsî*, to his father Ea the Craftsman, the
    Counsellor of Heaven and Earth.

---

12. The line numbers correspond to those of the Sippar copy. For the new material
in lines 1–26, I have drawn freely from the translation of Al-Rawi, "Tablets from the
Sippar Library," 8–9. The composite translation presented here includes the information
in the new fragments. Grayson used the same three sources available to Güterbock: a
Neo-Assyrian version (which he labeled A) and two Neo-Babylonian fragments (B and
C; Grayson, *Assyrian and Babylonian Chronicles*, 145). The new fragments published by
Finkel will be cited here as D (BM 39202) and E (BM 47733). The new Sippar copy
published by Al-Rawi will be designated as F (IM 124470). Textual variants are listed
in Grayson. Only those variants that result in a different translation are mentioned here.

20. 'Let Babylon, the city chosen in my heart, be exalted in all lands . . . ,

21. Esagil, the exalted shrine . . . to the border of all heaven and earth . . . ,

22. The Lord of lords, who dwells in the shrine, from east to west . . . ,

23. May he shepherd the Blackheaded People like sheep . . . ,

24. Let the city be elevated. Of (all) countries. . . .' "

25. Lord Nudimmud [put into effect] the words that he had said to him . . .

26. From heaven's base to heaven's summit he honored him . . .

27. Secondly (?), Anu and Enlil (and) the great gods, looked on him with steady favor[13] . . . and their word (is) true (?). . . .

28. "Let him be the leader of the Upper and Lower Lands . . .

29. May the great gods of heaven and earth tremble at his mighty sanctuary . . .

30. Raise the head of Esagil, of Ekua, the palace of heaven (and) earth, like heaven . . . their hearts

31. May its foundation constantly to the end of time like heaven and earth be. . . .

32. By means of your offering I understood the matter that you mentioned, and [I shall grant you (?)] life of long days. . . ."[14]

33. Apart from my order, a decision was given, a worthy decree for . . .

34. [F]or the gods of that city, the great gods of heaven and earth, he ab[andoned? . . .][15]

35. for the life of the renovation (?), monthly and yearly . . . to his decision . . . [no] god will go up against it and whoever's heart . . .

36. At his command, the hostile gods are bound (and) clothed in filthy [garments? . . .]

37. . . . whoever sins against the gods of that city, his star will not stand in heaven . . .

38. (His ?) royal dominion will end, his scepter will be carried off, his treasury will be turned into a ruin and [a waste land (?)].

39. . . . the king of the entire heavens and earth (said) thus: "The gods of heaven and earth . . .

40. and the conduct of each former king, of which I hear again and again, to . . .

---

13. On the idiom *kīniš naplusu*, see CAD K 385.

14. Lit.: 'the life of far distant days'.

15. Reading the end of line 34 as *ú-sa-aḫ-[ḫa-ru . . .]*. *Saḫaru* in the D-stem means 'to turn aside from, or expel' (*AHw* 1006).

41. Akka, son of Enmebaragesi, . . .
42. Enmekiri the king of Uruk, ravaged the people . . . .[16]

Reverse

1. The wise man, Adapa . . .
2. He heard [in] his pure sanctuary and he cursed Enmekiri . . .
3. . . . I gave[17] royal dominion over all lands to him and . . . his rites . . .
4. I made beautiful . . . like the "writing of the heavens" (constellations) and in Esagil . . .
5. The king who administers the entire heavens and earth, the first-born son. . . [18]
6. In the reign of Puzur-Nirah king of Akshak, the freshwater fisherman[19] of Esagil . . .
7. They were catching fish for the meal of the Lord of Fish[20]. . . the second lieutenants of the king took away the fish. The fisherman . . .
8. When the eighth day had passed,[21] the freshwater fisherman was catching fish . . .
9. In the house of Ku-Baba, the alewife . . . they brought near [to Esagi]l . . .
10. At that time . . . newly for Esagil . . .[22]
11. Ku-Baba gave bread to the freshwater fisherman, (and) she gave water . . . he qui[ckly offered (the food)][23] to Esagil . . .
12. The great lord Marduk[24] looked kindly upon her and said as follows: "So be it!"[25]
13. He has given royal dominion of all lands entirely over to Ku-Baba.[26]

---

16. Grayson has shown that *nammaššû* can mean 'people' in this context, rather than the expected 'animals' (*Assyrian and Babylonian Chronicles*, 147), and CAD N/1 234.

17. Text F has *iddinšumma* 'he gave'.

18. Text F has 'the whole of heaven and earth for his 3,020(?) . . . years . . .' (Al-Rawi, "Tablets from the Sippar Library," 5 and 9).

19. Von Soden, *AHw* 1260, translates 'Binnenfischer'; and see Grayson's note, *Assyrian and Babylonian Chronicles*, 147.

20. *Bēl nūne* according to Weidner is Marduk (Grayson, *Assyrian and Babylonian Chronicles*, 147).

21. On the idiom *ûme ina nasāḫi*, see CAD N/2 10–11. Text F appears to read 'seven days' instead of 'eight'.

22. This line is missing in all but text F.

23. Reading an Š-stem of *ḫamāṭu* (*AHw* 316), as suggested by Grayson, *Assyrian and Babylonian Chronicles*, 148.

24. Text F has 'Marduk the King, (son) of the Prince of Apsu'. See n. 31 below.

25. So von Soden takes the expression *šī lu kī'am* (GAG 124c); see CAD K 327.

26. Text F adds 'the alewife'.

14. Ur-Zababa[27] [commanded[28] (Sargon)] to exchange the wine libations for Esagil to . . .

15. But Sargon did not exchange (them). (Instead) he was very attentive[29] and he quickly offered[30] (the fish) to Esagil . . .

16. Marduk, the son of the prince of Apsu,[31] looked joyfully upon him and he gave him royal dominion over the four quarters.[32]

17. He acted as provisioner for Esagil. All who sat upon a throne [brought] their tribute to Babylon . . . [33]

18. As for him, he [neglected] the word that Bel spoke;[34] he dug up the dust of its pit and opposite Agade he built (another) city and [he called] its name Babylon.[35]

19. Enlil changed what he had said, and from east to west[36] they (his subjects) were hostile toward him. Sleeplessness set in.[37]

20. Naram-Sin ravaged the people[38] of Babylon. Twice he summoned the Gutian army against him (Naram-Sin)[39]

---

27. On the textual difficulties in this line, see Grayson's notes (*Assyrian and Babylonian Chronicles*,148, his line 46).

28. Grayson's reconstruction: $i[q(?)-bi(?)]$.

29. From *na³ādu*, CAD N/1 4. Güterbock translates 'er zeigte sich fromm' ("Historische Tradition," 54).

30. The new fragment E has confirmed Grayson's reconstruction of the verb (*Assyrian and Babylonian Chronicles*, 148).

31. The new fragments correct an earlier reading of this appellation. In the bilingual fragment D, the Sumerian line has a clear NUN ('prince') that was originally mistaken for É (*bītu* 'house') and translated by Grayson " 'the son of the Temple' of Apsu" (*Assyrian and Babylonian Chronicles*, 148). But both the Akkadian line of D as well as E confirm the reading of the NUN: DUMU *ru-bé-e šá ap-si-i* 'the son of the Prince of Apsu' (now see also F rev. 12, where the same title appears). Marduk's father, Enki (Ea), is referred to as *rubûm*(NUN) *ra-bi-um* ('the mighty prince') in the epilogue to Hammurapi's law code (rev. XXVI.98).

32. The expression is *kibrāt arba³i* 'the four quarters', i.e., the entire world (CAD K 331).

33. Thanks to fragment E, this line is now nearly complete: *za-ni-nu-⟨ut⟩ é-sag-íl e-pu-uš gi-mir a-šib* BARAG(*parakki*) *a-na ba-bi-lim* [*b*]*i-ᵈlatᵈ-su-n*[*u*] . . . .

34. The reading of this phrase is uncertain. Following the suggestions of Finkel ("Bilingual Chronicle Fragments," 73) I tentatively read the beginning of the line as ᵈšuᵈ-ú ᵈaᵈ-[*mat* ᵈEN *i*]*q-bu-šu* [*i-x-* . . .]. The independent pronoun is in *casus pendens* with a resumptive pronominal suffix on the verb.

35. Text F reverses Sargon's action, claiming he built a city opposite Babylon that he named Agade (Al-Rawi, "Tablets from the Sippar Library," 10).

36. Lit.: 'from the rising of the sun until the setting of the sun', CAD E 258–59.

37. Source B has *la ṣa-la-la i-ᵈmiᵈ?-i*[*d*?] 'he (Marduk) afflicted him (Sargon) with sleeplessness'. This tradition has parallels in other chronicle literature (see CAD Ṣ 67).

38. See parallel line 42.

39. Assuming that Marduk has called the invading armies against Naram-Sin. But Al-Rawi assumes Naram-Sin has called up the Gutian army against it (i.e., Babylon; "Tablets from the Sippar Library," 10).

21. and [put to flight ?] his people as with the goad of a donkey driver. He (Marduk) has given his royal dominion to the Gutian army.

22. The Gutians, who were a disgruntled people,[40] exhibited no divine reverence. They did not know how to set the cults and ordinances in order.

23. Utu-hegal, the freshwater fisherman, caught a fish for donation (to Marduk) in the region of the sea edge.[41]

24. That fish was not offered to another god until it was offered to the great lord Marduk.

25. (But) the Gutians took from his hand the fish, which was already boiled but not offered . . .[42]

26. [By] his noble decree, he denied the Gutian army the royal dominion of his land,[43] and he gave (it) to Utu-hegal.

27. Utu-hegal, the freshwater fisherman, laid his hands on his (Marduk's) city with evil intent, but the river carried off his corpse.[44]

28. To Šulgi son of Ur-Nammu he (Marduk) gave royal dominion of all lands, [but]

29. his (Marduk's) cult observances[45] he did not fulfill, his purification rites he defiled, and his sin . . .

30. Amar-Sin, his son, exchanged the large oxen and the (sheep) sacrifices of the New Year Festival of Esagil . . .[46]

31. Goring by an ox was foretold for him[47] and he died (?) from the "bite" of his shoe.[48]

32. Šu-Sin, for the well-being of his life, made Esagil like the "writing of the heavens" (constellations).

---

40. The word is *tazzimtu*, which Güterbock translates 'mürrische Menschen' ("Historische Tradition," 55).

41. Lit.: 'at the Entrance of the Breast of the Sea', which may have been a geographical name.

42. The phrase is *nūna bašla la ṭuḫḫa* 'a fish boiled but not yet served' (see CAD B 140).

43. Lit.: 'he took the Gutian army away from the kingship of his land'.

44. Note the wordplay using *abālu*. The play is created by repeating the verb in a different tense to dramatize the reversal of Utu-hegal's fortunes: he laid (preterite *ūbilma*) his hands on Babylon with evil intent, but the river carried off (perfect *itbal*) his corpse. This is "antanaclasis," i.e., a single word repeated with a different sense.

45. Grayson restored this line by conjecture (*Assyrian and Babylonian Chronicles*, 150) and the restoration was confirmed by Finkel's D source ("Bilingual Chronicle Fragments," 73).

46. This phrase is in Grayson's text C (*Assyrian and Babylonian Chronicles*, 151, see especially the commentary note) and confirmed by text F.

47. The discovery of text F has now cleared up the difficulties in this line. It was partially supplied by D, and Finkel restored to 'he was felled by a goring ox" ("Bilingual Chronicle Fragments," 74).

48. Ivan Starr's work on historical omens has demonstrated that there was probably more than one tradition about the unhappy demise of Amar-Sin ("Notes on Some Published and Unpublished Historical Omens," *JCS* 29 [1977] 160–62).

33. . . . that divine Šulgi did, Imbi-Sin his son . . . his sin . . .
34. . . . an earlier king, (your) predecessor . . . it is as you desire.
35. More than his father, Ea . . . heaven and earth . . . did not create;
     Anu and Ishtar . . .
36. His exalted son, the great lord Marduk, [King] of the gods,
     Prince(?) of the Gods . . .
37. His grandson Nabu, who . . . will name the king . . .
38. To his descendant, king Sumu-la-il, whose name Anu named . . .
39. To benefit yourself and . . . all of it . . .
40. [It will remain (?)] in your possession until distant days(?) . . . ."
     Tablet of Marduk-eṭir, son of Eṭir-[. . .] of . . . ; a worshipper of
     Nabu. Return if lost.

SIMILARITIES TO OLD TESTAMENT HISTORIOGRAPHY

One of the most important similarities between Old Testament historiography and the Weidner Chronicle is the so-called *Unheilsherrscher*
motif. This literary motif was first identified by Güterbock, who called
attention to the prominent role Naram-Sin played in later traditions of
Sumero-Akkadian literature.[49] For well over a millennium, this Sargonic
ruler was blamed for the downfall of the Akkadian empire because of sins
for which he was primarily responsible. *Unheilsherrscher* may be translated
'calamitous ruler', but Güterbock's term has no adequate English equivalent that retains both the active guilt of Naram-Sin's actions and the near
tragic nature of his reign.[50]

In a recent survey of the *Unheilsherrscher* motif in Mesopotamian literature, Carl D. Evans analyzed the Weidner Chronicle as one of the "pertinent texts" in which this device is found.[51] The chronicle, however,
differs from other sources in that Naram-Sin is but one of several rulers
who are guilty of sins that ruin. A unique feature of this chronicle is the

---

49. Güterbock, "Historische Tradition," 75–76.

50. Many legendary texts portray Naram-Sin as a king who suffers from hubris and
who refuses to follow divine advice (e.g., The Curse of Agade, the Cuthaean Legend of
Naram-Sin). J. J. Finkelstein suggested that "calamitous ruler" best describes the Mesopotamian scribal perception of Naram-Sin ("Mesopotamian Historiography," *PAPS* 107
[1963] 467). See Gurney's "ill-fated ruler" (O. Gurney, "The Cuthean Legend of
Naram-Sin," *Anatolian Studies* 5 [1955] 96).

51. Carl D. Evans, "Naram-Sin and Jeroboam: The Archetypal *Unheilsherrscher* in Mesopotamia and Biblical Historiography," in *Scripture in Context II: More Essays on the Comparative Method* (ed. W. W. Hallo, J. C. Moyer, and L. G. Perdue; Winona Lake, Ind.:
Eisenbrauns, 1983) 99–109. Piotr Michalowski has also identified this Chronicle as a "full
expression" of the *Unheilsherrscher* motif ("Amar-Suᵓena and the Historical Tradition," in
Essays on the Ancient Near East in Memory of Jacob Joel Finkelstein [ed. M. deJ. Ellis; Hamden, Conn.: Archon, 1977] 156).

use of cycles of "good" or "bad" kings as a propagandistic ploy challenging contemporary rulers to avoid the same fate as that of Naram-Sin.[52]

Evans argues that diverse materials from Mesopotamia (inscriptions, date formulas, rock reliefs, etc.) contradict this negative portrayal of Naram-Sin and that, in fact, he enjoyed one of the most prosperous and successful reigns in Mesopotamian history. Furthermore, the sins of which the various kings are accused are entirely anachronistic, since they ruled long before Babylon and Esagil were built. Therefore, the literary typology casts an important early ruler as "calamitous" against the evidence that his role in history was actually fortuitous.

It is this literary typology that Evans sees so prevalent in the Deuteronomistic presentation. He argues that sources more or less contemporaneous with Jeroboam I portray him as "an Israelite hero." But the first edition of the Deuteronomistic History (hereafter Dtr) presents the Jeroboam of tradition as "Israel's historiographical counterpart to the Naram-Sin of Mesopotamia's *Unheilsherrscher* tradition."[53] His sins are likewise said to be anachronistic. Dtr was allegedly defending the new theology of Josiah and imposing Josianic exclusivity on Jeroboam. The prophetic denouncement of 1 Kings 13 is a *vaticinium ex eventu* to depict the consequences of Jeroboam's "bad" reign and thereby warn the reader to support Josiah's reforms. Just as the Weidner Chronicle condemns rulers for sins against a cult that had not yet been instituted, so Dtr charges Jeroboam with sins against the law of the single sanctuary, which came into force long after his time.

Evans avers that the complex of materials in 1 Kgs 11:26–14:20 presents a picture of Jeroboam I that is distinctive in the Old Testament. Thus Dtr was propagandistic in defense of Josiah, contending that the Josianic reforms must be supported, lest Judah fall victim to the same fate as Israel before her. Likewise, it is possible that the Weidner Chronicle was written in defense of the religious reforms of Nebuchadnezzar I, when Marduk was elevated to the head of the Babylonian pantheon.[54]

I agree that there are general similarities between these themes in the Books of Kings and the Weidner Chronicle. However, at least two important observations should be noted here. First, Evans uses 2 Kgs 17:22–23 to show how Dtr used the cause-effect correlation between

---

52. Viewing the past as alternating periods of bliss and disaster has long been accepted as a feature of Mesopotamian historiosophy. See Güterbock, "Historische Tradition," 2–3, and Speiser, "Ancient Mesopotamia," 56.

53. Evans, "Naram-Sin and Jeroboam," 114.

54. W. G. Lambert, "The Reign of Nebuchadnezzar I: A Turning Point in the History of Ancient Mesopotamian Religion," in *The Seed of Wisdom: Essays in Honour of T. J. Meek* (ed. W. S. McCullough; Toronto: University of Toronto Press, 1964) 3–13.

Jeroboam's sins and the fall of Israel.[55] But in the immediate context, the author has been concerned most with the *corporate* sins of the nation (17:16–18a). Most scholars attribute the divergent views to the two editions of Dtr. The emphasis on Jeroboam's role in the fall of the nation was the concern of Dtr[1] (the first Deuteronomistic edition of Kings), whereas the second edition (Dtr[2]) highlighted national responsibility.[56] But the point here is that, unlike the Naram-Sin traditions, the biblical historiography connects and combines the guilt of Jeroboam with the corporate sins of the nation.

A further remark is in order concerning the way in which the *Unheilsherrscher* appears in the traditions of Israel *vis-à-vis* Judah. The references dealing with Jeroboam and the fall of Israel (1 Kgs 14:15–16 and 2 Kgs 17:22–23) are more parallel to the Naram-Sin literary traditions. The king responsible for the sin stood early in the cultural history and set the tone for successive rulers. But in Judah this was not the case. Rather, the decline of the nation was paralleled with a steady decline of monarchic leadership. There was a climax of royal degradation, as it were, from Asa to Manasseh, from general hubris to child sacrifice. So Manasseh was credited with the fall of the nation, even though he was late in the cultural history.

A second similarity between the Weidner Chronicle and biblical historiography goes beyond a thematic observation such as the *Unheilsherrscher* motif and brings us to an important controversy of recent decades, that is, the role of deity in historical events.[57] During what has come to be called the "biblical theology" movement, it was commonly asserted that Israel was unique among the other nations of the ancient Near East because of her unique views of the past. She alone perceived divine intervention as revelatory and, therefore, she alone gave considerable weight to past events. Other ancient Near Eastern philosophers were limited to the cyclic patterns of nature myths and were incapable of historical reflection. Von Rad makes this fundamental distinction his

---

55. Evans, "Naram-Sin and Jeroboam," 97–98.

56. Mordechai Cogan and Hayim Tadmor, *II Kings: A New Translation with Introduction and Commentary* (AB 11; Garden City, New York: Doubleday, 1988) 207. For general overview, see F. M. Cross, "The Themes of the Book of Kings and the Structure of the Deuteronomistic History," *Canaanite Myth and Hebrew Epic* (Cambridge: Harvard University Press, 1973) 274–89. One wonders if these views are divergent at all. The connection between corporate responsibility and the personal culpability of the leadership is certainly known elsewhere in the prophetic literature (see for example Isa 9:8–21 [Heb. 9:7–20]).

57. For a recent survey of the salient points and main protagonists, see John H. Walton, *Ancient Israelite Literature in Its Cultural Context* (Grand Rapids: Zondervan, 1989) 120–22.

methodological centerpiece. He asserts flatly that the theological parameters of the Old Testament are "conspicuously restricted compared
with the theologies of other nations" and that the Israelites expressed
themselves theologically "in one aspect only, namely as a continuing divine activity in history."[58] This formulation of course provided the basis
for his emphasis on the "credos" of Israel's faith.[59] But perhaps the classic
expression of this method was G. Ernest Wright's assertion that Israel represents a "mutation" or a "radical revolution" in the ancient Near East,
rather than an evolutionary development. This distinctiveness was expressly evident in Israel's peculiar interest in history in contrast with the
pagan concern for the cycles of nature and sympathetic magic.[60]

This approach may be said to have formed a scholarly consensus until
the late 1960s. The most challenging blow to the consensus was Bertil
Albrektson's acclaimed essay, in which he argued that the idea of historical events as divine manifestations is not unique to Israel and that
the Old Testament, like Mesopotamian literature, has little evidence of a
divine "plan" that is being worked out in history.[61] Likewise, H. W. F.
Saggs denied that Israel was unique in this regard. He maintained that
Mesopotamians believed in divine intervention, but unlike Albrektson, he argued that both cultures accepted the idea of a divine plan
within history. Israel was unique only in relative emphasis, not in basic
principle.[62]

In light of this discussion, I return to the Weidner Chronicle with
these questions: did the author perceive divine intervention in history,
and was there a divine plan? The evidence has led me to believe that
the idea of divine intervention was similar in these two cultures. On
the other hand, the possibility of divine plan in history will be treated
below as a dissimilarity.

Although the text of the opening section is broken, the contents of
Gula's night vision are clear. First the actions of Ea (lines 25–26) and

58. Gerhard von Rad, *Old Testament Theology* (2 vols.; New York: Harper & Row,
1962–65) 1.106. See also the comments of Walther Eichrodt on this topic (*Theology of
the Old Testament* [2 vols.; Philadelphia: Westminster, 1961] 1.41).

59. Ibid., 121–28. Similarly, see Walther Zimmerli, *Old Testament in Outline* (Edinburgh: T. & T. Clark, 1978) 24–25.

60. G. Ernest Wright, *The Old Testament against Its Environment* (London: SCM,
1950) 15 and 71–76. And on the distinctiveness of Israel, see Brevard S. Childs, *Biblical
Theology in Crisis* (Philadelphia: Westminster, 1970) esp. pp. 47–50.

61. Bertil Albrektson, *History and the Gods: An Essay on the Idea of Historical Events as
Divine Manifestations in the Ancient Near East and in Israel* (Lund: Gleerup, 1967).

62. H. W. F. Saggs, *The Encounter with the Divine in Mesopotamia and Israel* (London:
Athlone, 1978) 64–92. For similar conclusions, see now Maria deJ. Ellis, "Observations
on Mesopotamian Oracles and Prophetic Texts: Literary and Historiographic Considerations," *JCS* 41 (1989) 180–86.

then the speech of Anu and Enlil (lines 27–31) establish a decree in which the heavenly assembly sets a course protecting the Marduk cult at Babylon. Thus line 37 states emphatically, "Whoever sins against the gods of that city, his star will not stand in heaven." And the next line probably continues this curse: "(His ?) royal dominion will end, his scepter will be carried off, his treasury will be turned into a ruin and [a waste land (?)]."

Then in the second section, the chronicle proceeds to discuss the thirteen rulers chosen for inclusion. In each case, Bel responds according to the actions of the ruler. Wherever the ruler's behavior is acceptable, Bel grants "royal dominion" (*šarrūtu*, lines rev. 3, 13, 16, 21, 28). On two occasions, this is preceded by a favorable stare from Marduk: Bel "looked joyfully upon him/her" (lines rev. 12, 16). But in other cases, the deity plagued the ruler and took the privilege of royal dominion from him. So Sargon lost his position and suffered from insomnia (line rev. 19). Likewise, Bel summoned the Gutian army against Naram-Sin (line rev. 21) and, although it is less specific, Utu-hegal's fate (line rev. 27) is probably intended to be a direct act of Marduk.

Here there can be little question that the deity is not limited to a narrow realm of cyclic nature but is acting in history. And in the case of the Gutian army, Marduk is using a foreign people to punish a king for unfaithfulness (line rev. 20). The similarity to the biblical view of history as God's judgment upon apostate kings cannot be avoided (especially in the Books of Kings). Albrektson and others have noted these similarities and asserted that here, as elsewhere in ancient Mesopotamian literature, "history is a revelation of divine judgment."[63] Against the common assumptions of some biblical theologians, Marduk was not limited to the cycles of nature and sympathetic magic, but could reveal his displeasure or approval through historical deeds.

DIVERGENCES FROM OLD TESTAMENT HISTORIOGRAPHY

Despite the similarities, this comparison of the Weidner Chronicle with biblical historiography reveals several decisive differences. Even a casual reading of this document discloses one of the characteristic features of Mesopotamian literature, that is, list-science. In cuneiform literature, there was a scribal propensity to make lists of syllabaries, bilingual vocabularies, plants and animals, astral phenomena, deities, and

---

63. Albrektson, *History and the Gods*, 102–3; and see also Saggs, *Encounter with the Divine*, 78–79.

so on.[64] So here, in the chronicle proper (lines 41–rev. 38), the author simply lists kings pertinent to his purpose. There follows for each ruler a brief evaluative statement regarding his treatment of the people and particularly his concern for the Marduk cult at Esagil.

The development and literary alterations of the list-science may be traced throughout Mesopotamian history.[65] The lists were originally intended as tools for teaching and philological research. Thus the first lists were of cuneiform signs, sign groups, or words arranged simply in vertical columns. During the Old Babylonian Period, these lists were first used to categorize other items, not limited to philological interests: grammatical texts, synonym lists, dialect equivalents, legal formulas, enumerations of gods and goddesses, astrological observations, and stones and plants.

The question of the origins of Mesopotamian chronography becomes a pertinent question at this point. The relationship between the chronicle tradition and the lists is most obviously discernible when one tries to distinguish between certain chronicles and king lists. In some cases a definite connection can be established between chronicles and earlier date lists; in other cases it appears that historical data were extracted from astronomical lists to create chronicles. And the debate continues about the possible origin of the chronicles in the omen literature, which is a list of a different sort.[66] At any rate, it seems clear that the chronographic tradition in Mesopotamia has its roots in the various forms of the older list-science.

This use of lists must be counted as one of the distinct differences between Mesopotamian historiography and the Old Testament. The Old Testament also uses lists occasionally (e.g., Num 7:12–83, Josh 12:9–24, and 1 Kgs 4:1–19). But in each of these cases, the list serves to add some important detail to a larger literary unit. Josh 12:9–24 is a summary that

---

64. For the development and significance of the *Listenwissenschaft* in Mesopotamia see Jack Goody, *The Domestication of the Savage Mind* (Cambridge: Cambridge University Press, 1977) 74–111. On the relationship between list-science and historiography, see S. Moscati, *The Face of the Ancient Orient: A Panorama of Near Eastern Civilization in Pre-Classical Times* (Garden City, N. Y.: Doubleday, 1962) 321–22; and Gese, "Idea of History," 52.

65. Goody, *Domestication of the Savage Mind*, 80–99; and A. L. Oppenheim, *Ancient Mesopotamia: Portrait of a Dead Civilization* (Chicago: University of Chicago Press, 1977) 244–49.

66. Finkelstein argued that the chronicles are dependent on omen literature ("Mesopotamian Historiography," 470–71). But this has been refuted by Grayson, who denies that divination played any essential role in the origin "of the chronographic literature of ancient Mesopotamia" ("Divination and the Babylonian Chronicles," *La Divination en Mésopotamie ancienne* [Compte rendu de la Rencontre assyriologique internationale 14; Paris: Presses Universitaires de France, 1966] 76).

serves as a climax in which the author emphasizes the completion of God's gift of "inheritance" to his people. The lists in 1 Kgs 4:1–19 serve to build the case for the glory of the Solomonic kingdom and, at the same time, they add historical validity to the presentation.[67] Of course it is well known that the Books of Kings are structured around documents that were king lists, perhaps not unlike Assyrian and Babylonian king lists. But in Israel, list-science was definitely subsidiary to the mainline development of Israelite literature.

In the "historiographic" traditions of Sumero-Akkadian literature— the chronicles, royal inscriptions, and historical-literary texts—one discovers the "raw materials" for history-writing. These correspond to the Israelite sources that listed important items and observations about history, used by the authors of the Books of Kings. But in neither the Mesopotamian traditions nor in the early Israelite sources can one speak of genuine historiography. It was only in the use made of these sources by biblical authors that writing about the past moved beyond lists. In fact there are no Israelite copies of these raw materials themselves, only reconstructions or extrapolations from the biblical text. Thus one can only speculate about the nature of The Book of the Acts of Solomon (1 Kgs 11:41) or The Book of the Chronicles of the Kings of Israel (1 Kgs 14:19) or The Book of the Chronicles of the Kings of Judah (1 Kgs 14:29).[68]

Various attempts have been made to explain the appearance of historiography in Israel. Recently David Damrosch has suggested that Israelite historiography developed as a historicizing of older poetic epic.[69] The confluence of poetic epic and historical chronicle was a development that was under way in Mesopotamia in the second millennium B.C. But the process accelerated and redirected in the Hebrew tradition, resulting in literary composition on a new level of power and beauty previously unknown in the ancient Near East.[70]

In this regard the new emphasis on literary art only bears out the differences between Israel and Mesopotamia. However one tries to explain the difference, the Mesopotamian *literati* never moved beyond chronicle to genuine historiography. Akkadian literature has nothing to

---

67. These lists of officials appear to have been taken directly from official royal documents, since the list of taxation officials comes from a broken source.

68. Albrektson admits this major difference between Israel and Mesopotamia (*History and the Gods*, 114 n. 52). For a recent suggestion on how the compilers of Samuel and Kings may have relied on contemporary records, see A. R. Millard, "Israelite and Aramean History in the Light of Inscriptions," *TynBul* 41 (1990) 261–75.

69. David Damrosch, *The Narrative Covenant: Transformations of Genre in the Growth of Biblical Literature* (San Francisco: Harper & Row, 1987).

70. Ibid., 1–3.

compare to Israelite characterization, interpretive presentation of past events, multiple causal factors, or presentation of both negative and positive aspects of events and characters. And the debate in literary circles about historicity[71] in no way weakens the observation that the literary artistry of the Old Testament is unprecedented in the ancient Near East.[72]

At this point I return to the question of divine plan in history. As I have demonstrated, the Weidner Chronicle assumes that Marduk was active in history and was not limited to a single narrow realm, that of nature. But the question of divine plan in history remains. Albrektson has argued that the concept of a divine plan in history is not clearly stated in the Old Testament, as is commonly assumed. He concludes that the idea of the deity's purposeful control of history and the perception of events as a realization of divine intentions are common to the ancient Near East.[73]

It is true that both the Weidner Chronicle and the Old Testament historical narratives are tendentious. But a closer examination of these documents proves them to be radically dissimilar, both in the motives behind the *Tendenz* and its result. The motive of the Weidner Chronicle is obviously propagandistic, aiming to warn the reader to take care to provide for the Esagil cult, lest he suffer the fate of former rulers who were not so careful. But the causal forces at work in this document are located in the mythical deliberations of Ea, Anu, and Enlil, in which divine decrees are set in force for all time. Thus, the emphasis is on maintaining ritual performance in order to insure the throne. It must be admitted that the chronicle's line of causation reaches back beyond history to the divine realm. Here reality is established, and earthly kings are advised not to neglect the forces of that reality.

By contrast, the historical sections of the Old Testament are primarily concerned with maintaining the blessings of the covenant. This is no less tendentious, but the causal line reaches back to a moment in history when the deity established a relationship with the nation. Reality is established in the events of the nation's inception, not in the divine

---

71. I refer here to Alter's "prose fiction," or "fictionalized history," as he sometimes calls it (Robert Alter, *The Art of Biblical Narrative* [New York: Basic Books, 1981] 23–46). See the objections of Meir Sternberg, *The Poetics of Biblical Narrative: Ideological Literature and the Drama of Reading* (Bloomington: Indiana University Press, 1987) 23–35.

72. For illustration of the literary differences between Israel and her neighbors, see Dorothy Irvin, "The Joseph and Moses Stories as Narrative in the Light of Ancient Near Eastern Narrative," in *Israelite and Judaean History* (ed. J. H. Hayes and J. M. Miller; Philadelphia: Westminster, 1977) 180–203, esp. 190.

73. He opines further that these concepts are almost clearer in Mesopotamian literature than in the Old Testament (Albrektson, *History and the Gods*, 68–97, esp. 93 and 96).

realm of myth. And readers are urged to maintain the ritual only as it pertains to maintenance of the covenant relationship.

It could be asserted that the Weidner Chronicle shows a divine plan as clearly as the Old Testament. But this would be a misleading assertion. Marduk's only plan in history, as discernible from this chronicle, is to provide an eternal supply of fish for the Esagil temple complex. So, as Lambert has demonstrated for Mesopotamian culture in general, the gods determined social norms or destinies (*šimtu*) for society in order to maintain the *status quo*,[74] but social norms and destinies are not the same as a plan in history. In Israel God's actions in history were intended to maintain his holy standards in society. These actions also displayed God's working in history to accomplish the plan that he had established. Thus, Israel's "culture [was] historicist, Mesopotamian culture [was] non-historicist."[75]

As shown above, the chronicle literature of Mesopotamia can be traced in most cases to primitive list-science, though some look to the omen literature for the origins of the genre. The author of the Weidner Chronicle was at least familiar with omen literature, and in at least one or two cases "may have used omens or omen collections as source material."[76] But regardless of its affinities with omen literature, the very combination of the divine vision (lines 14–38) with the chronicle proper (lines 41–rev. 38) is enough to illustrate the intimacy between the divine realm and the human realm. In Mesopotamia, the world was an all-encompassing cosmic machine, of which the gods and people were only parts.[77] But illustrated in Israelite historiography is the fundamental idea of a God who is beyond nature, who created the world and gave it to humanity. Even more crucial is the conviction that he broke into his creation and established a relationship with Israel.

Thus the fundamental difference between Israel's and Mesopotamia's historiographical traditions was their view of divinity. This difference may best be called a distinction between *transcendence* and *continuity*.[78] Israel's God stood outside the created order, and thus his actions in his-

---

74. W. G. Lambert, "History and the Gods: A Review Article," *Or* n.s. 39 (1970) 171–72.

75. Jacob Licht, "Biblical Historicism," in *History, Historiography and Interpretation: Studies in Biblical and Cuneiform Literatures* (ed. H. Tadmor and M. Weinfeld; Jerusalem: Magnes, 1983) 111.

76. Grayson, *Assyrian and Babylonian Chronicles*, 44.

77. "The gods were seen as immanent in the created world, each having its own sphere of power and interest, and all were associated into a political organization" (Tikva Frymer-Kensky, "Biblical Cosmology," in *Backgrounds for the Bible* [ed. M. P. O'Connor and D. N. Freedman; Winona Lake, Ind.: Eisenbrauns, 1987] 235–36).

78. As used recently by John N. Oswalt, "Golden Calves and the 'Bull of Jacob': The Impact on Israel of Its Religious Environment," in *Israel's Apostasy and Restoration: Essays in Honor of Roland K. Harrison* (ed. A. Gileadi; Grand Rapids: Baker, 1988) 9–18.

tory were viewed from a totally different perspective. In Mesopotamia divine actions in history were reflections of parallel actions in the divine realm.

CONCLUSION

Many ideas and literary forms of the Old Testament are paralleled in the literature of the ancient Near East, such as temple patterns, agricultural feasts, and so forth. Albrektson's history "as divine revelation" (his chapter 6) may reflect similar ideas in Mesopotamia and Israel. But a conviction that the gods are active in historical events is not the same as a concept of divine self-disclosure or even of an abstract concept of history. Indeed the contents of the Weidner Chronicle and the chronicle literature in general demonstrate the fact that the Mesopotamians lacked the compulsion to organize systematically their observations about the past.[79] As Oppenheim noted in his survey of the Mesopotamian "stream of tradition":

> There is a noticeable absence of historical literature; that is, texts are lacking that would attest to the awareness of the scribes of the existence of a historical continuum in the Mesopotamian civilization of which they themselves and their tradition were only a part.[80]

In light of the recent works of Albrektson and Saggs, it appears that the leading proponents of the biblical theology movement overstated the case for the uniqueness of Israel. But certainly the recent emphasis on the similarities is overstated as well. The fact remains that the Israelite covenant-centered religion was intimately tied to historical summaries (Deuteronomy 1–4, Joshua 24, Exod 19:4). This concept of history as revelation may not be absolutely unique to Israel, as the biblical theology movement maintained. But only Israel had a transcendent God, and therefore her perspective on divine events in history was radically different. Ancient Near Eastern polytheism was bound to minimize the significance of history because any individual deity was limited in his sphere of influence by the other deities at work in the universe.[81]

Simply put, the similarities between Israel and Mesopotamia are cultural and formal; the differences are ideological and essential.[82] The emphasis on the differences in their views of history (as with their views of

---

79. As was asserted long ago by Speiser, "Ancient Mesopotamia," 38; Moscati, *Face of the Ancient Orient*, 321–22; and others.

80. Oppenheim, *Ancient Mesopotamia*, 19.

81. A point brought out by Lambert in his review of Albrektson's work ("History and the Gods," 171–72).

82. *Contra* Saggs, *Encounter with the Divine*, 8, 76, and 187–88.

creation, the flood, etc.) have certainly been overstated. Certain distinct similarities are unquestionable, and these are usually due to a shared cultural *Weltanschauung*. But there are also marked differences, and the question becomes: how does one explain the differences in light of a shared cultural background? The similarities among closely related cultures are understandable; it is the distinctions that require explanation. In other words, the similarities serve only to throw into bold contrast the differences. By overemphasizing the similarities, one misses the significance of this small, seemingly trivial nation of the ancient East with its astonishing claims for itself and its God.[83]

83. Stephen Ausband, in his work on cultural myths, has noted that beneath the radically different mythic traditions of societies, "there is a constant and uniform need—a uniformly human need—to find a way of dealing with the unending human questions about necessity, chance, purpose, and the meaning of life." The uniqueness of Old Testament Israel can only be explained by her monotheism, which led her to find the answers to these questions in history, rather than myth (*Myth and Meaning, Myth and Order* [Macon, Ga.: Mercer University Press, 1983] ix).

History and Legend in Early
Hittite Historiography

Gregory McMahon

University of New Hampshire

Hittite historical writing of the Empire period, particularly the two versions of the annals of Muršili II (1339–1306 B.C.)[1] and the Apology of Ḫattušili III (1275–1250 B.C.),[2] seems to be fairly well known among scholars of the ancient Near East. Non-Hittitologists may also be familiar with attempts at historiography from the Old Hittite kingdom, such as the Telipinu Proclamation[3] or the Political Testament of Ḫattušili I (1650–1620 B.C.).[4] In this paper I introduce several other texts from the Hittite corpus that are somewhat harder to categorize but that have historiographical elements.[5]

Texts discussed (with *Catalogue des Textes Hittites* number):

Anitta Text (CTH 1)	Edited E. Neu, StBoT 18
Zalpa Text (CTH 3)	Edited H. Otten, StBoT 17
Siege of Uršu (CTH 7)	H. G. Güterbock, *ZA* 44 (1938) 114ff.
Cannibal Text (CTH 17)	H. G. Güterbock, *ZA* 44 (1938) 104ff.
Palace Chronicle (CTH 8)	H. G. Güterbock, *ZA* 44 (1938) 100ff.

1. CTH 61. Both the Ten Year Annals and the Extended Annals are edited by A. Goetze, *Die Annalen des Muršiliš* (Leipzig: Hinrichs, 1933). The Ten Year Annals are also edited by J.-P. Grélois, "Les annales décennales de Mursili II (CTH 61,1)," *Hethitica* 9 (1988) 17–155.

2. CTH 81. H. Otten (ed.), *Die Apologie Ḫattušiliš III* (StBoT 24; Wiesbaden: Harrassowitz, 1981). An English translation is available in E. H. Sturtevant and G. Bechtel, *A Hittite Chrestomathy* (Philadelphia: Linguistic Society of America, 1935) 65–83. This text is discussed by H. M. Wolf, *The Apology of Ḫattušiliš Compared with Other Political Self-Justification of the Ancient Near East* (dissertation, Brandeis University, 1967).

3. CTH 19. I. Hoffmann (ed.), *Der Erlass Telipinus* (THeth 11; Heidelberg: Carl Winter Universitätsverlag, 1984). An English translation is available in Sturtevant and Bechtel, *Hittite Chrestomathy*, 183–93. Telipinu reigned ca. 1525–1500 B.C.

4. CTH 6. F. Sommer and A. Falkenstein (eds.), *Die hethitisch-akkadische Bilingue des Ḫattušili I (Labarna II)* (Munich: Bayerischen Akademie der Wissenschaften, 1938).

5. Two extremely important studies provide a foundation for any work on Hittite historiography: H. G. Güterbock, "Die historische Tradition und ihre literarische Gestaltung

A tendency discernible in the historiography of many ancient Mediterranean cultures was to formalize in writing the material concerning the history of the culture antecedent to the chronicler. Early writers in a culture, as a kind of initial task, seemed to gravitate to the composition of works that incorporate the stories of their culture's earliest-remembered time. Thus the epic poetry of Homer, the oldest known Greek literature, focuses not on his own time but on a distant but remembered past. The earliest-known author of Old Testament historical writing was concerned, among other things, with recording the history of his people before his own period. For the Hittites, this tendency manifests itself in several documents that treat Hittite history before their first securely attested king, Ḫattušili I, or that bear the marks of literature created to describe the period of the earliest well-attested kings. It is my purpose to discuss these "legendary" Hittite materials and to define what it is about them that causes modern historians to view them as "legendary."

The terms *historical, legendary,* and *mythological* are admittedly difficult to define. Acknowledging the arbitrary nature of my definition, I suggest that Hittite *historical* writing is usually the recounting of contemporary events from the first-person point of view. *Legendary* texts record mostly human activity that seems "superhuman" or beyond normal human experience. *Mythology* focuses on the activities of the gods.

The earliest-known Hittite text is the Anitta Text,[6] discovered in the archives at Ḫattuša. This document, straightforward in the information contained, poses certain problems for understanding. It is written in the first person by Anitta, King of Kuššara, with references to his own and his father's activities, mostly military. Included in the list of deeds is the destruction of the later Hittite capital of Ḫattuša, and yet the extant copy of the text was stored in the tablet archives of that very city, Ḫattuša. Neu, in his edition, has demonstrated convincingly that this text is not a translation from another language, such as Akkadian.[7] Güterbock has recently suggested that Anitta, whose name occurs in Old Assyrian tablets from Kaneš (modern Kültepe), may have been a native Hittite who spoke that language and was the king who first required scribes of the Babylonian tradition (perhaps from Mari) to adapt their cuneiform system to the

---

bei Babyloniern und Hethitern bis 1200," *ZA* 42 (1934) 1–91; Part 2: *ZA* 44 (1938) 45–149; and H. A. Hoffner, "Histories and Historians of the Ancient Near East: The Hittites," *Or* 49 (1980) 283–332.

6. Anitta is a somewhat shadowy figure who is not securely dated but who lived before the earliest datable Hittite king, Ḫattušili I (ca. 1650–1620 B.C.). The Anitta text is CTH 1 and was edited by E. Neu, *Der Anitta-Text* (StBoT 18; Wiesbaden: Harrassowitz, 1974).

7. Ibid., 132–35.

writing of Hittite.[8] What interests me here is the existence from the very beginning of Hittite history of a document that has all the basic elements of an annals text. Where did this form come from, and why does it first appear in a culture that had only very recently learned to write? This earliest text includes elements of later annalistic traditions among Hittites and Assyrians, such as first-person narration, emphasis on military activity, and focus exclusively on the king. Thus Hittite literature begins with a fairly well-developed historiographical tradition. Although the impulse for writing the text may not have been the disinterested pursuit of recording the past, its style is more or less "objective," with no particular agenda besides the obvious one of glorifying the exploits of the king. The extant version of these annals is probably a copy done in the early Old Hittite period (1650–1500 B.C.). Whether or not Anitta is "Hittite" and possibly an ancestor of the documented kings beginning with Ḫattušili I, the Hittites considered the text sufficiently important and/or interesting to preserve a copy in their archives. It was thus available to serve as a model for early Hittite forays into annalistic historiography. Van Seters, in his 1983 analysis, attempts to minimize the importance of this text by explaining it as nothing more than a compilation of a number of individual inscriptions, each of which could have been based on Mesopotamian prototypes.[9] Certainly the opening of the text is an odd one for an annal and resembles most closely the opening formula of a Mesopotamian letter. Even so, if Mesopotamia provided the form for all the supposed individual inscriptions, why is the text not in Akkadian? Even if the text did originate as a compilation, one should not minimize the innovation involved in creating a connected text, a kind of history, albeit with little or no attempt to date the individual events described therein.

Parallel to this very early Hittite tendency to record events of a king's reign in annal form is a tradition, attested in only a few texts, of treating Hittite history either before or contemporary with the earliest well-attested kings in a style that might be called *legend*. A distinction between an official *historiography* and a series of legendary *histories* was proposed by Güterbock in his doctoral dissertation, subsequently published in *Zeitschrift für Assyriologie* in the 1930s. Perhaps the best example of this is the Zalpa text.[10] Among the several copies of this text is one in the ductus of the Old Hittite kingdom, so its early date is secure. The story revolves

8. H. G. Güterbock, "Hittite Historiography: A Survey," *History, Historiography and Interpretation: Studies in Biblical and Cuneiform Literature* (ed. H. Tadmor and M. Weinfeld; Jerusalem: Magnes, 1983) 24–25.

9. J. Van Seters, *In Search of History* (New Haven: Yale University Press, 1983) 106–7.

10. CTH 3. H. Otten (ed.), *Eine althethitische Erzählung um die Stadt Zalpa* (StBoT 17; Wiesbaden: Harrassowitz, 1973).

around the queen of Kaneš, the site of the most important Old Assyrian *kārum* or trading colony and perhaps the original Hittite home city. This queen gave birth to thirty sons at once and, apparently in shock at what she had done, abandoned them to the river in a basket. Carried along by the river to the Black Sea, the boys were rescued at Zalpa and reared by "the gods." Later the same queen gave birth to a brood of thirty daughters, who stay with her in Kaneš. In a predictable plot, which still resonates in the twentieth-century mind three and one-half millennia later, the boys went seeking their mother and eventually came to Kaneš. Their mother, not recognizing them, gave her daughters to them. The resolution of what for the Hittites would have been an unacceptable situation is lost in a break in the tablet. When the text again becomes legible the narration has moved into the historic period and mentions the king (probably Muršili I, 1620–1590 B.C.), the father of the king (Ḫattušili I), and the grandfather of the king (Labarna?). Thus the first part of the text is not located specifically in time, while the latter part is carefully fixed by the reigns of several kings.

Scholars have unanimously described this text as "legendary." What makes it so is both the superhuman attributes of the queen and the obviously contrived nature of a plot that depicts a potentially tragic situation for the offspring of the queen. In fact, the text has very attractive literary qualities, as it sets up rather deliberately a situation rife with tragedy, anticipating in some ways the contrived plots involving tragedy among the Greeks and their cultural heirs much later. The text apparently reflects the impulse to record traditional material about relations between the Hittite homeland and the Black Sea district, which came under Hittite control for a while in the Old Hittite period. The historical portion of the text depicts conflict between these two regions. The story thus has an etiological function, to explain this conflict, and I assume therefore that the warnings of the one brother who recognized his sisters were disregarded and that enmity between Kaneš and Zalpa was explained as the result of the consummation of the mass incestuous marriage lost in the break.

The gods in the Zalpa story play more of a role than in the other "legendary" material, but even here they are not central to the plot. They provide only the mechanism for basing the sons at Zalpa; the interest of the story stems from the purely human relationships depicted therein. Hoffner, in his excellent survey of Hittite historiography,[11] points out that the Zalpa text functions the same way as a treaty preamble or the introduction to the Telipinu proclamation, by giving a

---

11. Hoffner, "Histories and Historians," 291.

historical introduction and then describing the current state of affairs stemming from the previous history.

A text usually entitled the Siege of Uršu, which seems to date from the reign of Ḫattušili I, may also be characterized as a legendary text. The setting is historical; the king is well documented from other sources, and the siege of the city is described elsewhere as one of Ḫattušili's conquests. However, the text describes a situation that, as well as can be made out in a fragmentary tablet, appears to be rather contrived. It consists of a series of confrontations between the king and various incompetent officers who cannot seem to put his plans for the taking of the city Uršu into action. There is no discernible attempt to place these conversations in order; chronology is not important to the story. The "plot" seems designed simply to present the king in the best light as he struggles to conquer, a basic role for a king, in the midst of a corps of incompetent lieutenants.

This kind of apparently contrived scenario is somewhat reminiscent of the hero epic from Mesopotamia and very strongly reminds one of similar scenes in Egyptian historiographic writings. For instance, the stela of Kamose depicts a council of war in which only the king has the courage and vision to pursue the necessary course of action. The Siege of Uršu does not resemble annals, which typically contain descriptions of marches and booty taken, but rather is mostly dialogue, in a very "literary" style. It seems to exemplify a process that is the reverse of the Zalpa story as recorded. The Uršu text takes a historical event (historical in the sense of having occurred in the historical period) and creates a legend around it, while the Zalpa text seems to take legendary material from a prehistoric time and work it into a historical narrative.

Fragmentary texts from the reign of Muršili I concerning his wars with neighbors, especially the Hurrians, exhibit a similar process, creating a literary plot based on the king's historically documented experiences. Included in this group for Muršili I is the Cannibal Text, a fragmentary tablet depicting an episode involving cannibalism during the king's Hurrian wars. Laroche manifests his understanding of these texts as legendary by cataloging them under a different number than another group of texts that record Muršili's Hurrian wars in a more annalistic style.

The other major text from this early historical period that appears to be a didactic piece of literature set in the historic period is the so-called Palace Chronicle. As pointed out by Hoffner, this text is not really a chronicle, since it attempts no systematic chronology, nor are the episodes dependent for their meaning on a chronological hierarchy. The text is a series of anecdotes about events in the palace, probably to be dated to the reign of Muršili I. It includes stories of events from the reign of the king's father (Ḫattušili I) as well. The point of each vignette is not always clear, but the general purpose is to illustrate potential problems within the state's administration by means of anecedotes illustrative of the ways in which an official might go wrong. The king may deal out quite harsh punishments to offenders. The tone and setting of the stories are such that they could be actual incidents, and it is not possible to assess the "historicity" of these accounts. However, as Hoffner points out, the text does name a number of officials attested in other documents from the reigns of Ḫattušili I and Muršili I.[12] Thus at least some of the characters are real. Recorded and/or contrived, the anecdotes illustrate a basic principle of historical writing, the selecting of the appropriate data in support of one's thesis or theme. Like some of the other "legendary" texts such as the Anitta Text and the Siege of Uršu, the document represents a historical writing process in which the records of a number of individual events are selected for their appropriateness to the theme and then worked into a larger text in a process of historical composition. The Palace Chronicle actually represents a more crude stage of this process than the older Anitta Text because there is no structure of causality among the individual anecdotes or integration into one flowing narrative. Nevertheless, it does represent an early attempt at the historical process, at reworking (or contriving) material that can be included in a historical text constructed around a central idea. The central idea is again the wisdom or discipline of the king.

One other group of texts should be mentioned in the context of the Hittite interest in legendary historiography. At least four major texts from Mesopotamia that demonstrate a legendary reading of history are known in Hittite translations from Ḫattuša. The King of Battle epic,[13] which describes Sargon the Great's foray into Anatolia, and the Naram-Sin legend[14] treat historically documented kings in a narrative that has taken on legendary proportions. The Epic of Gilgamesh, whose legendary elements are clear but whose protagonist is also probably a historical figure, is also extant in a Hittite translation.[15] The legend of Gurparanzaḫu, less well known than the others, also was of sufficient interest to the Hittites that they translated it into their own language.[16] Although these are not

---

12. Ibid., 302.
13. CTH 310. See Güterbock, "Historische Tradition 2," 45–49; idem, "Ein neues Bruchstück der Sargon-Erzählung 'König der Schlacht,'" *MDOG* 101 (1969) 14–26.
14. CTH 311. See Güterbock, "Historische Tradition 2," 49–67.
15. CTH 341. Complete translation of the Mesopotamian version of the epic by E. A. Speiser, *ANET,* 72–99, and A. K. Grayson, *ANET,* 503–7. A newer translation is M. G. Kovacs, *The Epic of Gilgamesh* (Palo Alto, Cal.: Stanford University Press, 1989).
16. CTH 362. See Güterbock, "Historische Tradition 2," 84–87.

native Hittite compositions, they do reflect the Hittite interest in legendary historiography. The Hittite and Mesopotamian legendary texts suggest that the Hittites did not make the distinctions modern historians would make between legendary and historical writing.

I have not included in this survey any of the mythological texts, a number of which are Hittite versions of Hattian prototypes and which therefore antedate the formation of the Hittite state. I have excluded them, both because they are not native Hittite compositions and therefore are an example primarily of Hittite cultural borrowing and also in recognition of the distinction, perhaps arbitrary, in genre between the supernatural stories of gods and the superhuman stories of legendary characters. In fact the role of the gods in Hittite legendary historiography is extremely small. There is almost no direct intervention in human affairs, certainly not the constant presence of the divine discernible in Homer or in the Old Testament accounts. Thus the Hittite mythological texts, in which the gods affect human beings very directly, and the early legendary and historiographical writings seem to reflect two different views of divine intervention. Hoffner, throughout his article on historiography in *Orientalia*, comments on the secular outlook and lack of divine intervention embodied in all the legendary stories from the Old Kingdom. In fact, as he notes, the older Hittite kings were much more self-reliant than their successors; it was really in the New Kingdom, under kings like Muršili II and Ḫattušili III, that divine patronage played such a large role in kingship.[17] I would note that in Hittite literature, mythology continues to be a productive literary form, with new texts being translated into Hittite right through the Empire period (1450–1200 B.C.). By contrast, the legendary material dries up after the early period; the "superhuman" activities of people are restricted to the legendary age, while the gods increasingly exercise their power in the human realm. What seems to continue from this early literary stage is the kind of legendary composition in which documented historical events are converted into literary historiography to fit a particular agenda. This is exemplified by the Introduction to the Telepinu Proclamation or the Apology of Ḫattušili III, which seem to be a continuation of the tradition of texts like the Siege of Uršu, in which the events are described in order to put the king in the best light.

The question of sources for the legendary texts of Hittite historiography is perhaps as difficult as the source question in Old Testament historiography. There is no evidence of a native "epic tradition" in Hittite literature that would justify positing an oral epic or epics from which

17. Hoffner, "Histories and Historians," 299.

these stories might be drawn. Day-to-day records are conspicuously absent from the Hittite corpus, probably because they were kept on relatively fragile wooden tablets. Some records of campaigns and booty might have served as sources for texts like the Siege of Uršu. Güterbock suggests that the Zalpa story had been living as an oral tradition long before it was written down; this is almost certainly true, but nothing is known of the form of oral traditions.[18] Van Seters's review of theories about the origins of Israelite legendary sources is sufficiently complex to illustrate how conjectural and arbitrary any discussion of proposed traditional oral sources must be.[19] Early Hittite historical compositions parallel the early historiography of the Israelites in that they are a first attempt by a people to create a historiography for themselves. A first attempt at written historiography must utilize a variety of sources, including oral ones, and the problems of recovering them seem to me to be equally difficult in the two fields.

The natures of the early Hebrew and Hittite historical writings do, I believe, differ significantly. For the Hittites, early historical writing was primarily concerned with kings or queens and their actions. This only became more entrenched in later Hittite historical writing. Often the writing is in the first person, introduced by the standard formula, "Thus speaks so and so, King of Ḫatti. . . ." Even under the monarchy, Israel had a different historiographic focus that encompassed a broader perspective on the state. As noted by Yamauchi, the literature sometimes included a critique of the king himself.[20] The data selected for inclusion by the Hebrew historical writers are unified by questions of morality and relationship with God and therefore do not necessarily cover all royal or political activities. For the Hittites, the focus on the king conditioned the nature of the historiography; it was not necessarily a pursuit of knowledge or a recording of history for its own sake, but rather a political pursuit. The problem of manuscript transmission and redaction is significantly less important for Hittite historiography because very often there is still extant what is probably the "original" composition. Even the later copies were removed from their originals only by a century or two and were still being copied by scribes in the same scribal tradition. In addition, the nature of the early Hittite historiographical texts is quite different from the early Hebrew texts as preserved, since the Hittite texts are short, discrete compositions dealing with one major theme, often only one event. The great complex of historical material and the need to

18. Güterbock, "Hittite Historiography," 28.

19. Van Seters, *In Search of History*, 211–27.

20. E. Yamauchi, "The Current State of Old Testament Historiography," in this volume, pp. 1–36.

organize it into a unified composition that obtains in the earliest preserved Hebrew historiography are lacking in the early examples of Hittite historiography.

As Hoffner points out in his survey of Hittite historiography, what one sees after analyzing all the Hittite historical texts is a series of individual views of history.[21] In the later historical texts one can see individual authors (Muršili II, Ḫattušili III) presenting their own views of the historical process. For the early period, parallel to the early development of historical writing as evidenced by the Anitta Text, the Hittites developed a number of legendary texts. These texts may involve independently documented figures in texts that one might call historicized legends.

The distinction between legend and history was, I believe, recognized by the Hittites, who stopped composing legendary texts quite early. This distinction is based on the difference between recording events that are within the bounds of normal human experience and those that chronicle events involving superhuman or extranormal activity, without extensive involvement by the gods. The genre of legend is not unique to Hittite historiography. The Hittite legends are, in fact, just one example of a strong tradition in the ancient Mediterranean world of legendary historiography in which superhuman figures shape the early destiny of a people. The Mesopotamian legendary texts such as the Naram-Sin Epic and the Gilgamesh Epic mentioned above demonstrate this tendency, as do Homer and Virgil. In the Old Testament, events are chronicled that are also beyond normal experience as presently understood. For people of any age who believe in Yhwh, the God of the Hebrews, such faith requires that extranormal accounts be interpreted not as legend, but as evidence of the activity of the divine in the human sphere. Here is an important distinction between Hittite legendary material and similar kinds of accounts in the Hebrew scriptures: the Hittite legends do not involve significant divine intervention, while the Hebrew accounts in general ascribe superhuman achievement to the activity of Yhwh on the terrestrial level. The Hittites manifested from the beginnings of their literacy a sensitivity to the power of historical or legendary writing in illustrating important themes. They, like the Hebrews, recorded and preserved stories of those who had made them what they were. Unlike the Hebrews, they often placed an emphasis on legendary, superhuman achievement rather than on the agency of the divine.

21. Hoffner, "Histories and Historians," 288.

The Historical Reliability
of the Hittite Annals

Herbert M. Wolf

Wheaton College

Among the major sources for studying the history of the ancient Near East are the various chronicles and annals written by different rulers. The best-known annals are probably those of the Assyrian kings, who kept important records for centuries, but scholars have not always given very "high grades" for the historical reliability of these annals. J. J. Finkelstein in his study of Mesopotamian historiography said that omen texts, not annals, are the best historical sources. Because of the historical information embedded in them, he believed that the omen texts "take precedence both in time and reliability over any other genre of Mesopotamian writing that purports to treat the events of the past."[1] Grayson and Van Seters have not been so high in their estimation of the omens,[2] but scholars have recognized that some annals were "eloquently exaggerated records of royal self-praise," as Hayim Tadmor describes them, a kind of "royal Assyrian propagandistic literature."[3] D. J. Wiseman has been a bit kinder in his evaluation of these annals. In his chapter on the "Historical Records of Assyria and Babylonia," in *Documents from Old Testament Times*, Wiseman says: "The Assyrian annals have been found to be generally reliable, though given to exaggeration in time of victory or silence on the rarer occasion of defeat."[4] Clearly, the possibility of this sort of

---

1. J. J. Finkelstein, "Mesopotamian Historiography," *PAPS* 107 (1963) 463.
2. A. Kirk Grayson, "Assyria and Babylonia," *Or* 49 (1980) 89–91; and J. Van Seters, *In Search of History* (New Haven, Conn.: Yale University Press, 1983) 56.
3. Hayim Tadmor, "Assyria and the West: The Ninth Century and Its Aftermath," *Unity and Diversity: Essays on the History, Literature and Religion of the Ancient Near East* (ed. Hans Goedicke and J. J. M. Roberts; Baltimore: Johns Hopkins University Press, 1975) 36.
4. D. J. Wiseman, "Historical Records of Assyria and Babylonia," in *Documents from Old Testament Times* (ed. D. Winton Thomas; New York: Thomas Nelson, 1958) 46.

skewing of the facts makes it difficult to assess the objectivity of the annals. The kings always wanted to look good in the eyes of the gods and in the eyes of the people, so the official records were usually carefully edited and self-serving.

Although the Assyrian annals are more famous than those from Anatolia, there are some notable examples of Hittite annals that have also been preserved. The king who contributed the most in this regard was Muršili II, who ruled toward the end of the fourteenth century. Albrecht Goetze, who translated the annals (into German), called the work "first-rank history" and spoke highly of its objectivity.[5] The Hittite annals include fewer building reports and dedication material than their Mesopotamian counterparts, and they do mention failures along with descriptions of the successful campaigns of the Hittite armies. Muršili also compiled the records of his famous father Šuppiluliuma, giving modern historians an opportunity to learn much about the accomplishments of the most powerful Hittite king of them all.

Interestingly, the burst of annalistic activity in Anatolia coincided with the beginning of the annals in Assyria. In an article about 2 Samuel, Alger Johns places the start of the Assyrian annals in the reign of Arik-den-ilu (1319–1308 B.C.).[6] Van Seters gives the credit for beginning the annals to the next king, Adad-nirari I, who ruled from 1306–1274 B.C.[7] Since Muršili lived at about the same time as these kings, there is a possibility that some "cross-fertilization" was taking place between the two areas.

However, it is also known that Muršili was influenced by the annalistic efforts of a king from the Hittite Old Kingdom named Hattušili I. Toward the end of the seventeenth century, Hattušili wrote about his accomplishments on a yearly basis, describing the cities he burned and the plunder he acquired. He wrote about the chariots, weapons, and statues found among the booty, while Muršili referred to the oxen and sheep he captured, as well as the captives who were brought to the capital.[8] Like Muršili and other Hittite kings, Hattušili I described his exploits in the first person. He mentioned the foreign cities and lands that he journeyed through with his army and methodically conquered. Both Hattušili and Muršili spoke of the gods who "ran before" them and en-

---

5. A. Goetze, *Die Annalen des Muršiliš* (Mitteilungen der Vorderasiatischen-Aegyptischen Gesellschaft 38; Leipzig: Hinrichs, 1933) 1.

6. Alger Johns, "Did David Use Assyrian-Type Annals?" *Andrews University Seminary Studies* 3 (1965) 97–109.

7. Van Seters, *In Search of History*, 61.

8. H. Otten, "Das Hethiterreich," in *Kulturgeschichte des Alten Orient* (ed. Hartmut Schökel; Stuttgart: Alfred Kröner, 1961) 339–41.

sured victory in battle. But Hattušili did not always use the same terminology to describe divine assistance in successive battles, in contrast to Muršili II, who used a repetitive style.[9] Another difference between the earlier and later annals is the lion symbolism applied to Hattušili I. Other Hittite annals scarcely used any similes at all, even though similes and metaphors are common in other literature, such as myth and ritual.[10] Although there were some differences between the earlier and later versions, it does seem clear that Muršili's scribes utilized the style of the annals of Hattušili I in their work. If this is true, one must acknowledge that the Hittites had a major role in the development of this genre.

The Hittites referred to the annals in a way that may help us understand their purpose. In the colophons of the ten-year annals of Muršili, the text is called The Manly Deeds (or Military Exploits) of Muršili. The word LÚ-*natar* is more literally rendered 'masculinity', a trait that was measured by prowess in battle and the ability to sire children. The royal inscriptions as well as the annals refer several times to this "proof of masculinity" or "military exploits."[11] The ten-year annals were clearly an attempt to prove Muršili's manhood by relating his ability to win battles. Toward the beginning of these annals, in paragraphs three and four, the text records the following defamatory remarks against Muršili: "He who sits on the throne is small and unable to defend the land of Hatti." These words were allegedly spoken by the Hittites' enemies, but some of the Hittites themselves were probably wondering about the new king's ability. So Muršili prayed to the sun-goddess of Arinna, who then proceeded to help him subjugate enemy lands during the next ten years. The writing of the annals helped celebrate these achievements and was perhaps "a partial payment of the vow made to the Sun-goddess."[12]

In light of such possible motivations and exaggerations, it is appropriate to examine my earlier statement about the greater historical reliability of the Hittite annals. After all, political propaganda was well known among the Hittites. As early as the reign of Hattušili I, the king was concerned with the royal image and took pains to portray himself as wise, just, and merciful.[13] Telepinu's Proclamation was designed to defend his usurpation of the throne, and the so-called Apology of Hattušili III is

---

9. H. A Hoffner, Jr., "Histories and Historians of the Ancient Near East: The Hittites," *Or* 49 (1980) 295–96.

10. Ibid., 297.

11. H. A. Hoffner, Jr., "Symbols for Masculinity and Femininity," *JBL* 85 (1966) 327.

12. H. A. Hoffner, Jr., "Propaganda and Political Justification in Hittite Historiography," *Unity and Diversity: Essays on the History, Literature and Religion of the Ancient Near East* (ed. Hans Goedicke and J. J. M. Roberts; Baltimore: Johns Hopkins University Press, 1975) 327.

13. Hoffner, "Histories and Historians," 301.

usually considered a tendentious account, excusing Hattušili's banishment of the legitimate king, Urhi-Tešub, in order to assume his throne.[14] Is there any reason not to assume that the annals were filled with half-truths and self-aggrandizement? Hoffner has pointed out that, unlike Telepinu and Hattušili III, there was no question about Muršili's right to the throne, only about his ability as a ruler.[15] Yet one wonders whether a king who wanted to prove his manliness would tell fewer lies than one who wanted to prove his right to rule.

Boasting was not absent even in the annals of Hattušili I, a king who claimed he was able to cross the Euphrates "on foot," that is, with the help of a bridge. Anticipating a challenge to this boast, Hattušili did acknowledge that Sargon the Great of Akkad was the only other king to cross the great Euphrates in this manner. This admission indicates that even in the Old Kingdom, rulers were interested in defending the truth of their statements in historical material.[16]

To assess the reliability of the annals, I would like to return to my earlier assertion that the Hittite annals refer to failures as well as victories, for if they do, a greater credibility is indeed likely. In the annals of Šuppiluliuma compiled by Muršili, there is the remarkable account of an Egyptian request to have Šuppiluliuma send a son to become the new Pharaoh.[17] King Tutankhamon had died, and while the Egyptians and Hittites were fighting over territory in Lebanon, his young widow sent envoys to ask the Hittite king to send one of his sons to become her husband. Suspicious of the request, King Šuppiluliuma sent a high official to Egypt to verify the story. The official returned with a letter from the queen assuring the Hittites that the offer was genuine in spite of the political implications. The Hittite annals were filled with letters to and from enemies, but none was quite like this one. So Šuppiluliuma dispatched a son to marry into the Egyptian royal family, but the delay proved to be costly. Apparently Egyptian noblemen had time to organize opposition to the plan, and they killed the Hittite prince as he traveled to Egypt. The death of this prince is noted in the Plague Prayers of Muršili, a reference that helps to verify the fact that a request for a son really did come from the Egyptian queen.[18]

14. Cf. O. R. Gurney, *The Hittites* (Baltimore: Penguin, 1961) 175–76; and H. M. Wolf, *The Apology of Hattusilis Compared with Other Political Self-Justifications of the Ancient Near East* (dissertation, Brandeis University, 1967).

15. Hoffner, "Propaganda and Political Justification," 50–51.

16. Hoffner, "Histories and Historians," 50–51.

17. A. Goetze, "Suppiluliumas and the Egyptian Queen," *ANET*, 319.

18. A. Goetze, "Plague Prayers of Mursilis," *ANET*, 395.

Since the episode ended in tragedy, it might have been interpreted as an example of poor judgment on the part of Šuppiluliuma. Could he not have guessed that such an alliance would be doomed to failure? Although it was an honor to have one's son married to an Egyptian queen, the likelihood of a foreigner being accepted as Pharaoh was not very great, as the Hyksos had learned two centuries earlier.[19] Yet in spite of these negative factors, the Hittite annals record the king's actions in considerable detail. Muršili's Plague Prayers also note that the Hittite incursion into Egyptian-controlled territory in retaliation for the death of the prince led to the plague that broke out among the prisoners and took the lives of many Hittites in the homeland. It marked a sad ending to the otherwise glorious reign of Šuppiluliuma.

The widespread nature of the plague does raise the possibility that the son dispatched to Egypt was himself a victim of this dread disease. Not all are convinced that the Egyptians killed the Hittite prince.[20] If he died as a result of the pestilence, the Hittite rulers might have concocted the story of murder for political reasons, so that their attacks against Egyptian-held territory would appear to have been provoked. The alleged invitation from the Egyptian queen could then be interpreted as boasting, for although it is known from the Amarna letters that foreign kings frequently wanted the Pharaoh to allow his princesses to marry their sons and form political alliances, no foreigners had ever been asked to assume a position of power in Egypt, let alone become the Pharaoh. Yet the consistent picture given both in the Hittite annals and in the Plague Prayers of Muršili is of a clear invitation from Tutankhamon's widow. The untimely death of the Hittite prince, whatever the cause, damaged the Hittite cause immeasurably. By referring to his death in their literature, the Hittites displayed a kind of objectivity not normally seen in the annals of other nations.

Within a matter of decades after the death of Šuppiluliuma there was another famous confrontation between the Egyptians and Hittites at Qadesh on the Orontes (1275 B.C.). The battle between Ramesses II and Hattušili III was something of a stalemate, though most feel that the Hittites did have the upper hand over their main competitors for domination of the Near East.[21] The relative indecisiveness of the outcome paved the way for the parity treaty concluded by Ramesses II and Hattušili III a few years later. Ramesses wrote on the walls of his temples that he had

19. John Bright, *A History of Israel* (Philadelphia: Westminster, 1972) 60–62.

20. Cyril Aldred, "Egypt: The Amarna Period and the End of the Eighteenth Dynasty," *CAH* 2/2.69.

21. S. Yeivin, "Canaan and Hittite Strategy in the Second Half of the Second Millennium B.C.," *JNES* 9 (1950) 106.

won a great victory, but the Hittites were much more subdued in their descriptions. In the Apology of Hattušili, which some scholars have compared with the annals of his father Muršili on a formal basis,[22] Hattušili described his role in the great campaign. At that time his brother Muwatalli was the king and gathered a large force to confront Ramesses. According to column II, lines 69–74 of the Apology, Hattušili was placed in command of the chariots of the Hittites and their allies. Since the chariotry played a key role in a surprise attack on the Egyptian forces that nearly overwhelmed Ramesses, one would expect Hattušili to describe his important contribution with considerable fanfare. But here is the total of what he says: "When my brother went into the land of Egypt, I led down to my brother into the land of Egypt troops and chariots from the lands I had resettled. I also took command of the chariots of my brother."[23] If more details were not known from other sources, one would think that the expedition was a minor one at best and that Hattušili had made little if any contribution. Perhaps the parity treaty helped tone down the rhetoric and kept Hattušili from boasting of his achievements. From a fragment of Hattushili's annals it is known that he considered Muwatalli's campaign against the Egyptians a victory for the Hittites, but again, few details are given.[24]

This sort of moderation in recounting events gives me good reason to believe that the historical references in Hittite literature, especially in the annals and the treaty prologues, are generally reliable. The Hittites did not seem to have the same tendency toward exaggeration found among the Assyrians and Egyptians, and this factor places their work in a more positive light. It also indicates that annalistic records may be quite objective and a great help to those who want to study history *per se* in the ancient Near East.

---

22. Annelies Kammenhuber, "Die hethitische Geschichtsschreibung," *Saeculum* 9 (1958) 153.

23. Wolf, *Apology of Hattusilis*, 58–60.

24. A. Goetze, "Hattusilis on Muwatallis' War against Egypt," *ANET*, 319.

The Structure of Joshua 1–11 and the Annals of Thutmose III

James K. Hoffmeier

Wheaton College

The "conquest narratives" in Joshua have received considerable scholarly attention in recent decades and for the most part have been given little historical credibility. They are generally viewed as etiological or so theologically and ideologically shaped as to be of little historical value. In fact, the notion that Israel entered Canaan by "conquest" is presently considered passé by many. John Van Seters has recently concluded that "the invasion of the land of Canaan by Israel under Joshua was an invention of DtrH."[1] Similarly, Robert Coote has said, "These periods [the exodus and conquest as described in the Old Testament] never existed."[2]

The roots of these modern perspectives go back at least to Albrecht Alt, who in 1925 argued that a migration/settlement model, rather than a military conquest, best explained the data.[3] Subsequently, Martin Noth and other influential scholars subscribed to this view.[4] William F. Albright and G. Ernest Wright were among those who supported the more traditional view, that a military conquest did take place. For Albright, his excavations at Tell Beit Mirsim (which he identified with Debir), revealing a massive conflagration around 1250 B.C., were compelling evidence that

---

1. J. Van Seters, "Joshua's Campaign and Near Eastern Historiography," *SJOT* 2 (1990) 12.
2. R. Coote, *Early Israel: A New Horizon* (Minneapolis, Minn.: Fortress, 1990) 3.
3. A. Alt, "Die Landnahme der Israeliten in Palästina," originally published in 1925, translated and reprinted in *Essays on Old Testament History and Religion* (Oxford: Blackwell, 1963) 135–69.
4. M. Noth, *The History of Israel* (London: Black, 1960) 53–84.

Joshua and the Israelites had conquered the city.[5] Similarly, Wright's observations at Beitîn (Bethel?) led him to the same conclusion.[6] More recent studies speak in terms of settlement and migration and not conquest. Israel Finkelstein believes that the Israelites abandoned their nomadic lifestyle for a more sedentary one in the hill country around 1200 B.C.[7] William G. Dever has recently described this interpretation of the archaeological and biblical record as "rapidly becoming a consensus."[8]

In this study I do not investigate archaeological questions concerning the nature and date of Israel's appearance in Canaan; rather, I focus on form- and source-critical questions of the "conquest" narratives, particularly Josh 10:28–42 and 11:11–14, and ways they relate to the rest of Joshua 1–11. These chapters in Joshua have not been compared to other Near Eastern military writings until Lawson Younger's recent monograph[9] and Van Seters's article, "Joshua's Campaign of Canaan and Near Eastern Historiography."[10] Younger's work is a thorough investigation that includes records from Egypt, Mesopotamia, and Anatolia from the second and first millenniums B.C. But, contrary to the title of the his study, Van Seters has restricted his investigation to just three Assyrian texts, one each from Sargon II, Esarhaddon, and Ashurbanipal from the very end of the eighth and the beginning of the seventh centuries. Van Seters's approach is not new. Twenty years ago Moshe Weinfeld used first-millennium Assyrian texts in precisely the same, selective manner to find support for a seventh-century date for D.[11] While the sources Van Seters cites nicely support his dating of the Deuteronomistic history to that period, he ignores Middle-Assyrian military texts, which Jeffrey Niehaus, in response to Weinfeld, has shown are the literary prototypes to those of the first millennium.[12] Furthermore, Van Seters has over-

5. W. F. Albright, "Archaeology and the Date of the Hebrew Conquest of Palestine," *BASOR* 58 (1935) 10.

6. G. E. Wright, *Biblical Archaeology* (Philadelphia: Westminster, 1962) 80–81. This interpretation of the evidence from Beitîn is upheld by Kelso, who directed the excavations there in 1954, 1957, and 1960; cf. W. F. Albright and James L. Kelso, *The Excavations of Bethel (1934–1960)* (AASOR 39; Cambridge, Mass.: American Schools of Oriental Research, 1968) 30–31.

7. I. Finkelstein, *The Archaeology of the Israelite Settlement* (Jerusalem: Israel Exploration Society, 1988).

8. W. G. Dever, " 'Hyksos,' Egyptian Destructions, and the End of the Palestinian Middle Bronze Age," *Levant* 22 (1990) 79 n.3.

9. K. L. Younger, Jr., *Ancient Conquest Accounts: A Study in Ancient Near Eastern and Biblical History Writing* (JSOTSup 98; Sheffield: JSOT Press, 1990) 226–28.

10. Van Seters, "Joshua's Campaign," 6–12.

11. M. Weinfeld, *Deuteronomy and the Deuteronomic School* (Oxford: Clarendon, 1972; repr. Winona Lake, Ind.: Eisenbrauns, 1992). Surprisingly, this work is not cited by Van Seters.

12. J. Niehaus, "Joshua and Ancient Near Eastern Warfare," *JETS* 31 (1988) 37–50.

looked Egyptian military inscriptions,[13] about which much has been written in recent years (see below).

I turn now to Josh 10:28–42 to show how recent Old Testament scholarship has interpreted it. Max Miller and Gene Tucker rightly described the passage as being "quite different from any which has preceded it in the book of Joshua."[14] It is made up of short, terse, stereotyped statements that recur throughout the section describing the conquest of Makkedah, Libnah, Lachish, Eglon, Hebron, and Debir, all in southern Canaan. J. Alberto Soggin,[15] as well as Miller and Tucker[16] and most recently Trent Butler,[17] believe an itinerary of some sort was behind this section. Numbers 33 contains a toponym list of Israel's travels with Moses from Egypt to Moab, and it is recognized on form-critical grounds to be an itinerary.[18] A comparison of Numbers 33, a genuine itinerary, with Joshua 10 shows little resemblance between the two. If an itinerary lay behind Josh 10:28–42, it has been embellished to such an extent that its original character is no longer discernible. This makes the suggestion that an itinerary is the source behind this segment of Joshua questionable.

Robert G. Boling claims that the narrative of "Joshua 2–11 seems to be drawn from older sources, related to those in Genesis, Exodus and Numbers"[19] but offers no specific suggestion. Surely there is theological significance to this anomalous unit, but John Hamlin's assertion that the stereotyped expressions are a "theological kind of writing, rather than factual reporting"[20] is simply not consistent with other known Near Eastern forms of military recording.[21] Younger's syntagmic analysis of Josh 10:28–42 and 11:11–14 is not unlike my own, reached independently more than fifteen years earlier, but never published.

---

13. Years ago I pointed out Van Seters's tendency to do this in his *Abraham in History and Tradition* (New Haven, Conn.: Yale University Press, 1975) in "Tents in Egypt and the Ancient Near East," *SSEA Newsletter* 7/3 (1977) 13–28.

14. J. M. Miller and G. Tucker, *The Book of Joshua* (CBC; Cambridge: Cambridge University Press, 1974) 88.

15. J. A. Soggin, *Joshua: A Commentary* (OTL; Philadelphia: Westminster, 1972) 131.

16. Miller and Tucker, *Joshua*, 88.

17. T. Butler, *Joshua* (WBC 7; Waco, Tex.: Word, 1983) 113.

18. G. W. Coats, "The Wilderness Itinerary," *CBQ* 34 (1972) 135–52; G. I. Davies, "The Wilderness Itineraries: A Comparative Study," *TynBul* 25 (1974) 46–81; idem, *The Way of the Wilderness* (SOTSM 5; Cambridge: Cambridge University Press, 1979); J. T. Walsh, "From Egypt to Moab: A Source Critical Analysis of the Wilderness Itinerary," *CBQ* 39 (1977) 20–33.

19. R. G. Boling, *Joshua: A New Translation with Introduction and Commentary* (AB 6; Garden City, N.Y.: Doubleday, 1982) 56.

20. J. Hamlin, *Joshua: Inheriting the Land* (ITC; Grand Rapids, Mich.: Eerdmans, 1983).

21. A point also made by Younger, *Ancient Conquest Accounts*, 261.

The following themes or expressions are repeatedly used throughout the narrative:

1. Departure of Joshua from conquered city
2. All Israel with him
3. Arrival at next city
4. Brief description of the military encounter with the city (siege, assault, take)
5. Yʜwʜ gives the town and its king into the hand of Israel
6. An attempt is made to date the campaign or its duration
7. Smiting city, its king, and people with the sword
8. Description of the extent of the destruction of the population
9. Comparing the present destruction (and the execution of its king) with a previous victory, usually the immediately preceding one.
10. An additional note about the campaign
11. Taking of booty

Younger isolates eight episodes comprised of eleven syntagms.[22] I too have isolated eleven recurring statements; however, I see only seven reports or entries, as the following chart illustrates.

	Makkedah 28	Libnah 29–30	Lachish 31–33	Eglon 34–35	Hebron 36–37	Debir 38–39	Hazor 11:10–14
1		O	O	O	O	O	?
2		O	O	O	O	O	
3		O	O	O	O	O	O
4	O	O	O	O	O	O	O
5		O	O				O
6	O		O	O			
7	O	O	O	O	O	O	O
8	O	O	O	O	O	O	O
9	O	O	O	O	O	O	
10			O			O	O
11							O

While Younger treats 10:33, which reports that the king of Gezer aided Lachish, as a separate pericope, I have included it with the Lachish episode of 10:31–32, which accounts for the seven reports I see. Younger isolates 10:40–42 as a summary statement concerning the foregoing conquest reports. While it does share some features with the preceding passage, it likely constitutes a separate pericope with a slightly different

22. Ibid., 226.

form. Further, I consider 11:10–14, the Hazor campaign, to have the same form as do the units in 10:28–39. Younger treats it separately. Beyond these differences, our observations are strikingly similar. Having recognized that there is a significant difference between the literary character of Josh 6:1–10:27 and that of 10:28–42 and 11:10–14, I wish to suggest what may be behind this different material. Younger's review of the recent treatment of Egyptian historiography, especially the studies of Anthony Spalinger and Donald Redford, along with some of the literary characteristics found in Egyptian military literature, is a helpful contribution to the current debate about the nature of the Joshua material. Here I would like to take the comparison of the Egyptian material a step further and suggest that an Egyptian scribal tradition may well have influenced the composition of Joshua 1–11.

Spalinger's several articles and his dissertation[23] are the first serious works on the forms and sources used to make up the Annals of Thutmose III since an article by Noth in 1943 and a small chapter in Hermann Grapow's 1947 book.[24] Spalinger believes that there were several sources behind the composition of the *annals,* the *daybook* and the *scribal war dairy* being the main ones. He believes that the scribal war diary was compiled by military scribes who accompanied the king on campaigns, reporting the "personal involvement" of the monarch in detail.[25] Redford rejects this suggestion because reference to a "daybook of the army" or "warfare" is not attested in Egyptian texts.[26]

Grapow demonstrated that the "daybook style" (*Tagebuchstil*) can be found as early as Pap. Bulaq 18 from the Thirteenth Dynasty, and vestiges are present in Pap. Anastasi III from the late Nineteenth Dynasty.[27] The *Tagebuchstil* is characterized by the use of bare infinitives and was by no means a literary composition. Daybooks have survived from a variety of periods and come from as early as the Twelfth-Dynasty Kahun Papyri.[28] Daybooks are more like the log of a ship than a flowing narrative,

---

23. Spalinger, "Some Notes on the Battle of Megiddo and Reflections on Egyptian Military Writing," *MDAIK* 30 (1974) 221–29; "A Critical Analysis of the 'Annals' of Thutmose III (*Stücke* V–VI)," *JARCE* 14 (1977) 41–54; the dissertation was published as *Aspects of the Military Documents of the Ancient Egyptians* (YNES 9; New Haven, Conn.: Yale University Press, 1982).

24. Noth, "Die Annalen Thutmose III. als Geschichtsquelle," *ZDPV* 66 (1943) 156–74; H. Grapow, *Studien zu den Annalen Thutmosis des Dritten und zu ihnen verwandten historischen Berichten des Neuen Reiches* (Berlin: 1947).

25. Spalinger, *Aspects of Military Documents,* 120–21.

26. Redford, *Pharaonic King-Lists, Annals and Day-Books: A Contribution to the Study of the Egyptian Sense of History* (Mississauga, Ont.: Benben, 1986) 122.

27. Grapow, *Studien,* 50–53.

28. Redford, *Pharaonic King-Lists,* 103. El-Lahun, of which Kahun was a part, was founded by Senusert II (ca. 1868–1862 B.C.), and the papyri would date from his time or

recording day-to-day accounts, comprised of repetitive entries and little variation. Redford has collected sixteen examples of what he believes are daybooks. The surviving daybooks include those concerned with tax records; the records of movement of Egyptian patrols in Nubia (the Semna Dispatches); the Daybook of the King's House of Sobekhotpe III(?), which records withdrawals and requisitions of food from the king's household;[29] a ship's log (Pap. Leiden I); and the Daybook of an Official from Egypt's eastern frontier.[30] The last example, from Pap. Anastasi III (verso 1ff.), is described by Redford as having a "rather rigid" format, beginning with the regnal year, a statement announcing the departure to and the arrival (*spr*) in Asia, and the 'coming' (*iit*) from Asia. These are followed by the name of the messenger and those who accompanied him (optional) and the number of letters he bears, including the names of the addressees.[31] A similar pattern can be seen in the entries for some of Thutmose III's lesser campaigns, such as in year 30 (ca. 1449 B.C.), the sixth campaign. This entry is structured as follows:[32]

1. Introduction (*Urk.* IV, 689.3–5):
   "Regnal year 30. Now his majesty was in the foreign land of Retenu on the 6th campaign of victory of his majesty."
2. The daybook summary (*Urk.* IV, 689.7–10, 12–15):
   "Arriving (*spr*) at the city of Kadesh, destroying it (*ski.s*),[33] felling its trees, and cutting its barley. Proceeding from *Ššryt*, arriving (*spr*) at the city of *Ḏȝmr*, arriving (*spr*) at the city of *Irttw*, doing likewise against it."
3. List of Tribute (*Urk.* IV, 689.17–690.10):
   ". . . male and female servants 181, horses 188, and so on."

---

or later in that dynasty. All Egyptian dates for the Middle through New Kingdom cited here follow the chronology of K. A. Kitchen, as proposed in "The Basics of Egyptian Chronology in Relation to the Bronze Age" and "Supplementary Notes on the The Basics of Egyptian Chronology," in *High, Middle or Low? Acts of an International Colloquium on Absolute Chronology in Gothenburg 20th–22nd August 1987*, part 1 (ed. Paul Åström; Studies in Mediterranean Archaeology and Literature 56; Gothenburg: Åström, 1987) 37–55. I have seen the second article from part 2, but only in the form of Prof. Kitchen's typescript, which he was kind enough to give me prior to its publication.

29. Sobekhotpe III reigned during the Thirteenth Dynasty, probably in the eighteenth century.

30. Redford, *Pharaonic King-Lists*, 103–21.

31. Ibid., 117.

32. The three-part outline presented here follows that of Spalinger, "Critical Analysis," 45. The translation, as with all other Egyptian texts, are my own, unless otherwise specified.

33. For a discussion of the significance of this word, see Hoffmeier, "Reconsidering Egypt's Part in the Termination of the Middle Bronze Age in Palestine," *Levant* 21 (1989) 183–84.

The introductory formula is used to begin each campaign in the annals, with little variation. The word *spr*, a regular feature in the daybooks, occurs repeatedly in the Annals, three times in the short entry for year 30.[34] It is used not only to announce the arrival of the king or Egyptian armies at the destination but also the safe return to Egypt.[35]

While the Joshua accounts do not number the campaigns or date them by regnal years, a similarity between the daybook summary and the entries of Josh 10:28–39 is striking indeed. A reading of Josh 10:29–30 illustrates the point:

> Then Joshua passed on from Makkedah, and all Israel with him, to Libnah, and fought against Libnah; and the Lord gave it also and its king into the hand of Israel; and he smote it with the edge of the sword, and every person in it; he left none remaining in it; and he did to its king as he had done to the king of Jericho (RSV).

The Libnah report, like the others in 10:28–42 and 11:10–14, contains terse, stereotyped expressions that are repeated frequently. The reports in Joshua 10 do not usually mention the taking of booty, a regular component of the brief Egyptian annal report. However, booty is mentioned in connection with the capture of Hazor (Josh 11:14).

The very brief report of year 30 in the Annals, 11 lines of text that take up a page and a half in Sethe's *Urk.* IV (689–90), contrasts with the lengthy report of the first campaign launched against the rebellious coalition at Megiddo. The latter occupies no less than 110 lines at Karnak, or 25 pages in *Urk.* IV (647–72). How do we account for the disproportionate amount of space given to one as compared with the other, not to mention the differences in style?

According to Redford,[36] a special document lay behind the first campaign because of its importance, and the primary source behind the remainder of the Annals was the Daybook [*hrwyt*] of the King's Palace, as witnessed by the statement toward the end of the report of the Megiddo campaign, which reads:

> All that his majesty did to this city and to that vile foe and his vile army were recorded on (its) day, by its name, by the name of the expedition, and by the names of the commanders of the troops. [. . .] They are recorded on a leather scroll in the temple of Amun to this day.[37]

---

34. For other occurrences see *Urk.* IV, 695.5; 696.17; 698.17; 710.3; 729.12, 15; 730.8.
35. *Urk.* IV, 695.5; 701.16.
36. Redford, *Pharaonic King-Lists*, 124–25.
37. *Urk.* IV, 661.14–662.6.

The theory that military records of campaigns were kept is further supported by the claim of the military scribe Tjaneny:

> I saw the victories of the king which he made over every foreign land.
> . . . It was I who recorded the victories which he achieved over all foreign lands, it being put into writing according to what was done.[38]

Redford concludes that the Daybook of the Palace, in combination with a unique document recording the first campaign, stand behind the Annals, rather than a War Diary plus a daybook, as Spalinger avers. He observes that the booty and tribute lists fit the daybook tradition and do not constitute a separate source, as Grapow and Noth had supposed.[39] The Daybook of the King's House of Sobekhotpe III illustrates this point. Lists of withdrawals or requisitions for certain temples or to the royal harem are recorded in this daybook, including incense, bread, fruit, and wine, not to mention *inw* (gifts, benevolences or tribute) from the South.[40]

Since elements of the daybook style are evident in the lengthy Megiddo campaign report, one wonders if the document in question was not just an expanded and embellished daybook. Regardless of whether Redford or Spalinger is correct regarding the exact nature of the sources behind Thutmose III's Annals, it is clear that both longer, well-developed narratives were used to describe some campaigns, as well as brief statements for others. The presence of the short statements in the Annals is due in part to the established, log-like tradition of the daybook. On the other hand, in a military setting, the scribe "had to record events as quickly as they occurred," notes Spalinger.[41] Further, he suggests, the short, terse reports recorded less important events, while the more "smoothly written narrative" was reserved "for the more detailed ones."[42] Thus it might be argued that the importance of a particular campaign was a factor in how much space was allotted to the report. The first campaign (Megiddo) and the Euphrates sortie (the eighth campaign) received considerably more coverage than the others. The first, being the longest of all, was evidently perceived in the Annals as the military highlight of Thutmose's career.[43]

---

38. *Urk.* IV, 1004.4, 9–10.
39. Redford, *Pharaonic King-Lists*, 124–25.
40. Ibid., 107–9.
41. Spalinger, *Aspects of Military Documents*, 123.
42. Spalinger, "Critical Analysis," 14, 46–47.
43. If one judges simply by the space allotted to the Megiddo campaign, as compared with the eighth campaign against Mitanni, Megiddo receives more coverage in the annals. Certainly R. O. Faulkner ("The Euphrates Campaign of Tuthmosis III," *JEA* 32 [1946] 39–42) is not wrong in seeing the eighth campaign as the military zenith of

A similar combination of reports exists in the Joshua 1–11 narratives:

1. The entry into Canaan and campaign against Jericho, Joshua's first military action in Canaan, receives the most detailed treatment (Joshua 1–6).
2. A lengthy report follows on the setback at Ai, followed by its defeat (Josh 7:1–8:28).
3. The report on Gibeon receives detailed treatment (Josh 10:1–11:14), perhaps owing to the uniqueness of the treaty made between Israel and the Hivites and Israel's defense of her vassal, undoubtedly a condition of the treaty, and because of the hailstorm, considered an act of divine intervention (Josh 10:11).
4. The entries on the campaigns against other southern Canaanite cities (Makkedah, Libnah, Lachish, Eglon, Hebron, and Debir) are very brief, daybook-like (Josh 10:28–39).
5. The campaign against Hazor (Josh 11:1–15), though short when compared with the Jericho and Ai narratives, is about as long as the combined reports in the previous section (Josh 10:28–39). Hazor is recognized by archaeologists as having been the dominant city in the Galilee area,[44] a point acknowledged in Josh 10:10. That Hazor's defeat is highlighted in Joshua is understandable. Van Seters considers the combination of long and short reports, clearly seen here, to be an idiosyncracy characteristic of the first millennium because this kind of mixing is found in Assyrian military texts.[45] However, the same practice is also found in second-millennium Egyptian military records.

A further comparison between Thutmose III's and Joshua's first campaigns is called for. The chart on the next page illustrates some of the structural similarities between the two. Some might argue that these similarities are superficial and demonstrate no literary relationship between the two, and that may be the case. But the structural similarity cannot be dismissed out of hand. Minimally, the similarities illustrate that the Joshua narrative is no orphan when compared to a piece of Egyptian military writing and that whatever ideological concerns may have shaped the Joshua narratives, they remain comparable to their counterparts elsewhere in the second-millennium Near East. Consequently, the structural

---

Thutmose III's career. The Megiddo campaign was politically important for Thutmose, allowing him to prove that he was no longer in Hatshepsut's shadow, not to mention the significance attached to securing Canaan for Egypt.

44. Piotr Bienkowski, "The Role of Hazor in the Late Bronze Age," *PEQ* 119 (1987) 50–61; Y. Yadin, *Hazor* (The Schweich Lectures 1970; London: British Academy, 1972).

45. Van Seters, "Joshua's Campaign," 7.

Annals of Thutmose III	*Joshua 1–6*
1. Divine commission to conquer and the march to Palestine (*Urk.* IV 647.1–649.1)	1. Divine commission to conquer and the assurance of victory (Josh 1:1–28
2. Thutmose calls for a war counsel to receive an intelligence report (*Urk.* IV 649.3–652.11)	2. Joshua dispatches spies to bring an intelligence report on Jericho (Joshua 2)
3. The march through the Aruna Pass to Megiddo (*Urk.* IV 652.13–655.9)	3. The march through the Jordan River (Josh 3:1–4:18)
4. Setting up camp south of Megiddo and preparations for war (*Urk.* IV 655.12–656.16)	4. Setting up camp at Gilgal and preparations for holy war (Josh 4:19–6:5)
5. The battle and siege of Megiddo (*Urk.* IV 657.2–661.13)	5. The siege of Jericho (Josh 6:6–14)
6. The surrender of Megiddo and presentation of tribute to Thutmose (*Urk.* IV 662.8–663.2)	6. The fall of Jericho and booty dedicated to Yahweh (Josh 6:15–25)

similarities, as well as the parallels in content, invite further scholarly investigation.

Indeed, it is noteworthy that upon the surrender of Megiddo, Pharaoh administered an oath of loyalty to his vassals or perhaps granted a legal pardon for their crime,[46] according to the Gebel Barkal Stela.[47] On the other hand, Joshua uttered an oath, cursing any future builder of Jericho (Josh 6:26).

After the campaign against Ai, the Israelites undertook a ceremony at Mt. Ebal (Josh 8:30–35). Andrew Hill has, in my opinion, rightly identified this as a divine land grant ceremony, like the royal deeds of Mesopotamia.[48] Just as *kudurru*-stones were used in Babylon in connection with land grants,[49] Moses directed the erection of a stone on which the words of the covenant–land grant deed were to be written: "When you pass over to enter the land which the Lord your God gives you . . ." (Deut 27:2–8).

46. The suggestion that pharaoh granted a pardon, *contra* the traditional interpretation of this expression, has been made by Scott Morschauser, "The End of the *Sḏf(ꜣ)-Tr(yt)* 'Oath,'" *JARCE* 25 (1988) 93–103.

47. *Urk.* IV, 1235.16–17.

48. A. Hill, "The Ebal Ceremony as Hebrew Land Grant," *JETS* 31 (1988) 399–406.

49. Ibid., 401–2.

That Pharaoh took Canaan and its plunder as a result of a divine gift (*di* or *rdi*) of Re or Amun is seen on numerous occasions in the Annals.[50] The reason for the first campaign is given as follows:

> . . . in order to overthrow that vile enemy, in order to widen the borders of Egypt according to the command of his father, Amun-re [being . . .], and being victorious that he might seize (foreign lands).[51]

The Egyptian practice of erecting a stela to indicate Egypt's hegemony and to mark the border of a conquered territory is well attested in the literature, as well as from the presence of stelae or fragments found on foreign soil. The Semna Stela of Senusert III and its duplicate found on the nearby island of Uronarti mark Egypt's southern border in Nubia. The stelae claim that the territory he controlled in the second cataract had been 'granted to me' (*swḏt n.i*).[52] Thutmose III records that he erected a stela beside that of his grandfather, Thutmose I, on the east side of the Euphrates.[53] He also set up two stelae on the west side of the Euphrates[54] and one at Niy.[55] A number of Nineteenth-Dynasty stelae have been discovered in Palestine and Phoenicia: two at Beth-shean belonging to Seti I and Ramesses II and three at Nahr el-Kelb belonging to Ramesses II.[56] Thus, it appears that the practice of erecting an inscribed stone as a claim of ownership in connection with a military campaign as reported in Josh 8:32 finds many parallels in the Middle and New Kingdom periods.

Another feature found in Joshua 10 is the summary (10:40–42) of preceding events (10:28–39), which Younger documents as a literary device found in Assyrian and Egyptian sources, such as in Ramesses II's Kadesh inscription and Thutmose III's Armant stela.[57] The word *shwy* introduces summaries in Egyptian inscriptions, as it does on the Armant stela, which contains "a summary of the deeds of valor and victory which this good god achieved."[58] A summary (*shwy*) can also introduce a list of booty and/or tribute. Year 31 in the Annals reads, "A summary of the plunder of his majesty from this year."[59]

---

50. *Urk.* IV, 647.7–9; IV; 684.9; 685.11.

51. *Urk.* IV, 648.14–649.1.

52. K. Sethe, *Ägyptische Lesestücke* (Leipzig: Hinrichs, 1924) 83.22.

53. *Urk.* IV, 697.3–5.

54. *Urk.* IV, 1232.10–11; 1246.2.

55. *Urk.* IV, 698.15.

56. John A. Wilson, "Egyptian Historical Texts," *ANET,* 253, 255.

57. Younger, *Ancient Conquest Accounts,* 231–32, 252–53.

58. *Urk.* IV, 1244.15.

59. *Urk.* IV, 690.15.

At this point it is helpful to review the literary components found in Thutmose III's Annals that have parallels in Joshua 1–11. Both employ long narratives to describe the most important campaigns and short, terse reports of less-significant actions using repetitive, stereotyped language. The summary statement is attested in both, as well as references to the booty taken (Josh 8:27, 11:14). The plunder from Jericho was not to be taken, but was to be devoted to Yahweh (Josh 6:19). In the Egyptian text, because Amun appointed the king to march into battle, the booty was presented to him.[60]

How does one account for these similarities? My thesis is that the parallels shown here between Thutmose III's Annals and Joshua 1–11 may be attributed to the Hebrews' borrowing of the Egyptian daybook scribal tradition for recording military actions.[61] The connections between Israel and Egypt, from the sojourn tradition through the days of Solomon, are well established.[62] The influence of Egyptian writing on Syria–Palestine has been noted by Ronald Williams:

> Egyptian hieroglyphic inscriptions on a multitude of scarabs and stelae and statues [from the Levant] testify to Egyptian influence from early times. This should occasion no surprise, as the region formed part of the Egyptian Empire during the Eighteenth to Twentieth Dynasties, and long before this time was in close contact through trade relations.[63]

Furthermore, an Egyptian scribal tradition is now recognized in some of the Amarna letters originating in Canaan.[64] Therefore, it is not improbable that elements of the Egyptian *Tagebuchstil* should be discernible in the conquest narratives of Joshua. Drawing a comparison with Thutmose III's annals does not necessarily give a date for the Joshua narratives, since elements of this genre are found in Egypt in the Ramesside era, as well as

---

60. *Urk.* IV, 647.5–9; 684.9–17; 710.13–14; 734.13–16.

61. Additional parallels are adduced by Younger, *Ancient Conquest Accounts*, 165–94, 241–66.

62. J. K. Hoffmeier, "The Arm of God versus the Arm of Pharaoh in the Exodus Narratives," *Biblica* 67 (1986) 378–87; idem, "Egypt as an Arm of Flesh: A Prophetic Response," in *Israel's Apostasy and Restoration: Essays in Honor of Roland K. Harrison* (ed. A. Gileadi; Grand Rapids, Mich.: Baker, 1988) 79–95.

63. R. Williams, "Writing," *IBD* 4.911.

64. See E. Edel, *Der Brief des ägyptischen Wesirs Pasijara an den Hethiterkönig Hattusili und verwandte Keilschriftbriefe* (Nachrichten der Akademie der Wissenschaften in Göttingen 1, Phil-hist. Klasse Jahrgang no. 4; Göttingen: Akademie der Wissenschaften, 1978) 134–35; Zipora Cochavi-Rainey, "Egyptian Influence in the Akkadian Texts Written by Egyptian Scribes in the Fourteen and Thirteenth Centuries B.C.," *JNES* 49 (1990) 57–65; Richard S. Hess, "The Amarna Letters from Pharaoh: Their Role in Canaanite Scribal Tradition" (paper presented at the Society of Biblical Literature Annual meeting in New Orleans, La., November 19, 1990; publication forthcoming); idem, "Rhetorical Forms in EA 162," *UF* 22 (1990) 137–48; see also Hoffmeier, "Arm of God," 384–86.

in the military documents of the Twenty-Fifth Dynasty.[65] However, the late period, it must be recalled, was one of literary and artistic renaissance, and thus the occurrences of the annals genre in the eighth and seventh centuries in Egypt likely represent archaisms.

To limit one's study of literary parallels to one geographical region (Assyria) and restrict the time period of the sources to only the first millennium B.C., as Weinfeld and Van Seters have done, is to select evidence that fits one's assumptions, namely, that DtrH is from the seventh century. By contrast, Younger provides a comprehensive investigation of military writings from around the Near East that spans both the first and second millennia. His investigation shows that if there is any literary influence on the Hebrew writer of Joshua it could just as likely have come in the second millennium. Van Seters rightly says of the DtrH, "His historiographic method is to write past history in the form and style of contemporary historical texts."[66] The question is: which "contemporary historical texts" influenced DtrH?

Van Seters considers data that first-millennium Assyrian kings received oracles encouraging them before a military campaign to be compelling evidence in favor of a first-millennium date for DtrH.[67] However, Niehaus has demonstrated that pre-campaign oracles are also attested in second-millennium Assyrian texts.[68]

Based on just two references to Assyrian monarchs who crossed a river during flood stage in the spring of the year, Van Seters is prepared to identify the theme as an Assyrian topos utilized by DtrH when composing the crossing of the Jordan episode by the Israelites.[69] It should be recalled that spring was the time when kings in the Near East went to battle. This tradition is reflected in 2 Sam 11:1, which states, "In the spring of the year, the time when kings go forth to battle. . . ."[70] On this point Robert Gordon has said, "Spring was the time for launching military campaigns, when the winter rains had stopped and the male population was not yet involved in harvesting."[71] One of the inscriptions cited

---

65. Spalinger, *Aspects*, 126–27.

66. Van Seters, "Joshua's Campaign of Canaan," 11–12.

67. Ibid., 7.

68. Niehaus, "Joshua and Ancient Near Eastern Warfare," 37–42; see also his contribution to this volume, "The Warrior and His God: The Covenant Foundation of History and Historiography" (pp. 299–312).

69. Van Seters, "Joshua's Campaign," 6–7.

70. One recognizes that "the spring of the year" (RSV) literally reads "the turn of the year," which most commentators acknowledge refers to the spring. Cf. P. K. McCarter, *II Samuel* (AB 9; Garden City, N.Y.: Doubleday, 1984) 284–85; A. A. Anderson, *2 Samuel* (WBC 11; Dallas: Word, 1989) 152–53; Robert Gordon, *1 & 2 Samuel: A Commentary* (Grand Rapids, Mich.: Zondervan, 1986) 252.

71. Gordon, *I & II Samuel*, 252.

by Van Seters, that of Sargon II, specifically places the crossing of the Tigris and Euphrates "at the highest flood, the high water of the spring of the year."[72] Similarly, Josh 3:15 reports, "The Jordan overflows all its banks throughout the time of harvest." The spring (grain) harvest in Canaan had just occurred: the people ate the grain of the land in connection with the Feast of Unleavened Bread after arriving in Canaan (Josh 5:10–12).

In reaching his conclusion, Van Seters fails to mention that the motif of the warring king crossing a raging river is attested in sources of the second millennium B.C. In his major study of Hittite historiography published in 1980,[73] Harry Hoffner discussed a reference to the crossing of the Euphrates " 'on foot' (i.e., over a bridge)" by Hattusili I (ca. 1650). Van Seters knew about this text, for he discusses it in *In Search of History*[74] but apparently chose to ignore it as a parallel to both the Neo-Assyrian texts and DtrH. What is noteworthy about Hattusili's statement is his claim to be emulating the earlier feat of Sargon the Great (ca. 2371–2316 B.C.).[75] Since the earliest Neo-Assyrian reference to the monarch crossing the river is that of Sargon II, it appears that he was trying to live up to standard of his namesake, Sargon of Akkad.[76] The fact that centuries later, in the second millennium B.C., Hattusili I could liken himself to the great Sargon, which in turn is echoed nearly a millennium later by the Assyrian Sargon, demonstrates both the tendency to repeat achievements of past heroes and the durability of the literary motifs used to described them.[77] Furthermore, the fact that military campaigns were launched during the spring in Canaan and Mesopotamia, when rivers were at flood stage, was a seasonal reality with which ancient armies had to cope, not a literary convention to be dismissed as being historically insignificant.

---

72. Luckenbill, *ARAB* II, §195.

73. H. Hoffner, "Histories and Historians of the Ancient Near East: The Hittites," *Or* 49 (1980) 294–95, 297. On the question of the historicity of this boast, see H. M. Wolf, "The Historical Reliability of the Hittite Annals," in this volume, pp. 159–64.

74. Van Seters, *In Search of History: Historiography in the Ancient World and the Origins of Biblical History* (New Haven, Conn.: Yale University Press, 1983) 107–8.

75. *KBo* X 2 iii 29–31; Hoffner, "Histories and Historians," 297.

76. On Sargon the Great as an exemplar for later generations of kings, cf. Brian Lewis, *The Sargon Legend: A Study of the Akkadian Text and the Tale of the Hero Who Was Exposed at Birth* (ASOR Dissertation Series 4; Cambridge, Mass.: American Schools of Oriental Research, 1980) 109–10; Sidney Smith, "Esarhaddon and Sennacherib," *CAH* 3.46.

77. This is especially true in Egypt of military and athletic motifs. Cf. J. K. Hoffmeier, "Hunting Desert Game with the Bow: A Brief Examination," *SSEA Newsletter* 6/2 (1975) 8–13; idem, "Comments on an Unusual Hunt Scene from the New Kingdom," *Journal of the Society for the Study of Egyptian Antiquities* 10 (1980) 195–200; idem, "Arm of God," 278–87.

Most of the other observations made by Van Seters for connecting DtrH with Assyrian military writing of the first millennium, such as the humiliating of captured kings (see Josh 10:22–27) and the spreading of the fame and terror of the victorious monarch, resulting in the downfall or submission of enemy states, is documented by Niehaus as occurring as early as Middle Assyrian texts.[78] In addition, the idea of a king's fame and terror overwhelming his enemies in battle is ubiquitous in inscriptions of the Empire period in Egypt, as I pointed out some years ago.[79] A few examples suffice for the present study.

Of Ahmose it is said, "His battle cry is in the lands of Fenkhu, his majesty's fear (*snḏ*) is within this land like Min when he comes."[80] Thutmose I claims of the deity, "You have made strong [my] awe (*šfšft*) [in their bodies] [my] battle cry [is throughout] their lands."[81] The following boast is made of Thutmose II, "Fear (*snḏ*) of him is throughout the land, his awe (*šfšft*) is in the Islands of the Aegean."[82] Of Thutmose III it is said: "You [the god Dedun] create his (the king's) awe (*šfšft*) in the hearts of tribesmen and bedouin." Once again, it is clear that what Van Seters believes to be a motif found in Neo-Assyrian texts and Joshua is also well documented much earlier than the Neo-Assyrian sources, in the second millennium.

Van Seters, like Weinfeld before him, fails to show a *unique* connection between the Joshua narratives and first-millennium Assyrian texts. Neither of these scholars even considers Egyptian military writings in his comparative study or investigates second-millennium Assyrian or Hittite sources. This essay and the works of Niehaus and Younger show that second-millennium texts cannot be excluded from the corpus of sources if true comparative literary analysis is to be achieved.

Based on the Egyptian evidence presented here, the New Kingdom period, when Israel would most likely have departed from Egypt and entered Canaan, proves to be the most likely time for the Egyptian daybook scribal tradition to have been embraced by Israelite scribes and thus to leave its mark on the composition of Joshua 1–11.

78. Niehaus, "Joshua and Ancient Near Eastern Warfare," 42–45.
79. J. K. Hoffmeier, "Some Egyptian Motifs Related to Enemies and Warfare and Their Old Testament Counterparts," *Egyptological Miscellanies: A Tribute to Professor Ronald J. Williams* (ed. J. K. Hoffmeier and E. S. Meltzer; Ancient World 6; Chicago: Ares, 1983) 53–70.
80. *Urk.* IV, 18.6–7.
81. *Urk.* IV, 272.1–2.
82. *Urk.* IV, 138.1–4.

Joshua 10:12–15 and Mesopotamian Celestial Omen Texts

John H. Walton
Moody Bible Institute

In Joshua 10 the coalition of Amorite cities in southern Palestine decided to attack the fortified town of Gibeon. The people from Gibeon
had recently made a treaty with the Israelites that the Amorites considered
an act of treachery. The proposed strike was probably punitive as well as
being an attempt to prevent the Israelites from having access to this stra-
tegically located, fortified city. When Joshua received word that Gibeon
was under siege, he gathered the Israelites for an all-night forced march in
order to execute a surprise, lightning strike on the attacking Amorites.
The fifteen-mile march taxed the endurance of his soldiers, and they lost
a night's sleep. Joshua was desperate for divine intervention, and his dar-
ing prayer, along with its results, is recorded in vv. 12–15.

The nature of Joshua's request has been interpreted in a number of
different ways. The earliest interpretation is represented in the Wisdom
of Sirach. Speaking of Joshua's accomplishments, he says: "Was not the
sun stayed by his hand, and one day increased to two?" (Sir 46:4). The
same perspective is expressed by Josephus: "Moreover it happened that
the day was lengthened, that the night might not come on too soon, and
be an obstruction to the zeal of the Hebrews in pursuing their enemies"
(*Ant.* 5.1.17). The belief that the length of the day was actually increased
(presumably by the slowing of the earth's rotation) was maintained
throughout history, being affirmed by the Septuagint translators, Augustine, Jerome, Calvin, and Luther.[1] The Jewish rabbinic writers likewise

---

1. Augustine, *City of God*, 21.8; Jerome, *Against Jovinianus*, 2.15, and in the Vulgate
translation; Calvin, *Commentary on Joshua* (Grand Rapids, Eerdmans, repr. 1949) 154: the
sun was on the western horizon and was prevented from setting; Luther, *Commentary on
Habakkuk* (Luther's Works, ed. H. C. Oswald; St. Louis: Concordia, 1974) 3.

agreed (see *b. Sukk.* 28a), though Maimonides argued for the interpretation that the day merely appeared to be longer.[2] Apparently, alternate interpretations did not become prevalent until the nineteenth century.
C. F. Keil, a conservative, provided an early alternative explanation: because of the lack of ability of the Israelites to measure the length of the
day, he concluded that the day appeared to be longer because of all that
they were able to accomplish.[3] In the twentieth century, another theory
that has been proposed is that the heat of the sun was diminished in order for the Israelites be able to accomplish their task.[4]

Undoubtedly, some modern interpreters have found the traditional
view unacceptable on scientific grounds. Either their presuppositions rule
out the supernatural altogether, or they find the magnitude of such a miracle beyond comprehension and unnecessary to explain the victory recorded in the text. Yet even for some conservatives, such as Keil, the details
of the text suggest that the traditional interpretation is also inadequate.

In this regard there are two observations that need to be made concerning the details of the text. The first was made as early as Keil and has
been reaffirmed by numerous commentators after him, though it had
been overlooked by such careful exegetes as Calvin. The text clearly
identifies the sun as being over Gibeon and the moon as being over the
valley of Aijalon. This description places the sun in the east and the
moon in the west, thus indicating that the prayer was made in the morning.[5] In the traditional interpretation, it is assumed that dusk was approaching, and Joshua wanted to be able to keep the momentum that his
army had gained. He thus would have desired extended light. This logic
is lost if the prayer was made in the morning. An interpreter would have
to ask why Joshua was requesting an extension of daylight if it was still
midmorning at the latest. This interpretation suggests that he was not
asking for extended daylight at all.

A second observation concerns the narrator's comment about the day
in v. 14. Though the day is identified as unique in history, the reason
given for its uniqueness is not an astronomical phenomenon. Rather, the
day is unique because God listens to the voice of a man and fights for Israel. What does this mean? Certainly God had orchestrated supernatural

2. Maimonides, *Guide for the Perplexed*, chap. 35.

3. C. F. Keil, *Joshua* (1863; repr. Grand Rapids: Eerdmans, 1950) 110.

4. For a brief summary of the views and their supporters see John Holladay, "The
Day(s) the Moon Stood Still," *JBL* 87 (1968) 166. See also K. Lawson Younger, Jr., *An-
cient Conquest Accounts: A Study in Ancient Near Eastern History Writing* (JSOTSup 98;
Sheffield: JSOT Press, 1990) 212–20.

5. Keil, *Joshua*, 108–9. Substantiation by Holladay, "Day(s) the Moon Stood Still,"
170 n. 16.

interventions in the past. The text, however, points out that the human initiation of the petition for God's intervention is the unique element. Never before had a person presumed to state what sort of supernatural strategy he wanted God to perpetrate on behalf of Israel. God granted Joshua the privilege of taking the initiative in devising the strategy. This is what the narrator identifies as the singular distinguishing feature of the day. As a result, the reader is not obliged to interpret the behavior of the sun and moon as being uniquely miraculous.

One must return to the text, then, to discover what its language and logic suggest Joshua intended when he addressed the sun and moon. If it was still morning, what could Joshua have had in mind? How could the sun and moon have any impact on the outcome of the battle?

One source of information concerning the importance of the sun and moon for battle is celestial omen texts from Mesopotamia.[6] Examination of these texts reveals significant relationship between the movements of the sun and the moon and military activity. Ancient societies used a lunar calendar, periodically adjusted to the solar year by the addition of an extra month. The beginning of a month was calculated by the first appearance of the new moon. The most important calculation, however, came in the middle of the month, at the full-moon phase. The first day of the full moon was identified by the fact that the moon set just minutes after sunrise. Consequently, for a few minutes the moon and sun were both fully visible on opposite horizons (the moon in the west and the sun in the east). Ideally, the first day of the full moon fell on the 14th of the month. This was a good sign because it indicated that the ancients' calculations were accurate, that the month would be the proper length, and that the new crescent would be seen on the 30th day. Consequently, one of the omens reads:

> When the moon and sun are seen with one another on the 14th, there will be silence, the land will be satisfied; the gods intend Akkad for happiness. Joy in the heart of the people. The cattle of Akkad will lie down securely in the pasture-places.[7]

---

6. Publication of these texts may be found in R. Campbell Thompson, *Reports of the Magicians and Astrologers of Nineveh and Babylon* (London: Luzac, 1900), with additional texts in L. Waterman, *Royal Correspondence of the Assyrian Empire* (Ann Arbor: University of Michigan Press, 1930–36), vol. 4. Some of Thompson's texts have been republished by S. Parpola, *Letters from Assyrian Scholars to the Kings Esarhaddon and Assurbanipal* (AOAT 5/1; Neukirchen-Vluyn: Neukirchener Verlag, 1970); too late for this article, all of these texts have been republished by Herman Hunger, *Astrological Reports to Assyrian Kings* (State Archives of Assyria 8; Helsinki: University of Helsinki Press, 1992).

7. Thompson, *Reports of the Magicians*, 124:6–9.

On the other hand, when the opposition of moon and sun took place on one of the other days or weather conditions limited the ability to see when the opposition took place, it was considered a bad omen. For instance:

> When the moon and sun are seen with each other on the 15th day a powerful enemy will raise his weapons against the land. The enemy will destroy the gate of my city.[8]

In the ancient Near East, great significance was attached to omens. If an army was going into battle, the omens would be consulted to see what they portended for the day. In the midsection of the month, the celestial omens were undoubtedly considered key indicators of the day on which battle should be joined. One can see, then, that the movement of the sun and moon potentially played a significant role in time of war, especially when a battle was to be enjoined in the middle of the month. The fact that Joshua 10 indicates that the sun is in the east and the moon in the west suggests that it is indeed the middle of the month. It is at the time of the full moon that this positioning occurs.

The terminology encountered in the celestial omens helps to clarify further the situation in Joshua 10. The verb 'to wait' (Akk. $qu^{\prime\prime}\hat{u}$) is used in the texts to describe whether the sun and moon are seen together or not. If the moon does not 'wait' for the sun, it means that the moon sets before the sun rises. For example:

> When the moon does not wait for the sun and disappears, there will be raging of lions and wolves. It was seen with the sun on the 15th.[9]

Some texts express the same idea with a slightly different wording. Rather than saying that the moon does not wait for the sun, they portray *both* the sun and the moon as waiting, so that they are not seen together.

> When the moon and sun do not wait, but disappear, there will be raging of lions and wolves. It was seen with the sun on the 15th.[10]

The language of these texts demonstrates that the logic of coordinated movements of these heavenly bodies is not a major factor in the terminology. In addition to the verb 'to wait', another common verb in the omens is the verb 'to stand' (Akk. *izzuzu*). This verb generally conveys the visibility of one body in the sky, often relative to another body. When the moon 'stands', however, it is related to its 'course'. For in-

---

8. Ibid., 161:1–4.
9. Ibid., 140:1–3; cf. 153:1; 156:4; 158A:4.
10. Ibid., 160:1–3; cf. 157D:6; 159:5; 161:9–10; 171:1–3.

stance, when the moon is said to 'stand', it may mean that it does not move low enough on the horizon for the opposition to occur that would indicate the beginning of the full moon. This constitutes a negative omen on the 14th, when it is hoped that the two will "be seen together."

> When the moon stands in its course, the market will be low. On the 15th it was seen with the sun.[11]

The three most frequent observations, then, are:

1. The moon (and sun) does not wait, indicating that the moon disappears over the horizon before the sun rises. This occurs on the days before opposition takes place.
2. The moon and sun are seen together, indicating that they have appeared in opposition on their respective horizons on the first day of the full moon. This could also be expressed by the moon's 'standing' or 'waiting'.
3. The moon stands, indicating that it is not on the horizon but further up in the sky when the sun rises. This would occur on the days after the opposition took place.

The significance of this type of terminology is further confirmed in the canonical omen series known as Enūma Anu Enlil. In this 70-tablet series, lunar omens make up the first 22 tablets. Most extant texts of the series date to the Neo-Assyrian period (Assurbanipal's library), but fragments are available from as early as the Old Babylonian period and are geographically well dispersed.[12] F. Rochberg-Halton summarizes the use of the terminology pertinent to this study:

> In a lunar omen commentary the variation in the day of opposition is expressed in terms of the moon's velocity in its course, i.e., if it was slowed, opposition occurred early, or if accelerated, opposition occurred late.[13]

The text she refers to is 3:44–46:

> If the moon is slowed down (*ut-taḫ-ḫa-as*) in its course . . . it is seen with the sun on the 13th day; if the moon is steady (*ne-eḫ*) in its course . . . it

---

11. Ibid., 153:7–8; cf. 161:7–8; 37:r.3.
12. Publication of Enūma Anu Enlil is still quite limited. See C. Virolleaud, *L'Astrologie chaldéenne: Le Livre intitulé "Enuma (Anu) Bel"* (Paris: Geuthner 1905–12), E. Weidner, "Die astrologische Serie Enuma Anu Enlil," *AfO* 14 (1941–44) 172–95, 308–18; and F. Rochberg-Halton, *Aspects of Babylonian Celestial Divination: The Lunar Eclipse Tablets of Enuma Anu Enlil* (AfO Beiheft 22; Horn, Austria: Berger, 1988).
13. Rochberg-Halton, *Aspects of Babylonian Celestial Divination*, 39.

is seen with the sun on the 14th day; If the moon is sped up (*e-zi*) in its course . . . it is seen with the sun on the 15th day.[14]

Apart from the texts indicating the movements of the heavenly bodies in relation to the first day of the full moon in the middle of the month, there are others that discuss the first appearance of the new moon, which served as the indicator for the first day of the month. The day previous to this appearance is referred to as the day that completes the month. When the month has 30 days, as it should, the days are spoken of as being their proper length or full length.[15] This most likely has reference to what modern astronomers call *lunar days*, a term that describes $1/30$ of the mean synodic month, for which Babylonian astrologers simply used the word 'day'.[16]

Other astrological omens dealing with the planets and constellations provide meaning for the use of some of the other terminology that occurs in Joshua 10. One text describing the entry of Mars into the precincts of Cancer comments:

> In the midst (*ina libbi*) it did not stand (*izzuzu*), it did not wait (*emēdu*), and it did not rest (*kâšu*); it went forth (*uṣṣû*) hurriedly.[17]

With this understanding of the Mesopotamian omen literature I now turn my attention to the text of Josh 10:12–14. The key verbs for interpreting the section are *dmm*, usually translated 'stand still' and *ᶜmd*, usually rendered 'stop'. It has often been observed that the semantic range of *dmm* in Hebrew also includes the meaning 'to wait', as is evidenced in such passages as Lam 3:26 and Ps 37:7.[18] In both passages it is parallel to the root *yḥl* with the meaning 'to wait' and in the latter context cannot easily be translated in any other way.

Though the root *ᶜmd* can mean 'to stop', it is more frequently translated 'to stand'. 1 Sam 14:9, a noteworthy passage, is the only other place in the Old Testament where the two verbs are used together. There Jonathan discusses with his armor-bearer how they will respond to Philistine instruction.

Based on this brief lexical analysis, I translate the prayer of Joshua in Josh 10:12–13 as follows:

---

14. Ibid., 40.

15. Thompson, *Reports of the Magicians*, xx–xxi, and his note to text 1; for terminology see especially 205:3, *ūmi ša ušallimu*.

16. O. Neugebauer, *The Exact Sciences in Antiquity* (Providence, R.I.: Brown University Press, 1957) 128.

17. Thompson, *Reports of the Magicians*, 236:4–7.

18. A. Baumann, "*Damah*," *TDOT* 3.263. This was recognized as early as Keil, *Joshua*, 108.

O sun, wait over Gibeon and moon over the valley of Aijalon.
So the sun waited and the moon stood, before the nation took ven-
geance on its enemies.
Is it not written in the book of Jashar,
"The sun stood in the midst of the sky and did not hurry to set as on a
day of full length"?

All of the descriptive terminology in Josh 10:12–13 was familiar
from the omen texts and is best interpreted in that light. On the basis
of celestial omens found at Boghaz-Köy, Qatna, Alalakh, Emar, Mari,
and Ugarit, Rochberg-Halton concludes that even in the West there was
"widespread 2nd millennium interest in celestial omens."[19] It is therefore
quite likely that the Canaanites made extensive use of celestial omens and
that the Israelites were familiar with the details of this class of divination.
However, while the connection in terminology is clear enough to give
the general direction of interpretation, the specifics of interpretation are
still far from certain. If one assumes, then, that an omen was involved
and that the request and the description of the event use astrological terminology, there are still a number of alternatives for interpreting the text.

The significance of the celestial omens to the text of Joshua 10 was
first recognized by the renowned linguist, Robert Dick Wilson, in an article in the *Princeton Theological Review* in 1918.[20] He was inclined, however, to translate the verb *dmm* as 'to be eclipsed'.[21] He thought Joshua
had requested and received an eclipse. As Barry Beitzel has recently
pointed out, however, this poses a problem for the chronology.

> We know exactly when solar eclipses that were observable in central Pal-
> estine took place between the years 1500 and 1000 B.C.—August 19,
> 1157 (8:35 A.M.), September 30, 1131 (12:35 P.M.) and November 23,
> 1041 (7:40 A.M.). None of those dates correlates even closely with the
> period of the conquest, no matter which of the two principal dates one
> assigns the Exodus from Egypt.[22]

It should further be noted that a solar eclipse cannot take place when
the sun is in the east and the moon in the west. Solar eclipses can occur
only at new moon (i.e., time of conjunction), and lunar eclipses can
occur only at full moon phase (i.e., time of opposition).

---

19. Rochberg-Halton, *Aspects of Babylonian Celestial Divination*, 30.

20. Robert Dick Wilson, "Understanding 'The Sun Stood Still,'" *Princeton Theological
Review* 16 (1918) 46–54; repr. in *Classical Evangelical Essays* (ed. Walter C. Kaiser; Grand
Rapids: Baker, 1972) 61–66.

21. Based on a syllabary of synonyms (CT 19) that listed *atalû*, *adiru*, and *daʾamu*
together.

22. B. Beitzel, *The Moody Atlas of Bible Lands* (Chicago: Moody, 1985) 97. It is on
this basis that J. F. A. Sawyer dates Joshua 10 ("Joshua 10:12–14 and the Solar Eclipse of
30 September 1131 B.C.," *PEQ* 104 [1972] 139–46).

More recently, John Holladay explored the issue and concluded that Joshua was seeking a good omen for himself and the armies of Israel.

> The first stich is a prayer (or incantation) that the sun and moon will "stand" in opposition on a day favorable to "the nation" (most probably the fourteenth of the month) rather than to her enemies. The second and third stichoi, then, simply report a favorable outcome to the prayer, "the nation" in effect gaining its ascendancy over "its enemies" during those few fateful minutes of opposition when the great lunar and solar orbs "stood" in the balance.[23]

But there are several difficulties with Holladay's view as well. First, it assumes that Joshua believed in omens and was seeking a favorable one for the benefit of his army. While it is not difficult to believe that many of the Israelites believed in omens and their significance, the prohibitions against divination practices make it much less likely that Joshua would have been portrayed as giving any credence to them. Second, the narrator's wording of the results suggests that Joshua was asking for a negative omen, for the text states that the conditions were not those of a "full-length day," that is to say, a favorable day.

I would like to offer the following interpretation of the text as a tentative explanation for the details given in the biblical account. Based on the use of the verbs 'wait' and 'stand' in the celestial omens and the timing of the prayer, stated as being approximately sunrise, one must conclude that the moon was moving toward the western horizon while the early rays of the sun were becoming visible on the eastern horizon. If the previous day had been cloudy, Joshua and the Israelites would not have known whether opposition had occurred already or not. Whatever day of the month it happened to be, the Amorites would be watching the sunrise very carefully to determine whether or not this would be a propitious day for battle. If it was the 14th of the month, Joshua would have known that the Amorites were hoping for the opposition of the sun and moon to occur as a favorable omen. If it was the 15th, they would have been hoping that opposition would not occur. Joshua, as a good general, would have hoped that the enemy would receive a bad omen, greatly damaging their morale. Though he himself was not swayed by omens, he knew of their great significance to the enemy and perhaps the impact they had on his own army. The terminology suggests he requested that the sun and moon wait or stand, in opposition; because of this request, I infer that it was the 15th of the month. The result reported is that the request was answered, eventuating in Israel avenging herself on the enemy. Some have objected that the text says the heavenly bodies performed

23. Holladay, "Day(s) the Moon Stood Still," 166–78.

their requested actions 'until' the battle was complete.[24] However, Waltke and O'Connor list the meaning 'before' for ʿ*ad* in passages in which the action prior to the preposition is antecedent to and in preparation for the action in the clause introduced by ʿ*ad*.[25] Though the account of the prayer comes after the report of the hailstorm in the text, the particle that introduces v. 12 (ʾ*az*) does not suggest that the prayer of Joshua was subsequent to the routing hailstorm.[26] Rather, the narrator's priority is to describe the part played by God's victory-producing special effects before explaining Joshua's unusual request.

The citation from the Book of Jashar in v. 13 is used to confirm the statement that "the sun stood in the midst of the sky." This wording does not demand that the event occurred at midday. Rather, the sky was viewed as having various segments, one major segment being below the horizon, others being above the horizon, and so on. One possibility is that the sun 'stood' in its half of the sky (that is, the eastern half). 'Standing' in the celestial omens refers to taking a position in relation to another body. The wording in Joshua is not significantly different from the statement in the celestial omens that the moon "stood in its course."

The movement of the sun is further explained in v. 13 by the statement that it did not hurry to set. The Hebrew verb used here regularly refers to the setting of the sun, but that does not mean that setting is imminent. From the time that the sun rises it is moving toward setting. Since the sun is in the east, this is simply to be understood as another way of saying that the sun 'waited' or 'stood'.

The description of the event ends by comparing the conditions of this day to a "full-length day." When the full moon comes on the 14th, and the month has the proper number of days, then each of the days of the month is a "full-length" day. This is what constitutes a good omen. In this text, the sun and moon do not act as they would on a "full-length" day. So, again, I assume that the day in question is the 15th of the month. If that is the case, when opposition occurred, it indicated that the month did not contain "full-length" days.

---

24. Younger, *Ancient Conquest Accounts*, 214.

25. B. Waltke and M. O'Connor, *Introduction to Biblical Hebrew Syntax* (Winona Lake, Ind.: Eisenbrauns, 1990) §11.2.12b/p. 215; see Gen 43:25, Exod 22:25, Num 10:21, and 2 Kgs 16:11. This possibility would negate the criticisms of M. Weinfeld ("Divine Intervention in War in Ancient Israel and in the Ancient Near East," in *History, Historiography and Interpretation* [ed. H. Tadmor and M. Weinfeld; Jerusalem: Magnes, 1984] 146) and P. D. Miller (*The Divine Warrior in Early Israel* [Cambridge: Harvard University Press, 1973] 126).

26. Younger, *Ancient Conquest Accounts*, 211.

I would like to emphasize again that in this interpretation, the omen was not requested because Joshua believed in omens. Rather, it was because he knew that his enemies did. Joshua therefore sought to use their own superstitions against them. It is of passing interest that even in the rabbinic work *Pirqe Rabbi Eliezer*, a similar perspective is adopted.

> Joshua noticed that the heathen were using sorcery to make the heavenly hosts intercede for them in the fight against the Israelites, so Joshua invoked the name of the Lord to make them be still.[27]

Whether this reconstruction of the events of Joshua 10 is accurate or not is difficult to prove. But the evidence from the celestial observations does make it clear that the wording of Joshua's prayer should be understood as technical terminology used for the normal and regular movements of the heavenly bodies. Another point in favor of my view is the fact that it offers a logical reason for Joshua to focus on the sun and moon. A final piece of evidence from the incantation literature of Mesopotamia shows how common this type of language was. In a first-millennium *balag*-lamentation entitled "He Is a Storm, At the Healing," the first nine lines describe the anger of the gods. Lines ten through fifteen contain the following:

> The heavens continually rumbled, the earth continually shook;
> The sun lay at the horizon
> The moon stopped still in the midst of the sky
> In the sky the great lights disappeared
> An evil storm . . . the nations
> A deluge swept over the lands.[28]

It is therefore a distortion of the biblical text to suggest that Joshua was requesting that the rotation of heavenly bodies actually cease. Some will complain that this interpretation makes the event far too common and ordinary. After all, the opposition might have occurred even if Joshua had not prayed. Where is the supernatural in this? In response I can only point out that even in prayers today one often prays for something to happen and when it does, considers it a marvelous answer to prayer. The role of God is not diminished just because the event prayed for might have happened without human prayers.

---

27. *Pirqe R. El.*, §52; cited from L. Ginzberg (ed.), *Legends of the Jews* (Philadephia: Jewish Publication Society, 1947) 4.11.

28. Mark Cohen, *The Canonical Lamentations of Ancient Mesopotamia* (Potomac, Md.: Capital Decisions, 1988) 2.427–39.

Asking Historical Questions of Joshua 13–19: Recent Discussion Concerning the Date of the Boundary Lists

Richard S. Hess

Glasgow Bible College, Scotland

EARLY STUDY

Albrecht Alt has provided the foundation on which virtually all historical-geographical work on Joshua 13–19 is based.[1] He accomplished this by making two important observations. First, he recognized that the integrity of the material in these chapters was antecedent to any editorial activity. As a result, he argued that the historical issues addressed by the text of Joshua 13–19 are not dependent on the particular literary source to which they may be assigned or to the date of that source.[2] Of course this realization does not alter the fact that profound changes might have been introduced into the text by later editorial activity. Instead, it permits liberty in the use of archaeological and ancient Near Eastern data to identify and date this particular text. This is especially true because the text is filled with place-names that correlate (1) with archaeological sites having records of occupation and (2) with datable ancient Near Eastern texts that mention these sites.

Second, Alt distinguished two primary forms of literature in these chapters. He found town lists that describe regions comprising tribal allotments. He also noted boundary descriptions separating one tribe from

---

1. See especially A. Alt's "Judas Gaue unter Josia," *PJ* 21 (1925) 100–116; repr. in *Kleine Schriften zur Geschichte des Volkes Israel* (Munich: Beck, 1953) 2.276–88. For a summary of Alt's views with bibliography, see my "Tribes, Territories of the," *ISBE* 4.907.

2. Despite the assignment of Joshua 13–19 to a Priestly source, the recognition that its content derives from earlier sources and must be evaluated on the merits of those sources is argued by F. M. Cross Jr. and G. E. Wright, "The Boundary and Province Lists of the Kingdom of Judah," *JBL* 75 (1956) 202 n. 1.

another. Sometimes the two types are clearly separated from one another: the town lists are identified by districts and the boundary descriptions are noted by the words that connect one place-name to another, describing the boundary as running from **x** to **y**. This is particularly true in the south, for example, in the case of the tribe of Judah. In some regions, however, the distinction is not so clear. There is also some dispute about where the boundary descriptions cease and the town lists begin, as in the case of the northern tribal allotments.[3] Nevertheless, the distinction has become better understood in more recent discussions. My concern in this paper is with the boundary descriptions.

In an article published in 1927, Alt dated most boundary descriptions to the period before the Monarchy, specifically the latter part of the premonarchic era.[4] The single boundary description that was not composed before the Monarchy is the boundary description of the tribe of Judah. Alt dates this description to the time of Josiah. He pointed out that another passage, Judges 1, describes the seven tribes west of the Jordan, with Levi, Simeon, Dan, and Issachar missing. However, Judges 1 presumes that Israel possesses all of the land of Canaan and that no territory is omitted.

The certainty with which the presumption of possession of all of Canaan is expressed in Judges 1 indicates that it should be dated before the period of the Monarchy and the inception of Israel's statehood. The boundary descriptions in the book of Joshua, then, should be dated earlier than Judges 1, since Judges 1 presumes their existence. Alt argued that the administrative divisions of the Monarchy are best understood as being derived from the boundaries in Joshua. Later development can also be seen in the regional list of Solomon in 1 Kings 4. By his time, Issachar was a separate territory, distinct from its neighbors in a way not found in Joshua.

Martin Noth accepted Alt's description in general, but identified two levels in the boundary descriptions.[5] The earliest stratum simply was comprised of *lists* of place-names that served as fixed boundary points for the tribes. Later editors added the connecting verbs that now appear in the text. This view seems to have been followed by K. Elliger[6] and William F. Albright, but Albright dated the final composition of the descriptions to

---

3. Hess, "Tribes, Territories of the," 907–10.

4. A. Alt, "Das System der Stammesgrenzen im Buche Joshua," *Sellin Festschrift: Beiträge zur Religionsgeschichte und Archäologie Palästinas* (Leipzig: Deichert, 1927) 13–24; repr. in *Kleine Schriften zur Geschichte des Volkes Israel* (Munich: Beck, 1953) 1.193–202.

5. See especially M. Noth, "Studien zu den historisch-geographischen Dokumenten des Josuabuches," *ZDPV* 58 (1935) 185–255; idem, *Das Buch Josua* (2d ed.; HAT 1/7; Tübingen: Mohr, 1953).

6. K. Elliger, "Tribes, Territories of," *IDB* 4.701–10.

the period of David and in particular to the time of his census.[7] Y. Kaufmann followed Alt, however, in dating the boundary descriptions to the period before the Monarchy. He assigned them to the time before the migration of the tribe of Dan north to the region around the city of Dan.[8] He considered the boundary descriptions to be a historical record of ethnic groups rather than an administrative or political document. His argument in favor of this was based on the appearance of the towns on Benjamin's border in the lists of border towns of other tribes. No administrative text, he argued, would allow such confusion regarding a border.

Yohanan Aharoni also followed Alt in positing a late premonarchic date for the tribal boundaries;[9] however, he suggested three new aspects to the analysis of Joshua 13–19. First, he maintained that most border descriptions were *abbreviated* to some extent. In order to prove his point, he noted the detailed descriptions around Jerusalem on the Benjamin–Judah boundary and suggested that they were an example of a boundary description in its *unabbreviated* form. Since the remaining boundary descriptions did not have this detail, they must have been abbreviated. Second, he noticed that the borders of Judah are not included. Instead, Judah's southern, eastern, and western boundaries correspond to those of Canaan as found in Numbers 34.[10] The northern border of Judah coincides with the border of Benjamin. Thus, among the tribes west of the Jordan, only the border descriptions of Benjamin, Ephraim, Manasseh, Asher, Zebulun, and Naphtali are preserved in Joshua. Third, Aharoni thought that the boundary lists originated in the context of a covenant of the northern tribes during the period of the Judges. His attempt to relate the border description to the covenant that formed the tribal league demonstrates his concern to place this material within the greater context of Joshua.

RECENT CONTRIBUTIONS

The collapse of Noth's hypothesis that premonarchical Israel was composed of a tribal amphictyony renewed the question about the origins of the

---

7. William F. Albright, "The Administrative Divisions of Israel and Judah," *JPOS* 5 (1925) 17–54.

8. Y. Kaufmann, *The Biblical Account of the Conquest of Canaan* (Jerusalem: Magnes, 1985).

9. Y. Aharoni, *The Land of the Bible: A Historical Geography* (rev. ed.; Philadelphia: Westminster, 1979) 248–62.

10. The Transjordan region occupied by Gad and Reuben was not part of Canaan, as defined by the Egyptian New Kingdom administration. See Z. Kallai, "The Boundaries of Canaan and the Land of Israel in the Bible," *Eretz-Israel* 12 (1975) 27–34 [Hebrew]. For the question of Machir and the region of Bashan, see idem, "Conquest and Settlement of Trans-Jordan: A Historiographical Study," *ZDPV* 99 (1983) 110–18.

tribal boundary system.[11] If there was no organization of tribes before the Monarchy, there was no need for a boundary system to exist.

Z. Kallai's English edition of his study of Joshua 13–19 provides the most thoroughgoing case for a *monarchical date* for the boundary descriptions.[12] He presents four points to establish this date:

1. The area outlined by the boundary descriptions is the same as the borders of David's census and of Solomon's districts.
2. The territory is complete, with no gaps.
3. Dan and Simeon do not appear in the boundary system.
4. Specific examples such as the borders in the Jezreel Valley, the borders claimed by Benjamin and Asher, and the Solomonic annexation of Gezer point to a monarchic date.

As is apparent from the arguments, the basic assumption behind Kallai's analysis is that a historical reality is presumed by the boundary descriptions. If a historical reality is assumed, then Kallai is correct that the only time when there was any memory of Israel's occupation and control of an area equal to the twelve tribes under a single authority was during the period of the United Monarchy. There is no evidence in the biblical text that Israel ever occupied the complete extent of the tribal areas attributed to the period of the Judges. Indeed, this is made explicit by the first chapter of Judges, which details the areas allocated but not occupied by Israel. For this reason, the weight of Kallai's argument does not depend on the details of Israelite territorial gains during the Monarchy. These at most serve to enhance the argument. Rather, Kallai's case is based on the identification of a historical period when the occupation of the land was achieved on a scale equivalent to that described in Joshua 13–19. Thus, it is not important that the Solomonic administrative divisions do not match the internal tribal borders that existed between tribes. It is possible for administrative divisions to change for a variety of rea-

---

11. For the hypothesis, see M. Noth, *Das System der Zwölf Stämme Israels* (BWANT 4/1; Stuttgart, 1930; repr. Darmstadt: Wissenschaftliche Buchgesellschaft, 1966). For a recent critique, see N. P. Lemche, *Early Israel: Anthropological and Historical Studies on the Israelite Society before the Monarchy* (VTSup 37; Leiden: Brill, 1985) 286–87. As Lemche goes on to point out, the collapse of one theory does not prove the alternative hypothesis, that the border descriptions date to the time of the United Monarchy. It might be added that the problems created by the use of the term *amphictyony* do not by themselves invalidate the existence of some sort of tribal league or association in the premonarchic period.

12. Z. Kallai, *Historical Geography of the Bible: The Tribal Territories of Israel* (Jerusalem: Magnes/Leiden: Brill, 1986) 277–325. This work forms a comprehensive revision of his earlier work, *The Tribes of Israel: A Study in the Historical Geography of the Bible* (Jerusalem: Bialik, 1967 [Hebrew]). See also his "Tribes, Territories of," *IDBSup* (ed. Keith Crim et al.; Nashville: Abingdon, 1976) 920–23; idem, "The United Monarchy of Israel: A Focal Point in Israelite Historiography," *IEJ* 27 (1977) 103–9.

sons. What is important about the Solomonic administrative divisions, as is also true of the geographical description that accompanies David's census, is that they describe a region whose outline is equivalent to that described by the sum of the tribal territories. The important point is that the external borders, that is, Israel's borders with its neighbors, had not changed. The Solomonic administrative divisions also suggest that all of the area within the external borders was occupied and controlled by the son of David; that is, there were no gaps in the area ruled. This interpretation is in accord with the description of Joshua 13–19 and adds further weight to a monarchic date for the boundary descriptions.

Alt and other scholars did not agree. They did not feel it necessary to identify a historical period when Israel actually controlled all of the land lying within the outline of the boundary descriptions. This Kallai defined as a historical reality. However, attributing the boundary descriptions to a period when Israel did not occupy the land so described is not the same as denying the descriptions any historicity. Thus some scholars felt that it was possible to attribute a partial or complete idealism to the boundary descriptions, suggesting that the land was divided among the tribes at a date when a complete occupation of the land was not yet realized. Alt and others who dated the boundary descriptions to the period before the Monarchy identified clues in the text that led them to believe that some of the descriptions included parts of the country that was not yet conquered. For example, the boundaries of the tribes of the hill country, such as Ephraim, Manasseh, and Judah, are described in more detail, but the descriptions become increasingly schematic as the boundaries are drawn westward into the Shephelah and onto the coastal plain. This reflects the initial settlement in the hill country by these tribes. The scribes describing the boundaries were unaware of geographical detail to the west, and so the border descriptions there included fewer sites.

Nadav Na°aman has provided another major contribution to the recent study of the boundary descriptions and their date.[13] He challenged Alt's date of the boundary lists and agreed with Kallai that they must be monarchic. Na°aman's challenge was based on the question, What purpose could these boundaries have served before the Monarchy? He disputed Alt's theory that the boundaries served to prevent tribal arguments. He argued that the tribes were "scattered and fragmented."[14] They did not require border delineations nor was there a central authority to enforce them. Furthermore, division of the entire land was unnecessary,

13. N. Na°aman, *Borders and Districts in Biblcal Historiography* (Jerusalem Biblical Studies 4; Jerusalem: Simor, 1986) esp. 75–117.
14. Ibid., 85.

since much of it was not occupied by the tribes. Na³aman argued for a date for the tribal boundaries during the reign of David. He considered its purpose to be historiographic or political rather than administrative: it served to legitimize David's rule over newly acquired lands in Canaan by identifying them as divinely allotted in the time of Joshua.[15]

Thus Kallai argued for a monarchic date of the boundary lists on the basis of the need for the description to agree with the area comprising the land actually occupied by Israel. And Na³aman agreed, noting as his fundamental objection to a premonarchic date for the Israelite tribal boundary system the lack of a purpose that such a document would serve.

ANOTHER DATE FOR THE BOUNDARY LISTS?

Although the present tendency is to move the date of the initial composition of Israelite tribal boundary lists to the period of the Monarchy, I believe that the subject should be reevaluated from the perspective of several matters that have come to light regarding the literature of Joshua and the archaeology of the Late Bronze–Early Iron age transition.

1. Na³aman's doctoral thesis, studying the fourteenth-century B.C. Canaan of the Amarna letters, has been followed by careful studies examining the boundaries of the Canaanite city-states that comprised Canaan at that time.[16] Although the Amarna letters do not provide detailed boundary descriptions such as those found in the book of Joshua, it is possible to reconstruct some city-state boundaries by studying the places mentioned, the claims made by rulers of various city-states, and the topography of the land. Again, it was Alt who first suggested this approach,

---

15. For both Kallai and Na³aman, the historiographical purpose extends to the artificial creation of the southern border of Canaan, which is understood as derivative from the boundary descriptions and not vice versa, *contra* Aharoni. Cf. Z. Kallai, "Territorial Patterns, Biblical Historiography and Scribal Tradition: A Programmatic Survey," *ZAW* 93 (1981) 428; idem, "The Southern Border of the Land of Israel: Pattern and Application," *VT* 37 (1987) 438; N. Na³aman, "The Inheritances of the Cis-Jordanian Tribes of Israel and the 'Land that Yet Remaineth,'" *EI* 16 (1982) 152–58 [Heb.]; Eng. summary, 257*; idem, *Borders and Districts*, 64.

16. N. Na³aman, *The Political Disposition and Historical Development of Eretz-Israel according to the Amarna Letters* (Ph.D. diss., Tel Aviv University, 1975 [Heb.]); idem, "The Canaanite City-States in the Late Bronze Age and the Inheritances of the Israelite Tribes," *Tarbiz* 55 (1986) 463–88 [Heb.]; idem, "Historical-Geographical Aspects of the Amarna Tablets," *Proceedings of the Ninth World Congress of Jewish Studies, Panel Sessions: Bible Studies and Ancient Near East* (ed. M. Goshen-Gottstein; Jerusalem: Magnes, 1988) 17–26; idem, "Canaanite Jerusalem and Its Central Hill Country Neighbours in the Second Millennium B.C.E.," *UF* 24 (1992) 275–91.

using as an example from the Amarna letters the ruler Labaya of Shechem, who controlled a territory occupied by Ephraim and Manasseh.[17]

Naᵓaman agrees with this approach and goes on to equate other Late Bronze Age city-states with tribal territories. Some of his more intriguing identifications include correspondences between the city-state of Gezer and Dan's territory, between Hazor's territory and that of Naphtali, and between Shim(r)on and the allotment of Zebulon. Naᵓaman discusses the territory comprising the allotment of Issachar, though this is more complicated since Issachar's boundary list was not preserved in Joshua. In fact, all of the Cisjordanian tribes with boundary lists are mentioned, with the exception of Judah and Asher. The border of Judah is problematic for a number of reasons. There is evidence that there were nomadic groups in the Judean hills, but scholars continue to dispute the borders of various city-states, especially Hebron and Jerusalem. Asher's boundary was perhaps a composite of several important city-states along the Mediterranean Coast. Of course Naᵓaman points out differences in detail between the boundaries described in the two groups of texts. Most evident is the obvious fact that there are more city-states listed than there are tribal territories. Thus, the correspondences are approximate, not precise. Nevertheless, it is significant that at no other time in the history of Old Testament Israel were regions demarcated in a way that so closely resembles the tribal allotments in Joshua. If one were to date Joshua 13–19 solely on the basis of the period in which the known political-geographical divisions most closely correspond to the boundary descriptions, the closest correspondence would be with the Late Bronze Age world of the Amarna correspondence.

Thus, the borders outlined in Joshua 13–19 appear at least in part to reflect traditions extending back in time to the Late Bronze Age city-states of Canaan. Attempts to date the boundary descriptions to the time of the Monarchy must reckon with geographical realities that precede the period of the Monarchy. In this light it is appropriate to question Naᵓaman's dating of the boundary descriptions. His concern was with the written documents themselves rather than the principles of division of the land. His question was less historical (whether there were tribes occupying the land allotted to them in the Monarchy) than literary (whether the tribes possessed a document that defined their boundaries in a way similar to the description in Joshua 13–19). His negative answer to the question of the possession of the document brings me back to the problem of the reason for such a document.

17. Alt, "Das System," 198 n. 5.

2. M. Weinfeld has demonstrated that the literary position of Joshua 13–19, immediately following the conquest account of chaps. 1–12, is not unique to the Hebrew tradition.[18] It is found in other literary sources, especially classical sources. The examples that he cites demonstrate that the chapters in Joshua concerned with allocation of the land were not inserted at random but describe the logical and necessary consequences of the occupation of a new land by a group of people. This analysis determines nothing about the date of the boundary descriptions or any of the narratives to which Weinfeld refers, but it does show that the distribution of land was considered the next step after conquest in cultures throughout the Mediterranean.[19] Consequently, allocation and boundary descriptions had a purpose and significance, one that was tied closely to the initial occupation of the land. Apparently, a rationale existed for preserving such materials in the initial accounts of Israel's appearance in the land. As I will yet demonstrate, the origins of this tradition hark back to second millennium B.C. treaty structure.

3. I. Finkelstein's work has been used a great deal in recent discussions on Israel's appeareance in Canaan.[20] Finkelstein collected evidence from surveys throughout the area of what was once ancient Canaan. He summarizes the results of this intensive and extensive canvassing of the land, and his conclusions suggest that the transition from the Late Bronze Age to the Early Iron Age (ca. 1200 B.C.) was marked by the sudden appearance of many new village sites throughout Canaan, especially in the

18. M. Weinfeld, "The Extent of the Promised Land: The Status of Transjordan," *Das Land Israel in biblischer Zeit: Jerusalem-Symposium 1981 der hebräischen Universität und der Georg-August-Universität* (ed. G. Strecker; GTA 25; Göttingen: Vandenhoeck & Ruprecht, 1983) 63–65; idem, "The Pattern of the Israelite Settlement in Canaan," *Congress Volume: Jerusalem 1986* (VTSup 40; ed. J. A. Emerton; Leiden: Brill, 1988) 270–83.

19. M. Weinfeld, "Historical Facts behind the Israelite Settlement Pattern," *VT* 38 (1988) 324–32. Weinfeld attempts to reconstruct this process with an emphasis on the "camps" that are attributed to various places. He suggests that the portrayal of Joshua is typical of the Greek founder figure, i.e., as leader, builder, and legislator. He concludes with the observation:

> One must bear in mind that the priestly Shilonite traditions were kept and fostered for hundreds of years in ancient Israel, and therefore not all the details can be considered trustworthy. However, on the basis of the comparison with the Greek procedure of colonization one must admit that division of land according to divine lot, and also the resort to an oracle of the central shrine, so well preserved in the Shilonite tradition, constitute genuine features of the settlement process in ancient Israel, save that they underwent schematization and nationalization in the developed priestly literature (p. 332).

20. I. Finkelstein, *The Archaeology of the Israelite Settlement* (Jerusalem: Israel Exploration Society, 1988). See also L. Stager, "The Archaeology of the Family in Ancient Israel," *BASOR* 260 (1985) 2–5.

central hill country. In the century or two following that, numerous additional sites began to appear in the Galilee region to the north. The only region to experience a significant increase in the number of settlements after the Monarchy, however, was the region of Judah to the south.

An interesting correlation may be made between this evidence and the earliest extrabiblical reference to Israel, at the end of the thirteenth century B.C. in the stele of Merneptah. There Israel is described, not as a city-state, but as a separate ethnic group. No single population center sufficed to give Israel an identity, for the people were spread across the hill country and beyond, inhabiting numerous small villages. The Song of Deborah in Judges 5 also avoids describing Israel other than as a collection of tribes.[21] Could it then be that Joshua 13–19 also preserves an ancient record of the people of Israel? Perhaps the passage portrays a time when the various tribes in Israel could not yet be identified by the one or two cities that served as administrative centers, such as was true in the time of Solomon, as described in 1 Kgs 4:7–19. Could not Joshua 13–19 describe a time when tribal identity was preeminently important and when the topography of this identity, especially in the hill country, could be described only by means of natural landmarks and villages?[22]

21. This poem is widely regarded as among the earliest premonarchic literary pieces preserved in the Bible. See L. E. Stager, "Merneptah, Israel and the Sea Peoples: New Light on an Old Relief," *EI* 18 (1985) 56*–64*. However, Kallai believes that "it reflects the territorial image of the United Monarchy of David and Solomon" ("The Reality of the Land and the Bible," *Das Land Israel in biblischer Zeit: Jerusalem-Symposium 1981 der hebräischen Universität und der Georg-August-Universität* [GTA 25; ed. G. Strecker; Göttingen: Vandenhoeck & Ruprecht, 1983], 82). He bases this on:

(1) Historical problems he identifies in Judges 4–5 ("The Conquest of Northern Palestine in Joshua and Judges," *Proceedings of the Fifth World Congress of Jewish Studies* [Jerusalem: World Union of Jewish Studies, 1972], 1.129–34 [Heb.]; Eng. summary, 240–41).

(2) The view that premonarchic sources, which he identifies as Genesis 49 and Deuteronomy 33, assign to Zebulon a northern coastal area, while monarchic sources such as Joshua and Judges 5 position Zebulon entirely inland, with no coastal outlet ("Judah and Israel: A Study in Israelite Historiography," *IEJ* 28 [1978] 258–60).

For linguistic analysis and alternative historic reconstructions arguing for a premonarchic date, see P. C. Craigie, "The Song of Deborah and the Epic of Tukulti-Ninurta," *JBL* 88 (1969) 253–65; D. N. Freedman, "Early Israelite History in the Light of Early Israelite Poetry," *Unity and Diversity* (eds. H. Goedicke and J. J. M. Roberts; Baltimore: Johns Hopkins University Press, 1975) 3–35; repr. in *Pottery, Poetry, and Prophecy: Studies in Early Hebrew Poetry* (Winona Lake, Ind.: Eisenbrauns, 1980) 131–66; M. D. Coogan, "A Structural and Literary Analysis of the Song of Deborah," *CBQ* 40 (1978) 143–66; and, in addition to the article already cited, L. E. Stager, "The Song of Deborah: Why Some Tribes Answered the Call and Others Did Not," *BAR* 15/1 (1989) 50–64.

22. Villages presumably were preferred to cities as boundary markers because the use of villages did not arouse disagreement over control of an entire territory as the use of city-states might have. This issue, rather than political motivations, was probably the primary reason for avoiding naming Jerusalem in the boundary of Judah. Of course, villages had their own regions, determined according to agricultural interests. See D. C. Hopkins,

4. Research in the agriculture of highland Canaan in the second and first millennia B.C.,[23] as well as studies devoted to the importance of kinship patterns and lineages in the biblical genealogies of early Israel,[24] have demonstrated that "Israelite" groups would have needed increased stability once they began to settle in the highlands. The nature of terrace farming, for example, suggests a need for a stable population to provide large and long-term investments of labor in order to build and sustain terraces. Furthermore, large families were needed to provide the labor for clearing uncultivated land and rendering it productive, and thus long-term residence in and maintenance of the territory of one's family became a major concern. The labor-intensive nature of sowing, harvesting, and other seasonal activities required the cooperation not only of the extended family but also of entire villages. This in turn provided the economic basis for inter-village cooperation[25] and, finally, the need for agreements about boundaries between families and tribal groups. These boundaries surely served to minimize intertribal strife and to maximize cooperation necessary for economic well-being. Thus, strong motivation for boundaries developed during the period of settlement.

5. In his study, Alt also observed similarities between biblical border descriptions and those from other cultures, citing examples from Greece, Mesopotamia, and Egypt. However, discoveries since his time have brought to light the existence of West-Semitic lists of towns that were created for census purposes. Documents discovered at Ugarit, Mari, and Alalakh list place-names and define administrative duties. Many such documents in the West-Semitic world come from the Late Bronze Age. Although this may simply be an accident of archaeological discovery, it appears more likely that the existence of such documentation for the Late

---

The Highlands of Canaan (The Social World of Biblical Antiquity 3; Sheffield: Almond Press, 1985) 237–41. However, the territorial borders of a village reached only as far as the point where the territory of the next village began. They did not include other villages.

23. See O. Borowski, *Agriculture in Iron Age Israel: The Evidence from Archaeology and the Bible* (Winona Lake, Ind.: Eisenbrauns, 1987).

24. See T. J. Prewitt, "Kinship Structures and the Genesis Genealogies," *JNES* 40 (1981) 87–98; R. A. Oden, Jr., "Jacob as Father, Husband, and Nephew: Kinship Studies and the Patriarchal Narratives," *JBL* 102 (1983) 189–205; N. Jay, "Sacrifice, Descent and the Patriarchs," *VT* 38 (1988) 52–70.

25. On these points and their importance in the parallel situation of the Biqa in modern Lebanon, see L. Marfoe, "The Integrative Transformation: Patterns of Socio-Political Organization in Southern Syria," *BASOR* 234 (1979) 1–42, esp. 20–23. Cf. also F. S. Frick, "Ecology, Agriculture and Patterns of Settlement," *The World of Ancient Israel: Sociological, Anthropological, and Political Perspectives* (ed. R. E. Clements; Cambridge: Cambridge University Press, 1989) 67–93.

Bronze Age (including the Mycenean world of Greece), documentation that exceeds anything that has been preserved from succeeding centuries in the West-Semitic world, is evidence for a widespread cultural interest. Perhaps the Israelites encountered this administrative system throughout the city-states of Canaan.[26] The Canaanite scribal tradition was of some antiquity,[27] and Israel's adaptation of the system for its own purposes would have been natural and expected. Israelite use of Late Bronze Age Canaanite wisdom traditions has already been suggested for the pre-monarchic period, and there is evidence of a similarity in rhetorical forms between the Amarna texts from Jerusalem and the Psalms.[28] Therefore, the borrowing and adapting of other scribal conventions would not have been without precedent during the period of the Judges.

Noth's theory that boundary descriptions were originally lists of names with connecting phrases added later derives from awareness of such lists. The distinction of the boundary lists is the presence of connecting phrases. They demonstrate a genre that appears in other biblical passages outlining borders.

Descriptions of this type are not unique to the Bible in the West-Semitic world. Examples of border descriptions in cuneiform texts of the

---

26. In addition to the fourteenth-century B.C. Amarna texts discovered in Egypt that report the presence of Canaanite vassals from city-states located within the borders of Joshua 13–19, Late Bronze Age cuneiform texts suggesting scribal traditions have been found at Kamid el-Loz, Tell el-Hesi, and the archaeological sites identified as Megiddo, Taanach, Shechem, Aphek, and Gezer. See D. O. Edzard, "Amarna und die Archive seiner Korrespondenten," *Biblical Archaeology Today: Proceedings of the International Congress on Biblical Archaeology, Jerusalem, April 1984* (eds. A. Biran et al.; Jerusalem: Israel Exploration Society, 1985) 248–59. To these should also be added the cuneiform fragments found in a Late Bronze II stratum at Pella. See R. G. Khouri, *The Antiquities of the Jordan Rift Valley* (Amman: Al Kutba, 1988) 23 and photograph.

27. For administrative records from Canaan, see both the Hazor cuneiform fragments and the recently discovered Hebron text. The Hazor texts include fragments of liver models, a lawsuit, and a lexical text, all dated to the Middle Bronze Age. For a summary and bibliography, see A. Malamat, *Mari and the Early Israelite Experience* (Schweich Lectures 1984; Oxford: Oxford University Press, 1989) 55–56. For the Hebron text, see M. Anbar and N. Naʾaman, "An Account Tablet of Sheep from Ancient Hebron," *Tel Aviv* 13–14 (1986–87) 3–12; M. Anbar, "A Cuneiform Tablet of the 17th–16th Centuries B.C. Discovered at Hebron," *Qadmoniot* 22 (1989) 94–95 [Heb.]. Concerned with sacrifice and also dated to the Middle Bronze Age, the Hebron text provides further evidence of a scribal tradition in the cities of the hill country of Canaan during the second millennium B.C. As at Hazor, the discovery of this document suggests the presence of other types of administrative records.

28. For suggestions concerning wisdom conventions, see R. N. Whybray, "Wisdom Literature in the Reigns of David and Solomon," *Studies in the Period of David and Solomon and Other Essays: Papers Read at the International Symposium for Biblical Studies, Tokyo, 5–7 December 1979* (ed. T. Ishida; Winona Lake, Ind.: Eisenbrauns, 1982) 13–26. For the similarity of rhetorical forms, see R. S. Hess, "Hebrew Psalms and Amarna Correspondence from Jerusalem: Some Comparisons and Implications," *ZAW* 101 (1989) 249–65.

Late Bronze Age also have been found. Among other places, they appear
in documents describing agreements between leaders of separate nations
or city-states. M. E. J. Richardson has identified a series of Akkadian
documents from Ugarit that represent a boundary agreement originally
made between Niqmadu, king of Ugarit, and Šuppiluliuma of Carchemish.[29] This agreement was renewed by later kings. Richardson examined the tradition of the boundary description preserved from generation
to generation by these documents and observed similarities in these
boundary descriptions, despite minor variations. For instance there are
small changes in the spelling of specific place-names that may be compared to the differences between some of the names in the Masoretic
Text and their spelling in the Septuagint. He also found that additional
place-names were inserted in later lists. These names may have been used
to delineate further the boundary or to reflect the emergence of new
towns and population centers from one generation to the next. Richardson also noted that the appearance of connecting prepositions between
the town names could not be predicted. This was frequently true for the
use of the preposition *a-du* (more commonly Akkadian *adi*), which is
regularly translated in connection with place-names as 'up to' or 'as far
as'.[30] Richardson argued that this demonstrates that boundary descriptions with prepositions may already have existed in the Late Bronze Age.
This theory renders unnecessary Noth's hypothesis that the boundary descriptions of Joshua were originally town lists to which connecting
phrases were added later.

Another boundary description is found in the Hittite treaty between
Tudhaliyas IV, ruler of the Hittites, and Ulmi-Teshub of Dattasa.[31] Lines

29. M. Richardson, "Hebrew Toponyms," *TynBul* 20 (1969) 97–98. The editions of
the texts to which he refers are all published by J. Nougayrol in PRU 4. They include
RS 17.340 (48–52); RS 17.369A (52); RS 17.237 (63–65); RS 17.62 (65–67); RS
17.339A (67–68); and RS 17.366 (68–69). I thank A. R. Millard for directing me to
Richardson's article. Private contractual documents from West-Semitic populations
with similar cultures may be found in land sales at Late Bronze Age Emar. Many of
these texts assume the form of: (1) measurement of a property's length; (2) the identification of houses or lands bordering on the right side, on the left side, on the back side,
and on the front side; (3) the seller and/or buyer; and (4) the price paid. See, e.g., texts
no. 76, 109, 110, 111, and 122 on pp. 82–84, 114–17, and 129–30, in D. Arnaud, *Emar
6/3: Textes sumériens et accadiens* (Recherches au pays d'Aštata; Paris: Éditions recherche
sur les civilisations, 1986).

30. CAD A/1 115, entry #1.

31. E. Forrer, *Keilschrifttexte aus Boghazköi* 4 (Wissenschaftliche Veröffentlichung der
Deutschen Orient-Gesellschaft 30/4; Leipzig: Hinrichs, 1920) 10; transliteration, E. Forrer,
Forschungen I (Berlin: printed by the author, 1926) 6–8; corrections, A. Goetze, "Rand-
noten zu Forrers 'Forschungen,'" *Kleinasiatische Forschungen* 1 (1927–30) 125–36 [125–27];
translation, E. Cavaignac, "Dadasa-Dattassa," *Revue hittite et asianique* 10 (1933) 65–76,
esp. 67–72; D. J. McCarthy, *Treaty and Covenant: A Study in Form in the Ancient Oriental*

15–32 (recto) recount a lengthy border description of the land that Tudhaliyas allotted to Ulmi-Teshub. In this case also there are connecting phrases that join a variety of landmarks and place-names. Thus, there is evidence of boundary descriptions resembling those in Joshua 13–19 in the international relations of the Hittites and the Syrian city-states of Carchemish and Ugarit.

More important is the context in which these boundary descriptions occur, in treaty documents (or renewals of earlier treaties) between a variety of national and city-state powers. The treaty context of Joshua 13–19 is clearly suggested by Joshua 24, a fact already noted by scholars such as Aharoni.[32] Chapters 13–19 could have formed part of an early Israelite covenant with God.[33] The allotment of land in ancient Near Eastern treaty texts served to guarantee land to those on either side of the border. It provided a legal document to which appeal could be made in disputes involving ownership of towns or pieces of land. It also defined the area for which a ruler was responsible. And it was of sufficient importance to be renewed whenever new rulers appeared on the throne.

The biblical memory of a divinely appointed allotment administered by tribal and family leaders (Josh 14:1–2) suggests that territorial division was of critical importance to Israel and that it had divine sanction. As with the Late Bronze Age Syrian and Anatolian texts, it could guarantee the integrity of the people's land and define the areas in which they had responsibility. Like the Ugaritic text, it was subject to renewal with the appearance of a new generation. However, Israel was not yet an established state. If the Late Bronze Age parallels suggest anything, it is in terms of a formal similarity. Surely, to date these texts before the Monarchy creates the problem of the unreality of these descriptions, a problem stated with clarity by Kallai and Naᵓaman. Much of the land did not belong to the tribes inhabiting only the hill country; the answer to this problem is that the portrayal is idealistic.

Documents and in the Old Testament (AnBib 21A; Rome: Pontifical Biblical Institute, 1978) 302–5.

32. Aharoni, *Land of the Bible*, 248.

33. Recent arguments for a first-millennium date for the entry of covenant forms and concepts into Israelite culture, such as those collected by E. W. Nicholson (*Deuteronomy and Tradition* [Oxford: Oxford University Press, 1986]) and reviewed by R. Davidson ("Covenant Ideology in Ancient Israel," *The World of Ancient Israel: Sociological, Anthropological, and Political Perspectives* [ed. R. E. Clements; Cambridge: Cambridge University Press, 1989] 323–47) remain unconvincing insofar as they fail to consider (1) the presence of historical prologue and blessings elements, which are virtually unique to treaties of the second millennium, and (2) the presence of the Hebrew expression for covenant, *br[y]t*, in West-Semitic texts of the second millennium B.C. See K. A. Kitchen, "The Rise and Fall of Covenant, Law, and Treaty," *TynBul* 40 (1989) 118–35.

Why is this the case? Two of the arguments already considered hint at possible explanations. Perhaps Israel took over the broad "map" of Late Bronze Age Canaan as suggested by Naᵓaman's analysis of the Amarna texts and their implicit city-state divisions. Also, the promotion of highland agriculture, along with a rapidly expanding population, could easily have led to a desire for an extended border system. Although idealistic at the time, anticipation of continued prosperity and growth as experienced by the early generations of settlers would naturally lead to the extension of borders.

6. A final consideration is the tribal nature of early "Israelite" groups in the highlands. As studies of West-Semitic tribes of second-millennium B.C. Mari have shown, tribal groups sometimes fluctuated between a sedentary and nonsedentary existence.[34] Such movements were not easily susceptible to control by a central authority. They also threatened the existence of other settled groups. Of course, tribal and family movements are well known from the Bible in the early Israelite period. The most famous was the migration of the tribe of Dan. Migrations of this kind were of great concern to the authorities whose traditions were preserved in the biblical text. For that reason a major migration, such as the one by the tribe of Dan, was carefully described (and so justified) as corresponding to the "Israelite Conquest," though on the smaller scale of a single tribe.[35]

Such concern illustrates the potential for problems encountered by various tribes living side by side. This is evident from the continual strife of the Israelites during the period of the Judges with their external enemies.

But of special interest is the intertribal conflict found in the narratives of Judges 19–21 and suggested by recent work demonstrating the inevitable competition for the relatively scarce resources of the Canaanite highlands.[36] There was a need from the beginning of the settlement to

---

34. J. T. Luke, *Pastoralism and Politics in the Mari Period* (Ph.D. diss., University of Michigan, 1965); M. B. Rowton, "Enclosed Nomadism," *Journal of the Economic and Social History of the Orient* 17 (1974) 1–30; V. H. Matthews, *Pastoral Nomadism in the Mari Kingdom (ca. 1830–1760 B.C.)* (ASOR Dissertation Series 3; Missoula, Mont.: Scholars Press, 1978); Malamat, *Mari and the Early Israelite Experience*, 34–52 (with additional bibliography). Naᵓaman (*Borders and Districts*, 94) makes the same observation. However, he stresses the movement of people between tribal groups that diminished any clear tribal division in the period before the Monarchy and implies the lack of need for boundary descriptions until the Monarchy. It is not clear how his argument accounts for early sources, such as Judges 5, which do show evidence of distinct tribal entities during the period of the Judges.

35. A. Malamat, "The Danite Migration and the Pan-Israelite Exodus-Conquest: A Biblical Narrative Pattern," *Bib* 51 (1970) 1–16. Malamat reverses the biblical sequence.

36. See no. 4 above, p. 200. See also I. Finkelstein, "The Emergence of the Monarchy in Israel: The Environmental and Socio-Economic Aspects," *JSOT* 44 (1989) 58–63. For

delineate tribal occupation areas. That this potential for conflict was eventually resolved by the formation of the Monarchy[37] does not alter the fact that the premonarchical society faced these problems.[38]

An agreement that defined territorial allotments and was backed by the force and witness of divinely recognized authority would have served as a useful instrument in the early stages of occupation and development. As a political tool it would have discouraged competition between various groups by appealing to divinely ordained divisions, just as the treaty curses provided sanctions for violations. As time went by, later generations would have continued to find the allotments important and useful. They served to apportion the land as it was gradually occupied. It was just as important that they also functioned to provide all of the people with two types of identity: an affiliation with one tribe and an affiliation with a unity of various tribes. As the incidents in Judges 4–5 and 19–21 demonstrate, the ideal of unity was not always realized. However, this fact in no way diminishes the perceived need for such a document.

These observations argue for a reconsideration of the hypothesis that the period preceding the Monarchy was formative, both for the creation of the territorial divisions that became the boundary descriptions of Joshua 13–19 and for the literary production of something not unlike these descriptions. On the basis of the present evidence, Alt's attempt to trace the origins of this material to the premonarchic period cannot be ruled out of consideration.

---

nonsedentary and pastoral tribal groups in the Late Bronze Age highlands, see idem, "The Land of Ephraim Survey," *Tel Aviv* 15–16 (1988–89) 143–45; idem, " 'Dimorphic Chiefdoms' in the Hill Country of Israel during the Middle and Late Bronze Ages," *The II International Congress on Biblical Archaeology, Jerusalem, 24 June–4 July 1990: Abstracts* (Jerusalem: Israel Exploration Society, 1990) 24.

37. Frick, *Formation of the State in Ancient Israel*; C. Hauer, "From Alt to Anthropology: The Rise of the Israelite State," *JSOT* 36 (1986) 3–15; K. W. Whitelam, "Recreating the History of Israel," *JSOT* 35 (1986) 45–70; Finkelstein, "Emergence of the Monarchy," 58–61.

38. The problems revolving around the nature of early Israel as a tribal society have not been resolved. An important starting point for discussion is Lemche's *Early Israel* (esp. pp. 416–32). See also the review of recent studies by J. W. Rogerson, "Anthropology and the Old Testament," *The World of Ancient Israel: Sociological, Anthropological and Political Perspectives: Essays by Members of the Society for Old Testament Study* (ed. R. E. Clements; Cambridge: Cambridge University Press, 1989) 17–37.

Judges 1 in Its Near Eastern Literary Context

K. Lawson Younger Jr.

LeTourneau University

INTRODUCTION

As the ancient historian (whether Near Eastern, biblical, or otherwise) reconstructed "historical" referents into a coherent description, he produced a figurative account, a "re-presenting representation."[1] This was true even if the narrative mode was selected for the presentation.[2] This is because a narrative historian is not only a presenter of the *events* of history, but also a *presenter* of the events of history. He is a literary artist! Moreover, the historical narratives of the ancient Near East provide the literary milieu that broadens the horizon of the biblical text. Only when these things are recognized can the biblical text's horizon begin to merge with ours.

Judges 1 has often been considered the "other" account of Israel's appearance in the land of Canaan, the account that preserves a more accurate picture than its counterpart in Joshua. This is because Judges is usually considered to be a supplemented composition that presents the settlement as piecemeal and incomplete. It is also argued that Judges 1

---

1. H. White uses the term *allegory*, but in my opinion this term is overcoded with certain connotations that negate its usefulness. But his point that historical narrative is fundamentally figurative is valid and useful ("The Question of Narrative in Contemporary Historical Theory," *History and Theory* 23 [1984] 24–25). This is in spite of the persistence of the historicist view of history in biblical studies (see, e.g., M. Brettler, "The Book of Judges: Literature as Politics," *JBL* 103 [1989] 395–98). Ancient Near Eastern conquest accounts are figurative in three ways: (1) the structural and ideological codes that are the apparatus for the text's production; (2) the themes or motifs that the text utilizes; and (3) the usage of rhetorical figures in the accounts. See P. Stambovsky, "Metaphor and Historical Understanding," *History and Theory* 27 (1988) 125–34.

2. As opposed to the poetry. For poetry as a mode of history writing, see now: W. T. Koopmans, *Joshua 24 as Poetic Narrative* (JSOTSup 93; Sheffield: JSOT Press, 1990) 415–18.

displays a tribal perspective and a geographic arrangement of discourse, whereas Joshua has a "pan-Israelite" perspective. And since it appears logical that tribal entities came before national unity, Judges 1 must therefore preserve the more genuine narrative.

Because the Assyrian summary inscriptions were also often written with a geographic orientation, they are helpful in providing the modern historian with a better understanding of the narrative in Judges 1. My purpose in this article is to investigate the literary structure of the Assyrian summary inscriptions in order to place Judges 1 in its context of ancient Near Eastern history-writing.[3]

ASSYRIAN SUMMARY TEXTS

In order to understand the Assyrian summary inscriptions, it is necessary first to contrast them with the Assryian annalistic texts. Assyrian annalistic-text narration is arranged chronologically. Events are usually represented by stereotyped syntagms that build an iterative scheme, and hyperbole and other rhetorical figures are regularly employed. The annals of Ashurnasirpal II,[4] a collection of various inscriptions recorded in his Kalah Inscription,[5] provide an excellent example.[6] In them there are two annalistic passages that evince a chronological framework and also stereotyped syntagms building a repetitive scheme.[7]

First Annalistic Section (i 43–ii 125a)

The first section rehearses the campaigns from Ashurnasirpal's accession to his fifth regnal year. These can be charted in the following manner:

---

3. In other words, joining the analysis with the contextual method. See most recently W. W. Hallo, "Compare and Contrast: The Contextual Approach to Biblical Literature," in *The Bible in the Light of Cuneiform Literature: Scripture in Context III* (ANETS 8; ed. W. W. Hallo, B. W. Jones and G. L. Mattingly; Lewiston: Edwin Mellen, 1990) 1–30.

4. For a new model for the growth of the Assyrian Empire during the reign of Ashurnasirpal II, see M. Liverani, "The Growth of the Assryian Empire in the Habur/Middle Euphrates Area: A New Paradigm," *SAAB* 2 (1988) 81–98.

5. According to A. K. Grayson's analysis, "Studies in Neo-Assyrian History: The Ninth Century B.C.," *BiOr* 33 (1976) 138–40; and H. W. F. Saggs, *The Might That Was Assyria* (London: Sidgwick & Jackson, 1984) 72–76.

6. A. K. Grayson, *ARI* 2.CI.1.

7. Space does not allow a complete analysis here. For a full listing and discussion of the Assyrian syntagms, see Younger, *Ancient Conquest Accounts: A Study in Ancient Near Eastern and Biblical History Writing* (JSOTSup 98; Sheffield: JSOT Press, 1990) 70–79; and E. Badalì et al., "Studies on the Annals of Assurnasirpal II, Part 1: Morphological Analysis," *Vicino Oriente* 5 (1982–83) 13–73.

Year	Campaign	Passage	Locations
883 B.C.	2 campaigns	i 43–i 68	Kirruru, Gilzanu, and Ḫabḫu
		i 69–i 100	Suru (belonging to Bit Halupe) and Bit Adini
882 B.C.	1 campaign	i 101–ii 22	Kašiari and Šubaru
881 B.C.	2 campaigns	ii 23–ii 32	Babitu Pass
		ii. 33–ii. 48	Mt. Nisir and Lullumu
880 B.C.	1 campaign	ii 49–ii 85	Babitu Pass to Hashmar Pass, and Zamua
879 B.C.	1 campaign	ii 86–ii 125a	Kadmuhu, Mt. Kašiari, Tušḫan, and Ḫabḫu

Fig. 1.

In the account of the campaign of 883 B.C., though the text states, "In my accession year (and) in my first regnal year . . ." (1.43), it is clear that there was no campaign in the accession year. The two narrated campaigns actually occurred in the first full regnal year.[8] These campaigns were fought to consolidate Ashurnasirpal's initial kingdom. The campaigns of 882 B.C. were to the north, while the campaigns of 881 and 880 were to the east. The campaign of 879 was to the north again.

Second Annalistic Section (iii 1–iii 113)

The second passage covers the sixth to eighteenth regnal years:[9]

Year	Campaign	Passage	Locations
878 B.C.	5 Campaigns	iii 1–iii 25	Habur River and Euphrates, including the taking of a Babylonian town
		iii 26–iii 49	Laqe (Ḫindanu) and Suhu
		iii 50–iii 55	Bit-Adini (Kaprabu)
		iii 56–iii 84	Carchemish★
		iii 84–iii 92	Lebanon and the Great Sea★
866 B.C.	1 Campaign	iii 92–iii 113	Kummuhu and Amedu

Fig. 2.   ★*The Carchemish-Mediterranean Narrative*

8. See Grayson, "Studies in Neo-Assyrian History," 138.

9. In this section there is inconsistency in the method of quoting dates that may be due to the eclectic form of the text. The narration also may have been streamlined because of space limitations.

The campaigns recorded for the year 878 B.C. were conducted in the west and southwest, with expansion in mind. These campaigns (actually years 878, 877, 876, 875, and 874[?]B.C.) have probably been telescoped into a single-year presentation. The geographic goals of the campaigns recorded for this year were Bit Adini and Carchemish.[10] The last recorded year again focused on the northwest.

While a full exposition will not be presented here, it is important to acknowledge that the main conquest account in the book of Joshua uses the same type of iterative scheme encountered in many annalistic texts from the ancient Near East.[11] The Joshua account is simulated or artificial in its structure. The writer/historian used the same techniques as any literary artist to arrange or fashion his materials. The narrative only approaches a representation of the reality it purports to describe, as is true of any historical narrative.[12]

The Assyrian summary or display inscriptions are often arranged geographically.[13] Grayson explains:

> Military campaigns are not normally described in chronological order but, most commonly, they are grouped according to geography.[14]

---

10. Grayson, "Studies in Neo-Assyrian History," 139; J. A. Brinkman, *A Political History of Post-Kassite Babylonia 1158–722 B.C.* (AnOr 43; Rome: Pontifical Biblical Institute, 1968) 390–94; and W. Schramm, *Einleitung in die assyrischen Königsinschriften II, 934–722 v. Chr.* (Handbuch der Orientalistik 5/1/2; Leiden: Brill, 1973) 27–28. Brinkman argues that there were two campaigns in two successive years, stating, "New official editions of royal inscriptions would hardly have been prepared for the short space of time it would have taken Ashurnasirpal to go directly from Carchemish to the Mediterranean" (p. 393). In support of his argument, Brinkman also refers to a text from Ashur, which records that Ashurnasirpal reached *māt Ḫatti*, but makes no reference to the Mediterranean (ibid., 139 n. 2191). Grayson agrees. Schramm, however, claims that the texts studied by Brinkman offer in themselves no compelling evidence for two campaigns. In fact, the mention of hostages is itself an argument in favor of only one expedition (p. 28).

While a case can be made for both conclusions, W. de Filippi argues that the ambiguity of the respective passages lies in the fact that while the scribes had to record events that were not part of a campaign of conquest, the records, nevertheless, had to be construed so as to convey the closest approximation to the accepted scheme of military triumph that could be produced without the narrative becoming purely fictitious at this point. See W. de Filippi, "The Royal Inscription of Assur-Nasir-Apli II (883–859 B.C.): A Study of the Chronology of the Calah Inscriptions Together with an Edition of Two of These Texts," *Assur* 1/7 (1977) 28. But another explanation for this literary wording may lie in the derivation of "campaigns" from "itineraries" in Assyrian history writing.

11. See Younger, *Ancient Conquest Accounts*, 197–266. Cf. also J. Hoffmeier's paper, "The Structure of Joshua 1–11 and the Annals of Thutmose III," above (pp. 165–79).

12. See White, "Question of Narrative," 59; and Younger, *Ancient Conquest Accounts*, 25–46.

13. This is not to say that annalistic texts cannot contain geographic presentations, especially in the case of itineraries contained in the annalistic narration (e.g., the Ḫabur River campaigns of Adad-nirari II, Tukulti-Ninurta II, and Ashurnasirpal II).

14. A. K. Grayson, "Histories and Historians of the Ancient Near East: Assyria and Babylonia," *Or* 49 (1980) 152. H. Tadmor states: "A distinctive feature of this type . . .

Usually a summary inscription is much shorter than any edition of royal annals, especially since it was inscribed on a surface of limited space, such as a commemorative stele or a slab. It ordinarily contained the following elements:

> (a) a prologue, consisting of invocation to the gods and the king's titulature; (b) a geographically arranged summary of events; (c) the main section explaining the circumstances leading to the composition of the inscription, introduced by the formula *ina ūmēšuma* = 'at that time'; (d) an epilogue with maledictions.[15]

It is also important to remember that summary/display inscriptions use an expositional or representational time ratio, depicting relatively long periods in brief spans of reading time. The language tends to summarize the time represented and in so doing is generally nonspecific and nonconcrete. It describes a static world in general terms; in contrast, a central narration introduces scenes of dynamic action that bring about change and movement and complications.[16]

An example that illustrates this is the Standard Inscription[17] of Ashurnasirpal II. It is geographically and ideologically arranged:[18]

> When Aššur, the lord who called me by name (and) made my kingship great, entrusted his merciless weapon in my lordly arms, I felled with the sword in the midst of battle the wide-spread troops of the Lullumu. With the aid of Šamaš and Adad, my divine helpers, I thundered like Adad, the destroyer, against the armies of the lands of Nairi, Ḫabḫu, the Shubaru, and Nirbu. The king who subdued at his feet (the area) from the opposite bank of the Tigris to Mount Lebanon and the Great Sea, the entire lands of Laqu (and) Suhu including the city of Rapiqu. He conquered from the source of the Subnat River to Urartu. I annexed within the borders of my

---

is the condensation of early with later events into one geographically but not chronologically coherent narrative" ("The Historical Inscriptions of Adad-Nirari III," *Iraq* 35 [1973] 141).

15. Tadmor, "Historical Inscriptions of Adad-Nirari III," 141.

16. L. Klein, *The Triumph of Irony in the Book of Judges* (JSOTSup 68; Sheffield: Almond Press, 1989) 193–95.

17. S. M. Paley, *King of the World: Ashur-nasir-pal II of Assyria 883–859 B.C.* (New York: Brooklyn Museum, 1976) 115–44.

18. Another excellent example of this phenomenon can be seen in Ashurbanipal's inscriptions. Grayson argues that "incidents are narrated primarily according to geographic proximity and, although the sequence varies somewhat from one edition to another, in all editions a general pattern is apparent: first districts in the west appear, then the north, east, south, and southwest in that order. Such a grouping bears no relation to the chronological sequence of events as a glaring example will suffice to show. The campaign against Kirbitu definitely occurred in 668 but it is narrated in Edition B (also the fragmentary Editions C, D, and E, and the Annals Tablet) after the first campaign against Egypt (667) because subsequent to the Egyptian campaign, Egyptians were transported to Kirbitu" (A. K. Grayson, "The Chronology of the Reign of Ashurbanipal," *ZA* 70 [1980] 245).

land (the area) from the passes of Mount Kirruru to the land of Gilzanu, from the opposite bank of the Lower Zab to the city of Til-Bari which is upstream from Zaban, from Til-Sha-Abtani to Til-Sha-Zabdani, the cities of Hirimu, Harutu, fortresses of Karduniash (Babylonia). I counted as people of my land (the inhabitants) from the pass of Mount Babite to Mount Hashmar. In the lands over which I ruled I appointed my governors. They did obeisance.

JUDGES 1: INTRODUCTION

In the past many scholars interpreted Judges 1 as being an early conflation of differing components that preserve a greater degree of reliability than the book of Joshua concerning the origins of ancient Israel. For this reason, they considered the book of Judges to begin with the Deuteronomistic editor's introduction in 2:6ff. Many literary critics ascribed this chapter to the early Yahwistic Pentateuchal source, viewing it as J's counterpart to the conquest narratives in the first half of Joshua.[19] They considered it older because it seemed to represent a view of the settlement that was piecemeal and incomplete and therefore closer to the facts than the deuteronomic presentation of a single invasion, as in Joshua. Thus S. R. Driver asserted:

> This section of the book consists of fragments of an old account of the conquest of Canaan—not by united Israel under the leadership of Joshua, but—by the individual efforts of the separate tribes.[20]

A few interpreters have felt that the varying components were a sign that Judges is unreliable. G. E. Wright argued that Judges 1 is not "a unified document," and

> . . . it is thus clear that Judges 1 presents many problems, because it is a collection of miscellaneous fragments of *varying dates* and *varying reliability*. To represent it or even some part of it as the earliest and most reliable account of the conquest of Canaan is to oversimplify the whole problem.[21]

Recently, a number of scholars have postulated that Judges 1 is a late composite, achieving a kind of unity that serves as a framework for

---

19. See G. F. Moore, *Critical and Exegetical Commentary on Judges* (ICC; Edinburgh: T. & T. Clark, 1895) xxxii–xxxiii, 3–100; S. Mowinckel, *Tetrateuch-Pentateuch-Hexateuch: Die Berichte über die Landnahme in den drei altisraelitischen Geschichtswerken* (BZAW 90; Berlin: de Gruyter, 1964) 17–33.

20. S. R. Driver, *An Introduction to the Literature of the Old Testament* (8th ed.; International Theological Library; Edinburgh: T. & T. Clark, 1962) 162.

21. G. E. Wright, "The Literary and Historical Problem of Joshua 10 and Judges 1," *JNES* 5 (1946) 109.

the rest of the book. This theory revived confidence in the general reliability of the text of Judges, as over against Joshua. Thus, for example, J. Gray argues that Judges 1 is the work of a later redactor's hand and that the deuteronomistic historian's account begins properly at 2:6 and runs to 3:6. In Judg 1:2–21, however, "the redactor draws upon older historical traditions" that are not used in Joshua.[22] Moreover, Judg 1:1–2:5 (except for the redactor's additions) is considered a much "more sober account,"[23] primarily because it does not seem to reflect an "all-Israel" political condition. So on the one hand Judges 1 is a later (probably) exilic, redactional "recapitulation of the settlement of Canaan," but on the other hand, it preserves an earlier and more accurate history of that settlement.

A. G. Auld also argued that "Judges 1:1–21, far from being an early historical narrative (whether from J or not), is in fact a late composition—itself much supplemented," but it contains a more accurate picture of the settlement than Joshua.[24] Another scholar who believes that the section was part of the latest framework to be attached to the book is Robert Boling.[25] However, he does not consider Judges 1 to be a rival account of the conquest or a corrective to the normative statement concerning the conquest of the land but rather a review of the performance of the generation that outlived Joshua, when Othniel was one of the few remembered links. He states:

> It is compiled from various sources, some superior to the Joshua account (e.g. vss. 22–25), others much more problematical (e.g. vss. 5–8). The purpose is to indicate the contrast between the situation under Joshua, the great war leader, and the subsequent deterioration of federation structure and the concomitant erosion of Yahwist loyalties.[26]

In a different vein, John Van Seters maintains that the passage is basically a unity, "except for a few possible additions," but he argues that it is

22. J. Gray, *Joshua, Judges and Ruth* (The Century Bible; London: Nelson, 1967) 188–89. The exceptions are Caleb's occupation of Hebron (Judg 1:20; cf. Josh 14:6–15) and Othniel's occupation of Kirjath-sepher (Judg 1:11–15 = Josh 15:16 and 19). The section (Judg 1:2–21) is falsely portrayed as occurring "after the death of Joshua" (1:1), since the actual beginning of the deuteronomistic history is recorded in Judg 2:6, "after Joshua had dismissed the Israelites. . . ." The incident of the angel at Bochim by Bethel (Judg 2:1–5) is considered redactional because of its etiological, mythical overtones.

23. Ibid., 194.

24. A. G. Auld, "Judges 1 and History: A Reconsideration," *VT* 25 (1975) 276. However, Judg 1:1–2 are, according to Auld, the work of a "post-Deuteronomistic Judaean editor" ("Review of Boling's Judges: The Framework of Judges and the Deuteronomists," *JSOT* 1 [1976] 45).

25. R. Boling, *Judges: Introduction, Translation and Commentary* (AB 6A; Garden City, N.Y.: Doubleday, 1975) 29–38.

26. Ibid., 66.

not the work of the Yahwist or the deuteronomist, but the work of P.[27] Finally, Brettler has recently argued that the author/editor of this introductory section formed the material in order to present a pro-Judean bias. In fact, this author/editor ". . . not only selected and organized material to match his pro-Judean bias, but actually rewrote traditional material to suggest Judean supremacy."[28] His argument is partially based on the geographic arrangement found in Judges 1. It is in this type of literary structuring that the Assyrian summary inscriptions may provide an aid to interpretation.

Analysis

While the majority of commentators claim that the phrase "after the death of Joshua" is an interpolation, Polzin compares it to a phrase at the beginning of the book of Joshua, "after the death of Moses," because he recognizes the relationship between Judges and the book of Joshua as a whole. He considers the phrase to be part of the narrator's style, so that the "Book of Judges, like Joshua, briefly recapitulates the previous book before interpreting it further."[29] According to Polzin, Judges recapitulates the basic thesis of Joshua (how much of the land Israel would occupy) before going on to the central concern of Judges, *why* the people could not completely occupy the land.[30] He does not consider Judges 1 to be a summary of the book of Joshua but rather a summary of the events after Joshua's death, conveying the same point as the book of Joshua.[31] In Polzin's view,

---

27. J. Van Seters, *In Search of History: Historiography in the Ancient World and the Origins of Biblical History* (New Haven, Conn.: Yale University Press, 1983) 338–42.

28. M. Brettler, "The Book of Judges: Literature as Politics," *JBL* 108 (1989) 402. Cf. Auld, "Judges 1." However, a pro-Judean redaction is very doubtful, since Judah is negatively portrayed in Judges (see Judges 20; and B. Webb, *The Book of Judges* [JSOTSup 46; Sheffield: JSOT Press, 1987], 192–98).

29. R. Polzin, *Moses and the Deuteronomist: A Literary Study of the Deuteronomic History* (New York: Seabury, 1980) 148.

30. Ibid.

31. Ibid., 147, *contra* A. E. Cundall (*Judges, Ruth: An Introduction and Commentary* [TOTC; London: Tyndale, 1968] 21) and most others. The phrase "after the death of Joshua" is a temporal clause that has close parallels in Josh 1:1; 2 Sam 1:1, and 2:1. The latter contains the same question-answer sequence found in Judg 1:1:

> Afterwards,
>   David asked the LORD:
>   "Shall I go up (ʿlh) to one of the towns of Judah?"
>   And the LORD answered:
>   "Go up."

See fig. 3 (p. 215, below). See also in this regard, B. Waltke and M. O'Connor, *An Introduction to Biblical Hebrew Syntax* (Winona Lake, Ind.: Eisenbrauns, 1990) 554. Furthermore

the question becomes why Israel survived this period at all in view of their continued apostasy.[32]

Judges 1 (and in a sense Judges as a whole) is a highly stylized, geographically-arranged account. It arbitrarily begins with Judah and ends with Dan (maintaining a south–north orientation). It is structured concentrically, with Judah and the House of Joseph purposely playing major parallel roles in the narrative. The section manifests a structure that has been described best by B. Webb:[33]

Fig. 3. *Judges 1:1–2:5*

A_1 The assembled Israelites ask Yahweh, "Who will go up . . . ? ($^c lh$) (1:1–2a)

         a   Prologue: Yahweh's promise (1:2b)

         b   Judah/Simeon alliance (1:3)

B_1 Judah goes up   x   Judah's successful wars,   Up (1:4–8)
     (1:2b–21)   including Calebites/
                          Kenizzites (1:4–16)   Down (1:9–16)

         b′   Judah/Simeon alliance (1:17)

         a′(c′)   Codicil:* Yahweh's presence with Judah, but with qualifications: (1) positive, (2) negative (1:18–21)

         a   Ellipsis: Prologue: Yahweh's promise

         b   The House of Joseph (1:22)

B_2 Joseph goes up   x   Wars of the House of Joseph including
     (1:22–36)   (in addition to Manasseh and
                          Ephraim) Zebulun, Asher, Naptali, and Dan (1:23–34)

         b′   The House of Joseph (1:35)

         a′   Codicil (1:36)

A_2 The Messenger of Yahweh goes up ($^c lh$) to indict the assembled Israelites (2:1–5)

*A codicil is a short writing or addition to a will that modifies it in some way.

---

the phrase $š^{\mathfrak{o}} l$ $byhwh$ 'inquire of the LORD' expresses the idea of obtaining a declaration of the divine will and is substantially the same as $š^{\mathfrak{o}} l$ $bmšpṭ$ $h^{\mathfrak{o}} wrym$ 'inquire of the judgment of the Urim' (Num 27:21), in which the divine will is obtained through the Urim and Thummim of the high priest.

32. Polzin, *Moses and the Deuteronomist*, 161, 211.

33. This is a modification of Barry Webb's analysis (*Judges*, 90–92).

Webb also pointed out that

> . . . in the all-Israel assembly (A₁) which opens this larger unit the activity of B_1B_2 is anticipated; in the all-Israel assembly (A₂) which closes the unit, the activity of B_1B_2 is reviewed and evaluated.[34]

Moreover, he observed that there are two elements that enhance the coherence and intelligibility of the text:

> 1. The key word ᶜlh ('to go up') in 1:1–2:5. By its frequency and distribution it serves to unify this extended segment of text and to demarcate the several units of which it is composed.
>
> 2. The compositional parallel between the Judah and Joseph section within chapter 1 throws the treatment of the Canaanite informer in the Bethel campaign (first item in the Joseph section) into sharp relief against the treatment of the Canaanite lord of Bezeq in the Bezeq campaign (first item in the Judah section). This comparison helps us to perceive more clearly the basic shift that has already begun to take place at this point in the relationship between Israelites and Canaanites in spite of the fact that the second section, like the first, begins with a notable victory.[35]

Furthermore, Judges 1 utilizes its south-to-north geographic arrangement of the tribal episodes in order to foreshadow the geographic orientation of the Judges cycle in 3:7–16:31.

Fig. 4.

Judah + Simeon	South
Benjamin	
House of Jospeh	
Manasseh	
Ephraim	
Zebulun	
Asher	
Naphtali	
Dan	North

In addition, there is a literary movement that finds its climax in the Dan episode.[36]

---

34. Webb, *Judges*, 103.

35. Concerning the translation "lord of Bezeq," see now S. Layton, *Archaic Features of Canaanite Names in the Hebrew Bible* (HSM 47; Atlanta: Scholars Press, 1990) 117.

36. Regarding the moral or spiritual movement in Judg 1:1–2:5, B. S. Childs notes that the function of the prologue in the book of Judges is to highlight the disobedience of the Israel that succeeded the era of Joshua. He concludes: "That the introduction performs this negative role is made explicit in 2:1–5 which confirms the judgment of God on the nation's disobedience" (*Introduction to the Old Testament as Scripture* [Philadelphia: Fortress, 1979], 259).

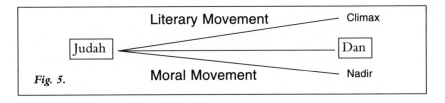

Fig. 5.

The moral or spiritual decline is evident from the very beginning of the book of Judges. Klein puts it this way:

> Yahweh (1:1) tells Israel (here Judah) specifically what to do, but Israel only partially heeds Yahweh's command: Judah immediately establishes a battle pact with his brother Simeon. Thus, from the outset, Israel exerts self-determination, evidencing automatic trust in *human* perception. These verses may be regarded as introducing the ironic configuration of the book—implicit difference in perception between Yahweh and Israel and Israel's insistence on following human perception.[37]

In like fashion, the cycles of the judges (3:6–16:31) have their climax and nadir in the person of Samson.[38]

Similar to the summary/display inscriptions, Judges 1 uses the expositional or representational time ratio, depicting relatively long periods in brief spans of reading time. This can be contrasted to the "time norm" of the central narrative of Judg 3:6–16:31 or the Assyrian annals' episodic narration.[39] The expositional time ratio is exploited by the writer in

---

37. Klein, *Triumph of Irony*, 23.

38. Webb, *Judges*, 177–79; C. Exum, "The Centre Cannot Hold: Thematic and Textual Instabilities in Judges," *CBQ* 52 (1990) 423–25.

39. See Klein's discussion of expositional time in *Triumph of Irony*, 12. Expositional passages may foreshadow the main narrative by introducing motifs and/or paradigms. The book of Judges does both. Some of the mininarratives in the first chapter contain motifs that recur at significant points in the rest of the book (Webb, *Judges*, 119):

Judges	First Reference	Theme	Recurrence
1:4–7	The lord of Bezek	Negative portrayal of (Canaanite) kingship	Cushan-rishathaim, Eglon, Jabin (Gideon, Abimelech)
		Retribution	Abimelech (9:56–57)
1:11–15	Achsah	The woman with initiative who exercises power over men	Deborah, Jael the "certain woman" who kills Abimelech (Jephthah's daughter, Delilah)
1:22–26	Conquest of Bethel	Conquest by devious means	Ehud, Jael, (Gideon), Delilah, (Samson), the conquest of Gibeah
2:1–5	Messenger of Yahweh	Confrontational message	The prophet of Yahweh (Judg 6:7–10), Yahweh himself (Judg 10:10–16)

stacatto snippets to move the reader to the climax/nadir of this opening section.

Since language can render only one thing at a time, concurrence itself cannot but emerge in sequence. Even a narrative that favors the strictest chronology must at least mark time as its shifts or spreads out in space from one arena to another.[40] Thus the snippets portray:

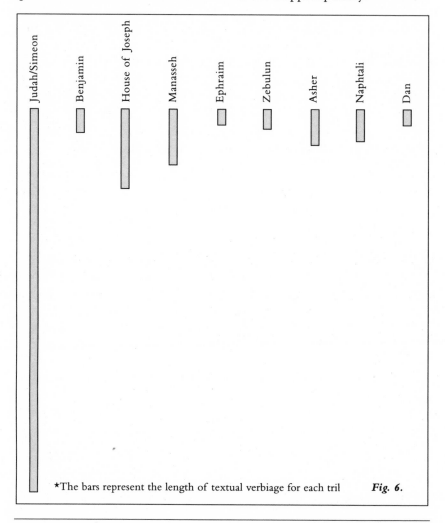

*The bars represent the length of textual verbiage for each tril   *Fig. 6.*

Because the texts are intimately tied to the book as a whole, one must consider the strong possibility that Judg 1:1–2:5 and 2:6–3:6 are not later framework additions but integral parts of the book (*contra* Boling).

40. M. Sternberg, "Time and Space in Biblical (Hi)story Telling: The Grand Chronology," *The Book and the Text: The Bible and Literary Theory* (ed. by Regina Schwartz; Oxford: Blackwell, 1990) 81–145, esp. 96–123.

This juxtaposition of the events narrated in Judges 1 (and for that matter in the Assyrian summary inscriptions) neutralizes and reshapes our very sense of time and distance. It has the power, not only to bring together under one umbrella events that are remote chronologically, but even to clothe simultaneity in the guise of sequence. The use of this structuring pattern in Judges 1 enhances the downward moral-spiritual movement mentioned above.

Indeed, a two-sided failure in the process of subjugation is observable in a four-stage decline in Israelite spirituality.[41] On one side, Judg 1:1–36 states that in many cases the subjugating tribe "did not drive out (*l' hwryš*)" the local population (vv. 19, 21, 27, 29, 30, 31, and 33). In only one case is the excuse for this failure to drive out the Canaanites attributed to inferior Israelite armament (v. 19). Rather, the impact of the formula is to state that this was an intentional failure to wipe out the population. In fact, this point is explicitly made in the somewhat parenthetical statement of v. 28: "When Israel became strong, they pressed the Canaanites into forced labor but never drove them out completely." Thus the writer/editor explains the failure to subjugate the promised land completely as being "the deliberate violation of older injunctions which commanded the removal of the nations of Canaan."[42] This failure climaxes in the case of the Danites through the ellipsis of this formula (*l' hwryš*). The writer emphasizes the fact that not only did the Danites fail to drive out the inhabitants of their allotment, they themselves were instead oppressed/confined by the Amorites and not allowed to come down into the plain (*ʿmq*)! Note that the only place from which Judah could not drive out the Canaanites was the plain (*ʿmq*).

Judges 1:1–36 uses the verb 'to live' (*yšb*) to illustrate on the other side this four-stage decline of Israelite spirituality. Beginning with Judah there is an absence of any statement concerning Canaanites living among Judah. Next, however, it is stated that the Canaanites lived among the tribes of Benjamin, Manasseh, Ephraim, and Zebulun (although Zebulun subjected them to forced labor). But then it is stated that the tribes of Asher and Naphtali lived among the Canaanites (although Naphtali subjected them to forced labor). And finally, the Danites were oppressed (*lḥṣ*,[43] within the same semantic field as Heb. *ms* 'forced labor'; cf. Exod 3:9) by the Amorites. Fig. 7 envisions this two-sided failure in the process

---

41. Cf. Webb, *Judges*, 97–101. He also notes the uses of *l' hwryš* and *ms* as "the focus shifts from conquest to co-existence" (p. 101).

42. See M. Fishbane, *Biblical Interpretation in Ancient Israel* (Oxford: Clarendon, 1985) 203.

43. The introduction of *lḥṣ* is ominous, foreshadowing things to come (see 2:18, 4:3, 6:9, and 10:12).

		Fig. 7. The Four-Stage Moral Decline in Judges 1 (with Special Reference to *l^ɔ hwryš* and *yšb*)	
1	Judah + Simeon	Initial success both tribal and individual. Judah drove out (*yrš*) the Canaanites. But did not drive out (*l^ɔ hwryš*) *in the plains*. No statement concerning Canaanites living among Judah or Simeon.	
2	Benjamin	Did not drive Jebusites out (*l^ɔ hwryš*). Jebusites live among them (*yšb*).	
	House of Joseph	Initial "arrangement" (at Bethel) through trickery.	
	Manasseh	Did not drive Canaanites out (*l^ɔ hwryš*). Canaanites live among them (*yšb*).	
		(*Parenthesis: Commentary*)	[When the Israelites are strong, they press the Canaanites into forced labor, but they never drive them out completely.]
	Ephraim	Did not drive Canaanites out (*l^ɔ hwryš*). Canaanites live among them (*yšb*).	
	Zebulun	Did not drive Canaanites out (*l^ɔ hwryš*). Canaanites live among them (*yšb*), *but are subject to forced labor* (*ms*).	
3	Asher	Did not drive Canaanites out (*l^ɔ hwryš*). Asherites live among the Canaanites (*yšb*), the inhabitants of the land.	
	Naphtali	Did not drive Canaanites out (*l^ɔ hwryš*). Naphtalites live among the Canaanites (*yšb*), the inhabitants of the land; *but the inhabitants are subject to forced labor* (*ms*).	
4	Dan	No statement concerning driving out. No statement concerning Canaanites living among Danites. Instead, Danites are *oppressed/confined* (*lḥṣ*); and not even allowed to come *into the plains*.	

of subjugation. That the narrator of Judges 1 has structured his account to emphasize this moral decline is evident from a comparison with the nar-

---

Fig. 8. The Allotments of Joshua 15–19
(with Special Reference to *l^{ɔ} hwryš* and *yšb*)

Judah	Unable to drive out (*l^{ɔ} ywklw hwryš*) the Jebusites. Jebusites live among them (*yšb*).	Josh 15:63
House of Joseph	Bethel mentioned.	
Ephraim	Did not drive Canaanites out (*l^{ɔ} hwryš*). Canaanites live among them (*yšb*); *but are subject to forced labor (ms).*	Josh 16:10
Manasseh	Unable to drive Canaanites out (*l^{ɔ} yklw hwryš*). Canaanites determined to live among them (*yšb*). [When Israel was strong, they pressed the Canaanites into forced labor; but they never drove them out completely.]	Josh 17:12
Benjamin	No statement concerning *l^{ɔ} hwryš* or *yšb*.	
Simeon	No statement concerning *l^{ɔ} hwryš* or *yšb*.	
Zebulun	No statement concerning *l^{ɔ} hwryš* or *yšb*.	
Issachar	No statement concerning *l^{ɔ} hwryš* or *yšb*.	
Asher	No statement concerning *l^{ɔ} hwryš* or *yšb*.	
Naphtali	No statement concerning *l^{ɔ} hwryš* or *yšb*.	
Dan	When the allotment of the Danites was lost to them, the Danites went up and fought against Leshem (Laish), and after capturing it and putting it to the sword, they took possession of it and settled in it, calling Leshsem "Dan" after their ancestor Dan.	Josh 19:47

ration in Joshua 15–19 of the tribal allotments and their allusion (or lack thereof) to *l^{ɔ} hwryš* and *yšb* in the context of each individual tribe. This can be seen clearly in fig. 8.

Note the differences. Judah is pictured in a more negative light in Josh 15:63 than in Judges 1 (they are "unable to drive out the Jebusites" and "the Jebusites live among them," respectively). Dan, on the other hand, is not depicted as negatively in Joshua as in Judges. Benjamin, Simeon, Zebulun, Issachar (an ellipsis in Judges), Asher, and Naphtali do not receive any negative treatment in Joshua. The order of Manasseh

and Ephraim in Judges 1 is the reverse of Joshua's arrangement so that
concentric patterning in the second stage might be accomplished with
the parenthetical commentary at the center. Note also that the comment
concerning the 'forced labor' (Heb. *ms*) of the Canaanites has been
moved from the description of Ephraim to Zebulun in order to close out
the second stage (note also Naphtali at the end of the third stage). Finally,
in Judges 1, Benjamin and Simeon are ordered so as to achieve a more
"pure" north–south arrangement.

Thus the "conquest account" in Judges 1 utilizes an artificial aesthetic
structure to accomplish its narration, just as the "conquest" and "allotment" accounts in the book of Joshua, but with a different orientation.[44]

While Judges 1 could be a later editorial addition, its historical accuracy is not dependent on a "supposed" non–all-Israel perspective. With
its geographic summary arrangement that reflects a degree of artificiality
(esp. with reference to the arrangement of the major judges), the text
evinces an impositional structure on a par with Joshua 9–12, although of
a dissimilar kind. Thus to posit that Judges is more historically reliable
than Joshua, without taking this imposed structure into account, appears
to me to be naive. Brettler has correctly observed this impositional structure, although he interprets it as pro-Judean.[45] This would certainly be
the case if there were not links with the rest of the book that portray all
the tribes, including Judah, in a negative manner.

Moreover, Judg 1:1–2:5 is really only the first of a two-fold introduction in which 2:6–3:6 functions to reveal the cyclical patterning of
the historical presentation that will dominate the main section of the
book (3:7–16:31). Klein correctly recognizes the parallelism of 1:1–2:5
and 2:6–3:6. The first section narrates from the point of view of the
Israelites and the second from the point of view of Yahweh. This dual
narration of the settlement of the land produces the potential for irony.[46]
Thus, in one sense, there is danger in interpreting 1:1–2:5 alone, because the writer/editor has purposely laid the one beside the other to
produce the effect desired. It is interesting to note that Esarhaddon's
Nineveh A inscriptions are another excellent example of this type of
double introduction.[47]

---

44. Only in Judg 1:1–8 are the typical, stereotyped syntagms of conquest accounts
encountered. If Judg 1:8 is utilizing stereotyped phrases, then *bny yhwdh* (Josh 15:63) and
bny bnymn (Judg 1:21) may not have had the ability (notice the use of *ykl* in Josh 15:63)
to *hwryš* 'drive out' (in a permanent sense) the Jebusites from Jerusalem.

45. Brettler, "Book of Judges," 395–400.

46. Klein, *Triumph of Irony*, 13.

47. See R. Borger, *Die Inschriften Asarhaddons: König von Assyrien* (AfO Beiheft; Graz:
by the author, 1956) 36–64 (I 1–7 and II 12–39). See also Grayson, "Histories and Historians," 154 n. 67; and H. Tadmor, "Autobiographical Apology in the Royal Assyrian

Thus, while in 1:1–2:5 success and failure are intermingled, the overall impression is increasingly negative, a pattern mirrored in the book of Judges as a whole.[48] And whereas the first part of the introduction (1:1–2:5) deals primarily with Israel's military failure, the second part (2:6–3:5) deals exclusively with the nation's religious failure, providing a cyclical account to reinforce and interpret 1:1–2:5 and to foreshadow the cyclical patterns to come: *disobedience–punishment : mercy–rest*. This type of cyclical history writing is not unique to ancient Israel. It can be observed in other ancient Near Eastern contexts. For example, Esarhaddon's Babylon inscriptions manifest a similar structure.[49] J. Brinkman discovered the following cyclical pattern in these incriptions: *divine alienation–devastation : divine reconciliation–reconstruction.* Moreover, the cycle is used in Esarhaddon's Babylon inscriptions as "a religious explanation (answering the question 'why')" for the destruction of Babylon.[50]

Accordingly, the "cycles" themselves in Judges 3:6–16:31 (often considered part of the so-called deuteronomistic framework) are arranged so as to point to the decline in the character of the judges as illustrative of the chaos of the time. However, as others have noted, the consistency of the pattern breaks down.[51] This is no happenstance. Cheryl Exum aptly remarks:

> Rather than attributing the lack of consistency in the framework pattern to careless redaction, I take it as a sign of further dissolution. The political and moral instability depicted in Judges is reflected in the textual instability. The framework deconstructs itself, so to speak, and the cycle of apostasy and deliverance becomes increasingly murky.[52]

Literature," *History, Historiography and Interpretation: Studies in Biblical Cuneiform Literature* (ed. H. Tadmor and M. Weinfeld; Jerusalem: Magnes, 1983) 36–57.

48. Exum, "Centre Cannot Hold," 413. See also her fine observations concerning the minor judges in the context of this "deconstruction" or "disruption" (p. 421).

49. Borger, *Inschriften Asarhaddons*, 12–15. See also Barbara N. Porter, *Symbols of Power: Figurative Aspects of Esarhaddon's Babylonian Policy (681–669 B.C.)* (Ph.D. diss., University of Pennsylvania, 1987); and A. Tsukimoto, "A New Esarhaddon Prism Fragment Concerning the Restoration of Babylon," *Annual Review of the Royal Inscriptions of Mesopotamia Project* 8 (1990) 63–69. For this cyclical pattern in Judges, see Polzin, *Moses and the Deuteronomist*, 140–50.

50. J. A. Brinkman, "Through a Glass Darkly: Esarhaddon's Retrospects on the Downfall of Babylon," in *Studies in Literature from the Ancient Near East by Members of the American Oriental Society: Dedicated to Samuel Noah Kramer* (ed. J. M. Sasson, J. A. Wakin, and P. W. Kroll; AOS 65; New Haven, Conn.: American Oriental Society, 1984) 35–42 = *JAOS* 103 (1983) 35–42.

51. See the excellent discussion of this point in F. E. Greenspahn, "The Theology of the Framework of Judges," *VT* 36 (1986) 385–96. Furthermore, each judge may be seen as a microcosm of the nation. See A. Hauser, "Unity and Diversity in Early Israel before Samuel," *JETS* 22 (1979) 289–303.

52. Exum, "Centre Cannot Hold," 412. This "deconstruction" that marks the moral decline in the relationship between Israel and Yahweh can also be seen in the characterization

In the narrative sequence of Judg 1:1–2:5 and 2:6–3:6, juxtaposition is used to communicate concurrence of events, or simultaneity. Judg 2:6–3:6 returns chronologically to the beginning of the book and functions as a flashback to the same characters and events as 1:1, amplifying the exposition.[53] Rather than hastening the march of events through ellipsis, the discourse suspends it along one line while tracing its parallel.

Furthermore, the double introduction is balanced by a double conclusion (chaps. 17–18 and 20–21), often misleadingly called "appendixes or additions." The double introduction and double conclusion (or better: "coda")[54] form a type of inclusio:[55]

A	Foreign wars of subjugation with the *ḥerem* being applied (1:1–2:5)
	B Difficulties with religious idols (2:6–3:6)
	B′ Difficulties with religious idols (17–18)
A′	Civil wars with the *ḥerem* being applied (20–21)

Fig. 9

---

of the women of the book, degenerating from the outspoken Achsah (1:12–15), to Deborah and Jael (Judges 4–5), to the "certain woman" (9:53), to Jephthah's daughter (11:53), to Delilah (16:4–22), and finally to the completely dependent and silent women of Judges 19–21. See Webb, *Judges*, 31 and K. R. R. Gros Louis, "The Book of Judges," *Literary Interpretations of Biblical Narratives* (ed. K. R. R. Gros Louis, J. S. Ackerman, and T. S. Warshaw; Nashville: Abingdon, 1974) 144–45.

53. Klein, *Triumph of Irony*, 12. This is preferable to the idea that Judg 2:6–10 is the *Wiederaufnahme* ('the resumptive repetition') of Josh 24:28–31, so that Judges 1 is seen as an inserted, fragmentary compilation and Judg 2:11 is the actual beginning of the book. See I. Seeligmann, "Hebräische Erzählung und biblische Geschichtsschreibung," *TZ* 18 (1962) 322–24. Evidence does, however, seem to point to the priority of Josh 24:28–31 over Judg 2:6–10 (see W. T. Koopmans, *Joshua 24*, 363–69).

54. Webb's term (*Judges*, 181–203). The unity of this section is apparent from the use of the refrain:

A . . . . . . In those days there was no king . . .
        Every man did what right in his own eyes (17:6)
             B . . . . . In those days there was no king . . . (18:1)
                 (Ellipsis)
             B′ . . . . . . In those days there was no king . . . (19:1)
                 (Ellipsis)
A′ . . . . . . In those days there was no king . . .
        Every man did what was right in his own eyes (21:25)

55. Exum, "Centre Cannot Hold," 413 and 429; and Boling, *Judges*, 29–38.

In Judg 17–21, Israel's enemy is no longer external but internal. Cyclical time is exhausted, and the period is predominantly characterized by absence: "In those days there was no king in Israel."[56] Polzin explains it this way:

> If the book's first chapter begins with an effective psychological portrait of the process whereby Israel, after Joshua's death, progressively went from certainty to confusion . . . the book's finale [chaps. 19–21] now completes with a flourish the paradoxical picture of confusion within certainty, obscurity in clarity, that has occupied its pages from the start . . . here [chaps. 19–21] the narrator is intent upon intensifying the doubt and confusion in Israel with which he began his story in Judges 1.[57]

CONCLUSIONS

A number of things can be observed from the inscriptions as a whole and the biblical episodes analyzed in particular. First, since Judges 1 is geographically arranged, the tribe is the natural focus of the narrative. This does not mean, however, that a unified Israel is not in view in the chapter. To the contrary, the concept of a unified Israel permeates the chapter (and book).[58] Note for example the very first verse:[59]

---

56. Ibid., 425. Compare Sternberg's remarks: "Apparently, then, the book moves in canonical order, only to finish with a couple of retrospects on the distant past. In fact, however, it juxtaposes the two final episodes to all the preceding episodes and to each other through the formula 'In those days there was no king in Israel; every man did what was right in his own eyes', repeated (with variations) at key points. It occurs at the outset of the 'appendix', twice for good retrospective measure (17:6; 18:1), recurs at its conclusion, which doubles as that of Judges (21:25), and also at the joint between its components (19:1). Beginning, middle, end: this loaded refrain calls for a repatterning of the whole Book of Judges. It seeks to replace nothing less than the book's principle of unity by effecting a switch in temporal framework and perspective, for example from the cycles of *post*-Joshuite (1:1; 2:6–23) sin and deliverance to a bird's-eye view of the *pre*-monarchical age, from a chaotic narrative past and present ('In those days') to a stable narrative future ('king of Israel'), from divine overlordship to human institutions of government, tribal as against royal" ("Time and Space," 109).

57. Polzin, *Moses and the Deuteronomist*, 200, 202.

58. To the narrator, the Israel of this period represented one nation. While it is possible that this was the retrojection of a later perception into an earlier period, D. Block has argued convincingly that the Israel that confronts us in the Book of Judges viewed itself as one nation ("The Period of the Judges: Religious Disintegration under Tribal Rule," in *Israel's Apostasy and Restoration: Essays in Honor of Roland K. Harrison* [ed. A. Gileadi; Grand Rapids, Mich.: Baker, 1988], 41–45; and idem, " 'Israel'–'Sons of Israel': A Study in Hebrew Eponymic Usage," *SR* 13 [1984] 301–26).

59. This cannot be excised as the work of a later Judean or pan-Israelite editor, since it is an integral part of the narrative (see fig. 3 on the structure of Judges 1:1–2:5, p. 215 above).

> After the death of Joshua,
> the people of Israel inquired of Yahweh,
>> "Who shall go up first for us [*lnw=yśr⁾l*]
>> against the Canaanites, to fight against them?"[60]

Furthermore, emphasis on the tribe does not cause a contradiction (as is often asserted)[61] about who conquered Hebron—Caleb, Judah, or Joshua—since credit in battle can be and often is given to individuals, regiments, and/or generals. One example will suffice. During the Second World War the bridge over the Rhine at Remagen was captured before the Nazis could destroy it. This bridgehead allowed the U.S. army to continue its advance and penetrate the heartland of Germany. On different occasions credit has sometimes been given to individuals (Mason, Thompson, etc.), the division (the 1st army), or the general (Hodges). The biblical text has preserved the individual (Caleb: Joshua 14), the tribe (Judah: Judges 1), and the leader (Joshua: Joshua 11). One may choose to reject the historicity of the accounts (just as one may choose to reject the historicity of the referents in the accounts of the battle for the bridge at Remagen), but there is no contradiction in literary principle.[62]

The "Israel" of Judges 1 is probably the same entity as in Judges 5, the Song of Deborah. *Israel* is mentioned in the Song seven times. The Song describes the war as a *national* war from the very first line: "When locks were loosed in *Israel.*"[63] The Song is to be sung to Yahweh, the God of *Israel.*" Verse 7 describes the situation "in *Israel*" when "Deborah arose, arose a mother in *Israel.*" Thus, regardless of the tribal delineation within it, the Song emphasizes the national entity, Israel, a supratribal subject of

---

60. This question assumes independence of action from the outset. Moreover, Yahweh answers in the imperative "Judah shall go up." As Klein has correctly noted, "Yahweh tells Israel (here Judah) specifically what to do, but Israel only partially heeds Yahweh's command: Judah immediately establishes a battle pact with his brother Simeon. Thus, from the outset, Israel exerts self-determination, evidencing automatic trust in human perception. These verses may be regarded as introducing the ironic configuration of the book—the implicit difference in perception between Yahweh and Israel and Israel's insistence on following human perception" (*Triumph of Irony*, 23). This only contributes more to the moral movement depicted in the narrative (see fig. 5 on the Moral Movement in Judges 1 above, p. 217).

61. See for example Auld, "Judges 1," 266.

62. The division (the 1st army) and the general (Hodges) are historically accurate. I have purposely given false information concerning individuals (Mason, Thompson, etc.) in order to illustrate my point.

63. For this translation of *pr⁽wt*, see: W. W. Hallo, "The Cultic Setting of Sumerian Poetry," *Actes de la XVIIᵉ rencontre assyriologique internationale* 17 (1970) 132. Cf. The Epic of Tukulti-Ninurta, V A.48 and also VI B.46 (see P. Machinist, *The Epic of Tukulti-Ninurta I: A Study in Middle Assyrian Literature* [Ph.D. diss., Yale University, 1978]).

historical action that existed *before* the war with the Canaanites.[64] Unfortunately, this fact is ignored in many reconstructions of Israelite origins.

Second, since both Joshua and Judges are figurative accounts utilizing either an iterative scheme of stereotyped syntagms or an artificial geographic arrangement, they narrate two aspects of one process: initial victory and subjugation. There is a difference between an initial victory and a subjugation that many interpreters ignore.[65] This difference is also observable in the conquests of Ashurnasirpal II and others. Liverani recently argued that the better model for the expansion and conquest of the Assyrians under Ashurnasirpal is a meshing process rather than an "expanding oil stain."[66] While some of Ashurnasirpal's campaigns brought certain areas under more direct Assyrian control, sometimes even through agricultural colonization, others simply "softened up" new areas for later subjugation. Similarly, while the conquest account in Joshua narrates in a partial and selective manner the initial victory that "softened up" the land, the partial, selective account of Judges 1 narrates the failure to subjugate that land later.[67] Importantly, then, Judges 1 stresses the incompleteness of that subjugation, so that while there may have been some sort of initial victory, Israel did not follow up and take advantage of this. The account in Judges 1 is no more and no less reliable than the account in Joshua. Both are highly stylized narrations re-presenting or imposing structures on the "historical" referents.[68]

64. On the question of tribal participation, see now K. L. Younger, "Heads! Tails! or the Whole Coin?! Contextual Method and Intertextual Analysis: Judges 4 and 5," *The Biblical Canon in Comparative Perspective: Scripture in Context IV* (ed. K. L. Younger, W. W. Hallo, and B. F. Batto; ANETS 11; Lewiston, N.Y.: Edwin Mellen, 1991). Also see Moshé Anbar, "Changement des noms des tribus nomades dans la relation d'un même événement," *Bib* 49 (1968) 221–32.

65. Brettler does not maintain a distinction between the initial conquest and subjugation of the land in his analysis of Judges 1 ("Book of Judges," 399). But numerous examples of initial conquest and later subjugation can be cited. The example of Damdammusa from the Annals of Ashurnasirpal II is a case in point. In the narrative of i 101–ii 2 above, the city Damdammusa (which Ashurnasirpal calls 'my royal city') is seized and is brought under Assyrian control, and yet in iii 105–iii 109 the city is called "the fortified city of the man of Bit-Zamani" and is conquered once again.

66. Liverani, "Growth of the Assyrian Empire," 91–92.

67. Ideologically, as writers of this sort often do, the writer of the text of Joshua manifests an unreal, utopian conception of the land of Israel (see Y. Kaufmann, *The Biblical Account of the Conquest of Canaan* [2d ed.; Jerusalem: Magnes, 1985], 72). This is true not only in the overall borders, but in the idealized tribal allotments and priestly and Levitical cities. In this regard, even the disproportionate attention given to the capture of Jericho (as opposed to the southern and northern campaigns) only reinforces the ideological orientation of the book.

68. It is important to note that the Standard Summary inscription of Ashurnasirpal II is included in the Kalah inscription. Thus summary and annalistic texts could be joined to create a more complicated document; just so, there is no difficulty in encountering both in the biblical texts.

Deborah among the Judges: The Perspective of the Hebrew Historian

Daniel I. Block

Bethel Theological Seminary

The advances made in the study of Old Testament historiography in the past fifteen or twenty years have been breathtaking. The most significant have occurred on two fronts. The often sterile preoccupation with source and form-critical issues and speculative historical reconstructionism that had preoccupied scholars for more than a century has, to a large extent, given way to a more holistic literary approach.[1] One of the most welcome results is an increased appreciation for the compositional artistry of Hebrew authors. Unfortunately, on occasion literary interpreters have become so intoxicated with the artistry of the ancient historians that their achievements are almost as "excavative"[2] as the efforts of previous generations of scholars. Because literary strategy preoccupies the new generation, it often pays inadequate attention to authorial intention. However, when reflection on literary strategy has occurred, exciting new dimensions of the message of the ancient historians have been discovered.

---

1. Leading the way in this hermeneutical revolution have been among others, Jacob Licht, *Storytelling in the Bible* (Jerusalem: Magnes, 1978); Robert Alter, *The Art of Biblical Narrative* (New York: Basic Books, 1981); Adele Berlin, *Poetics and Interpretation of Biblical Narrative* (Bible and Literature Series 9; Sheffield: Almond, 1983); and Meir Sternberg, *The Poetics of Biblical Narrative: Ideological Literature and the Drama of Reading* (Bloomington, Ind.: Indiana University Press, 1985). The *Journal for the Study of the Old Testament* is devoted largely to publication of articles in this vein. See also *Beyond Form Criticism: Essays in Old Testament Literary Criticism* (ed. P. House; Sources for Biblical and Theological Study 2; Winona Lake, Ind.: Eisenbrauns, 1992).

2. An expression used by Alter (*Art of Biblical Narrative*, 13) of older source and form-critical approaches. However, the criticism leveled by Alter at these approaches often applies to his own literary handling of specific texts.

Simultaneous with these literary advances has come an increased awareness of the fact that the Hebrew historians were children of their own ages. Their work should not be judged according to modern standards of historiography in which the value of a work is directly proportional to an author's objectivity and emotional detachment from the events reported. On the contrary, like the chroniclers of Egyptian and Babylonian affairs, Hebrew historians were polemicists. Although the Christian classification of a certain segment of the Old Testament as "historical books" overlooks this fact completely, it was not lost to the ancient Hebrew scribes who referred to these same works as "The Former Prophets." Their authors wore their biases on their sleeves. The sooner these biases are recognized, the more valid interpretation will be.

These advances in literary criticism have also influenced recent work on the book of Judges. To be sure, some scholars in conservative circles continue to moralize about the primary figures in the book. Taking their cue from Heb 11:32, they look on Barak, Gideon, Jephthah, and Samson as heroes of faith whose qualities are to be emulated by contemporary believers.[3] However, this picture of these men is difficult to reconcile with the portrait presented by the author of Judges. On the other hand, many scholars continue to speculate about the history of the text, unraveling layers of tradition with remarkable exegetical dexterity. In the process, the sources from which the editors of the present biblical text have drawn their material are chronologically rearranged and given a life and meaning of their own.[4] These sources obviously tell the reader more about the times in which they were produced than the events they purport to describe. Nevertheless, the rearrangement provides a basis for reconstructing a political and social history of Israel.

In increasing numbers, scholars have found the moralizing and source-critical approaches to be wanting and have been turning to a more holistic literary investigation of the book of Judges.[5] However, the conclusions

3. See Leon J. Wood, *Distressing Days of the Judges* (Grand Rapids: Zondervan, 1975); C. J. Goslinga, *Joshua, Judges, Ruth* (Bible Student's Commentary; Grand Rapids, Mich.: Zondervan, 1986). This idealizing of the judges by the author of Hebrews follows a long-standing custom, as is evident from Sir 46:11–12.

4. Among the most notable examples are R. G. Boling, *Judges: A New Translation with Introduction and Commentary* (AB 6A; Garden City, N.Y.: Doubleday, 1975), and J. A. Soggin, *Judges: A Commentary* (OTL; Philadelphia: Westminster, 1981). See the seminal work by Martin Noth, *The Deuteronomistic History* (JSOTSup 15; Sheffield: JSOT Press, 1981) 1–110 (translation of *Überlieferungsgeschichtliche Studien*, 3d ed., 1967). See also the more recent essay by S. Warner, "The Dating of the Period of the Judges," *VT* 28 (1978) 455–63.

5. See further D. I. Block, "The Period of the Judges: Religious Disintegration under Tribal Rule," *Israel's Apostasy and Restoration: Essays in Honor of Roland K. Harrison* (ed. A. Gileadi; Grand Rapids, Mich.: Baker, 1988) 39–58; idem., "Echo Narrative Technique

drawn from their studies have not been uniform. While the literary qualities of the book are gaining increased appreciation, considerable divergence of opinion on the central thesis of the author remains. This applies to the macroscopic level of the book and to the interpretation of individual units as well. Whereas I tend to view Judges as a prophetic work lamenting the Canaanization of Israelite society, some continue to interpret it essentially as a pro-Judaean political tractate in defense of the Davidic monarchy.[6] Thus Marc Brettler posits, "This book was composed as a political allegory fostering the Davidic monarchy" and in so doing represents "a polemic against Ephraimite, namely, northern, kingship."[7] To be sure, the observation repeated four times, "In those days there was no king in Israel; everyone did what was right in his own eyes" (17:6, 18:1, 19:1, and 21:25), highlights a political reality, and the anti-Ephraimite stance of many of the narratives is undeniable,[8] but this hardly represents the overall tenor of the book.

Disagreement over the interpretation of individual units is also common. The noticeable ambiguity of the author has not only contributed to the richness of the composition, but it has also invited a variety of interpretations. In this paper I address one such unit, the story of Deborah and Barak, told in both narrative (4:1–24) and poetic form (5:1–31). Specifically, I am concerned with the author's presentation of the role of Deborah in the flow of historical events. What part did she play in this period of rapid and widespread Canaanization of Israelite society? The author himself seems to offer three possibilities: (1) he identifies her explicitly as a 'prophet' of Yahweh (*nĕbîʾâ*, 4:4); (2) he informs the reader that she 'judged' (*špṭ*) Israel (4:5); and (3) he describes her involvement in the 'deliverance' (*yšʿ*) of the nation from a foreign enemy. She was a remarkable woman! The degeneracy of her times and the general lack of leadership within the nation thrust her remarkable position into even sharper relief.

Yet, while the account appears to paint her with bold definitive strokes, it raises a host of questions concerning the author's view of her actual status in Israel. Was she really a prophet? A judge? A deliverer?

---

in Hebrew Literature: A Study in Judges 19," *WTJ* 52 (1990) 325–36. See the monographs by Robert Polzin, *Moses and the Deuteronomist: A Literary Study of the Deuteronomic History* (New York: Seabury, 1980), esp. 146–204; Barry G. Webb, *The Book of Judges: An Integrated Reading* (JSOTSup 46; Sheffield: Sheffield Academic Press, 1987); and Lillian R. Klein, *The Triumph of Irony in the Book of Judges* (JSOTSup 68; Sheffield: Almond Press, 1988); not to mention a spate of articles on specific texts.

7. Marc Brettler, "The Book of Judges: Literature as Politics," *JBL* 108 (1989) 416.

8. Ibid., 416. In contrast, see the excellent literary and "theological" interpretation of Y. Amit, "Judges 4: Its Content and Form," *JSOT* 39 (1987) 89–111.

Each of these questions calls for further reflection. Without a "closer reading" of the text one might arrive at premature conclusions. I wish to examine the presentation of her involvement in each of these roles in reverse order. In the process the search for a clearer understanding of her perceived place in history should also yield an increased appreciation for the methodology of one ancient Hebrew historian.

DEBORAH: THE DELIVERER OF ISRAEL?

Deborah has usually been viewed as one of the heroic deliverers of Israel during the dark days of the Judges. To be sure, she is nowhere explicitly referred to as a 'savior' (*môšîᶜâ*)[9] or as having 'saved' (*hôšîᶜâ*) Israel 'from the hand' (*mikkap/miyyad*) of her enemies[10] or to have brought salvation to them.[11] However, it is obvious that her portrayal in this role does not depend on the presence of technical terms, and many view her primarily as the one who delivered the Israelites from the oppression of Jabin, the Canaanite king, and his general, Sisera.[12] Cundall introduces her as "the savior of her people and the only woman in the distinguished company of the Judges."[13] Commenting on 5:6–8, he notes that a "desperate situation obtained until Deborah arose to effect the deliverance of the nation."[14] This conclusion is not surprising for several reasons.

First of all, in the stereotypical structuring of the accounts of the six deliverances, she is introduced at precisely the point where one would expect the naming of a judge. While making some allowances for variations in order, the accounts share a common structure that may be summarized as follows:

1. An announcement: "The Israelites did evil in the sight of Yahweh."
2. A statement of Yahweh's response (e.g., he sold them into an enemy's hands).
3. A notice of how long Israel was subservient to the enemy.

---

9. See Judg 2:16; 3:9, and 15. Also 1 Sam 11:3; 2 Sam 22:42 = Ps 18:42; and 2 Kgs 13:5.

10. See Judg 2:16, 6:14, 8:22, 12:2, 13:5; 1 Sam 4:3, 9:16; 2 Kgs 16:7; and Neh 9:27. Also Judg 3:31, 6:15, 10:1; and 1 Sam 10:27 (all without *mikkap/miyyad*).

11. See Judg 15:18, 1 Sam 11:9 (see v. 13 with Yahweh as subject), 2 Kgs 5:1, and 1 Chr 19:12.

12. The problems involved in the identification of these men and their relationship to one another is amply dealt with in the literature and need not detain us here.

13. A. E. Cundall, *Judges and Ruth* (TOTC; Downers Grove, Ill.: InterVarsity, 1968) 82.

14. Ibid., 95.

4. A reference to Israel's 'crying' (*zā ͨaq/ṣā ͨaq*) to Yahweh.
5. An announcement of Yahweh's 'raising up' (*hēqîm*) of a deliverer.
6. A description of the way deliverance was achieved.
7. A concluding note about the length of time the land had rest.

The fact that the first cycle, the story of Othniel and his victory over Cushan-Rishathaim, offers few details beyond this skeletal outline reinforces its purpose as a paradigmatic introduction to the sequence of narratives that follows.[15] They tend to expand on individual phases of this structure, but the basic pattern is preserved throughout. Judges 4 follows this pattern precisely, with the exception of no. 5; it lacks a formal announcement of the raising up of a deliverer. However, at precisely the point where that person's name is expected, Deborah is introduced.

Second, Deborah is actively involved in effecting the deliverance. She accompanies Barak when the troops of Zebulun and Naphtali are marshaled (4:10); she appears to march out into battle with them (4:10b, 14); like general Ehud in the previous account, she announces in advance that Yahweh has delivered the enemy into their hands.[16] The author thereby invites the reader to think of Deborah as a female version of Ehud.

Third, in Deborah's response to Barak's hesitation she hints at her role: "I will go with you, but the honor that comes from the adventure on which we are embarking shall not be yours; for Yahweh will sell Sisera into the hands of a woman" (v. 9). Reading the story to its conclusion, this prediction is fulfilled in Jael. But did Deborah know that this would be the outcome? Or did she anticipate that she would come home with the glory of victory? At this point the author invites the reader to think so.

Fourth, in the poem that follows, Deborah's appearance in Israel coincides with the return of security in the countryside (5:6–8). In fact, although the verses that follow are extremely difficult to interpret, they

---

15. Brettler treats it as an allegory "which sets the tone for the book of Judges as a whole" ("Book of Judges," 404–5).
16. The verbal echo of 3:28 in 4:14 is intentional:

3:28	4:14
wayyō ͻmer [ͻēhûd]	*wattō ͻmer dĕbōrâ*
ͻ*ălēhem*	ͻ*el bārāq*
ridĕpû ͨ*aḥăray*	*qûm*
kî	*kî*
	zeh hayyôm ͻ*ăšer*
nātan yhwh	*nātan yhwh*
ͻ*et* ͻ*ōyĕbêkem*	ͻ*et sîsĕrā* ͻ
ͻ*et mô* ͻ*āb*	
bĕyedkem	*bĕyādekā*

leave the impression that Deborah was involved in marshaling the troops. Furthermore, when named alongside Barak, she is given priority, supporting the view that credit for the victory was primarily hers. Admittedly, this poem represents an independent source, but its very inclusion here requires its interpretation within the context of the surrounding narrative.[17]

Fifth, the description of Sisera, Jabin's army commander, 'sitting/ruling' in Harosheth of the Gentiles finds an answer in the description of Deborah, 'sitting/ruling' under her own palm tree. This striking lexical link suggests that Deborah was viewed as the Israelite counterpart to Sisera. In the same way that Sisera served as the viceroy of Jabin, so Deborah apparently functioned on behalf of Yahweh.

Finally, Deborah is explicitly described as judging Israel (4:5). While momentarily delaying discussion of the judicial function involved in this expression, I observe that the succeeding deliverers are also identified as judges (*šōpĕtîm*). In fact, in the preamble to the "Book of Deliverers" (3:7–16:31), the author explicitly describes the role of judges (*šōpĕtîm*) soteriologically: "Then Yahweh raised up judges who delivered (*hōšî^câ*) them from the hands of those who plundered them" (2:16; see v. 18). By referring to Deborah as a 'judge' (*šōpĕtâ*), the author invites the reader to interpret her as one of these judges. G. F. Moore found the weight of this evidence so convincing that he argued for translating *hî^ šōpĕtâ ^et yiśrā^ēl* as 'she delivered Israel' (4:4).[18] He found parallels to Deborah in the German Veleda, who supported Civilis in his efforts to throw off the Roman yoke, and Joan of Arc, the devout maid from Domrémy, Champagne, who led the French forces in delivering her land from England.[19]

Upon a closer reading, however, one realizes that the presentation of Deborah as a savior of her people is more apparent than real.[20] The "al-

---

17. The relationship between the prose and poetic accounts of these events has been discussed many times. In general the poetic version, because it is the older account, is considered more reliable for recreating history. In fact, B. Halpern has argued that, although obviously the work of a clever intellect, chap. 4 represents a garbled and unreliable interpretation of chap. 5 ("The Resourceful Israelite Historian: The Song of Deborah and Israelite Historiography," *HTR* 76 [1983] 379–401). However, the reliability of the poem (by virtue of its antiquity) is offset by its nature as a work of poetry. Like Exodus 15, which offers an enthusiastic celebration of the events described in Exodus 14, the aim of the Song of Deborah and Barak is to inspire, not to chronicle events. For a pessimistic view of the value of Judges 5 in reconstructing the history of premonarchic Israel, see A. Caquot, "Les tribus de Israël dans le Cantique de Débora (Judg 5:13–17)," *Sem* 36 (1986) 47–70.

18. G. F. Moore, *A Critical and Exegetical Commentary on Judges* (ICC; Edinburgh: T. & T. Clark, 1895) 114.

19. Ibid., 112–13.

20. See Polzin's comment "that the story is all about how things are not what they seem" (*Moses and the Deuteronomist*, 163).

together enigmatic"[21] nature of the narrative raises numerous questions. If the author considered Deborah one of the deliverers of Israel,

1. Why is she not introduced as one whom Yahweh had raised up?
2. Why is there no reference to her inspiration and empowerment by Yahweh's Spirit (*rûaḥ yhwh*), as the reader has witnessed in the life of Othniel (3:10) and will observe in Gideon (6:34), Jephthah (11:29), and Samson (14:19 and 15:14)?
3. Why does she need Barak to accomplish the deliverance?
4. Why is the verb *yšᶜ* 'to save' never applied to her?
5. Why does she say "Yahweh will sell Sisera into the hands of a woman," instead of "into my hands"?
6. Why does the author observe that "she went up with Barak" (4:10) but avoid placing her at the head of the troops?
7. Why does Deborah announce to Barak, "This day Yahweh has given Sisera into *your* hands," rather than "my hands" (4:14)?
8. Why is she entirely absent from the description of the actual battle (4:15–17)?
9. Why did the poet prefer the title "mother in Israel" to "savior of Israel" (5:7)?
10. Why does the poet avoid the root (*qûm*), let alone referring to Yahweh as the causative subject, when he speaks of Deborah's rise (5:7, *šqm*, 2 times).

There is an additional reason not to place Deborah in a class with the rest of the deliverer judges: her character. Her presence as a woman in a man's world has often been noted.[22] However, equally striking is the qualitative contrast between her character and those of the rest of the deliverers. To be sure, the narrative says nothing negative about Othniel, but then the account of him as the first judge is relatively colorless, casting him as a paradigm against which to view the rest. Ehud's personality is not criticized overtly, but at the end of the account the author leaves the reader wondering whether he is to be viewed as a hero or as a villain. Granted, he was raised by Yahweh as the agent of deliverance, but his treacherous tactics look for all the world like typical Canaanite behavior. But after Deborah there was an obvious deterioration in the quality of the individuals called on to deliver Israel. Far from being solutions to the

---

21. So also Klein, *Triumph of Irony*, 42.

22. See K. R. R. Gros Louis, "The Book of Judges," *Literary Interpretations of Biblical Narratives* (ed. K. R. R. Gros Louis et al.; Nashville: Abingdon, 1974) 148; B. Lindars, "Deborah's Song: Women in the Old Testament," *BJRL* 65 (1983) 158–75, esp. 172–75; Jo Ann Hackett, "Women's Studies and the Hebrew Bible," in *The Future of Biblical Studies: The Hebrew Scriptures* (ed. R. E. Friedman and H. G. M. Williamson; Atlanta: Scholars Press, 1989) 154–55.

Canaanization of Israelite thought and ethic, Gideon, Jephthah, and Samson were themselves all parts of the problem. The narrator seems to have arranged the accounts of the judges deliberately to demonstrate that with each cycle the apostasy snowballed. These were not noblemen; they were "antiheroes."[23] But Deborah was different. She was the only one the narrator cast in an unequivocally positive light. She was the only one who was involved in the service of Yahweh prior to her engagement in the deliverance. She stands out as a lonely figure indeed.[24]

Could it be that, by inviting a consideration of Deborah among the savior judges, the narrator has led his readers up the proverbial garden path? She appears on the surface to be a deliverer, but this could be a ruse. Significantly, in later lists of the deliverers, Barak's name appears, but never Deborah's.[25]

DEBORAH: A JUDGE OF ISRAEL?

The assertion that Deborah judged Israel seems so straightforward that it seems unnecessary to question it here. The narrator even provides several additional details about the ways in which her role was carried out. In the first place, she used to sit under the palm of Deborah. As already suggested, the term *yāšab* 'to sit' hints at some official governmental function. The location of her "capital," "under the palm of Deborah,"[26] may have been unpretentious, but it was well known. In fact, her central location between Ramah and Bethel in the highlands of Ephraim made her accessible to the entire nation.

But what attracted the Israelites to this woman sitting in the shade of the palm tree? Was she an early version of Margaret Thatcher, whom General Haig characterized as "the best man in the British cabinet"?[27] The narrator observes almost tautologically that the Israelites came to her 'for judgment' (*lammišpāṭ*). But what does this mean?

Traditionally, scholars have interpreted this to mean that she was exercising a judicial function. According to Stek, the narrator presents

---

23. An expression used by Brettler, "Book of Judges," 407. However, he interprets the sequence of deliverers politically, with the southern representatives (Othniel and Ehud) cast in a more favorable light than their northern counterparts. But the fact that Deborah was an Ephraimite casts some doubt on Brettler's thesis.

24. Boling (*Judges*, 94) describes Deborah as an "honorable honorary judge," in contrast to the "dishonorable divinely appointed judge Samson."

25. See 1 Sam 12:9–11 and Heb 11:32.

26. On the expression see the commentaries.

27. As cited by A. G. Auld, *Joshua, Judges, and Ruth* (Daily Study Bible; Philadelphia: Westminster, 1984) 154.

her as "the source of justice where the wronged in Israel can secure redress and the oppressed relief."[28] The NIV translates *lammišpāṭ* accordingly, 'to have their disputes decided'. Analogues of this type of judicial "sitting" are common in the Old Testament. To cite just one example, according to Exodus 18:16, Moses explained his own "sitting" thus: "Whenever they have a dispute, it comes to me, and I judge between a person and his neighbor." By this interpretation, Deborah held what Soggin calls a "forensic office."[29]

Though traditional, this interpretation is open to question on several counts. First, in the present context it is difficult to see a connection between such a judicial function and her role in the rest of the narrative. Stek's suggestion that her role in settling disputes might have awakened expectations that she would emerge as a liberator of the tribes from Jabin's harsh rule is speculative, overestimating her role as savior.[30]

Second, the narrator does not mention whether she continued judging Israel after the defeat of Jabin, let alone how long she judged. This is not the way he handles the judges who apparently succeeded her.[31] To be sure, the land had rest for forty years (5:31), but this fact is attributed to the efforts of God and the Israelites (4:23–24). By the time of this rest, Deborah was already out of the picture. In fact, the author seems to have had no interest in relaying any judicial activity by Deborah at all.

Third, the comparison between the activities of Deborah and Samuel, as described in 1 Sam 7:15-17, is less supportive than it seems on first sight. In 1 Samuel, Samuel was obviously presented as a "judge" after the order of Deborah,[32] but the differences should not be overlooked.

---

28. John H. Stek, "The Bee and the Mountain Goat: A Literary Reading of Judges 4," *A Tribute to Gleason Archer* (ed. W. C. Kaiser and R. F. Youngblood; Chicago: Moody, 1986) 62.

29. Soggin, *Judges*, 72.

30. Stek, "Bee and Mountain Goat," 62.

31. See Judg 12:7 (Jephthah), 15:20, and 16:31 (Samson). See also the archival notes regarding Tola (10:1–2), Jair (10:3–5), Ibzan (12:8–10), Elon (12:11–12), and Abdon (12:13–15).

32. In so doing, the narrator of 1 Samuel has distanced him from the deliverer judges. As a matter of fact, the view that the narratives of the charismatic judges actually continue through the life of Samuel should be rejected.

1. Nowhere is Samuel portrayed as a *môšîaᶜ* 'savior', raised up by Yahweh to deliver Israel from an enemy oppressor.

2. Nowhere is Samuel described as marshaling the troops and leading them into battle. His role in 1 Samuel 7 is quite different. In fact, in 8:20 the people lament that he has not been a deliverer.

3. His character does not fit the pattern of the judges in the book of Judges.

4. His role as reformer bears a greater resemblance to Yahweh's *malʾāk* 'envoy' in Judg 2:1 and the prophet in 6:7–10, than to the judges.

1. The text declares explicitly that Samuel's term as judge was life-long.
2. Samuel carried out his duties as a circuit judge, presiding annually at Bethel, Gilgal, and Mizpeh.
3. Samuel was also engaged in cultic activity, as his construction of the altar to Yahweh at Ramah indicates.

Unfortunately, as in the case of Deborah, the nature of the *mišpāṭ* 'judgment' that Samuel executed is not indicated. The text declares simply that he 'judged' Israel. Furthermore, not only does the construction of the altar indicate a priestly role, the events in the preceding and succeeding accounts are evidence of a national, prophetic role. In view of his standing in the community, it would not be surprising to find that the people also brought their civil cases to Samuel; however, nowhere is Samuel (or Deborah, for that matter) portrayed as actually holding court and settling disputes among the citizens.

The case for Deborah's being a legal functionary rests entirely upon the presence of the root *špṭ*: "She was judging (*šōpĕṭâ*) Israel at that time" (4:4); "the sons of Israel came to her for judgment (*lammišpāṭ*)" (4:5). But does this mean that she was settling legal disputes and criminal cases among the Israelites, as is commonly supposed? Probably not.

A judicial interpretation of the root *špṭ* is not required in this context. In fact, there is not a single occurrence of the term in the book that requires a judicial interpretation. As noted above, where their roles are defined, the "judges" are presented primarily as deliverers. Even in the formulaic comments that an individual "judged" Israel so many years,[33] the word may carry the more general meaning 'to govern'. This interpretation accords well with its meaning in a number of texts outside of Judges, where the sense 'to rule' is intended,[34] as well as with the meaning of the cognates in Ugaritic and Akkadian.[35] In each instance in

---

33. Judg 10:2, 3; 12:7, 9, 11, 14; 15:20; and 16:31. See also 3:10; 12:8, and 13.

34. See 2 Kgs 15:5; Isa 40:23 *šōpĕṭîm*//*rōzĕnîm* 'ruler', which in Judg 5:3 is paired with *mĕlākîm*; Amos 2:3, //*śarîm*; Ps 2:10, //*mĕlākîm*; 94:2; and 148:11, //*mĕlākîm*, *śarîm*. G. Liedke argues that in Hebrew the root *špṭ* refers fundamentally to a restoration of *šālôm* and is then used with the derived sense of 'to govern' (*THAT* 2.999–1001).

35. *Ugaritic:* While *špṭ* is clearly used in a judicial sense when paired with *dn* (CTA 16:6.34.47, 17.5.8, and 19.1.25), elsewhere it is paired with *mlk* (CTA 2.3.18, 6.6.29) and with *ytb* 'to sit [as king]' (*Ug* V 2.1.3; *KTU* 1.108, 1.113). For a discussion of these texts, see F. C. Fensham, "The Ugaritic Root *špṭ*," *JNSL* 12 (1984) 63–69. See also H. Cazelles, "*Mtpt* à Ugarit," *Or* 53 (1984) 177–82.

Akkadian: Based on the usage of *šāpiṭum* in the Mari tablets, T. J. Mafico concludes, "The *šāpiṭum* was appointed by the higher ruling authorities primarily to assist in the administration of a territory as a 'ruler' or 'governor'" ("The Term *šāpiṭum* in Akkadian Documents," *JNSL* 13 [1987] 72).

Judges the context must determine the meaning. Since the narrator has applied the term *šōpēṭ* unconventionally to 'deliverers' in other contexts, the possibility should be allowed that a special usage is intended here as well.[36] Furthermore, one wonders why the narrator would have made this passing reference to the settlement of relatively petty civil disputes when the issue in the chapter is a national crisis.

Second, the term *mišpāṭ* in particular does not need to be understood as denoting a legal decision. Several specific features of Judg 4:5 hint that something more than routine judicial cases was involved. On the one hand, those who came to Deborah for "judgment" are referred to as *běnê yiśrāʾēl* ('sons of Israel'), an expression that is used consistently in the book as a collective, referring to the nation as a whole rather than particular individuals.[37] On the other hand, the articular construction *lammišpāṭ* 'for *the* judgment' is deliberate and suggests that a particular issue is in mind, not a series of cases or a routine fulfillment of professional duties. As already observed, the context informs the reader what that issue is: the oppression at the hands of Jabin and the Canaanites.

This leads me to a third consideration, the relationship of the word *mišpāṭ* to the verb *ṣāʿaq*. J. S. Ackerman has argued convincingly that the action described in v. 5 represents an exposition on v. 3a, "the sons of Israel cried out (*ṣāʿaq*) to Yahweh."[38] He observes that in the narratives on the United Monarchy, *ṣāʿaq* and *mišpāṭ* were closely related. When subjects appealed (*ṣāʿaq*) to a king for help in a matter, his pronouncement in response was designated his *mišpāṭ* (cf. 1 Kgs 20:39–40). In 2 Kgs 6:26 a woman cried out (*ṣāʿaq*) to the King of Israel for help (*hôšîʿâ*), but in this case he was unable to respond. According to 1 Kgs 3:16–28, when the two prostitutes came to Solomon to settle their dispute regarding the surviving son, the king's decision was designated his *mišpāṭ* (see also 2 Sam 15:1–6). This use of *mišpāṭ* applied particularly to life-threatening situations, as Job demonstrates in 19:7:

> Look! I cry out (*ṣāʿaq*), "Violence!"
> But I am not answered (*ʿānâ*).
> I shout aloud,
> But there is no response (*ʾēn mišpāṭ*).

---

36. See Boling's comment (*Judges*, 221) that "general observations about the origins of law in customary procedures do not alone determine the semantics of *mišpāṭ* in the Book of Judges."

37. See the brief discussion in Block, "Period of the Judges," as well as the fuller treatment of the expression in " 'Israel'–'Sons of Israel': A Study in Hebrew Eponymic Usage," *SR* 13 (1984) 301–26.

38. James S. Ackerman, "Prophecy and Warfare in Early Israel: A Study of the Deborah-Barak Story," *BASOR* 220 (1975) 11; following Boling, *Judges*, 81, 95.

In the book of Judges such cries ($ṣā^caq$ or its biform $zā^caq$) for deliverance were never addressed to a human authority; they were always directed to Yahweh.[39] In fact, in 10:14, when "the sons of Israel" made their appeal to him, he retorted sarcastically, "Go and cry out ($zā^caq$) to the gods whom you have chosen! Let them save ($hôšîa^c$) you from your distress ($ṣārâ$)!" It appears that when "the sons of Israel" came to Deborah for "the judgment," they were not asking her to solve their legal disputes but to give them the divine answer to their cries. She functioned as a representative of Yahweh.

DEBORAH: A PROPHET OF YAHWEH

In determining Deborah's role as perceived by the author of Judges, more careful attention should be paid to the manner in which he introduces her. In Judg 4:4 she is explicitly identified as a prophetess ($nĕbî^ʾâ$). While the etymology of $nābî^ʾ$ is uncertain,[40] the role of the prophet is clearly defined in texts such as Exod 4:15–16 and 7:1–2. A prophet served as a spokesperson for deity to the people. The designation deliberately places her in the line of succession to Moses (see Deut 18:15–22) and in the company of other female bearers of this title.[41]

Deborah's prophetic status and not her judicial office led the "sons of Israel" to come to her at the palm between Ramah and Bethel. They came to her to hear Yahweh's determination of their case, here designated $hammišpāṭ$. Although several of the cases adduced above to point out the connection between $ṣā^caq$ and $mišpāṭ$ involved legal decisions, this oracular use of $mišpāṭ$ is firmly attested elsewhere in the Old Testament.

The pocket containing the Urim and the Thummim, worn by the Israelite high priest, was designated $hōšen hammišpāṭ$ 'the pouch of the judgment' (Exod 28:30). Nowhere are the nature and function of these special stones spelled out, but Cassuto is certainly correct when he concludes: "They served as a means of inquiring of God, that is to say, of obtaining from the Deity, with the help of the priest, an answer concerning matters beyond human ken."[42] The usage of the Urim and the Thummim is clearly illustrated in Num 27:21, which describes the way Joshua was supposed to conduct the affairs of state when he succeeded Moses:

39. Judg 3:9, 15; 4:3; 6:6; 10:10. In every instance the subject is "the sons of Israel."
40. See J. Jeremias, "Nabiʾ Prophet," *THAT* 2.7–26.
41. Those named in the Old Testament include Miriam, Exod 15:20; Huldah, 2 Kgs 22:14; and Noadiah, Neh 6:14. See also Anna in Luke 2:36. Isaiah's wife is unnamed, Isa 8:3.
42. U. Cassuto, *A Commentary on the Book of Exodus* (Jerusalem: Magnes, 1967) 380.

He shall stand before Eleazar the priest, who shall inquire (*šā²al*) on his behalf by the judgment of Urim (*bĕmmišpaṭ ha²ûrîm*) before Yahweh. According to his (Yahweh's) mouth (*ʿal pîw*) they shall conduct their affairs,[43] that is Joshua himself, and the sons of Israel with him, and the entire congregation.

This procedure seems to have been followed in Joshua 7 (the determination of Achan as the guilty party), as well as in chaps. 18–19 (the apportionment of the tribal lands). In the case of the Gibeonites, the narrator states specifically that they did not "consult the mouth of Yahweh (*²et pî yhwh lō² šā²ālû*)" (9:14). This procedure was still followed after the death of Joshua. On several occasions in the book of Judges the Israelites seek a divine determination (*šā²al bayhwh*) concerning the conduct of their affairs. In Judg 1:1 the issue is leadership in the battle against the Canaanites and the conquest of tribal territory; in chap. 20 it is the manner in which to conduct the war against the Benjamites.

The latter passage is especially significant for several reasons. Three times "the sons of Israel" go up (*ʿālâ*) to Bethel to inquire of God (*šāʿal bē²lōhîm*, vv. 18 and 23; *bayhwh*, v. 27). In the last instance, the narrator adds an explanatory note concerning the reason they went to Bethel: the ark of the covenant of God was there in those days and Phinehas, the son of Eleazar, Aaron's son "stood before it" in those days. The practice continued into the monarchic period, though with mixed success. Saul is known to have consulted Yahweh on several occasions (see 1 Sam 14:36–42). However, the futility of his efforts in the end is summarized in 1 Sam 28:6: "When Saul inquired of Yahweh (*šāʿal bayhwh*) he refused to answer (*ʿānâ*) him either by dreams, or by Urim, or by prophets." David seems to have had more success. Not only did Yahweh inform him regarding the campaign against the Philistines (1 Sam 23:1–5), he also instructed him regarding his relations with Saul (23:6–12).[44]

Although the verb *ʿālâ* is used in its normal sense 'to go up' in the book of Judges (cf. 1:4), and the location of the palm of Deborah is expressly referred to as being "in the hill country of Ephraim," the affinities of Judges 4:4–5 with 20:18, 23, and 27 suggest that in 4:5 the verb *ʿālâ* assumes an almost technical sense of 'to go up [to the high place] to inquire [of the deity]'. Because Deborah stationed herself near Bethel, her oracle presented an alternative to the Urim and Thummim of the priesthood in town. The fact that the Israelites came to her instead of the priest reflects the failure of the established institution to maintain contact

---

43. The merism "they shall go out and they shall come in" may refer even more specifically to conducting the campaigns of conquest.

44. See also 1 Sam 30:7–8. The importance of the ephod in this case derives from the 'pouch of judgment', which was associated with it.

with God, a spiritual tragedy that is given explicit expression in the early chapters of 1 Samuel. According to 1 Sam 2:12–13, Eli's sons were 'scoundrels' (*běnê běliyyāʿal*), "they did not know Yahweh (*lōʾ yādĕʿû ʾet yhwh*) or the 'oracle' of the priests (*mišpāṭ hakkōhănîm*) with the people."[45] The narrator observes in 1 Sam 3:1 that "a word from Yahweh was rare in those days; visions were infrequent." In fact, when Yahweh spoke he deliberately bypassed the priest, who did not recognize the voice of God when he heard it (3:4–18). In this case the Israelites learned quickly that if they wanted a determination from Yahweh, they should go to Samuel, not Eli (3:19–21).[46] But one might conclude from Judges 4 that the demise of the priesthood antedated the ministry of Samuel. The people recognized that only by presenting their appeal to the prophet was there hope of receiving a *mišpāṭ* from Yahweh.

This interpretation of *mišpāṭ* sheds new light on other occurrences of the word. In Judg 13:12, in response to the divine messenger's announcement that his wife would have a son, Manoah asked, "What shall be the *mišpāṭ* ('pronouncement') of the boy, and what shall be his work (*maʿăśēhû*)?"[47] The fact that the messenger responded by informing him that the boy's mother was to adopt the diet of a Nazirite makes it unlikely that in this case *mišpāṭ* had to do simply with the way he should live. In requesting the boy's *mišpāṭ* and his *maʿăśeh*, Manoah was requesting further elaboration on the comment in v. 5, "He shall begin to deliver Israel." Interpreted this way, the verse finds a remarkable parallel in *Ug.* V 6.3–12, involving the exact Ugaritic counterpart, *mtpṭ*. While the fragmentary nature of the text inhibits clear understanding of the full text, the reading of line 3 is fairly secure:

> When he arrives at the lord of the great gods with a gift, he must ask a decision (*mtpṭ*) about the child.[48]

A few lines later the text reads:

> And your messenger will arrive with a gift;
> he will receive a decision (*mtpṭ*).[49]

It is clear that the issue in this passage is a divine determination concerning a child, perhaps at his birth or at a time of illness. As Cazelles has

---

45. The latter phrase is commonly interpreted as 'the customs of the priests'.

46. Verse 21 implies that there had been a protracted period when Yahweh's voice had not been heard at Shiloh. This suggests that the events described in Judges 20–21 transpired relatively early in this period of the Judges.

47. See the use of *maʿăśeh* in Judg 2:7, 10. On the word used in the sense of 'achievement', see Esth 10:2.

48. As translated by Fensham, "Ugaritic Root," 12, 68.

49. *Ug.* V 6.12. See Fensham, ibid.

observed, at Ugarit, as at Babylon, people's destinies (in this case a child's) were determined by the gods.[50] In a similar fashion, Manoah sought to learn from the messenger of Yahweh the destiny of his son, whose birth had been so auspiciously announced.

The variations in the translations of *mišpāṭ hammelek* in 1 Sam 8:10–11 indicate how difficult these verses are to interpret. While the translations are unanimous in rejecting a judicial interpretation of the word in this context,[51] none connects *šā'al*, which occurs in v. 10, with *mišpāṭ* in v. 11.[52] The *mišpāṭ hammelek* is nothing other than the oracle in the context, which is a response to an inquiry by the people before the prophet. Not only is it identified as "the words of Yahweh" (v. 10), it is cast in formal oracular style and concludes with a warning that, should the people cry out (*zāʿaq*) on account of the king's oppression, Yahweh would not answer (*ʿānâ*) them.[53]

Other narratives[54] and prophetic[55] texts that use the term *mišpāṭ* in similar ways could be discussed. However, the evidence presented above

50. H. Cazelles, "*Mṭpṭ*," 47.

51. NJPSV, 'practice of the king'; NASB, 'procedure of the king'; RSV, NRSV, 'ways of the king'; NIV, 'what the king will do'; NEB, 'what sort of king [will govern them]'.

52. Nor have scholars who have commented on this verse and the related text 1 Sam 10:25 connected *šā'al* with *mišpāṭ*. See J. J. M. Roberts: "The *mišpāṭ* of the kingdom that Samuel wrote in a document at Mizpeh (1 Sam 10:25) was probably a treaty specifying the rights and limitations of the king" ("In Defense of the Monarchy: The Contribution of Israelite Kingship to Biblical Theology," *Ancient Israelite Religion: Essays in Honor of Frank Moore Cross* [ed. P. D. Miller, P. D. Hanson, and S. D. McBride; Philadelphia: Fortress, 1987], 383); S. Talmon: "Now Samuel's speech hinges on the fundamental principle of the 'Rule of the King', which sets limits to the royal prerogative and defines the king's obligations" (" 'The Rule of the King': I Samuel 8:4–22," in *King, Cult and Calendar in Ancient Israel: Collected Studies* [Jerusalem: Magnes, 1986], 61); also: "The Law of the King and the Statute of the King probably preserve parts of a social contract which laid down quasi-constitutionally the rights and duties of the king" (idem, "Kingship and Ideology of the State," *King, Cult and Calendar*, 21).

53. This use of *mišpāṭ* compares with the use of *tôrâ* in 2 Sam 7:19, the difficulty of which is reflected in the variations in the translations: NJPSV, 'law for the people'; NASB, 'custom of man'; RSV, following emendation, 'future generations'; NRSV, 'instruction for the people'; NIV, 'usual way of dealing with man'; NEB, 'the lot of man embarked on a high career'. While the riddle of *'ādām* in the context remains, with the 'oracle' interpretation of *tôrâ*, the sense is clear. David recognized that the oracle delivered by Nathan represented a divine determination concerning his dynasty. In fact, the narrator tells us that the word of Yahweh came to the prophet at night (v. 4). For additional possible examples of the oracular use of *tôrâ*, see Isa 1:10; 8:16, 20; 30:8–10; 42:21; Jer 8:8; and Lam 2:9, *tôrâ/ḥāzôn*.

54. E.g., 2 Kgs 1:7. When Ahaziah, Ahab's successor suffered a serious accident, he sent his envoys (*mal'akîm*, v. 2) to inquire (*dāraš*) of Baal-zebub, the god of Ekron, whether or not he would recover. While not indicating the outcome of this inquiry, the text notes that on their return from Ekron the messengers ran into Elijah, who not only rebuked them for their journey but also proceeded to deliver his own divine determination. The Tishbite's message displays many qualities characteristic of a divine *mišpāṭ*: [cont.]

is sufficient for concluding that *mišpāṭ* was often used technically of 'an oracular divine determination' concerning an issue that was beyond human assessment. In fact, both the Hebrew and Ugaritic usages of the word correspond exactly to the Akkadian use of *dīnu*. While this root is employed most often in judicial contexts, it frequently refers to the decisions, determinations, or verdicts of the gods and to oracles in particular.[56] In Assyria such inquiries appear to have been addressed most often to Shamash, who dispensed his pronouncements through extispicy and other forms of divination.[57]

Extrabiblical analogues to the role played by Deborah in Judges are well documented. While ancient Mesopotamian kings regularly sought a divine determination prior to marching into battle,[58] such appeals were especially appropriate in critical situations. Thus Shalmaneser I of Assyria, whose reign (1274–1245 B.C.) was almost contemporary with the tenure of Deborah, wrote:

> The Qutu of which, like the stars of the sky, no one knows their number, skilled in murder, rebelliously turned against me (and) committed hostilities. I prayed to Ashur and the great gods, my lords, and they gave me a straight answer, a firm yes.[59]

Centuries later Esarhaddon wrote of his reaction to a palace revolt:

---

1. It is delivered by a prophet.
2. It occurs within the context of an inquiry of a deity concerning the welfare of an individual.
3. It is preceded by the messenger formula.
4. Its content is in keeping with a divine determination: the king shall die.
5. It is identified as a *mišpāṭ*. The last point is not obvious from most translations. However, the question was raised by Ahaziah when he received the report of Elijah's pronouncement, *meh mišpāṭ hāʾîš ʾăšer ʿālâ liqrāʾtēkem* 'What was the *mišpāṭ* of the man who met you [and declared to you these things]?' Although the messengers responded by reporting the nature of the prophet's dress, the LXX's rendering of *meh mišpāṭ* with *tis hē krisis* 'What is the judgment?' suits the context better than most modern readings. The description of Elijah's garb was not so much an answer to the king's question as a way of identifying this doomsayer. The king immediately recognized him as the prophet who had played such a prominent role in his father's life.
6. The purpose of the sequel is to confirm the divine word spoken through Elijah.

55. Hos 5:1; Mic 3:1–4; Isa 28:5, 41:1, 59:9–21; Ezek 21:26–27; Mal 2:13–3:1.
56. See CAD D 150–52.
57. For discussion see M. deJ. Ellis, "Observations on Mesopotamian Oracles and Prophetic Texts: Literary and Historiographic Considerations," *JCS* 41 (1989) 171–73.
58. See Nebuchadnezzar's divination as described in Ezek 21:23–32. For a study of this issue, see Manfred S. Weippert, " 'Heiliger Krieg' in Israel und Assyrien: Kritische Anmerkungen zu Gerhard von Rads Konzept des 'Heiligen Krieges im alten Israel,' " *ZAW* 84 (1972) 460–93.
59. As translated by A. K. Grayson, *ARI* 1.83. Grayson notes that the request was made by divination (n. 180).

But I, Esarhaddon, who never turns around in a battle, trusting in the great gods, his lords, soon heard of these sorry happenings and I cried out "Woe!" rent my princely robe and began to lament loudly. I became as mad as a lion, my soul was aflame and I (called up the gods by) clapping my hands, with regard to my (intention of) assuming the kingship, my paternal legacy. I prayed to Ashur, Sin, Shamash, Bel, Nebo and Nergal, (to) the Ishtar of Nineveh, the Ishtar of Arbela, and they agreed to give me an (oracle-)answer. By means of their correct (and) positive answer, they sent me the (following) trustworthy oracle (received by) extispicy: "Go (ahead), do not tarry! We will march with you, kill your enemies."[60]

Another text purports to preserve Ashur's response in greater detail:

As these rebels were rising against you,
driving you out,
and oppressing you.
You opened your mouth, "Look! Ashur!"
I have indeed heard your lament-appeal.
From the gate of heaven I am swooping down.
I will cast them down;
I will let fire devour them.
You shall remain standing between them.
I will remove them from you;
I will chase them off into the mountains.
I will rain fire-stones down upon them.
I will present your enemies as a sacrifice.
With their blood I will fill the river.
May men see it and praise me,
That I am Ashur, the Lord of the gods.[61]

But the practice of inquiring of the gods in times of crisis was also common among western Semites. Zakkur, the eighth-century B.C. king of Hamath,[62] describes his response to an alliance of sixteen kings who laid siege to Hadrach:

But I lifted up my hands to Baalshamayn, and Baalshamayn answered (*ᶜnh*) me. Baalshamayn spoke to me through seers (*byd ḥzyn*) and messengers (*byd ᶜddn*). Baalshamayn [said to me], "Fear not, because it was I who made you king, [and I shall stand] with you, and I shall deliver (*ʔḥṣlk*) you from all [these kings who] have forced a siege upon you."[63]

60. A. L. Oppenheim, "Esarhaddon," *ANET*, 289.

61. See J. Craig, *Assyrian and Babylonian Religious Texts* (Assyriologische Bibliothek 13; Leipzig: Hinrichs, 1885–87) 22–23. The transliterated text and a German translation are also provided by Weippert, "Heiliger Krieg," 481–82.

62. On Zakkur see most recently A. R. Millard, "The Homeland of Zakkur," *Sem* 39 (1990) 47–52.

63. As translated by J. C. L. Gibson, *Textbook of Syrian Semitic Inscriptions*, vol. 1: *Aramaic Inscriptions* (Oxford: Clarendon, 1975) 8–11. Such "answerers," referred to by *āpilu/*

The fear of Zakkur at the sight of these armies is reminiscent of the Moabite King Balak's reaction to the vast horde of Israelites camped at his doorstep (Numbers 22–24). In reality they posed no threat to him. However, being unaware of or disbelieving their peaceful designs *vis-à-vis* his nation, he appealed to the world-renowned prophet Balaam of Beor for a divine word of relief from this threat. In fact, he sought to dictate the nature of the divine pronouncement by demanding a curse upon Israel. Although the term *mišpāṭ* is never applied to Balaam's pronouncements, the oracles recorded in chaps. 23–24 may be interpreted as divine decisions. However, in Mic 6:5, Balaam's response is described by means of the word *ʿānâ*,[64] the semantic equivalent of *šāpaṭ* when used in the same context: "My people, remember what Balak king of Moab plotted (*yāʿaṣ*) against you, and how Balaam son of Beor responded (*ʿānâ*) to him" (NJPS).[65]

A similar use of *ʿānâ*, this time in conjunction with *zāʿaq*, a biform of *ṣāʿaq*, occurs in 1 Sam 7:8–10. In the face of a desperate Philistine threat, the Israelites appealed to Samuel, who is elsewhere identified as a prophet of Yahweh (*nābîʾ*, 3:20), a seer (*rōʾeh*, 9:9), and a man of God (*ʾîš ʾĕlōhîm*, 9:6), not to cease to cry out to Yahweh for their deliverance (*hôšîʿa*). As a part of the "crying-out ritual," Samuel offered up a whole burnt offering.[66] Yahweh responded (*ʿānâ*) with a thunderous routing of the Philistines.

In Judges 4, Deborah has assumed the role of these "seers" and "messengers" through whom appeal is made to the gods in times of distress, and who then relay the decision (*mišpāṭ*) of the gods to the inquirers. Though she is given the official designation *nĕbîʾâ* 'prophetess', the fact that she is referred to as the wife of Lapidoth may point to her lay status.[67]

āpiltu, feature prominently in the prophetic texts from Mari. See H. B. Huffmon, "Prophecy in the Mari Letters," *BA* 31 (1968) 105–12; repr. in *Biblical Archaeology Reader 3* (Garden City, N.Y.: Doubleday, 1970) 203–9.

64. See the Zakkur quotation directly above. For *ʿānâ* used as the divine response to *ṣāʿaq*, see the Job 19:7 text cited above, p. 239.

65. See the comment of A. Malamat in "A Forerunner of Biblical Prophecy: The Mari Documents," *Ancient Israelite Religion* (ed. P. D. Miller, P. D. Hanson, and S. D. McBride; Philadelphia: Fortress, 1987) 40: "The verb *ʿānāh* does not indicate here any response to a specific question that Balak put forward to Balaam but rather the prophetic oracle Balaam was compelled to deliver on behalf of Israel." Malamat provides discussion and full bibliography on the Mari prophecies up to 1986.

66. This act may provide a clue to the significance of the altar to Yahweh constructed at Ramah (7:17). Ramah was the site where he engaged in such inquisitory activity.

67. See also the reference to her as *ʾēm bĕyiśrāʾēl* 'mother in Israel' in 5:7. This affectionate title conjures up notions of warmth and security (see Jesus' lament in Matt 23:37, as well as the imagery of the eagle protecting its young in Deut 32:11). While no exact parallels occur in the Old Testament, masculine counterparts are found in several texts.

But neither her lay status nor her female gender would have been surprising in the second-millennium cultural milieu. As Malamat has observed, the Mari correspondence attests to an unusually high proportion of women among the lay prophets at that site.[68] Deborah, who sat under the palm tree[69] between Ramah and Bethel, posed an alternative to the degenerate priesthood. Through her Yahweh permitted himself to be inquired of,[70] even during the dark days of the Judges.

With this as a background, it is now possible to examine the ways in which Deborah fulfilled her prophetic role. Although there is no explicit reference to a commandment by Yahweh to perform the actions described, Judg 4:6–14 clearly reflects his favorable response to the Israelites' inquiry. The call of Barak was Yahweh's answer to the crisis. As Ackerman recognized, the historian has deliberately cast the succeeding narrative in the form of a call narrative.[71] Like the call of Gideon in chap. 6, this account should be subclassified as a protested call narrative on the basis of its structure and design.[72] A number of typical elements may be identified.

(1) The person called experienced a personal encounter with Yahweh or his messenger. Deborah's response to the inquiry of the Israelites was to dispatch (*šālaḥ*) her own representative(s) to call (*qārā᾿*) Barak of

---

Within Judges an apostate Levite is offered the honorific role of 'father' *᾿āb*) and priest, first to Micah's household (17:10) and then to the tribe of Dan (18:19). But nearer the usage under discussion is the ascription of the title to prophets: Elijah, by his disciple Elisha (2 Kgs 2:12); Elisha, by an unnamed king of Israel (2 Kgs 6:21) and by Joash, another king of Israel (2 Kgs 13:14). See also Hazael's reference to Ben-Hadad, king of Aram Damascus, as the "son of Elisha" in 2 Kgs 8:9. The sense of security associated with this type of title is reflected in Job's confession in 29:16–17:

> I was a father to the needy,
> And I looked into the case of the stranger.
> I broke the jaws of the wrongdoer,
> And I wrested prey from his teeth (NJPSV).

68. Malamat, "Forerunner of Biblical Prophecy," 43–44.

69. On the palm as a sacred symbol see Ursula Magen, *Assyrische Königsdarstellungen: Aspekte der Herrschaft* (Baghdader Forschungen 9; Mainz am Rhein: Von Zabern, 1986) 79–81.

70. This contrasts with the declarations of Yahweh's refusal to be inquired of in Ezek 14:3 and 20:1–3.

71. Ackerman, "Prophecy and Warfare," 5–13. He argues that it has all the elements of preprophetic call accounts, as identified by Wolfgang Richter, *Die sogenannten vorprophetischen Berufungsberichte* (Göttingen: Vandenhoeck & Ruprecht, 1970). On the nature and forms of call narratives, see also Norman C. Habel, "The Form and Significance of the Call Narratives," *ZAW* 77 (1965) 297–323; Rudolf Kilian, "Die prophetische Berufungsberichte," *Theologie im Wandel: Festschrift zum 150 jährigen Bestehen der katholisch-theologischen Fakultät an der Universität Tübingen 1817–1967* (Tübinger theologische Reihe 1; Munich: Wewel, 1967) 356–76; Walther Zimmerli, *Ezekiel 1* (Hermeneia; Philadelphia: Fortress, 1979) 97–101.

72. This interpretation is less strained than Ackerman's.

Kedesh-naphtali. No details of Deborah's initial meeting with Barak are given. Nevertheless, she entered the picture at precisely the same point as did the *mal⁾ak* of Yahweh in Judg 6:11.

(2) The person was presented with a statement of the task to which he/she was being called. In the narrative Deborah appears to have launched immediately into the commissioning of Barak. Although no reference is made to her having received any orders from Yahweh, the form of her commissioning speech reflects a clear self-consciousness of her prophetic status. On the one hand, she introduces her speech with a variation of the messenger formula:[73] *hălō⁾ ṣiwwâ yhwh ⁾ĕlōhê yiśrā⁾ēl lēk* . . . (Judg 4:6). The statement translates literally, 'Has Yahweh the God of Israel not commanded, "Go . . . "?' but in the context it signifies a firm declaration: 'Surely Yahweh has commanded . . . !'[74] On the other hand, in her charge she uses the first person. As an authorized representative of Yahweh, what she says was by definition what Yahweh says.

The commissioning speech itself consists of two parts. First, through a series of imperatives, Barak was charged to go (*lēk*) and deploy (*māšak*)[75] the troops at Mount Tabor. They were to consist of 10,000 men from Naphtali and Zebulun.[76] Second, Barak was promised Yahweh's personal involvement in the anticipated battle. The divine Commander would deploy (*māšak*) Sisera and all of his forces against Barak, but he would deliver them over into his hand.[77] As in the Gog oracle in Ezekiel 38–39, the enemy is portrayed as a puppet, with Yahweh at the controls. The one who sold Israel into the hands of Jabin would also engineer the enemy's defeat.

(3) The person expressed resistance and objected to the divine call. The most emphatic expressions of resistance to the call of Yahweh are found in the commissioning of Moses in Exodus 3–4. In Judges, in the

---

73. For a discussion of the messenger formula and its function, see Claus Westermann, *Basic Forms of Prophetic Speech* (Philadelphia: Fortress, 1967) 100–115. The most common form of the formula is *kh ⁾mr* PN 'Thus has PN declared'.

74. On the use of *hălō⁾*, literally 'Is it not', as an emphatic particle virtually synonymous with 'Behold', see M. L. Brown, " 'Is It Not?' or 'Indeed!': HL in Northwest Semitic," *MAARAV* 4 (1987) 201–19.

75. On this use of *māšak*, see Boling, *Judges*, 96; and Ackerman, "Prophecy and Warfare," 8.

76. For a form-critical study of charges to attack, see Robert Back, *Die Aufforderung zur flucht und zum Kampf in Alttestamentlichen Prophetenspruch* (Neukirchen-Vluyn: Neukirchener Verlag, 1962).

77. Two forms of the committal formula, which speaks fundamentally of the transfer of power, occur in the book: *nātan bĕyad* 'to give you into the hands of' (Judg 1:2; 2:14a, 23; 3:10, 28; 4:7, 14; 6:1; 7:7, 9, 15; 8:3, 7; 9:29; 11:30, 32; 12:3; 13:1; 15:12; 18:10; and 20:28); and *mākar bĕyad* 'to sell into the hands of' (2:14b; 3:8; 4:2, 9; and 10:7). *Nāpal bĕyad* 'to fall into the hands of' is a more passive expression (see 15:18).

description of Gideon's call to deliver the nation from the Midianites, his reluctance to obey was demonstrated by apologies for his insignificance in Israel (Judg 6:15; see also 1 Sam 9:21 and Jer 1:6) and by repeated demands for signs showing that Yahweh actually meant what he said. Barak's protestation was less overt: "If you go with me, I will go; but if you will not go with me, I will not go" (Judg 4:8). On the surface, this objection made Barak appear cowardly: he would not enter the fray unless he had Deborah beside him holding his hand. This impression is also reflected in the second part of Deborah's response. But at a deeper level, the objection reflects a recognition of Deborah's status. The request for the accompaniment of the prophet is a plea for the presence of Yahweh.[78]

(4) The person was reassured by promises of the presence of Yahweh and/or authenticating signs. Both elements are found here, albeit in veiled form. On the one hand, Deborah responds with a firm promise of her presence: *hālōk ʾēlēk ʿimmāk* 'I will surely go with you' (4:9). However, her answer signifies much more than merely the promise of a woman to accompany a man on an adventure of which he was afraid. It was neither accidental nor coincidental that this reassuring word was offered precisely at the point in a call narrative where a promise of the presence of God was expected.[79] Like Samuel in 1 Sam 7:10–11, Deborah clearly functioned as the *alter ego* of Yahweh. Her presence alone was enough to guarantee victory over the enemy.

A recognition of this fact exposes how misplaced are comments about Deborah the deliverer being filled with the Spirit of Yahweh in the present context. She was neither the deliverer, nor was her infusion with the divine Spirit the issue. In fact her presence with Barak would have made superfluous any reference to the Spirit's coming upon him prior to the battle (cf. Judg 3:10, 6:34, 11:29). Where a prophet was, there was the Spirit. According to Hebrew perceptions, the prophetic presence and the presence of the divine Spirit (*rûaḥ*) were two ways of concretizing the presence of Yahweh.

The validity of this assertion is borne out by the Samuel narratives. As long as Samuel was with Saul, the new king felt relatively secure; however, with the anointing of David, Samuel shifted his allegiance, leaving Saul totally vulnerable to all hostile forces. But what happened cannot be understood without a more careful investigation of the interplay between Samuel the prophet and the Spirit of Yahweh.[80] The basis of Samuel's role as the symbol of the divine presence is found in the narrator's comment,

78. See below, section (4).
79. See Exod 3:12; Judg 6:16; 1 Sam 10:7; and Jer 1:8.
80. For a beginning, see David M. Howard, Jr., "The Transfer of Power from Saul to David in 1 Sam 16:13–14," *JETS* 32 (1989) 473–84.

"Yahweh was with him [Samuel] and permitted none of his words to fall"
(1 Sam 3:19). But another key to his ministry exists in the interplay
between his activity and that of the Spirit of Yahweh. Although the issue
demands further investigation, the dimensions of this relationship in
1 Samuel may be preliminarily summarized as follows:

1. Samuel was able to predict the operation of the Spirit of Yahweh
   and through it exercise "control" over another person. In 10:6–
   10 that person was Saul.
2. Samuel interpreted the presence of the Spirit and the other
   signs as confirmations of God's presence with Saul (10:7).
3. At the proper signal, namely, Samuel's turning to leave, God
   changed Saul's heart, and all of the predicted signs were fulfilled, including the arresting power of the Spirit.
4. When Saul was arrested by the Spirit, he began to behave like a
   prophet (10:9–10).
5. Samuel's presence in the Philistine battle (chap. 7) was the same
   as the presence of the Spirit of Yahweh in the battle with the
   Ammonites (11:6).
6. The operation of the Spirit was directly related to Samuel's
   anointing activity. As soon as Samuel anointed David, the
   Spirit left Saul and came upon the new king-elect.
7. When Samuel abandoned Saul, the abandonment of the Spirit
   followed (chaps. 15–16). All of this Saul interpreted as abandonment by God (28:15).
8. Because of the presence of the Spirit on the newly anointed
   king-elect, when Samuel left David, the presence of the Spirit
   served as a sign of God's presence, in place of Samuel.
9. With the departure of Samuel and the Spirit of Yahweh, Saul
   was left wide open for God to send upon him an evil spirit (*rûaḥ
   rāʿâ*, 16:14; cf. 19:9). Yahweh then began to take an active part
   in destroying Saul.
10. When the rejected king later made overtures to Samuel, the
    Spirit of God drove him out of control (19:19–24).

However, the ultimate declaration of Samuel as the *alter ego* of God
came from the lips of the necromancer of Endor. When she saw Samuel
emerging she declared, "I see [a] god (*ʾĕlōhîm*) coming up out of the
earth" (1 Sam 28:13). Since Deborah also served as the *alter ego* of Yahweh, her presence was required by Barak to ensure the success of the
mission. However, even while she was reassuring Barak of her support,
she offered him an authenticating, if ironic, sign. Just as God had promised Moses in Exod 3:12 that he would know that it was he who had sent

him when he brought his people out of Egypt back to that mountain, so the sign offered Barak was proleptic: Yahweh would sell Sisera into the hands of a woman. This would be the divine confirmation of his call and the involvement of Yahweh in the event.

Whereas the stronger form of the committal formula (*mākar běyad*) served to strengthen the certainty of victory, the prediction that the honor would go to a woman was deflating. Whether or not she was expressing displeasure at Barak's hesitation to go without her is not clear. In any case, her introduction of the issue of gender will complicate the rest of the narrative. Since Deborah has been the only female participant in the story up to this point, the reader's first impulse is to anticipate that she will emerge as the heroine of the story. The actual result catches everyone by surprise, for Deborah's role was merely to be a spokesperson to stand in for Yahweh. In that capacity she promised to go with Barak and offered him a sign of the eventual success of the mission.

For the moment, however, the narrator turns the reader's attention back to her promise. Twice in Judg 4:9–10 he announces that she fulfilled the pledge and went with General Barak. The call and commission have been completed. Barak marched off to battle with the symbol of Yahweh's presence at his side.

However, her prophetic responsibilities were not yet completed. From the subsequent account of the battle, it is apparent that Deborah had no real military role. In the first place, Sisera marshaled his forces in response to Barak's arrival on Mount Tabor. He seemed unaware of the presence of Deborah. Second, it was Barak who came down the mountain with 10,000 troops following him. Third, the battle that ensued is described as involving the forces of Barak and the armies of Sisera. By this point Deborah has disappeared from the description completely.

But this does not mean that she was not involved. At the critical moment, she announces that the time for the attack has come. Yahweh was about to deliver Sisera into his hands; after all, he had gone out before them. After this declaration, all that is left for the narrator to report is that Yahweh routed Sisera and his entire army before Barak. But Deborah's exclusively prophetic role in the narrative was not compromised. Throughout she functioned entirely as a spokeswoman and representative of Yahweh.

CONCLUSION

One important question remains. After pinpointing the narrator's view of Deborah's role in the events described, one must ask what her role is in the overall thesis of the book. Surely the narrator's agenda is nobler than simply posing a riddle to his readers: Who was this person called Deborah? Somehow the manner in which she is portrayed must serve his broader aims.

The answer to the question of her role is realized only when attention is directed away from the human participants in this drama to the real hero, Yahweh himself.[81] In the end Israel was saved. But to whom did the credit belong? Who rescued the nation? By means of a succession of rapidly moving scenes the author has presented the reader with several candidates. Was it Deborah? Barak? Jael? If the reader's interest is only at the human level, he or she walks away from the drama puzzled. But the author wishes the reader to know that this story is not simply a performance being acted out on a stage by characters who have the freedom to write their own script and determine their own moves. Behind the stage stands one who is above all, the one who determines the roles and who pulls the strings. The epilogue says it well: "So God subdued on that day Jabin the king of Canaan before the sons of Israel" (4:23). It is the saving activity of Yahweh, the divine warrior, that is celebrated in the Song of Deborah and Barak. While humans played their parts, ultimately it was Yahweh who was to be blessed.

This theological dimension has determined the shape of the account from the beginning. The issue that led to the crisis in the first place was that the Israelites had violated the will of God (4:1). The Canaanites were deliberately brought in by him as agents of punishment, expressing Yahweh's displeasure with his people. It was in response to their cry for help that Barak was raised up. However, no formal statement to this effect is given. In its place the narrator opens up a window into the mysterious workings of God. Whereas the reader puzzles over the way Yahweh raised up Othniel and Ehud, with Barak as with Gideon the issue is presented in full detail. Deborah was his agent. The silence of the priesthood in the book of Judges is deafening. But just because the people were in spiritual decline, it does not follow that Yahweh abandoned his people totally. He still had his representative. She sat, not at Bethel or Shiloh, where the ark was, but outside the town, receiving the pleas of the Israelites on Yahweh's behalf. Her commissioning of Barak represented the divine *mišpāṭ*. In fact, as his representative, she went the second mile. She accompanied him into battle, as a recognized representative and spokesperson for the Commander in Chief.

That was her role, no more and no less. By so doing she was granted full authority to take her place in line with the rest of God's servants the

---

81. For a discussion of the way the literary strategy of the account serves the theological purpose of the author, see Amit, "Judges 4," 39, 89–111.

prophets. While they served as agents of God's grace in every age, in no age was it more welcome (and undeserved) than in the dark days of the Judges. To borrow a note from the first century A.D. author Pseudo-Philo, in Deborah the grace of God was awakened; through her the works of the LORD were praised.[82]

82. The generally more sermonic tone of Pseudo-Philo's version of the Song of Deborah and Barak (32:1–18) and a concluding farewell address (33:1–6) lend support to this "prophetic" interpretation of Deborah's role. For a translation of these texts, see D. J. Harrington, in R. H. Charlesworth, ed., *The Old Testament Pseudepigrapha* (Garden City, N. Y.: Doubleday, 1985) 2.345–48.

Who Made the Kingmaker?
Reflections on Samuel and the
Institution of the Monarchy

Robert P. Gordon

The University of Cambridge

Well! I've often seen a cat without a grin, thought Alice; but a grin without a cat! It's the most curious thing I ever saw in all my life!

So, with due acknowledgement of Lewis Carroll's *Alice's Adventures in Wonderland*, begins an undergraduate lecture of mine entitled "Samuel and the Cheshire Cat." The point of this curious association is, of course, that, as modern research into the Samuel narratives has developed, the substantial figure of this man of several parts has tended to be reduced to grin-like insubstantiality. Just over fifty years ago W. A. Irwin was lamenting that we are "in the disturbing position of possessing not a single narrative of Samuel's activity that merits respect as good source material,"[1] and if that sounds extreme it is also fairly representative of a widespread and developing skepticism about the historiographical worth of the early Samuel narratives in general. Not so W. F. Albright, who, in his Goldenson Lecture published in 1961, found little difficulty in discovering a figure of flesh and blood behind the narratives and even managed to delve into the psyche of the sometime acolyte of Shiloh, whose sterner, ungrinning, character traits Albright attributed to "unhappy experiences as a boy in Shiloh."[2] From our vantage-point over thirty years later, Albright, not for the first time, gives the appearance of an egregious optimist.

---

1. W. A. Irwin, "Samuel and the Rise of the Monarchy," *AJSL* 58 (1941) 134.
2. W. F. Albright, *Samuel and the Beginnings of the Prophetic Movement* (Cincinnati: Hebrew Union College Press, 1961) 18.

The underlying problem with which we are engaged is partly the complex tradition-history often envisaged for the early chapters of 1 Samuel and partly the fact that we are dealing with narrative texts that are governed by interests other than the simply historiographical and that are therefore suspected of providing an inadequate basis for historical reconstruction. In such circumstances a wide epistemological gulf opens up between those who accord the biblical narratives referential status and those who do not. "How can we approach the social world of Iron Age I as biblical historians and still retain intellectual respectability?" asks J. W. Flanagan as he unveils his "social world," or "comparative sociological," approach to the study of this period.[3] Others also warn against the dangers of "text-based history," perhaps not so much because of antipathy to texts as out of frustration at being restricted to the theologically-filtered texts of the Old Testament so much of the time. Even such wary practitioners as J. M. Miller and J. H. Hayes, who recognize at least some kernel of historical truth in the Samuel narratives,[4] come under the condemnation of B. O. Long, who chides them for imagining that "holy books yield real history" and goes so far as to stigmatize their approach as "fundamentalist."[5] But Long, who is in turn labeled "fundamentalist" by Miller,[6] confuses the issue with his talk of "holy books," since it is difficult to keep the term free of ideas of canonicity and sacred scripture. The historical books of the Hebrew Bible were written to describe and account for the historical experience of the community of Israel; they became "holy," "canonical," "scripture" at a later stage.[7] Or perhaps we must add to Long's "holy books" the category of "holy stelae" to take in such hitherto respectable historical sources as the Mesha Stele and the Zakir Inscription, which mix in a little divine activity with their historical reminiscences. That the Old Testament historical books are theologically motivated is an argument against simplisms, but not against the entire historical quest.

In this paper I wish to consider briefly the historical backcloth to the emergence of the monarchy and then in more detail, but still selectively, the narrative traditions associated with Samuel of Ramah, whom I have

3. J. W. Flanagan, *David's Social Drama: A Hologram of Israel's Early Iron Age* (The Social World of Biblical Antiquity 7; Sheffield: Almond, 1988) 22.

4. See J. M. Miller and J. H. Hayes, *A History of Ancient Israel and Judah* (London: SCM/Philadelphia: Westminster, 1986) 134–35.

5. B. O. Long, "On Finding the Hidden Premises," *JSOT* 39 (1987) 10–14.

6. J. M. Miller, "In Defense of Writing a History of Israel," *JSOT* 39 (1987) 54.

7. See J. Barton (*Oracles of God: Perceptions of Ancient Prophecy in Israel after the Exile* [London: Darton, Longman and Todd, 1986] 115–16), making a similar point in connection with the recognition of "inspired prophecy" in the postprophetic era.

dignified as "kingmaker" in keeping with his portrayal in the biblical text.

THE PHILISTINES AND THE MONARCHY

K. W. Whitelam's characterization of 1 Samuel's explanation of the rise of the monarchy as "monocausal" is not far from the truth even if it fails to take account of the charge of maladministration by the sons of Samuel as mentioned in 8:1–5.[8] In the biblical texts it is principally the external pressure exerted by the Philistines to the west, with some Ammonite input from the east, that brings the monarchical question to the fore (8:20; 9:16; 10:1 [LXX], 5–7, and 27). For this reason I think that it is a mistake to divide too sharply between chaps. 7 and 8, for the account of "Samuel's victory" over the Philistines in chap. 7 offers a context for, and an implicit commentary on, the elders' request in 8:20 for a king "to go out before us and fight our battles."

There is nothing improbable about the Samuel storyline as far as it goes, and scarcely anyone would wish to deny that external factors such as Philistine pressure from the west impelled Israel towards its acceptance of monarchy; nevertheless, a number of recent studies of so-called "secondary states" have called in question the adequacy of the external ("exogenic") factor as an explanation of how Israel became a monarchy. The "secondary state" normally emerges as internal factors, such as social stratification, social conflict, population increase, and administrative needs, become agents for social and political change.[9] Of such there is little mention in the early chapters of Samuel, with the possible exception of the already-mentioned maladministration of Samuel's sons, cited as the ostensible reason for the elders' request for a king in 8:1–5. But to claim that the anthropological approach flies in the face of the literature and of the archaeology of the period would be an inappropriate response, and one that might be contested at either level. A more likely way forward is to consider why, from an internal Old Testament point of view, the Philistines are given such prominence as they are in 1 Samuel. Also involved, though I shall not dwell much on the point, is the question of what constitutes history-writing.

Reaction against event-laden, personality-focused, "Flavian" history-writing is understandably strong in the guild of modern historians.

8. K. W. Whitelam, "Recreating the History of Israel," *JSOT* 35 (1986) 62.
9. See the chapter entitled "The Formation of the Davidic State," in *The Emergence of Early Israel in Historical Perspective* (ed. R. B. Coote and K. W. Whitelam; The Social World of Biblical Antiquity 5; Sheffield: Almond, 1987) 139–66.

Accounts of peoples and periods that pay attention to social structures, the role of the ordinary citizen and the family unit are currently enjoying enhanced status. The names of various recent scholars (notably F. Braudel[10]) are associated with this approach, though the British-based historian from the previous generation, Lewis Namier, exemplifies an earlier preoccupation with history of this sort.[11] Now one of the most obvious things to be said about biblical history is that much of it is event-laden and personality-orientated, if this is not to misrepresent narrative characteristics that are found to some degree in most historical writing. Reading between the lines is often necessary before social, not to say sociological, inferences can be drawn. In the early chapters of 1 Samuel the narratives revolve around Eli and his sons, Samuel and his parents, and then Saul. To these it would be reasonable to add the Philistines as a kind of corporate persona also participating in events, and especially in the so-called "Ark Narrative" in 1 Samuel 4-6. That they were involved in some way in the events that precipitated the crisis whence emerged the Israelite monarchy is, as I have noted, not an issue for most students of the period. But what of the "monocausality" of the biblical text?

The answer appears to lie, at least partly, in the typological function of the Philistines within the Old Testament. Émigrés from the Mediterranean region (see Amos 9:7), they are indigenized Canaanites in the narrative texts of the Old Testament, where their extraneous origins would seldom be suspected. This presentation of them accords with their status as the archetypal enemy of Israel, for as quasi-autochthonous inhabitants of Palestine they inherit the mantle of the "inhabitants of the land," which in other Old Testament traditions is worn by the pre-Israelite peoples of Canaan. It is impossible to do justice within the limits of this paper to what is a major topic in itself, but we must develop this aspect of the typological Philistines a little further.

Wherever the Philistines appear in the biblical narratives, the territorial issue is likely to be present. This applies not least to the Philistines of Genesis, who are not quite so irenic as they are sometimes made out to be. The disputes over wells in Genesis 26 raise already in a patriarchal context the issue of territorial possession, for Isaac is told in a vision to remain in Philistine Gerar during a famine, in the following terms:

> Stay in this land and I will be with you and will bless you; for to you and to your descendants I will give all these lands (26:3).

---

10. F. Braudel, *On History* (London: Weidenfeld and Nicolson/Chicago: University of Chicago Press, 1980).

11. On Lewis Namier, see A. Cook, *History/Writing* (Cambridge: Cambridge University Press, 1988) 207–10.

He stayed there (v. 6) and planted crops and reaped a hundredfold "because the Lord blessed him" (v. 12). It is difficult to avoid the suggestion that claims to sovereignty over Philistine territory in the later period are being voiced already in the patriarchal traditions, just as they will be in some of the prophets (see Zeph 2:7; Zech 9:7). The Israelite claim to Philistine territory on an equal basis with (other) Canaanite land is also expressed in Josh 13:2, where the regions of the Philistines head the list of territories still to be taken over by the Israelites. Philistine cities are, accordingly, included in the tribal allocations of Joshua 13-19 (see 15:45-47).

The Old Testament presentation of what I have called the quasi-autochthonous Philistines is assisted by their association with gigantism, which finds parallels in the traditions relating to the pre-Israelite inhabitants of Canaan. We are familiar with the figure of Goliath of Gath and with certain Philistine "descendants of Rapha" with whom David's men were in contention (2 Sam 21:15-22). The Rephaim are included among the Canaanite inhabitants of the land in Gen 15:20 and are associated with gigantism partly through Og king of Bashan who, interestingly in view of the later Samuel references, is described as one of the last of the Rephaim (see Deut 3:11; Josh 12:4, and 13:12). The conflation with pre-Israelite tradition is further expressed in the association of the Philistines with the tall Anakim, descended from the Nephilim according to Num 13:33 (see Deut 1:28; 2:10, 21; and 9:2). In Josh 11:22 it is stated that there were no Anakim left in the land of Israel apart from those in Gaza, Gath, and Ashdod, while by a presumed misreading on the part of the Septuagint or its *Vorlage* the same relationship is indicated at Jer 47:5:

> Baldness has come upon Gaza;
> Ashkelon has perished.
> O remnant of the Anakim [MT *ᶜmqm* 'their valley'] how long will you
> gash yourselves?

The typological role of the Philistines as Israel's chief opponent in the land and as her ideological foe (another aspect that cannot be developed here) puts into perspective the depiction of them in 1 Samuel as a perpetual threat to the well-being of Israel and a primary cause of the political démarche that brought the monarchy into being. In all of this the three chapters of the so-called "Ark Narrative" (1 Samuel 4–6) are of crucial importance.[12] Their theological and ideological thrust is everywhere evident, and the significance of the issue being played out in this

---

12. Whether there ever was an "Ark Narrative" as such and whether, if there was, 2 Samuel 6 formed part of it are questions that need not be addressed here.

way at this point is quite strikingly apparent when one considers the low-key treatment of the decisive encounters of David with the Philistines in 2 Sam 5:17–25. The chapters of the "Ark Narrative" bear witness to this ideological concern in their various references and allusions to the Exodus tradition; David Daube found them a fruitful field for his *The Exodus Pattern in the Bible.*[13] But what are these Exodus references and allusions saying if not that the crisis described is serious enough to recall that in which the nation had its birth? A. F. Campbell's talk of a "caesura in the saving history" is, from this standpoint, words well spoken.[14]

So far I have concentrated on the possibility that the almost monocular view of the origins of the Israelite monarchy in 1 Samuel derives in part at least from the ideological significance given to the Philistines within the Old Testament, but that is not the same as parting company with the biblical tradition of Philistine hostility and its consequences. History and typology have both contributed to the proportions of 1 Samuel. And, since historical developments are in question, we may, at the same time as being grateful for sociological insights, look to our archaeologists in a reasonable expectation of further illumination. Such has recently been proffered on the monarchical issue by Israel Finkelstein, whose concern is with "settlement pattern" in the central hill country of Palestine.[15] His conclusion is that settlement in the western part of the area was a secondary development that resulted in friction with the Philistine inhabitants of the coastal plain.[16] If this were so, then Israelite expansion westward as well as Philistine interest in their neighbors' territory to the east would have made for the kinds of situations described in Judges and 1 Samuel. The monarchy emerged first in Benjaminite territory, says Finkelstein, because the population of this area suffered most directly from Philistine encroachments. Thus, for Finkelstein, the stimulus of Philistine aggression, facilitated by Israelite expansion, contributed to the circumstances in which Israel discovered its need of a monarchy. Obviously, Finkelstein's work will be subject to review and perhaps even reassessment, but it does illustrate the way in which the inexact science of surface archaeology may supplement or subvert the nebulous sciences of sociology and literary criticism.

13. D. Daube, *The Exodus Pattern in the Bible* (Westport, Conn.: Greenwood Press/London: Faber and Faber, 1963) 73–88.

14. A. F. Campbell, *The Ark Narrative (1 Samuel 4–6; 2 Samuel 6): A Form-Critical and Traditio-Historical Study* (SBLDS 16; Missoula, Mont.: Scholars Press, 1975) 212.

15. I. Finkelstein, "The Emergence of the Monarchy in Israel: The Environmental and Socio-Economic Aspects," *JSOT* 44 (1989) 43–74.

16. Ibid., 59–61, 63.

SAMUEL IN 1 SAMUEL

It is not possible to look at each of the several narratives in 1 Samuel in which Samuel features, nor, let it be said at the outset, is it my intention to try to prove the historicity of any of the events associated with the name of Samuel. Our task and our best hope is to consider the nature of the traditions that relate to the eponymous prophet in partial determination of the question, "Can any good thing come out of Ramah?"

The one biographical datum that most often manages to survive the sifting process where the Samuel narratives are concerned is the reference to "Samuel's circuit" in 7:15–17. Here, it is reckoned, is a credible picture of a minor judge operating within a restricted sphere, largely within Benjaminite territory.[17] On the other hand, the depiction of him as prophet, judge, and kingmaker to all Israel from Dan to Beersheba (cf. 3:20) is thought to have come about as the interests of prophetic circles and Deuteronomistic editors fashioned the narratives according to their own image. It is this impression of developing literary creativity and theological reflection that makes it difficult for many critical readers of these chapters to feel confident that what they read approximates to historical realities in the eleventh century B.C.

There have been attempts to push behind the present form of the individual narratives or to establish features that, from a common cultural point of view, deserve recognition as being, at the least, pre-Deuteronomistic. The account of the call of Samuel in chap. 3, recataloged by Robert Gnuse as "an auditory message dream" and negatively assessed as to its historical worth,[18] was earlier defended by R. R. Wilson, on the basis of anthropological comparison, as perhaps being more than mere literary invention.[19] However, Wilson's observations do not take us very far, since, as he himself recognizes, a correct description of an experience of "spirit-possession," as he terms it, is as much within the competence of a writer of fiction as of a history-writer. P. Weimar has argued in connection with chap. 7 that a pre-Deuteronomistic "Yahweh War" tradition underlies the account of Samuel's victory over the Philistines,[20] and, as is well known,

17. See A. D. H. Mayes, "The Period of the Judges and the Rise of the Monarchy," in *Israelite and Judaean History* (ed. J. H. Hayes and J. M. Miller; London: SCM/Philadelphia: Westminster, 1977) 321.

18. R. Gnuse, "A Reconsideration of the Form-Critical Structure in I Samuel 3: An Ancient Near Eastern Dream Theophany," *ZAW* 94 (1982) 379–90; idem, *The Dream Theophany of Samuel: Its Structure in Relation to Ancient Near Eastern Dreams and Its Theological Significance* (Lanham, Md.: University Press of America, 1984).

19. R. R. Wilson, "Anthropology and the Study of the Old Testament," *USQR* 34 (1979) 178–81.

20. P. Weimar, "Die Jahwekriegserzählungen in Exodus 14, Josua 10, Richter 4 und 1 Samuel 7," *Bib* 57 (1976) 63–69.

I. Mendelsohn sought to show that Samuel's portrait of a king in 8:11–18 better suited the period in which it is located than the later settings that are sometimes suggested for it.[21] And finally, T. Ishida holds that the narrative of Saul's meeting with Samuel in 9:1–10:16 is fundamentally a unity and originated ultimately in the lifetime of Saul.[22] For all that, each of these conclusions and the inferences drawn from them would be challenged by many or even, in one or two cases, by the great majority of scholars who have looked into them.

Some of the detail in the Samuel narratives plainly did not arise in the latest phase of the writing of the Old Testament books. Samuel's sleeping arrangements in the Shiloh sanctuary are no more likely to have appealed to Deuteronomistic editors and priestly tradents than they did to the punctuators of the Masoretic Text or the Targumic paraphraser who put the fledgling priest to bed in the Court of the Levites (3:3).[23] Again, the association of Samuel with the high place of Ramah (9:12–14) would have gained him instant dismissal from Jer 15:1 if he had been a seventh-century frequenter of Judean high places. The plurality of offices held by Samuel also provides a contrast with what was possible at a later date and has been cited in support of the basic genuineness of the traditions about him. To argue thus is, of course, to invoke the "criterion of dissimilarity" which, for present purposes, means the presence of features in a narrative despite their conflicting with what would be regarded as normative or appropriate in the period when the traditions crystallized in more or less their final literary form.

The reasoning of the "criterion of dissimilarity" may also be seen in James Barr's evaluation of the title "Anointed of Yahweh," as used of Saul in Samuel. In asserting that the title was already current within the lifetime of the first king of Israel, Barr is swayed by the fact that the term recurs in passages (e.g., 16:6 and 24:6) that are not obviously favorable towards Saul, and so "the very negativity of the picture of Saul which our sources give, rejected by Yahweh and rather a failure among men, makes all the more emphatic the fact that David still calls him 'the

---

21. I. Mendelsohn, "Samuel's Denunciation of Kingship in the Light of the Akkadian Documents from Ugarit," *BASOR* 143 (1956) 17–22; cf. A. F. Rainey, *Ras Shamra Parallels* II (ed. L. R. Fisher et al.; AnOr 50; Rome: Pontifical Biblical Institute, 1975) 93–98.

22. T. Ishida, *The Royal Dynasties in Ancient Israel: A Study on the Formation and Development of Royal-Dynastic Ideology* (BZAW 142; Berlin: de Gruyter, 1977) 43.

23. The anomalous positioning of the *atnah* at *šōkēb* ('was lying down') in the MT of the verse probably indicates unhappiness with the thought of Samuel sleeping "in the temple of the Lord." Note also the Qumranic fragment of "The Vision of Samuel" (4Q160), according to which Samuel "lay in front of Eli" (*Discoveries in the Judaean Desert of Jordan*, vol. 5: *Qumrân Cave 4* [ed. J. M. Allegro; Oxford: Clarendon, 1968] 9).

anointed of Yahweh.' "[24] As, however, the David traditions have been pushed more and more into the category of political propaganda, so the inclination to interpret Saul's designation as "Anointed of Yahweh" in this way has diminished. The propagandistic interpretation relates the expression only indirectly to Saul, to whom it is conveniently attached in order to teach the higher truth that David as the "Anointed of Yahweh" enjoys in his turn the sacrosanctity of one who rules by divine appointment.[25] In this case the historical value of the term as used of Saul would be nil, but if Barr were right then there would be a place for Samuel as the one who did the anointing. Of course, the currency of the term in Saul's lifetime would not by itself authenticate Samuel's part in the anointing, but who better?

The texts generally are insistent that Samuel was involved in the process by which Saul became Israel's king, yet this evidence is interpreted in strongly contrasting ways. The univocality of the narratives on the matter most naturally points to the conclusion that Samuel dominates the tradition because it was his role historically that gave rise to the tradition. Others, however, argue that Samuel makes his appearance in the installation narratives by courtesy of later prophetic circles for whom kingship under other than prophetic auspices was unacceptable. Yet this kind of argument can be double-edged when Saul is the king in question, since its effect is to tie Samuel, however reluctant his involvement, to a failed and rejected monarch. Would not Samuel's anointing of David have satisfied the prophetic coterie's craving for retrospective recognition? It is certainly not easy to imagine a northern prophet like Hosea contending for the inclusion of Saul's inauguration under the prophetic umbrella, but that is doubtless to venture too far into speculative realms.

THE BIRTH AND DEDICATION (1 SAMUEL 1−2)

In the remainder of this paper I shall concentrate on one facet of the Samuel tradition, in which Samuel and Saul have all unwittingly had their fates tangled together. A succession of writers on 1 Samuel have conjectured that the fourfold association of the Hebrew verb *šā'al* ('ask') with the name of Samuel in 1:17, 20, 27, and 28 (cf. 2:20) is not original but has come about because a tradition about the birth and dedication of

---

24. J. Barr, "Messiah," *Hastings' Dictionary of the Bible* (ed. F. C. Grant and H. H. Rowley; 2d ed.; Edinburgh: T. & T. Clark, 1963) 648.

25. See F. H. Cryer, "David's Rise to Power and the Death of Abner," *VT* 35 (1985) 391; Miller and Hayes, *History*, 155.

Saul has been expropriated and put to Samuel's account; and it is certainly true that *šā'al* provides a more satisfactory etymological basis for Saul's name than for Samuel's. We shall not detain ourselves with discussion of the detailed and, in my opinion, improbable hypotheses constructed on this observation by I. Hylander and J. Dus.[26] A modified version of their basic position is adopted and defended at some length by P. K. McCarter in his commentary on 1 Samuel. He offers three main arguments in support of the theory: the repeated wordplay involving *šā'al*, the formal similarity between 1:1 and 9:1, and a degree of correspondence between 1 Samuel 1 and Judges 13 that is sufficient to create the expectation that the former, like the latter, is intended to introduce a warrior figure of heroic dimensions.[27]

The second of these points requires little comment since the form of introduction, of Elkanah and Kish respectively, has parallels elsewhere (see Judg 13:2, 17:1), and only the presence of the genealogical matter is worthy of note. Whether there is any value at all in McCarter's second observation therefore depends a great deal on the validity of the other two arguments that he advances.

With regard to the wordplay on *šā'al*, the point that by Old Testament canons the root provides a passable etymology for the name Samuel has been sufficiently stated by a number of writers to require no further comment here. McCarter tries, however, to introduce a refinement when he argues that the purpose of 1 Sam 1:20 "is not to reinforce the etymological play on *š'l* but, on the contrary, to eclipse it or at least to modify it to the requirements of the name Samuel."[28] The justification for this conclusion is found in the word-order of the MT: " 'Samuel' because, 'From Yahweh I requested him,' " and according to McCarter "*miyyahweh* stands in the emphatic first position suggesting that it and not the verb is the intended referent of the etymology." If, however, we compare the naming of Moses and the accompanying explanation in Exod 2:10 we find precisely the same sort of word-order and without any special emphasis such as McCarter reads into 1 Sam 1:20: "She named him Moses, 'Because,' she said, 'from the water I drew him.' " McCarter's attempt, therefore, to catch an editor or compiler in the act of adapting a Saul etymology to suit Samuel's name is to be rejected as oversubtle.

---

26. I. Hylander, *Der literarische Samuel-Saul-Komplex (I. Sam. 1–15) traditionsgeschichtlich untersucht* (Uppsala: Almqvist and Wiksell, 1932) 9–62; J. Dus, "Die Geburtslegende Samuels, I. Sam. 1 (Eine traditionsgeschichtliche Untersuchung zu I. Sam. 1–3)," *RSO* 43 (1968) 163–94.

27. P. K. McCarter, *I Samuel: A New Translation with Introduction, Notes and Commentary* (AB 8; Garden City, N.Y.: Doubleday, 1980) 62–63, 65–66.

28. Ibid., 62.

In developing his third point McCarter assumes that 1 Samuel 1 is about the birth and dedication of a Nazirite. There is, of course, no explicit reference to Naziriteship in the chapter in its Masoretic recension, yet there are points of parallel that should not be overlooked (see especially 1:11), and we have also to take into account the direct references to Samuel's Nazirite status in the LXX at 1:11 (cf. 4QSam[a]) and in 4QSam[a] at 1:22.[29] I shall not, therefore, contest the description of Samuel in the MT as a Nazirite. There are correspondences between 1 Samuel 1 and Judges 13, which describes Samson's birth in terms of Nazirite dedication, and so the case for viewing 1 Samuel 1 as originally dealing with a Samson-like warrior figure begins to take shape.

Because references to Nazirites are rare in the Old Testament, it is possible to exaggerate the links between 1 Samuel 1 and Judges 13 to the level of an almost exclusive relationship, with obvious consequences for the reader's expectations about 1 Samuel 1. It is important, then, to establish the fact that the links are mainly with Nazirite status in general rather than with Judges 13 in particular. Indeed, McCarter himself may be found rejecting the LXX variant "until the day of his death" in 1:11 on the ground that it "shows the influence of Judg 13:7."[30] Literary readings of 1 Samuel 1 also have a bearing on the question. Read with an eye on intertextual concerns, this chapter could be understood to be setting up a deliberate contrast with Judges 13. In particular, Hannah's reference to the razor in v. 11 may be expressing the conviction that the same depilatory disaster as befell Samson (Judg 16:17–21) will not overtake the son whom she so earnestly seeks from God. Proceeding along similar lines, André Wénin sees in this verse, by what it says and what it omits saying about Samuel's being a Nazirite, an attempt to relativize the analogy between Samson and Samuel, even while drawing attention to it.[31]

Furthermore, even if 1 Samuel 1 is talking about full-blooded Naziriteship, it would not follow that a prophet figure like Samuel would fail to meet the expectations created by the narrative. It is true that the Nazirite of Judges 13 is a warrior figure, but then one of the few remaining Nazirite texts, namely Amos 2:11–12, links prophets and Nazirites in poetic parallelism and implies a close connection between the two groups. (Josephus's use of the term *prophet* for Samson, on the other

---

29. See E. C. Ulrich, *The Qumran Text of Samuel and Josephus* (HSM 19; Missoula, Mont.: Scholars Press, 1978) 39, 165.

30. McCarter, *I Samuel*, 54.

31. A. Wénin, *Samuel et l'instauration de la monarchie (1 S 1–12): Une Recherche littéraire sur le personnage* (Europäische Hochschulschriften, Reihe XXIII 342; Frankfurt am Main: Peter Lang, 1988) 50.

hand, is of little significance in view of his fairly loose descriptions of other Old Testament worthies as *prophets.*[32])

There is thus no reason to dispossess Samuel of the narrative of birth and dedication as it now stands in 1 Samuel 1, and we are spared the more extreme consequences of the rejected theory. For if the šāʾal theme originally belonged to Saul, the logic of the section that culminates in 1:28 ("he is lent [šāʾûl] to the Lord") would require that Saul spent his youth in the service of the Shiloh sanctuary. Since such an association between Saul and Shiloh is very difficult to square with the biblical data, McCarter's solution, following Dus, is to separate the Nazirite tradition from the Shiloh elements in the story: "So the Shilonite apprenticeship is not an original element from the tradition but, like the transferral of Saul's birth narrative, an innovation in the prophetic revision of the material which works to the aggrandizement of Samuel, who will become heir to the lost authority of the house of Eli."[33] Now this reconstruction of McCarter's is based on the premise that Shiloh no longer functioned as a cult center by the time of Saul, but even this assumption has been challenged by J. M. Miller and J. H. Hayes[34] and, in a major way, by D. G. Schley, whose published dissertation on Shiloh was written under the guidance of these same two specialists in Israelite history.[35]

Schley makes much of the šāʾal theme in 1 Samuel 1–2 as evidence that Saul was the original referent in the narrative *and* that the tradition linked him, and not Samuel, to Shiloh.[36] He also lays great emphasis on the references to Ahijah (from the Shilonite connection), who is with Saul in the battle preliminaries as reported in 14:3 and 18, and he expresses a strong preference for the MT of v. 18, according to which the ark of God was with Saul and his army at the time of the battle of Michmash.[37] Thus, Schley regards Saul as having had close links with the still-functioning priesthood of Shiloh through Eli's descendant Ahijah. For all this to be possible, of course, the tradition of the capture of the ark of God by the Philistines in 1 Samuel 4, as of the downgrading or even destruction of Shiloh that many have thought is implied in the narrative, has to be drastically reinterpreted. Schley and his mentors reject as an inference incorrectly drawn from 1 Samuel 4 and from the possibly related

---

32. See L. H. Feldman, "Prophets and Prophecy in Josephus," *JTS* n.s. 41 (1990) 389–91.

33. McCarter, *I Samuel*, 66.

34. Miller and Hayes, *History*, 125, 133.

35. D. G. Schley, *Shiloh: A Biblical City in Tradition and History* (JSOTSup 63; Sheffield: JSOT Press, 1989).

36. Ibid., 152–53.

37. Ibid., 153–54, 159–60.

references to Shiloh in Psalm 78 and Jeremiah 7 (cf. Jeremiah 26) the idea that the ark of God was captured and Shiloh was destroyed in the period represented by 1 Samuel 4.[38] Instead, they relocate the events of 1 Samuel 4 in the aftermath of Saul's defeat by the Philistines at Gilboa. Schley notes that Aphek, where the Israelites were defeated according to 1 Samuel 4, is mentioned in 29:1 as the muster-point for the Philistine contingents that proceeded to Gilboa, whence he finds encouragement for his reinterpretation of the earlier battle accounts.[39] Miller and Hayes are so sold on the same procedure in their 1986 volume that they refer at one point to Saul's defeat near Aphek, though an Aphek in the Jezreel area is otherwise unknown.[40] Finally, it should be noted that the supposed replacement of Saul by Samuel in 1 Samuel 1–2 is attributed by Schley to pro-Davidic editors of the account of David's rise: "the entire tradition of Samuel at Shiloh appears to have been theologically formulated rather than historically based."[41]

Schley and his colleagues are right when they say that 1 Samuel 4 does not expressly indicate that Shiloh was destroyed on the occasion described and that Ps 78:60–72, which Schley accepts as referring to the events of 1 Samuel 4, is likewise silent on this point. It seems to be generally agreed, moreover, that the archaeological evidence of destruction in the early Iron Age would as easily suit a date in Saul's reign as in the earlier period. But the abandonment or destruction of the Shiloh sanctuary before the rise of Saul is certainly not excluded by the evidence and may even be judged to be the more likely of the options. Schley is impressed by the absence of Shiloh from the list of places on Samuel's circuit in 7:15–17, as if this indicates that there never was a link between Samuel and Shiloh, yet the absence is adequately explained if by this time Shiloh had ceased to function. The apparent continuation of the Elide priesthood at Nob may still be explained satisfactorily in terms of the succession having perforce passed from Shiloh to Nob because of the Philistine depredations; no other special explanation is called for.[42] (Schley accepts the fact that 14:3 links Shiloh and Nob but sees this as a secondary feature "tying the Aaronite line of Eli to the independent line of Ahitub at Nob."[43])

The reference in the MT of 1 Sam 14:18 to the ark of God as being in the Israelite camp conflicts with the other relevant data in 1 Samuel

38. Ibid., 157–60, 167–83.
39. Ibid., 160, 195.
40. Miller and Hayes, *History*, 130, 133.
41. Schley, *Shiloh*, 156.
42. Pace Schley, ibid., 139–40.
43. Ibid., 159.

and is an old crux on that account. Schley prefers the MT reading to
the LXX's mention of the ephod, regarding the information that the ark
was in Kiriath-jearim all the days of Saul (cf. 1 Sam 7:2; 2 Sam 6:2) as
having been secondarily introduced into the Samuel tradition.[44] This is a
brave assumption as far as the text of 1 Sam 14:18 is concerned, for the
MT, as much as the LXX, is talking of an aborted oracular consultation,
for which the ephod was usually the appropriate instrument, as even the
associated vocabulary of 14:18–19 would suggest.

It should not require stating that the mention of Ahijah in 14:3,
whether as grandson[45] or great-grandson of Eli "the priest of Yahweh in
Shiloh," does not imply anything about the continuing function of the
Shilonite sanctuary; nevertheless, Schley chooses to see Ahijah as "a
younger priest of Shiloh, who serves as oracular priest of the ark."[46]
There is a further point to be made in relation to Ahijah. Schley makes
much of Saul's links with the Elides as legitimizing his rule and equally as
something to be played down by the "Davidic editors" of the Saul tradition. He refers to their needs to "separate Saul's monarchy from its very
real association with the sanctuary at Shiloh, the ancient Aaronite priesthood of Eli, and the ark."[47] The needs, as we can easily agree, were not
that pressing when 14:18 (MT) was allowed to slip through, but a couple
of other points deserve highlighting.

First, there would have been at least as much propaganda value for
David if the story of the fortunes of the ark of God had told how it had
been lost in battle by Saul at Gilboa and then recovered by David,
which is basically what happens in Schley's revised version of events.
As things are in the MT, the ark is recovered from the Philistines and
lodged in a halfway house before ever Saul or David appears on the
scene. If it really was lost at Gilboa, why did the "Davidic editors" not
ensure that the narrative recounted how, to his eternal glory, David recovered the ark for Yahweh and for Israel? All Schley has to offer on the
circumstances of the recovery is that David "was somehow able to secure
the return of the ark from Kiriath-Jearim."[48] He explains the "massive
revision" of the Saul traditions in terms of David's need of sacral legitimacy, which the extant narrative achieves for him by obliterating Saul's
connection with Shiloh and by showing how David reestablished the
Shiloh tradition. But one is entitled to ask whether this legitimacy based
on Shiloh finds support in the text. At best it is a thin line that connects

44. Ibid., 157–59.
45. Ibid.
46. Ibid., 195.
47. Ibid., 160.
48. Ibid., 198.

Shiloh with Jerusalem; by the time of David's reign Shiloh is a distant memory. And again, would not the account of David's recovery of the ark from the Philistines have worked wonders as regards his sacral legitimation? Furthermore, even if the narratives are relieved of every trace of misdemeanor on the part of the Elides, the historical reality is of a priesthood and sanctuary that, on either reading of the data, had been eclipsed by the time David became king. In that case, any attempts by Davidic editors to distance Saul from Shiloh become acts of significant kindness; they are rescuing him from a sinking ship. The significance of 14:3 is, I believe, better grasped by David Jobling:

> Saul is accompanied by Ahijah, a member of the rejected priestly house of Eli (14:3), and this first mention of an Elide after the disasters which befell Eli's family in ch. 4 triggers the response "rejected by Yhwh." His own royal glory gone, where else would we expect Saul to be than with a relative of "Glory gone"?[49]

Before we take leave of 1 Samuel 1–2, there are other aspects of the question that merit mentioning at the least. First, it is interesting to find so many scholars assuming that there was a birth narrative for Saul when no one in biblical antiquity seems to have thought to devise one for David. Secondly, there exists in 9:1–10:16, according to a common view, a legendary tale of Saul's introduction to his kingly destiny through his meeting with the prophet Samuel. Indeed, a more complicated version talks of two Saul narratives that have been conflated, the one about a visit to an anonymous seer and the other involving Samuel. None of this has a direct bearing on our discussion of 1 Samuel 1–2, yet it becomes clear that the argument about the fate of the once-favored, then rejected, Saul is pulling in opposite directions: he loses his birth story because of his fall from grace, yet he is awarded a royal anointing narrative or two (*honoris causa*) under the prophetic auspices of Samuel.

In this section I have argued that the Samuel traditions of 1 Samuel 1–2 have no prehistory of attachment to the figure of Saul and that they bind Samuel to the cult-center of Shiloh. At the same time, it should be recognized that sometimes strange and peculiarly effective narrative ploys are used by Old Testament writers, so that one should not reject *a priori* the possibility of a reworking of a Saul birth tradition in favor of Samuel. What could more powerfully make the point that, despite his position and achievements, Saul had to give place to Samuel in the judgment of God and of history? Yet that does not seem to be the way in which the author of 1 Samuel 1–2 crafted his account.

---

49. D. Jobling, "Saul's Fall and Jonathan's Rise: Tradition and Redaction in 1 Sam 14:1–46," *JBL* 95 (1976) 368.

How Did Saul Become King?
Literary Reading and
Historical Reconstruction

V. Philips Long

Covenant Theological Seminary

INTRODUCTION

"The heart of the discussion of Hebrew history-writing lies in the literary analysis of the books of Samuel." So writes John Van Seters in his controversial book *In Search of History.*[1] Such an assertion would, of course, be a gross exaggeration if intended categorically, but Van Seters is speaking only of his decision to focus on the books of Samuel in his discussion of Hebrew historiography. It is true, nevertheless, that the Samuel narratives often figure prominently in debates over the nature of biblical history-writing. Witness, for example, J. Licht's essay "Biblical Historicism"[2] or H. Donner's "Basic Elements of Old Testament Historiography Illustrated by the Saul Traditions."[3] Both of these focus on the so-called "rise of Saul" in 1 Samuel as exhibiting something of the essence of early Israelite history-writing. In this regard, such works are in line with G. von Rad's view that the beginnings of Israel's historiography as such are to be found in the "early monarchical period."[4] W. E. Evans can even speak of

---

1. J. Van Seters, *In Search of History: Historiography in the Ancient World and the Origins of Biblical History* (New Haven: Yale University Press, 1983) 247.

2. J. Licht, "Biblical Historicism," *History, Historiography and Interpretation: Studies in Biblical and Cuneiform Literatures* (ed. H. Tadmor and M. Weinfeld; Jerusalem: Magnes, 1983) 107–20.

3. H. Donner, "Basic Elements of Old Testament Historiography Illustrated by the Saul Traditions," *Die Ou-Testamentiese werkgemeenskap in Suid-Afrika* 24 (1981) 40–54.

4. E.g., von Rad writes: "It is amazing that we can name three major historical works which must have followed upon one another at relatively short intervals in this era—the history of David's rise to power (I Sam. XVI. 14–II Sam. v. 12), the history of the succession after David (II Sam. VI. 12, 20ff.–I Kings II), and the Jahwist's history" (*Old Testament*

271

a "general agreement" that the career of Saul marks "the threshold of
actual historical events in the Bible."[5] More recently, P. J. Arnold has
observed that "the events surrounding the establishment of the monarchy
at Gibeah are among the most crucial in biblical history. . . ."[6] My point
in reciting these comments is not to agree or disagree with them but simply to underscore the attention that is often given to the Saul narratives
in discussions of early Israelite historiography.[7]

   Despite this high level of interest, historical study of the Saul narratives
has yielded rather disappointing results. Archaeology has provided little
assistance in reconstructing the rise of Israel's first king, for, as A. Mazar
has recently pointed out, "the archaeological evidence for the period of
the United Monarchy is sparse" and "often controversial." More
specifically, "The time of Saul hardly finds any expression in the archaeological record."[8] Social-scientific and contextual-archaeological studies
are in the process of providing general background information, but
specific information about Israel's first kings must still be derived almost
exclusively from the literary deposit in scripture. Here one encounters a
basic problem, however, for a majority of scholars find the biblical account
of Saul's rise to the throne, as Licht puts it, "rather unconvincing as a
statement of fact."[9] Indeed, most would still subscribe to the verdict ren-

---

Theology [2 vols.; New York: Harper & Row, 1962], 1.48–49); cf. idem, "The Beginnings
of Historical Writing in Ancient Israel," *The Problem of the Hexateuch and Other Essays* (Edinburgh and London: Oliver & Boyd, 1966) 166–204. In this essay von Rad cites the
Succession Narrative as "the oldest specimen of ancient Israelite historical writing" (176;
cf. 192). In his "Zwei Überlieferungen von König Saul" (*Gesammelte Studien zum Alten
Testament* [ed. R. Smend; Munich: Chr. Kaiser, 1973], 2.199–211), von Rad cites the
battle report of 1 Samuel 13–14 as marking a breakthrough toward more truly historical
thinking and writing.

   5. W. E. Evans, "An Historical Reconstruction of the Emergence of Israelite Kingship
and the Reign of Saul," *Scripture in Context II: More Essays on the Comparative Method* (ed.
W. W. Hallo, J. C. Moyer. and L. G. Perdue; Winona Lake, Ind.: Eisenbrauns, 1983) 61.

   6. P. J. Arnold, *Gibeah: The Search for a Biblical City* (JSOTSup 79; Sheffield: JSOT
Press, 1990) 27.

   7. Attempts at setting the *terminus a quo* of history-writing in Israel are handicapped
from the start by the continuing debate over what exactly constitutes "history-writing."
If I may adopt a broad definition something like "a selective, interpretative, verbal representation of past events and persons," then it would seem unnecessary (and ill-
advised) to deny a place for history-writing in Israel in the premonarchical period.

   8. A. Mazar, *Archaeology of the Land of the Bible: 10,000–586 B.C.E.* (New York:
Doubleday, 1990) 371. The one possible exception to this generalization, viz., the Iron I
tower foundation at Tell el-Ful thought by Albright to represent the "Citadel of Saul," is
now regarded as far less certain evidence of Saulide construction than scholars had previously believed; see, most recently, Arnold, *Gibeah*, 51–52.

   9. Licht, "Biblical Historicism," 107.

dered back in 1932 by W. W. Cannon that "the events by which he [Saul] came to the throne are and will remain a mystery."[10]

This rather unhopeful verdict may derive from one or more of several basic lines of reasoning. For example, since the Enlightenment many scholars have subscribed to the notion that those writings that may appear in some respects to recount historical events but which make explicit or implicit reference to God or the gods as active participants in those events are automatically to be disqualified as "history."[11] Others, such as Dutch scholar K. A. D. Smelik, have argued that the ancient Near East provides too few "inspirerende voorbeelden" ('inspiring examples') of history-writing from around the time of David or Solomon to justify any expectation that Israel might have had a historiographical tradition stemming from that time.[12] As influential as these two assumptions are, by far the *most frequently cited reason* for the historical agnosticism regarding Saul's kingship is the belief that the biblical narratives recounting Saul's rise to power *simply do not make sense as a story*. That is to say, they do not constitute a coherent, sequential narrative. Tomoo Ishida speaks for a majority of scholars when he asserts that "it is futile from the outset to attempt reconstruction of a harmonious history from all the narratives."[13]

10. W. W. Cannon, "The Reign of Saul," *Theology* 25 (1932) 326.

11. David Friedrich Strauss, in his *Life of Jesus* (first published in 1835), offers a classic articulation of this viewpoint: "An account is not historical . . . when the narration is irreconcilable with the known and universal laws which govern the course of events. Now according to these laws, agreeing with all just philosophical conceptions and all credible experience, the absolute cause never disturbs the chain of secondary causes by single arbitrary acts of interposition, but rather manifests itself in the production of the aggregate of finite casualities [*sic*], and of their reciprocal action. When therefore we meet with an account of certain phenomena or events of which it is either expressly stated or implied that they were produced immediately by God himself (divine apparitions: voices from heaven and the like), or by human beings possessed of supernatural powers (miracles, prophecies), such an account is *in so far* to be considered as not historical. And inasmuch as, in general, the intermingling of the spiritual world with the human is found only in unauthentic records, and is irreconcilable with all just conceptions; so narratives of angels and of devils, of their appearing in human shape and interfering with human concerns, cannot possibly be received as historical" (the quotation is from Peter C. Hodgson's edition [New York: Fortress, 1972], 87–88). For a corrective to this view, see, e.g., A. R. Millard, "The Old Testament and History: Some Considerations," *FT* 110 (1983) 39–40.

12. K. A. D. Smelik, *Saul: De voorstelling van Israëls eerste koning in de Masoretische tekst van het Oude Testament* (Amsterdam: Drukkerij en Uitgeverij P. E. T., 1977) 76. This is not the place to launch a critique of Smelik's view, except perhaps to make the following brief observations: (1) it tends to underplay the significance of, for example, the royal apology literature so well attested from the chancelleries of the ancient Near East; and (2) it at any rate must assume that a truly new literary form can never arise spontaneously but only by means of an evolutionary development from earlier forms.

13. Tomoo Ishida, *The Royal Dynasties in Ancient Israel: A Study on the Formation and Development of Royal-Dynastic Ideology* (BZAW 142; Berlin: de Gruyter, 1977) 42.

Even the rather conservative (by contemporary standards) John Bright insists that "in view of these varying accounts, we cannot undertake to reconstruct the sequence of events" by which Saul became king.[14]

In this essay I am focusing on this last and most pervasive line of reasoning believed by the vast majority of scholars to discredit any attempt to reconstruct the historical rise of Saul from (all) the narratives of 1 Samuel.

PERCEIVED HINDRANCES TO A COHERENT LITERARY READING OF "SAUL'S RISE"

The literary, or logical, difficulties thought to stand in the way of a straightforward reading of the rise of Saul are basically three. First, since Wellhausen it has been customary in discussions of the rise of the Monarchy in 1 Samuel 8–12 to distinguish at least two originally independent narratives detectable on the basis of *discrepant attitudes to kingship*. Bright explains:

> The account of Saul's election comes to us in two (probably originally three) parallel narratives, one tacitly favorable to the monarchy, and the other bitterly hostile. The first (I Sam. 9:1 to 10:16) tells how Saul was privately anointed by Samuel in Ramah; it is continued in 13:3b, 4b–15. Woven with this narrative is the originally separate account (ch. 11) of Saul's victory over Ammon and his subsequent acclamation by the people at Gilgal. The other strand (chs. 8; 10:17–27; 12) has Samuel, having yielded with angry protests to popular demand, presiding over Saul's election at Mizpah.[15]

This quotation from Bright, highlighting the apparently contradictory promonarchical and antimonarchical sentiments of the assumed sources, touches also upon the second of the most-frequently cited literary inconcinnities in the biblical account of Saul's rise: namely, the fact that Saul appears to come to power by *too many different routes*. Did he come to power by distinguishing himself in battle against the Ammonites (as most historical critics believe), or as a result of his anointing followed by battle (as the combined promonarchical source would have it), or by lot-casting (as the antimonarchical source would have it)? The consensus of scholarly opinion is well summarized by H. Donner when he says of the pro- and antimonarchical accounts that "they contradict each other: Saul could not have become king in so many ways."[16] Even restricting himself

---

14. John Bright, *A History of Israel* (3d ed.; London: SCM/Philadelphia: Westminster, 1981) 188.

15. Ibid., 187–88.

16. Donner, "Basic Elements," 43.

to a consideration of the promonarchical source, W. A. Irwin insists that
"we are embarrassed by our very wealth! Either account [i.e., the anointing episode or the Ammonite victory] would suffice as an explanation of
this revolutionary change in Hebrew history, to be given both baffles
credence."[17]

To these two apparent difficulties, the differing attitudes towards the
monarchy and the multiple accession accounts, must be added a third.
This has to do with the much-discussed *crux interpretum* in the account
of Saul's anointing and first charge by Samuel. At the close of these
events, Samuel instructs Saul in 1 Sam 10:8 to go down to Gilgal and
wait for him, so that he may come and offer sacrifices and tell Saul what
he is to do. The problem is that this instruction comes on the heels of
10:7, in which Samuel tells Saul to "do what your hand finds to do."[18]
Assuming the v. 7 directive to be an unqualified authorization for Saul
to act whenever the need should arise, scholars have felt that v. 8 constitutes a blatant contradiction.[19] What v. 7 seems to authorize, "Do what
your hand finds to do," v. 8 seems to take away, "Go down to Gilgal"
and "wait." To make matters worse, the fulfillment of the injunction in
v. 8 does not come until chap. 13, all of which contributes to the impression that v. 8 must not be original to its present context in chap. 10 but
must be a later interpolation, perhaps a sort of "theological correction"
inserted by a later prophetic circle unhappy with the apparently free
hand being given Saul by Samuel in v. 7.[20] As a corollary to the assumption that v. 8 is secondary to chap. 10, scholars have customarily assumed
that the Gilgal episode in chap. 13 (i.e., vv. 4b, 7b–15a) must also be
secondary.[21]

17. W. A. Irwin, "Samuel and the Rise of the Monarchy," *AJSL* 58 (1941) 117.

18. This rendering is preferred to the NIV's "Do whatever your hand finds to do,"
which may reflect LXX's *poiei panta, hosa ean heurē hē cheir sou,* which in turn appears to
read ʿśh kl ʾśr where MT has ʿśh lk ʾśr. It is better to retain the MT and understand *lk* as
a *dativus ethicus*: on which see, e.g., GKC §119s; B. K. Waltke and M. O'Connor, *An Introduction to Biblical Hebrew Syntax* (Winona Lake, Ind.: Eisenbrauns, 1990) §11.2.10d.
The point is that Samuel's charge to Saul is not that he should do just *whatever* comes to
hand, as if Samuel himself does not have something specific in mind.

19. See, e.g., J. Wellhausen, *Prolegomena zur Geschichte Israels* (3d ed.; Berlin: Georg
Reimer, 1886) 268; K. D. Budde, *Die Bücher Samuel* (Kurzer Hand-Commentar zum
Alten Testament 8; Tübingen: Mohr, 1902) 69; R. J. Thompson, *Penitence and Sacrifice in
Early Israel outside the Levitical Law* (Leiden: Brill, 1963) 106; Stoebe, *Das erste Buch Sam-
uelis* (KAT 8/1; Gütersloh: Mohn, 1973) 210.

20. Cf. J. Kegler's characterization of 10:8 as a "theologische Korrektur" in *Politisches
geschehen und theologisches Verstehen: Zum Geschichtsverständnis in der frühen israelitischen
Königszeit* (Calwer Theologische Monographien 8; Stuttgart: Calwer, 1977) 264.

21. The following statement by T. Veijola (*Die ewige Dynastie: David und die Entstehung seiner Dynastie nach der deuteronomistischen Darstellung* [Annales academiae scientia-
rum Fennicae, Series B, 193; Helsinki: Suomalainen Tiedeakatemia, 1975], 55) is typical: "That the entire Gilgal episode in 1 Sam 13:7b–15a (which falls outside its present

How is one to evaluate these three arguments to the effect that the
biblical account of the rise of Saul is at points contradictory and inco-
herent and thus an unreliable source of historical information? It is my
contention that the data are now available to enable solutions to all
three problems. The first two I shall consider only briefly, since the
relevant insights necessary to their resolution have already been published by others.

Regarding the matter of monarchical attitudes, I found that once I
recognized with Tsevat, McCarthy, Childs, and others that the more antimonarchical chords are struck in the episodes involving assemblies
(natural contexts for the expression of strong opinions) and not so much
in the action reports, and once I asked with Eslinger "the simple question of who says what to whom," and once I followed Weiser, Ishida,
Crüsemann, and others in abandoning Wellhausen's mistaken notion
that antimonarchical sentiments arose only late in the history of Israel
and Judah, and once I learned to distinguish carefully between attitudes that are antimonarchical *per se* and those that are merely anti-Saul,
my sharpened vision revealed not a more clearly defined problem but the
absence of any problem at all.[22] Indeed, there is an increasing tendency in
recent discussions to play down the significance and even the validity of
Wellhausen's old promonarchical/antimonarchical opposition.

Regarding the second challenge to the literary coherence of the
biblical account of Saul's rise (i.e., the fact that Saul appears to have come
to power via several distinct pathways), the raw material for building a
solution has been provided in recent work by Baruch Halpern[23] and has
been further fashioned by Diana Edelman.[24] Halpern has argued on the
basis of both biblical and extrabiblical evidence that the process by which
leaders in early Israel came to power quite likely entailed three stages,
which we might describe simply as designation, demonstration, and

---

context) is a secondary insertion (along with its similarly isolated anticipation in 1 Sam
10:8), is no longer in need of demonstration" (my translation). Cf. in addition to the literature cited by Veijola, von Rad, "Zwei Überlieferungen," 203; Stoebe, *Das erste Buch
Samuelis*, 207; P. K. McCarter, *I Samuel* (AB 8; Garden City, N. Y.: Doubleday, 1980)
228.

22. For bibliography and discussion pertaining to all of the above, see my *Reign and
Rejection of King Saul: A Case for Literary and Theological Coherence* (SBLDS 118; Atlanta:
Scholars Press, 1989) 173–83.

23. Baruch Halpern, *The Constitution of the Monarchy in Israel* (HSM 25; Chico, Cal,.:
Scholars Press, 1981); idem, "The Uneasy Compromise: Israel between League and Mon-
archy," *Traditions in Transformation: Turning Points in Biblical Faith* (ed. B. Halpern and J. D.
Levenson; F. M. Cross Festschrift; Winona Lake, Ind.: Eisenbrauns, 1981) 59–96.

24. Diana Edelman, "Saul's Rescue of Jabesh-Gilead (1 Sam 11:1–11): Sorting Story
from History," *ZAW* 96 (1984) 195–209.

confirmation.[25] The process went something like this. An individual is first *designated* in some way as God's chosen instrument. The new appointee is then expected to *demonstrate* his special status and suitability for leadership by a feat of arms or military victory, whether real or merely ritual. Having thus distinguished himself publicly, he is in a position to be *confirmed* publicly as leader of God's people.

Both Halpern and Edelman attempt to elucidate the biblical account of Saul's rise on the basis of this tripartite pattern. Halpern isolates what he believes to be two complete exemplars of the accession pattern in the stretch of text from 1 Samuel 9–14.[26] The impetus for this discovery, however, appears to come more from Halpern's commitment to a theory of sources and doublets[27] than from the evidence of the texts themselves.[28] Edelman improves on Halpern's analysis by discerning but one instance of the accession pattern in 1 Samuel 9–11. In her view, the divine designation is represented by Saul's anointing in 9:1–10:16, the demonstration by his defeat of the Ammonites in 11:1–11, and the confirmation by the "renewal" of the kingdom in 11:14–15.[29]

Edelman's scheme is essentially correct insofar as it goes, but it leaves some unanswered questions. For example, it provides no explanation of the lot-casting episode in 10:17–27, which comes between the anointing and the Ammonite victory.[30] A further and more significant tension in Edelman's scheme has to do with Samuel's charge to Saul in 10:7 to "do what your hand finds to do." Edelman rightly recognizes that this charge implies some kind of military engagement, and she assumes that this must be none other than Saul's Ammonite victory. But she also recognizes—and herein lies the problem—that the real focus of 10:7 in context is not the Ammonites but the Philistines, and particularly the Philistine presence in Gibeah (which is to become the object of Jonathan's aggression in chap. 13). To come to terms with this awkward situation, some scholars postulate that the events of chap. 13 must have

25. While Halpern sometimes explicitly names only two stages, viz., designation and confirmation (*Constitution of the Monarchy*, 125, 173–74, and *passim*), it is clear that he presupposes a middle "demonstration" stage consisting of a real or ritual victory of some sort (ibid., 95, 178–74; "Uneasy Compromise," 72). On the validity of distinguishing three stages, see also Edelman, "Saul's Rescue," 198 n. 9.

26. Halpern, "Uneasy Compromise," 70.

27. He writes, "The first step in investigating Saul's election is, as the histories recognize, a division of the sources in 1 Samuel 8ff." (ibid., 63).

28. For a critical evaluation of Halpern's two-source theory, see my *Reign and Rejection*, 191–93.

29. Edelman, "Saul's Rescue," 197–99.

30. Edelman (ibid., 200–202) notes only that this episode "appears to augment the discussion of the first stage of the process of installing a king" and to look forward to the public coronation that will eventually occur in 11:14–15.

followed more closely on 10:7 in some hypothetical earlier stage of devel-opment.[31] In other words, they assume that episodes originally joined have now been redactionally put asunder.

This suggestion of textual dislocation brings me to the third and final challenge to the literary coherence of the rise of Saul as recounted in 1 Samuel. In what follows I shall attempt to demonstrate that this perceived difficulty actually offers the key to a rather straightforward synchronic reading of the narrative of Saul's rise.

SAUL'S "FIRST CHARGE" AS A TWO-STAGE AFFAIR

As mentioned earlier, the impression of textual dislocation derives from two felt tensions in the text: first, the apparently contradictory commands given to Saul by Samuel in back-to-back verses in chap. 10 (namely, "do what your hand finds to do" (v. 7) and "go down ahead of me to Gilgal [and] wait . . . until I come to you and tell you what you are to do" [v. 8]) and second, the fact that the trip to Gilgal is not made until chap. 13. I want to take these up in order.

It is my contention that the commands of 10:7–8 should be viewed not as contradictory but as complementary instructions, the execution of the second being contingent on the fulfillment of the first. This view seems to be quite in keeping with the larger narrative context, which runs as follows. After a divinely orchestrated meeting between the two principals in chap. 9, Samuel anoints Saul in 10:1 as the Lord's desig-nate to lead his people. Samuel then describes three signs that will confirm Saul in his new station (vv. 2–6). The third sign is to take place at Gibeah of God, where, as Samuel points out, there is a Philis-tine outpost (v. 5). This reference to a Philistine outpost is regarded by many scholars as at best superfluous, if not indeed out of place. No bet-ter justification is given for this opinion than that these scholars fail to see any reason why the biblical narrator should mention a Philistine in-stallation at this particular juncture in the narrative.[32] When one recalls,

---

31. Ibid., 200. In Edelman's *King Saul in the Historiography of Judah* (JSOTSup 121; Sheffield: JSOT, 1991), which became available after the present essay had been completed and submitted, she offers a more synchronic reading. Others who seek to explain the ap-parent relationship between chaps. 10 and 13 in traditio-historical terms include H. J. Stoebe, "Zur Topographie und Überlieferung der Schlacht von Mikmas, 1 Sam 13 und 14," *TZ* 21 (1965) 277–80; J. M. Miller, "Saul's Rise to Power: Some Observations Con-cerning 1 Sam 9:1–10:16; 10:26–11:15 and 13:2–14:46," *CBQ* 36 (1974) 162; T. N. D. Mettinger, *King and Messiah: The Civil and Sacral Legitimation of the Israelite Kings* (ConBOT 8; Lund: CWK Gleerup, 1976) 97; and most recently Arnold, *Gibeah*, 89–90.

32. E.g., McCarter (*I Samuel*, 182) remarks simply that "this notice is immaterial at this point and probably secondary, having been added along with the instructions in v. 8 as preparation for c[hap.] 13."

however, that Saul is being appointed specifically to deal with the Philistine menace (see the Lord's instructions to Samuel in 9:16), and that it is as soon as the three signs have come to pass that Saul is to do what his hand finds to do (10:7), then the reference to a Philistine presence at the site of the third and final sign takes on special significance. Indeed, there is much to commend the view that Samuel's reference to the Philistines in 10:5 represents a fairly obvious hint to Saul about what his hand should find to do.[33]

Against this background, and recalling the tripartite accession process worked out by Halpern and Edelman, I am prompted to ask what could possibly serve as a more appropriate *demonstration*, after Saul's divine *designation* by anointing, than that he should throw down the gauntlet to the Philistines by attacking one of their installations? Samuel, of course, realizes that such an act of provocation will signal only the beginning and not the end of trouble, and so he issues a second instruction to Saul in v. 8: "Go down ahead of me to Gilgal. I will surely come down to you to sacrifice burnt offerings and fellowship offerings, but you must wait seven days until I come to you and tell you what you are to do." In other words, as soon as Saul has done what his hand finds to do, thereby provoking the Philistines, he is to repair to Gilgal, where Samuel will join him in order to consecrate the ensuing battle with sacrifices and to give him further instructions.[34]

In this way, then, the two injunctions of 10:7–8 are seen to be, not contradictory, but complementary and sequentially contingent. There is still a problem, however, since the prescribed rendezvous in Gilgal does not take place until chap. 13. The wording of 13:8, which speaks of Saul's waiting "seven days, the time set by Samuel," leaves no room for doubt that the allusion is to 10:8. On this point there is universal agreement. What is often overlooked, however, is that a similar relationship exists between the report of Jonathan's attack on the Philistine outpost at Geba in 13:3 and Saul's first charge in 10:7. In other words, in 13:3 Jonathan is doing what Saul was instructed to do earlier in 10:7. As Stoebe succinctly

---

33. This understanding of the significance of 10:5 is attested already in the writings of grammarian and biblical commentator David Qimḥi (1160–1235), who pointed out that in reminding Saul of the Philistines in Gibeah-elohim, Samuel is "hinting to him that he should remove them from there and save Israel out of their hands" (*rmz lw ky hw⁾ ysyrm mšm wyšy^c yśr⁾l mydm*) (from Kimchi's commentary to 1 Sam 10:5 found in standard editions of the rabbinic Hebrew Bible). Other commentators who have sensed something of the significance of 10:5 include R. Kittel, *Geschichte des Volkes Israel* (7th ed.; Gotha: Klotz 1925) 2.82; A. Lods, *Israel from Its Beginnings to the Middle of the Eighth Century* (London: Kegan Paul, Trench, Trubner, 1932) 353; C. J. Goslinga, *Het eerste boek Samuël* (Commentaar op het Oude Testament; Kampen: Kok, 1968) 223; Smelik, *Saul*, 107.

34. For a discussion of the prophet's role in prebattle consecration and instruction, see my *Reign and Rejection* 61–63.

explains, "the deed that is here [13:3] ascribed to Jonathan is what one awaits as the continuation of Saul's Spirit-endowment in Gibeah and of the charge: 'Do what your hand finds to do' (10:7)."[35] It is noteworthy that Jonathan's provocative act in 13:3 is followed immediately by Saul going down to Gilgal to wait for Samuel (13:4). Thus, the two-stage procedure *envisaged* in chap. 10 (i.e., provocation of the Philistines followed by convocation in Gilgal) is actually *followed* in chap. 13. While this double attestation of the provocation/convocation pattern does not constitute a proof of the genuineness and originality of the pattern in either context, it does at least shift the burden of proof to those who wish to assert the contrary.

In view of the relationship between chaps. 10 and 13 highlighted above, one is faced with a final, very crucial question. How does one explain the rather large gap, in both narrative time and real time, between Samuel's two-part instruction to Saul in 10:7–8 and its evident fulfillment three chapters and several episodes later? Must the reader assume redactional or traditio-historical dislocation of originally sequential episodes? Or is one perhaps meant to understand that *Saul falters in his first assignment*, that he simply doesn't do what his hand finds to do, with the result that the execution of his second instruction, namely, the rendezvous with Samuel in Gilgal, is indefinitely delayed? This latter suggestion offers a promising explanation of the gap between the issuance of Saul's first charge in chap. 10 and its eventual fulfillment through the agency of Jonathan in chap. 13. The objection might be raised, however, that if the narrator intends for the reader to understand that Saul falters at the start, why does he not make this point explicitly, or overtly condemn Saul for his inaction? In addressing this objection, it will be helpful to contemplate a different kind of gap or gapping.

"GAPPING" AS LITERARY DEVICE AND THE GAP
BETWEEN 1 SAMUEL 10 AND 13

In his *Poetics of Biblical Narrative*, Meir Sternberg notes that all literary works establish "a system of gaps that must be filled in" by the reader in the process of reading.[36] Every literary work raises a number of questions in the mind of the reader, but it only provides explicit answers to a few of them. The remaining questions, the "gaps" as Sternberg calls

35. Stoebe, *Das erste Buch Samuelis*, 247 (my translation); cf. 207. More recently, Halpern (*Constitution of the Monarchy*, 155–56) has also drawn attention to the command/fulfilment relationship between 10:7 and 13:3.

36. Meir Sternberg, *The Poetics of Biblical Narrative: Ideological Literature and the Drama of Reading* (Bloomington: Indiana University Press, 1985) 186.

them, are to be answered or filled in by the reader on the basis of clues in the text itself. Sternberg illustrates the principle of "gapping" by citing in translation the following Hebrew nursery rhyme.

> Every day, that's the way
> Jonathan goes out to play.
> Climbed a tree. What did he see?
> Birdies: one, two, three!
>
> Naughty boy! What have we seen?
> There's a hole in your new jeans![37]

How did Jonathan tear his jeans? In the tree, of course. Even a child can draw this conclusion quite readily from the information given in the rhyme, though the point is never explicitly made. Of course, gap-filling may not always be as simple as this, especially in narratives as artful and sophisticated as the Samuel narratives. Sternberg writes: "Gap-filling ranges from simple linkages of elements, which the reader performs automatically, to intricate networks that are figured out consciously, laboriously, hesitantly, and with constant modifications in the light of additional information disclosed in later stages of reading."

It seems fair to say that the *literary* gap created by the *literal* gap between Saul's first charge (chap. 10) and its eventual fulfillment (chap. 13) is of the more difficult sort described above. That it should take conscious effort to fill it should not surprise us, for, as Sternberg remarks, "in works of greater complexity, the filling-in of gaps becomes much more difficult and therefore more conscious and anything but automatic." The test of any attempt at gap-filling is, of course, whether the hypothesis is "legitimated by the text."[38] While a full exploration of the question cannot be attempted within the confines of the present essay, one may at least trace in broad outline the manner in which my theory that Saul *falters* in the starting gate, as it were, makes possible a synchronic reading of the entire narrative sequence of his rise to power.

MAKING SENSE OF "SAUL'S RISE"

Immediately following the anointing episode in 1 Samuel 10, the text recounts a rather enigmatic conversation between Saul and his "uncle" (10:14–16), the significance of which has largely eluded scholars. In this conversation, Saul is reasonably loquacious on the topic of his search for his father's lost donkeys and even on his "chance" meeting

37. Ibid., 187.
38. Ibid., 186–88.

with Samuel, but he is absolutely silent, as the narrator informs us, on the matter of the kingship (v. 16b). Saul's unwillingness to mention the "big news" of the day has baffled most commentators.[39] But according to my understanding, Saul's reticence is readily explained as that of a man who is shrinking back from a fearful first duty as the "Lord's anointed" and who would just as soon not talk about it, at least not with one of such militant leanings as Uncle Abner (if that is who is in view).[40]

Moving on to the next episode (10:17–27), I would argue that Saul's failure to carry out his first charge also helps to explain why it is necessary for Samuel to convene an assembly in Mizpah and why there is a certain negative tone[41] to the proceedings there. Saul's inaction after his designation means that he has done nothing to gain public attention or to demonstrate his fitness as leader. In other words, the normal accession process, whereby designation was to be followed by demonstration that would then lead to confirmation, has stalled. The Mizpah assembly may be viewed as Samuel's attempt to bring Saul to public attention by a different route than that originally envisaged and to show by the lot-casting that Saul is the leader given by God in response to the people's request for a king (chap. 8). If this reading of the episode is basically correct, it becomes increasingly difficult to endorse the common understanding of Saul's hiding behind the baggage at the time of his selection (10:22) as evidence of laudable humility. One senses, rather, a timidity and fearfulness in the crouching "giant" (cf. 9:2) that will show itself again in the cringing "giant" of chap. 17, who shrinks back in fear and dismay before the Philistine's own giant (17:11). Moreover, if, as this theory would have it, Saul has yet done nothing to demonstrate his valor or fitness to lead in battle, it is not too surprising that some of the people protest when Saul is dragged from behind the baggage, "How can this one save us?" (10:27).

In chap. 11 Saul's rescue of Jabesh-gilead from the Ammonite threat finally provides the long-awaited *demonstration*, and the kingship is "renewed" (v. 14), that is, the accession process, derailed by Saul's initial faltering, is put back on track.[42] Read this way, the defeat of the

---

39. So, e.g., McCarter (*I Samuel*, 187–88 and n. 5), who admits that the "secrecy motif . . . has never been fully explained."

40. As I have noted elsewhere (*Reign and Rejection*, 209 n. 61), there is some debate about the identity of Saul's conversation partner in this episode, but such questions do not substantially affect the interpretation I am suggesting.

41. Noted, e.g., by J. Blenkinsopp ("The Quest of the Historical Saul," *No Famine in the Land: Studies in Honor of John L. McKenzie* [ed. J. W. Flanagan and A. W. Robinson; Missoula, Mont.: Scholars Press, 1975], 76); cf. McCarter, *I Samuel*, 196.

42. For a defense of this understanding of *ḥdš Piel* in v. 14, see my *Reign and Rejection*, 225–28.

Ammonites serves as a sort of substitute for the demonstration originally envisaged by Samuel in 10:7, which was to have been a provocation of the Philistines. After Saul's Ammonite victory, all the people are delighted with their new king, and chap. 11 concludes with the notice that "Saul and all the men of Israel rejoiced greatly there" in Gilgal (v. 15b). Only Samuel's name is missing from the list of celebrants.[43] In the next chapter, Samuel shows that he still has reservations about the experiment of kingship. After a stern rebuke of the people's misguided demand for a king, "even though the LORD was your king" (12:12), Samuel warns that kingship can still fail. The tenor of Samuel's pronouncements in chap. 12 suggests that human kingship, and in particular Israel's first king, must yet stand a test. The nature of this test, according to the interpretation proposed in this essay, is precisely described in Saul's "first charge" as recorded in 10:7–8. It is no mere coincidence, then, that the very next chapter recounts Jonathan's attack on the Philistine outpost in Geba (13:3)—phase one of Saul's first charge (cf. 10:7)—and, as its immediate sequel, Saul's retreat to Gilgal to await Samuel's arrival (13:4ff.)—phase two of the first charge (10:8).

Lamentably, Saul fails in the execution of phase two and receives a stinging rebuke from the belated Samuel (13:8–14). Samuel's reaction to Saul's failure has often been interpreted as excessively harsh—most recently, for example, by Walter Brueggemann, who speaks of the "posturing" and "peevishness" of Samuel.[44] But if my understanding of Saul's first charge and of its significance as background to the events of chap. 13 is basically on target, then such assessments of Samuel's behavior can no longer be "legitimated by the text."

The full significance of Saul's first charge will not be explored here, but one may at least observe that it seems designed to create an authority structure whereby human kingship can be accommodated within what remains essentially theocratic rule. In the new order established by Samuel in his first charge to Saul, the king is to become the standing military agent, but the prophet is to remain the recipient and mediator of the divine initiative.[45] If the king will but obey the word of the Lord as mediated by the prophet, then he will have proved himself suitable to occupy the throne in Israel (see 12:13–15, 24–25). Saul does not obey,

---

43. Perhaps sensitive to this omission, the LXX (mis)reads *šm š²wl*, if that was its *Vorlage*, as 'Samuel' (*šmw²l*); i.e., *kai euphranthē Samouēl kai pas Israēl hōste lian*.

44. Walter Brueggemann, *First and Second Samuel* (Interpretation; Louisville, Ky.: John Knox, 1990) 101.

45. On the mediatorial role of prophets in the monarchical period, see my *Reign and Rejection*, 60–65.

however, either in chap. 13 or subsequently in chap. 15, and it is for this fundamental failure that he is rejected.

CONCLUSION

My treatment of literary issues has of necessity been brief, but enough has been said to indicate that once the significance of Saul's first charge in 10:7–8 is recognized, a coherent and sequential reading of the biblical narratives recounting his rise to the throne is possible, and indeed plausible. Of course, simply establishing the literary coherence of the biblical account of Saul's rise does not constitute proof of its historicity, but then knock-down arguments and positive proofs in such matters are seldom if ever possible. What such an exercise does accomplish, however, is the removal of the most frequently cited basis of historical skepticism, namely, the notion that the biblical story of Saul's rise simply cannot be read sequentially as a coherent account. To pursue the matter of historicity further, one would need to investigate questions of literary genre, of overall rhetorical purpose as determined by the larger discourse unit, and the like. But such questions must remain for another time.

In Search of David:
The David Tradition
in Recent Study

Robert P. Gordon

The University of Cambridge

INTRODUCTION

It is easy to sympathize with Joel Rosenberg when he confesses that "something in us rebels . . . at the notion that the materials of II Samuel are *not* history."[1] The clear and frank delineation of character, the eyewitness impression, the ancillary thesis of a "Solomonic Enlightenment" that produced Israel's earliest history-writing—these and more besides helped to create a period lasting several decades during which events and personalities from David's reign seemed easily accessible to the modern interested reader of the books of Samuel. By the 1970s, however, David and the period of the United Monarchy were already beginning to cede their status as firm ground for the critical historian's feet.[2] This was in large measure owing to a reappraisal of the historical worth of the two basic components of the Davidic biography, the "History of David's Rise" (HDR) and the "Succession Narrative" (SN).

This reappraisal has been conducted on several fronts and against a background of justifiable skepticism about the existence of the so-called Solomonic Enlightenment. At this point I want to note only two of the considerations that have led to a radical reevaluation of HDR and SN. In the first place, the enhanced appreciation of the literary quality of these

---

1. J. Rosenburg, *King and Kin: Political Allegory in the Hebrew Bible* (Indiana Studies in Biblical Literature; Bloomington: Indiana University Press, 1986) 102.

2. See J. W. Flanagan, *David's Social Drama: A Hologram of Israel's Early Iron Age* (The Social World of Biblical Antiquity 7; Sheffield: Almond, 1988) 19.

writings has brought (as is common in such cases) an almost equal re-action against them as witnesses to real events in David's lifetime, this be-ing especially true of SN. In SN the vivid portrayal of persons and events, once explained by the writer's proximity to what he was recount-ing, began to be attributed to his imaginative and descriptive powers of writing. Secondly, the widespread and increasing characterization of both HDR and SN as "apology" or "propaganda" has played havoc with their reputation as historical reportage, with perhaps HDR the greater loser on this account, for, whereas attention to propagandist aspects of SN has concentrated largely on 1 Kings 1–2, large tracts of HDR have been sub-jected to this treatment.

It would be reasonable in the circumstances to hope for some external source of illumination or verification for at least the reign of David, but verification is as elusive for the first half of the tenth century B.C. as it is for the developments of the two centuries preceding it. The problem, which realistically may be defined as the total absence of archival and epigraphic material, remains virtually unchanged for the whole of the pre-exilic period. In particular, the Old Testament scarcely mentions in-scriptions celebrating the achievements of Israelite kings. If one considers the few relevant biblical references, it may be possible to understand why, for it is Saul who goes to Carmel in Judah to erect a stele "in his own honor," in commemoration of his victory over the Amalekites (1 Sam 15:12), and Absalom who, in the absence of a son and heir, erects a pillar to perpetuate his own name (2 Sam 18:18). Hadadezer of Zobah is also mentioned as having erected a commemorative stele in the Euphrates area, according to the reading in 1 Chr 18:3 (see, however, 2 Sam 8:3).[3] None of these is a role model for Israelite kingship; on the contrary, the idea of self-congratulation would have been offensive to the biblical his-torians for whom victories, even over Israel (cf. 2 Kgs 5:1), came from the hand of Yahweh. So the *res gestae* of David in 2 Samuel 8 twice attributes David's battle victories to Yahweh's involvement on his behalf (vv. 6, 14). One need not be surprised, then, at the Old Testament historians' silence about Israelite royal stelae. But what of the archaeological silence? Did the ideological ban operate at an even more basic level than that of history-writing? Giovanni Garbini thinks not, since the Israelite kings were prob-ably little different from their Near Eastern counterparts in their attitude to commemorative art. Systematic destruction and *damnatio memoriae* are

---

3. P. K. McCarter argues, with the aid of a revocalization of MT *lĕhāšîb* ('restore') to *lĕhōšîb* ('leave') in 2 Sam 8:3, that it is David who sets up a stele in the Euphrates region (*II Samuel: A New Translation with Introduction and Commentary* [AB 9; Garden City, N.Y.: Doubleday, 1984], 243, 247). However, this is a doubtful improvement on the MT, since the verb *yšb* (*Hiphil*) always takes a personal object in Biblical Hebrew.

made to account for the absence of artifacts.[4] One piece of evidence is offered, in the shape of an inscriptional fragment from Samaria bearing the single word ᵓšr ('which'?), made the basis by Garbini of the reconstructed reading, '(stele) which (King So-and-So of So-and-So placed . . .)'. Perhaps deuteronomistic-type ideology did not affect actual royal praxis, as Garbini argues, but as long as the dearth in royal inscriptional material continues, ideological factors will remain as possible explanations for the dearth. Meantime, the fact is that the literary or textual attestation for David's reign is restricted to Samuel–Kings and Chronicles. "The quest for the historical David, therefore, is primarily exegetical." [5]

This paper is mainly concerned with SN; nevertheless, a few recent studies discuss HDR and SN as parts of one grand "apology of David." K. W. Whitelam, whose interests moved away from text-based approaches in the later 1980s, discusses the David tradition in the context of ancient Near Eastern royal propaganda and suggests that as further propaganda works from the same general sociohistorical setting become available for discussion, so the location of the "Defense of David" within the genre will become clearer.[6] As it is, Whitelam draws comparisons with the Hittite Apology of Hattušiliš III and the Egyptian Prophecy of Neferti.[7] L. G. Perdue draws similar comparisons between the Testament of David (1 Kgs 2:1–12) and the Egyptian Instruction for Merikare and Instruction of Amenemhet.[8]

One of the more significant points about these nonbiblical texts is that they were written near the time of the circumstances that they address. This is reflected in McCarter's maximalist reading of HDR (which he sees as a "typical success story of the early Iron Age") and in his assertion that there is much material from the period of David and Solomon embedded within the David stories.[9] Perdue notes that his royal "instructions" come from a deceased or dying king and are meant to legitimate successors whose thrones are insecure.[10] Hayim Tadmor discusses "autobiographical apology in the royal Assyrian literature" in a 1983 essay and concludes that such apologies were generally written in conjunction with the appointment of a successor. He offers a brief comment

---

4. G. Garbini, *History and Ideology in Ancient Israel* (London: SCM/New York: Crossroad, 1988) 17–18.

5. P. K. McCarter, "The Historical David," *Int* 40 (1986) 117.

6. K. W. Whitelam, "The Defence of David," *JSOT* 29 (1984) 79.

7. Ibid.

8. L. G. Perdue, "The Testament of David and Egyptian Royal Instructions," *Scripture in Context II: More Essays on the Comparative Method* (ed. W. W. Hallo, J. C. Moyer, and L. G. Perdue; Winona Lake, Ind.: Eisenbrauns, 1983) 79–96.

9. McCarter, "Historical David," 119.

10. Perdue, "Testament of David," 96.

on the Davidic-Solomonic succession stories, which he accordingly dates to the reigns of these two kings.[11] Is the sociohistorical approach then being impelled towards the early dating of HDR and SN without regard for internal arguments to the contrary? This is not an aspect of the "location" of the "Defense of David" that Whitelam himself addresses in the article referred to above.

THE SUCCESSION NARRATIVE

As the discerning will judge from the title, part of this paper is taken up with John Van Seters' pronouncements on SN in his 1983 volume *In Search of History*. His overall conclusion is that, far from being a building block of some antiquity that was integrated into the Deuteronomistic History, SN is a large-scale interpolation into that work.[12] A number of difficulties with the standard view of SN have led Van Seters to this radical conclusion. He asks how SN, with its account of a very flawed and unexemplary King David, could form part of a work that presents him as the ideal Judean monarch.[13] The only reference to Davidic foibles after 1 Kings 2 comes in the concessive clause in 1 Kgs 15:5, "except in the matter of Uriah the Hittite," but Van Seters doubts the originality of this clause.[14] Then there are the particular problems presented by 1 Kings 1–2. Holding that 2:1–4 is completely deuteronomistic, Van Seters argues that these four verses are presupposed in v. 5 and that, therefore, the SN component that begins with this verse is postdeuteronomistic.[15] These chapters, moreover, present events in such a way as to contradict the more favorable depictions of David in previously established tradition. In the matter of the succession, David offends both by act and by omission, and so the process by which Solomon comes to succeed him is invalidated. Whereas it was God who should have designated Solomon as *nāgîd* ('leader'?), David took the responsibility upon himself.[16] In fact, as Van Seters notes, David acts throughout, "without oracle or revelation,"[17] which leaves Van Seters in little doubt about what the author of SN thought of the whole legitimizing process outlined in 1 Kings 1–2. In

---

11. H. Tadmor, "Autobiographical Apology in the Royal Assyrian Literature," in *History, Historiography and Interpretation: Studies in Biblical and Cuneiform Literatures* (ed. H. Tadmor and M. Weinfeld; Jerusalem: Magnes, 1983) 56–57.

12. J. Van Seters, *In Search of History: Historiography in the Ancient World and the Origins of Biblical History* (New Haven: Yale University Press, 1983) 277–91.

13. Ibid., 278.

14. Ibid., 290.

15. Ibid., 279.

16. Ibid., 288.

17. Ibid.

short, SN is viewed as an antilegitimation story written in contradiction of the theme of divine promise to David and his house. Since Van Seters concludes that SN is a postdeuteronomistic composition, it is not surprising, though it is not necessarily a corollary of his thesis, that he should entertain the possibility that SN is, in its entirety, a work of the imagination.[18] However, despite his radicalism, Van Seters still works with the concept of a "Succession Narrative," and he agrees with those scholars who think that its boundaries should be redrawn to include 2 Sam 2:8–4:12, for example, because this section shows David as weak and lacking in authority in a manner more typical of SN than of HDR.[19] Altogether, Van Seters has mounted a significant attack on the status of SN as "history" in any sense of the term, and it will be only by detailed argument that his case will be corroborated or refuted, which is why the present study is not inclined to linger in the shallow waters of "methodology."

If it is true that David is "the king after the Deuteronomist's own heart," to use Gerhard von Rad's fine coinage, then it is still necessary to inquire in what sense this applies before accepting Van Seters' judgment on the incompatibility of SN with the Deuteronomistic History (DH) in its portrayal of David. Above all, we may ask whether there is any difficulty in the standard doctrine that the Deuteronomist(s) could have regarded David as a seriously flawed individual and yet as having satisfied the basic deuteronomistic requirement of eschewal of pagan cults and loyalty to Yahweh. A distinction between David and Solomon is made on this basis in 1 Kgs 11:4–6, and the cultic criterion is, as is well known, regularly applied to the kings of Judah especially, in the books of Kings. Even if H.-D. Hoffmann's concentration on DH as a history of cult reform highlights one feature at the expense of others, it bears striking testimony to the importance of the cult in deuteronomistic thinking.[20] In other respects, the perspective of the Deuteronomist(s) may be "from the ground, from below Olympus, from amongst the participants,"[21] but as long as David supplies model obedience in the realm of cult he may emerge even from SN as a deuteronomistic paragon.

So far I have played along with Van Seters' assumption that the Deuteronomist(s) could not have been responsible for the editing or inclusion of SN because it supposedly contradicts the view of David expressed elsewhere in DH. This, as B. Halpern has suggested in his review of Van Seters, requires of the Deuteronomist(s) a degree of uniformity in the

---

18. Ibid., 286–87.
19. Ibid., 281–84.
20. H.-D. Hoffmann, *Reform und Reformen: Untersuchungen zu einem Grundthema der deuteronomistischen Geschichtsschreibung* (ATANT 66; Zürich: Theologischer Verlag, 1980).
21. Flanagan, *David's Social Drama*, 234.

presentation of David that Van Seters did not find in the Deuteronomistic account of Saul which, he believes, tolerates quite contradictory views of David's predecessor.[22] A basically similar point could be made about the "deuteronomistic" picture of David found within the confines of HDR, since the lying schemer of 1 Samuel 21, who later confesses that he has brought about the deaths of the priests at Nob (1 Sam 22:22), is a paler-than-usual messianic prototype.

I have noted that Van Seters raises problems in connection with the suturing of SN and deuteronomistic material in 1 Kings 2.[23] Whether he does or does not have a valid point here is difficult to judge, since assumptions must be made regarding the Deuteronomist's dealings with received material precisely at suture points. One of the more recent writers on 1 Kings 2, J. S. Rogers, finds predeuteronomistic material in 2:1–2 and might be held to have met Van Seters' point, though unfortunately Rogers does not indicate awareness of Van Seters' discussion.[24] The difference of opinion regarding the status of the early verses of 1 Kings 2 is unfortunate in view of the importance of 1 Kings 1–2 for Van Seters' thesis that SN is intended to overwrite the theme of divine promise and election in relation to the Davidic house.

However, even a subscriber to the concept of SN (as is Van Seters) might do well to consider whether 1 Kings 1–2 is so obviously tied to 2 Samuel 9–20 as to form part of the same discrete narrative entity. Apart from the interposition of the so-called "Samuel Appendix" (2 Samuel 21–24) between the torso and the tailpiece, there are stylistic grounds for distinguishing between the two, as may be judged from the comments of S. Bar-Efrat on the incidence of repetition in 1 Kings 1–2,[25] and from the more explicit observations of G. Keys on repetition and other stylistic features in these chapters as arguments against their inclusion in SN.[26] (We may also recall J. W. Flanagan's proposal of a Court History, originally limited to 2 Samuel 9–10 and 13–20 and later expanded to include narratives relating to the rise of Solomon.[27]) Thus there are grounds for

---

22. B. Halpern, Review of Van Seters, *In Search of History*, in *JBL* 104 (1985) 508.

23. Van Seters, *In Search of History*, 279.

24. J. S Rogers, "Narrative Stock and Deuteronomistic Elaboration in 1 Kings 2," *CBQ* 50 (1988) 407–9.

25. S. Bar-Efrat, *Narrative Art in the Bible* (JSOTSup 70; Sheffield: Almond, 1989) 218–23.

26. G. Keys, *The So-Called Succession Narrative: A Reappraisal of Leonhard Rost's Interpretation of II Samuel 9–20 and I Kings 1–2* (Ph.D. diss., Belfast: Queen's University, 1988) 68–90.

27. J. W. Flanagan, "Court History or Succession Document? A Study of 2 Samuel 9–20 and 1 Kings 1–2," *JBL* 91 (1972) 172–81. Note also the schema proposed by K. I. Parker for 1 Kings 1–11, with chaps. 1–2 acting as a "frame story" in parallel with 11:14–43 ("Repetition as a Structuring Device in 1 Kings 1–11," *JSOT* 42 [1988] 19–27).

observing a moratorium on hypotheses about SN that depend too heavily on 1 Kings 1–2.

But let us suppose, for the sake of argument, that 1 Kings 1–2 is of a piece with 2 Samuel 9–20. What are we to make of Van Seters' point that David appoints Solomon as his successor without ever a hint of a reference to divine oracle or guidance? Of course, this lack of attention to sacral issues is widely held to be a feature of SN in general, and one that distinguishes it very clearly from HDR. However, David consults the oracle in HDR because of the uncertainties of his pillar-to-post existence, whereas SN depicts him in different circumstances and in a different, but not necessarily reprehensible, frame of mind. The set of circumstances in SN that perhaps most nearly approximates to David's situation in HDR comes in 2 Samuel 15–19, where he is forced out of Jerusalem by Absalom. Oracular consultation is not a feature of David's behavior at this stage, yet the highest possible respect for the ark of God is in evidence:

> Then the king said to Zadok, "Carry the ark of God back into the city. If I find favor in the eyes of the Lord, he will bring me back and let me see both it and his habitation" (2 Sam 15:25).

This reference does not feature in Van Seters' discussion of the David tradition, but it does provoke the observation that if 1 Kings 1–2 is to be classed as part of SN, then it cannot be part of a sustained parody of David the secularized king, since no such parody exists.

For Van Seters, as was noted earlier, SN is an essay on the delegitimation of the kingship of David and his house. The prevenient tradition had lionized him and was providing the basis for a postexilic Davidic messianism that the author of SN wished to undermine.[28] Now, as far as can be judged, the "Samuel Appendix" (2 Samuel 21–24) forms part of the deuteronomistic work into which Van Seters believes SN to have been inserted,[29] yet he has nothing to say about those elements in the "Appendix" that frankly depict David as weak and in need of Yahweh's disciplining hand. If these elements were accepted by the Deuteronomist(s) alongside the generally more favorable portrayal of HDR, then the gate is open, possibly into the large field of SN.

Furthermore, the description of SN as designedly subversive of the David tradition seems ironic alongside two recent treatments of the "Samuel Appendix." David Gunn argues for the subversive character of the "Appendix" as "reinforcing rival views of David that have already

---

28. Van Seters, *In Search of History*, 361.

29. See the attempt by J. W. Rogerson, in his review of Van Seters (*JTS* n.s. 37 [1986] 451), to compile a list of the passages not original to Van Seters' version of DH.

come into focus," and he speaks of the "engineered collapse of reader-confidence" that it creates.[30] Walter Brueggemann sees the "Appendix" as an exercise in deconstruction, undermining the "high royal theology" of 2 Samuel 5–8 in particular, though 2 Samuel 9–20 is not excepted.[31] Here, then, are two scholars for whom the "Appendix" functions as a deconstruction of the presentation of David in earlier chapters of 2 Samuel. We shall certainly have to choose between Van Seters and these others, for a deconstruction of a deconstruction is more than any reader of SN should be asked to bear.

If the idea of a thoroughly unfavorable picture of David in SN is difficult to defend on a "Rostian" definition of its boundaries, the task is not made lighter by Van Seters' inclusion of 2 Samuel 2:8–4:12 with the other chapters. He includes 3:31ff. among sections from within 2:8–4:12 that display "a mastery of descriptive detail" characteristic of SN,[32] but he has failed to notice how this section and the section immediately preceding it contradict his view of SN as a delegitimizing account of David as Saul's successor. As I have noted elsewhere in reference to the second half of 2 Samuel 3, rarely has an Old Testament writer gone to such lengths, as has the writer of this passage, in order to preserve the good name of one of his characters.[33] In this respect at least, 2:8–4:12, with its insistence on David's innocence of involvement in the deaths of members of Saul's family, aligns itself more naturally with HDR than with SN. Van Seters, however, has annexed 2:8–4:12 to SN without giving thought to the possible consequences for his larger theory.

Finally, I wish to consider Van Seters' suggestion that what SN recounts is largely or wholly owing to the imagination of its author. A test case for the issue of facticity versus fictitiousness is provided by the appearance of Ishbosheth in 2 Samuel 2–4, since, according to Van Seters, there has been no mention of him previously in Samuel.[34] According to 1 Sam 14:49, Saul's sons were Jonathan, Ishvi, and Malki-Shua, while the three who are said to have died with him at Gilboa are named in 1 Sam 31:2 as Jonathan, Abinadab, and Malki-Shua. "Where did Ishbosheth come from?" asks Van Seters, who is concerned about certain tensions between 2 Sam 2:8–4:12 and HDR, and who resolves them by

---

30. D. M. Gunn, "New Directions in the Study of Biblical Hebrew Narrative," *JSOT* 39 (1987) 70–71.

31. W. Brueggemann, "2 Samuel 21–24: An Appendix of Deconstruction?" *CBQ* 50 (1988) 383–97.

32. Van Seters, *In Search of History,* 284.

33. R. P. Gordon, *1 and 2 Samuel: A Commentary* (Exeter: Paternoster/Grand Rapids, Mich.: Zondervan, 1986) 216.

34. Van Seters, *In Search of History,* 281.

his locating the section in SN, thus consigning Ishbosheth, his truncated kingdom, and the notion of civil war after Saul's death to the realm of fiction. On the difference in the names of Saul's second son in 1 Samuel 14 and 1 Samuel 31, he concludes that, however it is explained, it "does not allow for the survival of a fourth son in this story,"[35] and he attributes the existence of four names for Saul's sons in 1 Chr 9:39 to the author's "correction" of the record in the light of the narratives in SN. This amounts to treating Ishvi and Abinadab as the same person, which is not the only, or even the obvious, way of dealing with the data. It is quite possible that Ishvi in 1 Sam 14:49 and Ishbosheth in 2 Samuel are the same person, even if there remains a question as to why Ishbosheth, said to have been forty years old when he became king (2 Sam 2:10), apparently was uninvolved in the battle at Gilboa or, if present, was a previously unmentioned survivor of the debacle. Nor is it fair to dismiss the reference to Eshbaal (= Ishbosheth) in 1 Chr 9:39 as a mistaken "correction" deriving from the nonhistory of 2 Sam 2:8–4:12. (Van Seters does not note the occurrence of Eshbaal's name in 1 Chr 8:33 in the same basic genealogy.) Moreover, awareness on the part of the Chronicler that a son of Saul survived him apparently runs deeper than the genealogical additions in 1 Chr 8:33 and 9:39 suggest. When the Chronicler records the death of Saul and his sons in 1 Chr 10:6, he uses the following form of words: "So Saul and his three sons died, and all his *house* died together." This corresponds to 1 Sam 31:6, which has notable differences: "So Saul and his three sons and his armor-bearer and all his men died together *that day.*"

If we proceed on the reasonable assumption that the Chronicler used a text more or less the same as MT 1 Sam 31:6, then he can be credited with two significant departures from his lemma, namely, the substitution of "and all his house" for "and his armor-bearer and all his men" and the omission of "that day." The two alterations appear to be interdependent, inasmuch as the first is acceptable only if the second is made. By stating that Saul "and all his house" died at Gilboa, the Chronicler is telescoping his history, and not for the only time in a controversial career. His purpose would not have been served by dwelling on the civil war that intervened between Saul's death and David's installation as king over all Israel any more than it would have been served at a later point by a recapitulation of the Bathsheba episode and the Absalom rebellion, even though 1 Chr 20:1–3 gives evidence of abridgement from a longer text of the Samuel type.[36] So the Chronicler wishes to say that the house of Saul as

---

35. Ibid., 281 n. 150.
36. See H. G. M. Williamson, "A Response to A. G. Auld," *JSOT* 27 (1983) 36.

good as perished at Gilboa: Ishbosheth and his remnant Saulide kingdom
counted for nothing from the perspective of later history. But it would
have been a literal untruth to report that the whole house of Saul died at
Gilboa, and the Chronicler solves the problem by his omission of the
words "that day." We conclude, therefore, that when the Chronicler wrote
1 Chronicles 10 he acknowledged the unseen presence of Ishbosheth.

Van Seters also cites the case of Joab in support of his argument that
2 Sam 2:8–4:12 belongs with SN, since Joab, "mentioned previously
only in 1 Sam 26:6 as the brother of Abishai," appears in these chapters
as already a major figure who needs no introduction.[37] In development
of this point Van Seters footnotes the view that, whereas Joab is already
commander-in-chief of David's army in 2 Samuel 2, "in the original
account of the taking of Jerusalem (2 Sam 5:6–9; 1 Chr 11:4–9), Joab
became commander of the army only at that time."[38] First, we should
note that in 1 Sam 26:6 it is not Joab who is described as Abishai's
brother but Abishai who is introduced as Joab's brother, which is very
different. Second, in creating this conflict of evidence, Van Seters has relied entirely upon the additional material in 1 Chr 11:4–9, where alone
Joab's promotion comes as a reward for his part in the capture of Jerusalem. On the other hand, the recent study by J. P. Floss of the accounts of
the capture of Jerusalem concludes that the Chronicler's additions are not
reproduced from alternative sources but are his own composition.[39]
More to the point is Van Seters' own decision that the various sources
named by the Chronicler in his work are all fictitious and are intended to
disguise his obvious dependence on the Pentateuch and the Deuteronomistic History: "This was his way of seeking to justify and make credible
his numerous additions, alterations, and deletions."[40] This conclusion has,
however, been overlooked in his treatment of 1 Chronicles 11. Moreover, whereas in the case of Ishbosheth the Chronicler is represented as
having altered his genealogical information in order to take account of
SN, here he appears (*ex hypothesi*) to have elaborated upon his source in
a way that is contradicted by SN. This is by no means fatal for Van
Seters' case, but it is worthy of note all the same.

In general, Van Seters' approach to SN fails because contrary evidence is overlooked in his zeal to make the text conform to a particular

37. Van Seters, *In Search of History*, 283.
38. Ibid., 284 n. 158.
39. J. P. Floss, *David und Jerusalem: Ziele und Folgen des Stadteroberungsberichts 2 Sam 5,
6–9 literaturwissenschaftlich betrachtet* (Münchener Universitätsschriften; ATSAT 30; St. Ot-
tilien: EOS, 1987) 17–18.
40. Van Seters, *In Search of History*, 48.

theory. His interpretation of 1 Kings 1–2 (whether one regards the chapters as being in or out of SN matters little) has much in common with the redaction-critical work of L. Delekat and E. Würthwein, with whom he expresses his partial agreement, but it is no more convincing for that. The author of these chapters makes direct comparisons between Adonijah and Absalom, notes that David was not in the habit of crossing his ambitious son (1:6), recognizes that the lives of Solomon and Bathsheba will be at risk if Adonijah succeeds in his bid (1:12, 21), and has Adonijah acknowledge that the kingdom has come to Solomon "from the Lord" (2:15). Yet Van Seters sees the narrative as basically an attack on the legitimacy of the Davidic succession.

Others treat 1 Kings 1–2 very differently. McCarter thinks that Solomon is defended, even at cost to David's reputation,[41] while Rogers achieves the same end without mulcting David.[42] If opinions vary so drastically, perhaps the ancient author is less partisan than he is made out to be. Interestingly, B. Halpern supports his case for Solomonic legitimacy from references in 1 Kings 1 to sworn statements concerning Solomon's position as successor to David (vv. 11–14, 30; cf. 17),[43] whereas Van Seters, as we have seen, makes much of the fact that these statements have everything but the oracular authority that is required to validate them.[44] This is an important question that deserves special consideration along the lines of viewpoint and point of view, yet, as we have noted, the clearest affirmation of the legitimacy of Solomon's kingship is put into the mouth of Adonijah in 1 Kgs 2:15. If authorial intention is the crucial issue, then 2:15 is specially relevant. Furthermore, our discussion of Solomonic legitimacy has not even mentioned 2 Sam 12:24–25 and the conferring of the additional name Jedidiah upon Solomon "because the Lord loved him" (v. 25). In a version of SN that embraces 1 Kings 1–2, it is very unwise to interpret the later developments without taking into account this unambiguous statement of divine approval that puts Solomon in a unique position among David's sons as one specially favored from birth. Many a Near Eastern king is said similarly to have enjoyed divine patronage from birth. Unfortunately, Van Seters has nothing to say about 2 Sam 12:24–25 in his treatment of SN.

41. McCarter, " 'Plots, True or False': The Succession Narrative as Court Apologetic," *Int* 35 (1981) 360–61, 365–67.
42. Rogers, "Narrative Stock," 412–13.
43. B. Halpern, *The First Historians: The Hebrew Bible and History* (San Francisco: Harper & Row, 1988) 145.
44. Van Seters, *In Search of History*, 288.

"THE LIMITS OF SKEPTICISM"

Even if the attempt to rescue SN from the lumber room of Hebrew historiographical writing were to be judged successful, many basic questions would remain to be addressed. When did SN (or, the chapters that SN is generally thought to comprise) originate? Is there a dominant theme, or are there just an indeterminate number of themes, complementary or competing, mostly fashioned by autonomous readers in the late twentieth century? And, again, how serious is the problem of historical refraction, given the fact that SN is a work of literature deploying a wide range of narrative skills?

Neither HDR nor SN contains specific clues to the dating of the material found in them. In SN one or two features have been singled out as possibly favoring a particular period, usually in the post-Solomonic era, but otherwise dating tends to be based on impressions of proximity to, and involvement with, the events described. This is an approach that, in terms of the sociology of knowledge, succeeds to the extent that the particular theory enjoys the right kind of patronage. Furthermore, if "succession" is not the thread on which the stories in SN are beaded,[45] then a strong argument for binding these chapters to Solomon's reign has to be surrendered.

As is well known, von Rad canvassed the idea of a Solomonic Enlightenment that fostered, among other things, a secularized world view less beholden to the miraculous and to the dual-control interpretation of history. However, von Rad may have overstated the case, even for SN, since there are sufficient references to divine involvement in human affairs to rescue Yahweh from the fate of a superannuated celestial clock-winder.[46] Traditional piety also has its say,[47] and, if the entire account of Absalom's rebellion is to be viewed as the fulfillment of Nathan's pronouncement in 2 Sam 12:10–12, then there are limits to the usefulness of the concept of the "hidden hand of Yahweh" in SN. At the same time, there is a distinct absence of "the miraculous" in the David traditions. Perhaps the claim that, when the armies of David and Absalom met, "the forest claimed more lives that day than the sword" (2 Sam 18:8) hints at miraculous intervention in a way reminiscent of Joshua's hailstones (Josh 10:11) or the combatant stars of Deborah's song (Judg 5:20), but this would be atypical. It might be argued that the story of the rise and reign of David did not provide much scope for miracle-working, though David's single stone that felled Goliath seems to ricochet in reply (1 Sam 17:49).

45. See, for example, Keys, *The So-Called Succession Narrative*, 54–68.
46. See 2 Sam 11:27; 12:1, 15; 17:14.
47. See 2 Sam 14:14; 15:8, 25; 16:12.

Halpern has suggested that, when the Deuteronomist is leaning hard on archival sources, miracles become quite scarce; they occur for earlier (premonarchical) periods or in the Elijah-Elisha cycles, which may be presumed to have come to the Deuteronomist(s) with their main contours already established.[48] If this distinction is valid, and there appears to be some element of truth in it, perhaps it has relevance for the David traditions, which, as it happens, receive little attention in Halpern's *The First Historians*. Is it possible that what von Rad saw as a secularized account of a historical period evinces not so much a viewpoint on the nature of history as a relationship to the events and circumstances in question? Von Rad had, of course, accepted Rost's tenth-century B.C. dating of SN, which was based on its alleged eyewitness character, so that the early dating does not, in his case, arise as a corollary to his interpretation of SN's view of divine action in history. One obvious difference between the DH and SN is the absence in the latter of references to written sources, an absence that may be explained in more than one way. If SN were composed while the events described lay within living memory, its author may not have felt the need to consult external sources, to whatever extent they existed.[49] Or, the absence of backup references may simply indicate that we are reading a kind of "faction" in which historical interests are served to a greater or lesser extent. (That SN contains material [e.g., the "private scenes"] that does not necessarily come within the history-writer's province is self-evident.) The danger in all this is that the wish for a secure early dating of SN in order to strengthen its claims as "history" may father the thought and fashion the evidence, whereas, a proper appreciation of the David traditions as literature or as scripture does not depend on the recognition of their transmitted literary form as dating to the tenth century B.C., nor would their historical testimony necessarily be muted if a later date of origin could be proved.

There is another point to be made in relation to the Davidic narratives, namely that, if they do not reflect the interests of a period close to the one they purport to describe, it is not so easy, either, to treat them as expressions of the needs and interests of Judah in later stages of her history. Put another way, they would contribute little to Halpern's version of *Kulturgeschichte* as discussed in his 1988 volume.[50] An exception might be the anointed-of-Yahweh motif in HDR, were one to conclude that it was developed, not in recognition of Saul's status despite his failings, but

48. Halpern, *The First Historians*, 247–48.
49. The relationship of the account of the Ammonite War in 2 Samuel 10 and 12:26–31 to SN is disputed, but the possibility of SN's having incorporated a "source" at this point has to be admitted.
50. Halpern, *The First Historians*, 20, 22, etc.

in the interests of David and his successors in Jerusalem.[51] But this would be an excessively cynical way of reading HDR. Even though this writer would keep an open mind on the dating of the David traditions in Samuel–Kings, it must be conceded that, if it is "interests" that are to determine the time of writing, the attention paid in the narratives to Saulide claims and, in 1 Kings 1–2, to Solomon's accession and initial management of his kingdom favors an early rather than a later dating of substantial parts of the David-Solomon tradition.

As regards the general question of history in or behind the David narratives, there should be limits to one's skepticism, if I may borrow the title of William Hallo's presidential address to the 199th meeting of the American Oriental Society, held in New Orleans in March 1989.[52] The problem that Hallo addresses initially is that of putting together an account of ancient Near Eastern history, institutions, and society on the basis of the cuneiform evidence. He is responding both to a paper by Miguel Civil, published in 1980, and to a more widely diffused skepticism about the adequacy of the Mesopotamian sources for such an undertaking. The problem is not special to the Old Testament scene! Hallo acknowledges the need to sift carefully the contemporary evidence, especially evidence from the royal monuments, in order to penetrate behind the propagandistic tendencies to the historical core. This is precisely the kind of language that many a historian of ancient Israel feels bound to use of the Old Testament evidence, and the more so because of its tendency not to be contemporary with the events that it describes. But there should indeed be limits to our skepticism. After all, the one thing about which we can be fairly certain is that the nihilists (or Halpern's "negative fundamentalists") have got it wrong when they gratefully accept externally unattested names like those of David[53] and Solomon but deny that their reigns are at all accessible via the literature that purports to describe them.

51. As argued by F. H. Cryer, "David's Rise to Power and the Death of Abner," *VT* 35 (1985) 391.

52. W. W. Hallo, "The Limits of Skepticism," *JAOS* 110 (1990) 187–99.

53. A recently discovered inscription in Aramaic, found at Tel Dan and dating to the ninth century B.C., refers to the "house of David" (see A. Biran and J. Naveh, "An Aramaic Stele Fragment from Tel Dan," *IEJ* 43 [1993] 81–98).

The Warrior and His God:
The Covenant Foundation of
History and Historiography

Jeffrey J. Niehaus

Gordon-Conwell Theological Seminary

To speak of the warrior and his god in the ancient Near East is really to speak of the king and his god, for ancient Near Eastern historiography is, by and large, the memorials of royal deeds. The records intend to show that the kings lived lives of exemplary piety and obedience to the will of their gods. But these histories really record the boasts, as much as the valor, of those kings. Their accomplishments, many of which were infamously bloody, were done in the name of their gods.

The relationship between these ancient warrior-kings and their gods is of special interest because it provides the ancient Near Eastern cultural context for understanding the relationship between the kings and leaders of Israel and their God.

In this paper I consider this relationship in a logical progression. First, I examine the themes of election and covenant: the king as chosen by his god. Then, I examine the area of warfare, its divine institution, divine help in carrying it out, treaties that arise from it, and consecration of booty and of temples sometimes related to it. In order to limit this study to manageable proportions, I am focusing primarily on parallels offered by the Assyrian royal tradition, although I believe the same parallels might be drawn with Egyptian, Babylonian, or other sources.

ELECTION AND COVENANT

The divine election of kings was a well-understood doctrine in the ancient Near East. Indeed, according to the Sumerians, kingship itself was bestowed from heaven.[1] The gods decided where and by whom kingship would be exercised.[2] Sometimes (and often in poetic accounts), the kings were said to be the offspring of the gods.[3] The kings of Assyria clearly agreed with this theology. They always made it clear that they were the elect or "chosen" rulers of their land. For instance, Tiglath-pileser I (ca. 1115–1077 B.C.) styles himself the "beloved prince, your select one, attentive shepherd, whom in the steadfastness of your hearts you chose."[4] Similar claims are made, from Shamshi-Adad I (1814–1782 B.C.) to Ashurbanipal (668–627 B.C.).[5]

The Assyrian kings were called to shepherd the people of Assyria. So they called themselves "shepherds," looking after the "flock." The flock, of course, was the people of their gods. The concept of shepherding people as viceregents of the gods is well attested in Mesopotamia from very ancient times. Hammurapi (1792–1750 B.C.) said that he was called to shepherd the people of Babylon by the gods Anu and Enlil,[6] and the phrase, "the people of the god, Enlil," is attested from Shar-kali-sharri of Akkad (2212–2188 B.C.) to Ashurbanipal, who claimed, "I shepherded the people of the god, Enlil."[7]

Not only were the ancient kings shepherds by election. There is also evidence that they were so by covenant. Uru-inimgina[8] of Lagash (25th/24th century B.C.) was the lawgiver *par excellence* who made a covenant with the god Ningirsu stressing the observance of laws.[9] A great Hittite

---

1. See Thorkild Jacobsen, *The Sumerian King List* (Assyriological Studies 11; Chicago: University of Chicago Press, 1939), 70–71; A. L. Oppenheim, "The Sumerian King List," *ANET,* 265.

2. H. Frankfort, *Kingship and the Gods: A Study of Ancient Near Eastern Religion as the Integration of Society and Nature* (Chicago: University of Chicago Press, 1948) 237.

3. See Samuel N. Kramer, "Kingship in Sumer and Akkad: The Ideal King," *Le Palais et la royauté: XIXe Rencontre assyriologique internationale* (ed. P. Garelli; Paris: Geuthner, 1974), 163–66. Note also the description of the Assyrian king, Tukulti-Ninurta I, in W. G. Lambert, "Three Unpublished Fragments of the Tukulti-Ninurta Epic," *AfO* 18 (1957–58) 50–51: "By the fate assigned by Nudimmud his form is reckoned as divine nature / By the decree of the Lord of the Lands his forming proceeded smoothly *inside* the divine womb / He is the eternal image of Enlil."

4. *AKA,* 30, lines 18–20; *ARI* 2.5.

5. *ARTSM,* 48 (lines 12–17: Shamshi-Adad I), 183 (lines 22–26: Shalmaneser I), 234 (col. i, lines 21–31: Tukulti-Ninurta I); *AKA,* 260 (lines 17ff.: Ashurnasirpal II); R. Borger, *Die Inschriften Asarhaddons Königs von Assyrien* (AfO Beiheft 9; Graz: Im Selbstverlag der Herausgegebers, 1956), 96 (no. 65 verso 1–12: Esarhaddon); A. C. Piepkorn, *Historical Prism Inscriptions of Ashurbanipal* (Chicago: University of Chicago Press, 1933; henceforth, *HPIA*) 28 (lines 1–13: Ashurbanipal).

6. *CH* i 1–25; see xxiv rev. 10–15.

7. See Knut Tallqvist, *Akkadische Götterepitheta* (Leipzig: Harrassowitz, 1938), 182–83.

8. Formerly read *Urukagina*; see J. S. Cooper, *Sumerian and Akkadian Royal Inscriptions, vol. 1: Presargonic Inscriptions* (AOSTS 1; New Haven: American Oriental Society, 1988), 70.

9. Thureau-Dangin, *Die sumerischen und akkadischen Königsinschriften* (Leipzig: Hinrichs, 1907), 52ff.

sun hymn celebrates Shamash the sun-god as "Just lord of judgment" who rules all lands and "establishes custom and contract of the land."[10] From Babylon in the so-called "Prophetic Speech of Marduk" (probably from the reign of Nebuchadnezzar I, 1127–1105 B.C.), the god Marduk foretells that he will make a covenant with a human king whom he will raise up: "That prince will rule all lands. And/But I, O gods all, have a *covenant* with him. He will destroy Elam. Its cities he will cast down."[11] Still later, Ashurnasirpal II (883–859 B.C.) relates, "I founded the temples of the great gods within the city, and established the *covenant* of the great gods, my lords, within them."[12] So Shamash gives Hammurapi the law, that he might "bring justice to prevail in the land, to destroy the wicked and evil, that the strong may not injure the weak . . . to enlighten the land and to further the welfare of men . . . that orphans and widows may be protected in Babylon."[13] Like Hammurapi, Tukulti-Ninurta I (1244–1208 B.C.) of Assyria claims divine instruction for being a good ruler when he says, Ashur "teaches me just decisions."[14] Six centuries later, Esarhaddon says that the gods Sin and Shamash (the moon and sun gods, respectively) appointed him "to give just and righteous judgment to the land and the people."[15]

It seems clear from all this that Assyrian (and, for that matter, Mesopotamian) kings claimed to be chosen by their gods to rule their people. Not only so, but they were also given divine laws by which to rule. Evidence further suggests that such divine instruction was given in some sort of covenant relationship, although more evidence in this area is desirable. But it is against such a background that the calling and authority of the kings were understood.

Modern readers need to understand this calling and this authority if they are to appreciate the warfare of ancient Near Eastern kings, for they waged war in the name of their gods, and they were able to do so

---

10. H. G. Güterbock, "The Vocative in Hittite," *JAOS* 65 (1945) 251.

11. See D. I. Block, *The Gods of the Nations* (ETS Monograph 3; Jackson: Evangelical Theological Society, 1988), 175.

12. D. J. Wiseman, "A New Stela of Assur-nasir-pal II," *IRAQ* 14 (1952) 34 (col. ii, left rev., 59–60). I translate *mamītu* 'covenant', i.e., 'sworn agreement'. Wiseman with some doubt translates 'the spell (?) of the great gods'. But *mamītu* + *kunnu* is used of covenant establishment. See two examples from the Tukulti-Ninurta Epic: R. Campbell Thompson and R. W. Hutchinson, "The Excavations of the Temple of Nabu at Nineveh," *Archaeologia* 79; 2d series vol. 29 (1929) 130, 133 at col. v, line 16: *u-kin-nu ma-mi-ta*, where the covenant oath is in view; Thompson and M. E. L. Mallowan, "The British Museum Excavations at Nineveh," *University of Liverpool Annals of Archaeology and Anthropology* 20 (1933) 120, 124 at col. iv, line 9: "I will read aloud the tablet of the covenant/ sworn agreement (*mamītu*) between us and the Lord of heaven" (see CAD M/1 190).

13. *CH* i 30–45; xxiv rev. 60.

14. *ARTSM*, 234, lines 32–33.

15. Borger, *Inschriften Asarhaddons*, 2 (text 2, col. i, lines 31–34).

because they claimed divine calling and divinely imparted law or instruction as the foundation for all their actions. Since ancient Near Eastern historiography is, by and large, the record of their deeds, the conclusion is inevitable that history-writing itself was established on the theological foundations of divine election and covenant.

WARFARE

When the king set out to war, he did so by the express command of his god. So Tiglath-pileser I declares, "The god Ashur (and) the great gods, who magnify my sovereignty, . . . commanded me to extend the border of their land."[16] Esarhaddon some five centuries later made a similar claim.[17] When the kings set forth, they inquired of their gods whether to engage a particular foe or not. If the oracle gave them a firm yes, they proceeded, and, of course, were victorious.[18]

The kings also fought and won with the help of their gods. Their success was always based upon a supposedly obedient and trusting relationship with the gods. Tiglath-pileser I says of his enemies at one point that "they trusted in their own strength."[19] But the Assyrian king, by contrast, engaged them "with trust in the god Ashur, my Lord."[20] Such claims are common throughout Assyrian tradition.

Along with this trusting relationship, there was great affinity between the king and his gods. The affinity is made clear by the fact that the same phraseology is applied to both. For example, the king says of his enemies, "The splendor of my valor overwhelmed them."[21] But he also

16. *AKA*, 33–34, lines 46–49.

17. Borger, *Inschriften Asarhaddons*, 46 (text 27, episode 3, lines 30–31).

18. E.g., *ARTSM*, 184 (lines 32–34: Shalmaneser I); D. D. Luckenbill, *The Annals of Sennacherib* (Chicago: University of Chicago Press, 1924), 137 (line 29: Sennacherib); Borger, *Inschriften Asarhaddons*, 40 (text 27, episode 2, lines 13–14), 43 (text 27, episode 2, lines 59–61: both Esarhaddon); R. Campbell Thompson, *The Prisms of Esarhaddon and Ashurbanipal* (London: Oxford University Press, 1931), 31 (lines 18–19: Ashurbanipal).

19. *AKA*, 35–36, lines 68–69. See P. Rost, *Die Keilschrifttexte Tiglat-Pilesers III* (Leipzig: Pfeiffer, 1893), 12 (line 62: Tiglath-pileser III); *HCS*, 12 (line 66: Sargon II); Borger, *Inschriften Asarhaddons*, 50 (text 27, episode 6, line 27: Esarhaddon); Piepkorn, *Historical Prism*, 30 (line 56: Ashurbanipal).

20. *AKA*, 36, lines 70ff.; *ARTSM*, 136 (lines 22–26: Adad-Nirari I), 183 (lines 16–17: Shalmaneser I), 234 (col. 2, lines 8–9: Tukulti-Ninurta I). See Wolfgang Schramm, "Die Annalen des assyrischen Königs Tukulti-Ninurta II," *BiOr* 27 no. 3/4 (1970) 148 (verso 4: Tukulti-Ninurta II); *AKA*, 268 (line 42: Ashurnasirpal II); E. Michel, "Die Assur-Texte Salmanassars III.," *WO* 1 (1954–59) 456, line 20 (Shalmaneser III); *HCS*, 4 (line 13), 48 (line 314: both Sargon II); Luckenbill, *Annals*, 31 (lines 1–2: Sennacherib); Borger, *Inschriften Asarhaddons*, 48 (text 27, episode 5, verso line 9: Esarhaddon); Piepkorn, *Historical Prism*, 64 (line 14: Ashurbanipal).

21. See *AKA*, 48 (line 2b: Tiglath-pileser I). See *ANET*, 277–78 (Shalmaneser III); Luckenbill, *Annals*, 29 (lines 38–39: Sennacherib); Piepkorn, *Historical Prism*, 102 (line 23: Ashurbanipal).

says, "The terror, fear, and splendor of the god, Ashur, my lord, over-whelmed them."[22] His enemies are those "who in the face of my weapons had fled."[23] But they are also those who "in the face of the terrible weapons of Ashur, my lord, had fled."[24] Such phraseology is standard in the Assyrian tradition, spanning many centuries.

Not only did the kings have affinity with their gods on the battlefield. The gods even went so far as to interfere with the psyche of the king's foe. In this way the gods prepared the enemy for defeat. Assyrian records attest this concept of divine destruction of wisdom prior to divine punishment by warfare. In the "Tukulti-Ninurta Epic," one reads that Tukulti-Ninurta I (1244–1208 B.C.), King of Assyria, challenged Kashtiliash IV (1242–1235 B.C.), King of Kassite Babylon, to battle because the Kassite had broken covenant. Then we read, "But Kashtiliash, because he had broken the rule of the great gods, *was terrified*, and cried to Shamash [the overseer of covenants in Mesopotamian religion], and complained to the gods, and the command of the mighty king [i.e., Shamash] paralyzed his body like the *alu* ghost."[25] That is to say, Shamash bound the Kassite, filled him with fear of the gods, and caused him to change his mind and withdraw in a policy of retreat, which eventually lead to his overthrow. In a comparable letter of earlier date, the Babylonian king, Adad-shum-uṣur, taunted Ashurnarari III (1202–1197 B.C.) and Iluhadda of Assyria, claiming that Ashur and the great gods deranged them because of their sin.[26]

Because the ancient kings waged war for their gods, they assumed absolute rights over the defeated. Their job was to make manifest on earth the rule of their gods. They did so by conquering other peoples and bringing them into a vassal relationship. The kings were closely identified with their gods in this task. The interchangeability of phraseology as applied to them and their gods has demonstrated this affinity.

---

22. See *AKA*, 42 (lines 38–39: Tiglath-pileser I). See Schramm, "Annalen," 148 (verso 15: Tukulti-Ninurta II); *AKA*, 309 (line 46: Ashurnasirpal II); Rost, *Keilschrifttexte*, 60 (line 27: Tiglath-pileser III); E. F. Weidner, "Silka(he)ni, König von Musri: Ein Zeitgenosse Sargons II.," *AfO* 14 (1941–44) 50 (col. ix, lines 1–2: Sargon II); Luckenbill, *Annals*, 30 (line 54: Sennacherib); Borger, *Inschriften Assarhaddons*, 54 (text 27, episode 15, line 37: Esarhaddon); Piepkorn, *Historical Prism*, 70 (lines 4–5: Ashurbanipal).

23. See *AKA*, 37 (lines 85–86: Tiglath-pileser I). See *AKA*, 277 (line 47: Ashurnasirpal II); Rost, *Keilschrifttexte*, 78 (line 9: Tiglath-pileser III); *HCS* 26 (line 175: Sargon II); Luckenbill, *Annals*, 27 (line 3: Sennacherib); Borger, *Inschriften Asarhaddons* (text 27, episode 17, B III, line 41: Esarhaddon); Piepkorn, *Historical Prism*, 82–84 (lines 23–24: Ashurbanipal).

24. See *AKA*, 74 (lines 55–56: Tiglath-pileser I). See Luckenbill, *Annals*, 73 (lines 52–53: Sennacherib); Piepkorn, *Historical Prism*, 78 (lines 64–65), 82–84 (lines 23–24: both Ashurbanipal).

25. Thompson and Mallowan, "British Museum Excavations" (col. iv, lines 22–24, translation after CAD, emphasis mine).

26. E. Weidner, *Die Inschriften Tukulti-Ninurta I und seiner Nachfolger* (AfO Beiheft 12; Graz: Im Selbstverlag der Herausgegebers, 1959) 48 (text 42, lines 1–19); see *ARI* 1.135ff.

As Morton Cogan notes, the same phenomenon occurs in Assyrian oath administration to conquered vassals: "The interchangeability of terms points to functional equivalence. Swearing to serve the king was at the same time acknowledging the rule of the Assyrian god."[27]

Their authority as suzerains included the right to mutilate the conquered foe. The purpose of this was primarily to strike fear into their hearts, so that they would not even think of rebellion. Assyrian kings piled heaps of enemies' hands and heads before the foe's city gates.[28] They impaled their enemies and skinned them alive.[29] Tukulti-Ninurta I even boasts that he burned a whole city of rebellious vassals alive.[30]

Their authority was also expressed by another practice. Assyrian kings regularly captured the idols of the defeated. This act was supposed to indicate the superiority of the god Ashur and other Assyrian gods over the gods of the defeated. The act was logical: Assyria's gods had helped her win, so they must be more powerful than the enemy's gods. At the same time the enemy's gods were not to be dismissed, because they were, after all, gods. So they were captured and taken under the authority of Assyria's gods, just as the enemy was captured and taken under authority of Assyria's king.[31] Hence in Assyrian annals a very common phrase is, "I took/carried away their gods."[32]

CONSECRATION OF SPOIL AND TEMPLE BUILDING

Because their gods had made victory possible, the Assyrian kings always dedicated some of the booty of war to the gods in their temples. So Tiglath-pileser I says, "I dedicated one bronze mug and one bathtub of bronze from the booty and tribute of the land Kadmuhu to the god Ashur, my Lord. I gave 60 copper kettles, together with their gods, to

27. M. Cogan, *Imperialism and Religion* (Missoula, Mont.: Scholars Press, 1974), 45.

28. E.g., *ARI* 2.123 (Ashurnasirpal II); *ARI* 2.126 (Ashurnasirpal II); see Rost, *Keilschrifttexte*, 8–9 (Tiglath-pileser III).

29. E.g., *ARI* 2.76 (Ashur-Dan II); *ARI* 2.125 (Ashurnasirpal II); Luckenbill, *Annals*, 32 (Sennacherib).

30. *ARI* 1.103; see *ARI* 1.126 (Ashurnasirpal II).

31. As Cogan concludes, "Neo-Assyrian spoliation of divine images was meant to portray abandonment of the enemy by his own gods in submission to the superior might of Assyria's god, Ashur" (*Imperialism*, 40).

32. See *AKA*, 79 (lines 9–10: Tiglath-pileser I). See Luckenbill, *Annals*, 30 (line 62: Sennacherib); Borger, *Inschriften Asarhaddons*, 53 (text 27, episode 14, lines 1ff.: Esarhaddon); Thompson, *Prisms of Esarhaddon*, 34 (lines 1–4: Ashurbanipal). To date, the annals of Tiglath-pileser I afford the earliest example of such spoliation of images by Assyrian kings; see Cogan, *Imperialism*, 27.

the god Adad, who loves me."[33] Such offerings were standard long before and after this particular Assyrian king.[34]

Assyrian kings not only dedicated booty and tribute to their gods. They also built or renovated temples. This was part of their calling by the gods who had chosen them as worshipers. Assyrian annals for centuries contained building report sections, in which the kings followed their accounts of military campaigns with accounts of how they built, or rebuilt, the temples of various gods. So Ashurnasirpal II records:

> In Kalḫu, my royal metropolis, the temples which had not existed before, the temple of Enlil and Ninurta, I founded within it; the temple of Ea and Damkina, the temple of Adad and Šala, the temple of Gula, the temple of Sin, the temple of Nabu, the temple of *Ištar bêlit māti*, the temple of the Sibitti, the temple of Ištar-Kidmurri, the temples of the great gods anew within (the city) I founded and established the *covenant*[35] of the great gods my lords within them.[36]

He also records how, after the completion of the palace, he brought the gods into it and then regaled the people in honor of the gods:

> At the time when Aššur-naṣir-pal, king of Assyria, adorned the palace, the joy of the heart, even a palace embodying all the skill of Kalḫu, and when he invited into it Aššur, the great lord, and the gods of all the land. . . . When I adorned the palace of Kalḫu. . . . The happy peoples of all the lands together with the people of Kalḫu for ten days I feasted, wined, bathed, anointed and honoured them and then sent them back to their lands in peace and joy.[37]

THE LEADERS AND KINGS OF GOD'S PEOPLE:
ELECTION AND COVENANT

Like the kings of Assyria, the leaders and kings of Israel, were elected, or chosen by God, and a covenant with God was the foundation of their rule.[38] The theme of God's election is clear in the Old Testament.

---

33. See *AKA*, 44 (lines 58–62).

34. E.g., Georges Dossin, "L'Inscription de Fondation de Iaḫdun-lim, roi de Mari," *Syria* 32 (1955) 13 (lines 10–11: Yaḫdunlim); *AKA*, 372 (line 85: Ashurnasirpal I); Rost, *Keilschrifttexte*, 44 (lines 15–16: Tiglath-pileser III); Luckenbill, *Annals*, 74–75 (lines 79–80: Sennacherib).

35. See n. 7 above.

36. Wiseman, "New Stela of Assur-Nasir-Pal II," 30–31. See also A. L. Oppenheim, in *ANESTP*, 558–60.

37. Ibid., 31–32.

38. Indeed, Yahweh also raised up the kings of other nations, e.g., Hadad of Edom (1 Kgs 11:14), Rezon of Damascus (1 Kgs 11:23), Hazael of Damascus (1 Kgs 19:15), and of course Cyrus (Isa 44:28, 45:1–7), who is even called Yahweh's "anointed" (Isa 45:1).

Consider the case of Saul. We read that "the day before Saul came, the LORD had revealed this to Samuel: 'About this time tomorrow I will send you a man from the land of Benjamin. Anoint him leader over my people Israel'" (1 Sam 9:15–16). And again, "When Samuel caught sight of Saul, the LORD said to him, 'This is the man I spoke to you about; he will govern my people'" (1 Sam 9:17). Likewise, when Samuel sees David, the LORD tells him, "Rise and anoint him; he is the one" (1 Sam 16:12). Of course, although Assyrian kings claimed divine selection, their claims are not expressed in the same way in Assyrian royal inscriptions.

Israel's anointed kings also had a covenant foundation for their rule. That foundation is spelled out clearly enough in Deuteronomy: "When you enter the land the LORD your God is giving you and have taken possession of it and settled in it, and you say, 'Let us set a king over us like all the nations around us,' be sure to appoint over you the king the LORD your God chooses" (Deut 17:14–15).

Not only must the king be God's elect, but he also must be obedient to God's covenant, as is expressed in Deuteronomy 17:

> When he takes the throne of his kingdom, he is to write for himself on a scroll a copy of this law, taken from that of the priests, who are Levites. It is to be with him, and he is to read it all the days of his life so that he may learn to revere the LORD his God and follow carefully all the words of this law and these decrees and not consider himself better than his brothers and turn from the law to the right or the left. Then he and his descendants will reign a long time over his kingdom in Israel (Deut 17:18–20).

God was faithful to his covenant in choosing kings for his people, and whom he chose he also anointed and empowered. There is an interesting parallel in this respect: the Assyrian kings claimed to have a *melammu*, or divinely imparted aura about them. But in contrast, the divinely imparted Spirit of the LORD came upon the anointed kings of Israel. We read of Saul, for instance, that Samuel anointed him and that this symbolic anointing was followed by the Spirit's coming on him for rule:

> Then Samuel took a flask of oil and poured it on Saul's head and kissed him saying, "Has not the LORD anointed you leader over his inheritance? . . . The Spirit of the LORD will come upon you in power, and you will prophesy . . . and you will be changed into a different person. Once these signs are fulfilled, do whatever your hand finds to do, for God is with you" (1 Sam 10:1, 6–7).

Likewise, when Samuel anointed David, we read, "So Samuel took the horn of oil and anointed him in the presence of his brothers, and from that day on the Spirit of the LORD came upon David in power" (1 Sam 16:13).[39]

Like the Assyrian kings, the kings of Israel waged war in the name of the LORD, and they were able to do so because they had a divine calling and divinely imparted *tôrâ* ('law, instruction') as the foundation for all their actions. Like the kings of Assyria, the kings of Israel were divinely commissioned to wage war. As in Assyria, their warfare was meant to advance and make manifest the visible rule of the national God among men.

Consequently, it was necessary to proceed according to God's will. The king had to seek the LORD before embarking on battle. If the LORD was with him, victory would be his. So the kings, and indeed the earlier leaders of Israel, sought the LORD, just as their Assyrian counterparts sought their gods to see whether or not they should go up to battle. For instance, at the begining of the book of Judges one reads, "After the death of Joshua, the Israelites asked the LORD, 'Who will be the first to go up and fight for us against the Canaanites?' The LORD answered, 'Judah is to go; I have given the land into their hands' " (Judg 1:1–2).

Likewise, David desired to overtake the Amalekite raiders who had destroyed Ziklag and taken its people away captive:

> Then David said to Abiathar the priest, the son of Ahimelech, "Bring me the ephod." Abiathar brought it to him, and David inquired of the LORD, "Shall I pursue this raiding party? Will I overtake them?"
>
> "Pursue them," he answered. "You will certainly overtake them and succeed in the rescue" (1 Sam 30:7–8).

Examples of this sort may be multiplied: Israel against the Benjaminites (Judg 20:26–28); Jehoshaphat against Ammon, Moab, and Edom (2 Chr 20:5–17); and even Ahab against Aram (1 Kgs 22:5–28). These examples show well enough that the leaders of Israel sought the LORD before committing themselves to battle in his name.

Like the kings of Assyria, the kings and leaders of Israel fought and won with divine help. So it is written of the conquest in Joshua 10 that

> Joshua subdued the whole region, including the hill country, the Negev, the western foothills and the mountain slopes, together with all their kings . . . . All these kings and their lands Joshua conquered in one campaign, because the LORD, the God of Israel, fought for Israel (Josh 10:40–42).

---

39. See likewise the LORD's Spirit anointing of the judge Othniel (Judg 3:9–10).

Their success was always based upon an obedient and trusting relationship with their God. Of Hezekiah it says:

> Hezekiah trusted the LORD, the God of Israel. . . . He held fast to the
> LORD and did not cease to follow him; he kept the commands the LORD
> had given Moses. And the LORD was with him; he was successful in whatever he undertook. He rebelled against the king of Assyria and did not
> serve him. From watchtower to fortified city, he defeated the Philistines,
> as far as Gaza and its territory (2 Kgs 18:5–8).

So David declares, "The king trusts in the LORD; through the unfailing love of the Most High he will not be shaken" (Ps 21:7 [8]). And Asaph illustrates the principle in Psalm 44:

> I do not trust in my bow,
>   my sword does not bring me victory;
> but you give us victory over our enemies,
>   you put our adversaries to shame (Ps 44:6–7).

This principle, reflected in Assyria and in the realm of common grace, finds embodiment in the Old Testament not only in the relationship of the king to God but also of the people (cf. 1 Chr 5:18–20). Interestingly enough, the Old Testament presents in a true light the trust that Mesopotamian kings claimed to put in their gods. Habakkuk says, for instance, of the Babylonians:

> Dread and terrible are they;
> their justice and dignity proceed from *themselves* . . .
> guilty men, whose *own strength* is their god!
> . . . He sacrifices to his net
> and burns incense to his dragnet;
> for by his net he lives in luxury,
> and enjoys the choicest food.
> Is he then to keep on emptying his net,
> and mercilessly slaying nations for ever? (Hab 1:7, 11, 16–17)

So, in an ironic twist, the prophet believes that the Mesopotamians, who claimed to trust in their gods, were really the ones who "trusted in their own strength." Why? Because they had idolized their own power and desires and made them an object of worship. And according to the Torah they worshiped the demons behind those idols, as Deut 32:16–17 explains (cf. Lev 17:7). The kings and people of Israel who trusted the LORD, however, would not be put to shame and could advance the warfare for God's name.

Just as God could give victory to his people, he could deprive their enemies of wisdom, just as Assyria's god did. There are numerous examples of this in the Old Testament. Obadiah, for instance, says to Edom:

Will it not happen, on that day—
oracle of Yahweh—
that I will cause wise men to perish from Edom
and understanding from Mount Esau? (Obadiah 8)

Obadiah does not mean a literal and selective destruction of wise men but an obliteration of their wisdom. As their wisdom departs there will be, in effect, no more wise men in Edom. See the parallel passage, Jer 49:7: "Is there no longer *wisdom* in Teman?/Has counsel perished from the prudent?"; Isa 3:1–12, especially v. 12: "Youths oppress my people, women rule over them" (disappearance of wise leadership because of sin); Isa 19:11 (destruction of Egyptian wisdom); Isa 29:14 (destruction of wisdom out of Zion). Job likewise portrays God's sovereign ability to do this among nations:

He silences the lips of trusted advisers
　and takes away the discernment of elders . . .
He *deprives the leaders of the earth of their reason*;
　he sends them wandering through a trackless waste (Job 12:20–24).

In a similar way, Yahweh hardened the heart of Pharaoh (Exod 23:27) and the hearts of the Canaanites (Josh 11:20), leading them to defeats that were also God's judgment upon them. As Joshua says: "It was the LORD himself who hardened their hearts to wage war against Israel, so that he might destroy them totally, exterminating them without mercy, as the LORD had commanded Moses" (Josh 11:20).

Because the kings of Assyria waged war for their gods, they assumed absolute rights over the defeated. Their job was to make manifest on earth the rule of their gods. They did so by conquering other peoples and bringing them into a vassal relationship. The same may be said of Israel's kings. Although God commanded Israel to leave no survivors during the conquest period and to make no treaties with those nations, he did not set such standards for their relationship with nations outside the promised land. Indeed, he wanted his rule in Israel to stand as a testimony to other nations of his wisdom and righteousness (Deut 4:5–8).

Be this as it may, Israel's leaders both during and after the conquest followed the practices common to ancient Near Eastern warfare. Thus, just as the Assyrian kings killed their enemies and suspended their bodies for public view, Joshua executed the five kings of the southern coalition and suspended their bodies from five trees near the cave at Makkedah until sunset (Josh 10:16–27). In a similar spirit, David punished those who had murdered Ishbosheth, Saul's son, and who had thus shown contempt for a righteous man: "David gave an order to his men, and they killed them. They cut off their hands and feet and hung the bodies by the pool in Hebron" (2 Sam 4:12). But it must be added at this point that Israelite leaders generally did not show the blatant inhumanity that was characteristic of Assyrian rulers.

As we noted, the authority of Assyrian kings was also expressed by another practice. They regularly carried away the idols of the defeated. This act was supposed to indicate the superiority of the god Ashur and other Assyrian gods over the gods of the defeated.

The same theology is evident in the Philistine capture of the ark of the LORD, although that capture had consequences they had not forseen. They put the ark in Dagon's temple. And because this act symbolized the superiority of Dagon over God, the LORD smote them with plague to show that *he* was God, and not Dagon (1 Sam 4:1–7:1).

Indeed, the Old Testament makes it clear that the LORD's victory on behalf of Israel was also a victory over the gods of the enemy. This is especially clear in his defeat of Egypt, when he brought his people out: "On that same night I will pass through Egypt and strike down every firstborn, both men and animals; and *I will bring judgment on all the gods of Egypt. I am the* LORD" (Exod 12:12).

The book of Numbers reflects on this event in a similar vein:

> The Israelites set out from Ramses on the fifteenth day of the first month, the day after the Passover. They marched out boldly in full view of all the Egyptians, who were burying all their firstborn, whom the LORD had struck down among them; for *the* LORD *had brought judgment on their gods"* (Num 33:3–4).

The LORD was able to bring judgment on other gods because he alone was truly God. In the ancient Near East, as I have shown, the military victory of one people over another showed the superiority of their god(s) over the other(s). The spoliation of divine images was meant to reflect the same superiority. Like the Assyrians, the Philistines and other ancient Near Eastern peoples, the Israelites also took the idols of the foe. For instance, when the Philistines had come and deployed their troops in the Valley of Rephaim,

> David inquired of the LORD, "Shall I go and attack the Philistines? Will you hand them over to me?"
>
> The LORD answered him, "Go, for I will surely hand the Philistines over to you." So David went to Baal Perazim, and there he defeated them. . . . The Philistines abandoned their idols there, and David and his men carried them off (2 Sam 5:19–21).

David did not take them away to the temple of his God, however, to install them there as captive and subordinate gods. That is what a pagan king would have done. For the LORD had said, "You shall have no other

Gods in my presence" (Exod 20:3). Rather, as 1 Chr 14:12 relates, David took and burned the Philistine idols, knowing that they were in reality not gods.

Because their gods had made victory possible, the Assyrian kings always dedicated some of the booty of war to the gods in their temples. The writer of 1 Chronicles says that the Philistines did the same. The reader learns that, when they found Saul and his sons fallen on Mount Gilboa,

> . . . they stripped him and took his head and his armor, and sent messengers throughout the land of the Philistines to proclaim the news among their idols and their people. They put his armor in the temple of their gods and hung up his head in the temple of Dagon (1 Chr 10:9–10).

King David likewise, on a far larger scale, dedicated booty and tribute to the LORD:

> When Toi king of Hamath heard that David had defeated the entire army of Hadadezer, he sent his son Joram to King David to greet him and congratulate him on his victory in battle over Hadadezer, who had been at war with Toi. Joram brought with him articles of silver and gold and bronze. King David *dedicated these articles to the LORD,* as he had done *with the silver and gold from all the nations he had subdued*: Edom and Moab, the Ammonites, and the Philistines, and Amalek. He also dedicated the plunder taken from Hadadezer son of Rehob, King of Zobah (2 Sam 8:9–12).

The kings of Assyria, after they had established some measure of peace by subduing the nations around them, returned home from their military campaigns and built or renovated temples. I have cited one such account of temple building from the reign of Ashurnasirpal II. Similarly, the Bible records Solomon's letter to Hiram of Tyre: "Now the LORD my God has given me peace on every side, and there is no adversary or disaster. I intend, therefore, to build a temple for the Name of the LORD my God" (1 Kgs 5:4–5).

When the work on the temple was complete and it was dedicated, Solomon regaled the people, just as Ashurnasirpal did. The account is remarkably similar to that of the Assyrian king, who was Solomon's near-contemporary:

> So Solomon observed the festival at that time, and all Israel with him, a vast assembly, from Lebo Hamath to the Wadi of Egypt. They celebrated it before the LORD our God for seven days and seven days more, fourteen days in all. On the following day he sent the people away. They blessed the king and then went home, joyful and glad in heart for all the good the LORD had done for his servant David and his people Israel (1 Kgs 8:65–66).

REVIEW OF WAR PRACTICES AND CONCLUSION

It becomes obvious that certain war practices and theological assertions were common to Assyria and Israel—and indeed I suggest, throughout the ancient Near East. In both cases the king or leader marched at the command of his god. He always proceeded with the help of his god, because (supposedly) a trusting relationship existed between them. One way in which a god might, and often did, help his elect king in battle was to interfere with the "heart" or the psyche of the enemy, so as to work his defeat.

The king for his part was ruthless in the execution of his lofty commission. That commission was nothing less than to make manifest on earth the rule of his god. To do so he conquered other nations and peoples and brought them under a covenant relationship with his nation and himself (and hence, implicitly, with his gods). Their king became his vassal, their gods subordinate to his gods. In the conquest of vassals and the quelling of rebels, the king showed no mercy. Mutilations were common, although far more so, apparently, at the hands of Assyria than at the hands of Israel. The victorious king took the idols of the defeated. He also took abundant booty and dedicated a portion of it to his god. When his god had given him peace round about, he set himself the task of building or renovating the god's temple. Ideologically, the god was at the center of all of this. The king or leader was chosen by the god. He was called into some sort of covenant relationship with the god. In this relationship he received divine laws and instruction for the just administration of his land and people.

Differences there are, of course, because Israel believed that Yahweh was God, not some demonic counterfeit. But broadly speaking the rationale for war, the practice of war, the ideology and very phraseology of war were essentially the same in Israel, Assyria, and elsewhere in the ancient Near East. And in each case, there was a sense of covenant background, or commitment, and divinely imparted instruction that provided the basic rationale for war. Indeed, since the ancient Near Eastern annals purported to be history, this covenant relationship seems to have formed a basis or rationale for historiography itself.

The Oscillating Fortunes of "History" within Old Testament Theology

Elmer A. Martens

Mennonite Brethren Biblical Seminary

A theology of the Old Testament must come to terms with the historical dimension of the Old Testament. For the last sixty years, ever since Walther Eichrodt's volumes in 1930, there has been a pouring forth of books on Old Testament theology. These works seek to synthesize the message of the Old Testament theologically. Like ocean waves, the movement has crested and waned, but by one count more than forty full-orbed theologies have appeared.[1] Perched at the end of the twentieth century, modern scholars are at a peculiar vantage point to survey a random selection of these biblical theologies in order to discover what place they have given to "history" in their theologizing.

The purpose of this essay is to inquire about the place given to "history" in a representative selection of these theologies, and in the context of an assessment, to propose how best to deal with the historical component of theology. Following a sketch of the ebb and flow of the historical component within Old Testament theology, a taxonomy, together with assessments will follow; that is, a longitudinal overview will be followed by a cross-sectional taxonomy.

THE EBB AND FLOW: A DESCRIPTIVE OVERVIEW

I would like to begin this sketch about the incorporation of history into Old Testament theology by noting that the modern discipline of

Author's note: I wish to acknowledge with gratitude suggestions and responses to the paper by Abraham Friesen, Allen Guenther, Ben Ollenburger, V. Philips Long, and Stephen Reimer.

1. E. A. Martens, "The Multicolored Landscape of Old Testament Theology," *The Flowering of Old Testament Theology: A Reader in Twentieth-Century Old Testament Theology, 1930–1990* (SBTS 1; Winona Lake, Ind.: Eisenbrauns, 1992) 56–57.

biblical theology owes its genesis in part to the Enlightenmment.[2]
J. Philipp Gabler is customarily credited with launching the enterprise of
biblical theology in 1787 by distinguishing it from dogmatic theology.[3]
Gabler urged that the historical setting of a passage should be noted when
examining Scripture. The emphasis on history was meant to correct the
view that the Bible was a book of doctrines. Accordingly, biblical theology as a discipline from the first took account of the Scripture's historical
character.[4]

Heilsgeschichte

The discipline of biblical theology soon swung into territory dominated by philosophy (e.g., W. de Wette and W. Vatke), but in the middle of the nineteenth century it became realigned with history. J. C. K.
von Hoffmann of the Erlangen School countered the philosophical orientation by introducing the notion of *Heilsgeschichte* or Salvation History. Salvation History entails distinguishing between historical events
of general history, which are subject to empirical investigation, and the
events recorded in Scripture. The latter are distinct disclosures of God,
highlighting his redemptive acts and plans, and are grasped by faith. Von

2. W. Lemke's definition of *history* serves well. By *history* we mean temporal events
that "may involve both human as well as divine activity and are inclusive of deeds and
words, external objective facts and the subjective apprehension and interpretation of
these facts" (Werner Lemke, "Revelation through History in Recent Biblical Theology," *Int* 36 [1982] 39). Cf. J. Goldingay whose definition is nuanced in the direction of
a discipline that chronicles these events (J. Goldingay, " 'That You May Know that Yahweh is God': A Study in the Relationship between Theology and Historical Truth in the
Old Testament," *TynBul* 23 [1972] 60–61).

3. John Sandys-Wunsch and Laurence Eldridge, "J. P. Gabler and the Distinction between Biblical and Dogmatic Theology: Translation, Commentary, and Discussion of His
Originality," *SJT* 33 (1980) 33–158; also in "J. P. Gabler, "An Oration on the Proper Distinction between Biblical and Dogmatic Theology and the Specific Objectives of Each,"
Flowering of Old Testament Theology, 493–502; B. C. Ollenburger, "From Timeless Ideas to
the Essence of Religion: Method in Old Testament Theology before 1930," *Flowering of
Old Testament Theology*, 5.

4. Ludwig Baumgarten-Crusius in 1828 asserted: "The idea and the execution of biblical theology are joined essentially with historical interpretation, and each of them has developed in recent times in relation to the other" (quoted by Ollenburger, "Timeless
Ideas," 4).

Gabler has often been considered to have given the discipline a historical character
in the sense of grounding biblical theology historically; others, however, see him as
wanting to identify the historical so that one can then leave the historical behind and
concentrate on the theological. See the remarks of A. K. M. Adam, "Biblical Theology
and the Problem of Modernity: Von Wredestrasse zu Sackgasse," *Horizons in Biblical Theology* 12 (1990) 1–18; and B. C. Ollenburger, "Biblical Theology: Situating the Discipline," *Understanding the Word: Essays in Honor of Bernhard W. Anderson* (JSOTSup 37;
Sheffield: JSOT Press, 1985) 37–62.

Hoffmann divided the study of the Old Testament into two parts: the first dealt with Old Testament history; the second, with its theology. "The former reproduces the series of events recorded in the Old Testament as a continuous history. The latter describes the history of the proclamation of salvation implied in that history."[5] Scripture is regarded as documenting a historical process, one that culminates in Christ, from which vantage point the Old Testament must be examined. In this approach the unity of the Bible is an important consideration, along with progressive revelation and the notion that historical events are a medium of revelation. History within the Scripture partakes of a unique quality: it is a record of events through which God discloses himself and his salvation purposes.[6] Clearly von Hoffmann's approach puts the element of history very much in the foreground.

In the latter part of the nineteenth century, biblical theology was eclipsed. Books on the history of Israel, rather than on biblical theology, dominated. For four decades scholars were preoccupied with the history of religion. This interest in history is to be associated with the pervasiveness of the historical-critical method.[7] The anomaly is that excessive concern with history muted the theological enterprise. It is a paradox that in promoting the importance of the dimension of history as a way of making a theological statement, interest in theology became sidetracked. That is, an excessive concern with history, while initially aiding in the formulation of Old Testament theology, served in the end to choke the enterprise.

Walther Eichrodt

The eclipse of bibical theology ended with the appearance in 1933 of Walther Eichrodt's *Theology of the Old Testament*, but it is important first to make reference to his debate with Otto Eissfeldt in the 1920s.[8] The debate between Eissfeldt and Eichrodt was important, for it faced in a new way the challenges that historical investigation had brought. Eissfeldt proposed that historical-critical tools be applied rigidly so that the result

5. John Hayes and Frederick Prussner *Old Testament Theology: Its History and Development* (Atlanta: John Knox, 1985) 82.

6. For a bibliography on Salvation History, see H. Graf Reventlow, *Problems of Old Testament Theology in the Twentieth Century* (Philadelphia: Fortress, 1985) 91.

7. So Hayes and Prussner, *Old Testament Theology*, 127.

8. The two significant essays by O. Eissfeldt (1926) and W. Eichrodt (1929) now appear in English translation as "The History of Israelite-Jewish Religion and Old Testament Theology" and "Does Old Testament Theology Still Have Independent Significance within Old Testament Scholarship?" in *Flowering of Old Testament Theology*, 20–29 and 30–39, respectively.

would be a discipline that would occupy itself with *knowledge*, namely the discipline of "The History of Religion." A second discipline, "Old Testament Theology," using different tools, would occupy itself with the *faith*. Eichrodt resisted this suggestion and argued that the critical tools of historical investigation were appropriate to the discipline of Old Testament theology. A biblical theology should be informed by research into the historical aspects of the material.

Consequently, when Eichrodt writes about theology, he looks in two directions, one of which is the context of the ancient Near East. In so doing, Eichrodt acknowledges the importance of history. Historical matters, however, do not dominate his work, but as he explains, an "Old Testament theology presupposes the history of Israel." For him the main agenda is systematizing concepts. Still, individual religious concepts, such as covenant, around which he organizes his presentation, must not be treated without regard to its historical context. For example, he devotes twenty-four pages to "The History of the Covenant Concept." He begins with the element from Canaanite religion that endangered the Yahweh covenant.[9] Then, adopting the critical grid, the JEDP theory, he traces the historical development from the Yahwist source/tradition, through the prophets, and into Deuteronomic and Priestly material.[10] Eichrodt also discusses Salvation History.[11] He sees a difference between the Spirit's work during the time of the Judges and that in the time of the Monarchy, which was more fortified with institution. But his theologizing sits lightly on questions of historical factuality, nor does the rubric of history appear important in the organization of his work. Rather than make great distinctions based on time periods, Eichrodt frequently differentiates between priestly and prophetic nuances, between 'glory' (*kābôd*) and 'word'.[12] He repeatedly differentiates between Israelite understandings and the understanding of other people in her oriental environment.[13] He is expansive in discussing teleology in the context, not of history primarily, but of the structure of the cosmos.[14]

It should not escape those who are given to highlighting history that Eichrodt's Old Testament theology is not dominated by history. He succeeds in presenting a biblical theology without a heavy emphasis on Israelite history. To the extent that he introduces ancient Near East

---

9. Walther Eichrodt, *Theology of the Old Testament* (trans. J. Baker; OTL; 2 vols.; London: SCM/Philadelphia: Westminster, 1961–67) 1.32, 45.

10. See, for a similar approach, the discussion about the priesthood in ibid., 1.392ff.

11. Ibid., 2.50–57; see the "inner coherence of creation and history," 2.100ff.

12. Ibid., 2.52, 76.

13. E.g., creation, ibid., 2.96ff., 113ff.

14. Ibid., 2.109, 158.

material, he makes use of historical data of course, but the exposition of his theology is largely without resort to the category of history. Eichrodt demonstrates that it is possible to write a credible theology apart from an excessive preoccupation with the category of history.

Gerhard von Rad and G. Ernest Wright

G. von Rad, whose work in Old Testament theology appeared twenty-five years later, rivals Eichrodt's in its magisterial compass and innovative design but differs sharply from Eichrodt in what he makes of the rubric of history. Von Rad's greater attention to history is signaled by the subtitle of his first volume, *The Theology of Israel's Historical Traditions*, and in part 1, "A History of Jahwism and of the Sacral Institutions in Israel in Outline."[15] Von Rad leaves to the side the systematizing of concepts and elevates the historical dimension, not however by worrying about the facts the critical historian might establish. For von Rad, theology consists of tracing the traditions within the story. He stresses Israel's recital of her story, by which she appropriates the tradition and offers a confessional statement about her God. The Old Testament is a piece of literature with movement. It is also an address; that is, it is *kerygma*, a proclamation. This proclamation is one involving an understanding of the past. A theology of the Old Testament, in von Rad's view, is inextricably linked to Israel's history, her story. "Israel's faith is grounded in a theology of history."[16]

G. Ernest Wright, the American Old Testament archaeologist and theologian contemporary with von Rad, also gives the category of the historical a most prominent place. What is implied by the word *history*, however, is not the same for both. For von Rad, history is the transmission of traditions, such as the patriarchal and Exodus traditions, at first independent, but later fused to forge a *kerygma*. For Wright history is more closely associated with historical documentation, such as is possible through archaeology.[17] Wright is interested in what actually happened. For von Rad it is important that Israel conceptualized her relationship with God in historical terms, whether that history can be verified or not. Wright, as part of the biblical theology movement, is keen on establishing

15. Gerhard von Rad, *Old Testament Theology* (2 vols.; trans. D. M. G. Stalker; Edinburgh: Oliver and Boyd/New York: Harper & Row, 1962–65).

16. Ibid., 1.106. For a further discussion see G. Hasel, "The Problem of History in Old Testament Theology," *AUSS* 8 (1970) 23–50; and Reventlow, *Problems of Old Testament Theology*, 64–77.

17. Archaeological work at sites such as Hazor, Megiddo, and Gezer both illumined and in some sense confirmed parts of the biblical record about Solomon.

the unity of the entire Bible. Von Rad considers this goal to be misguided, if unity means a coherence of theme. Still, both Wright and von Rad lean hard on the historical factor as constitutive for theology; it is in the attention that each gives to the historical factor that one is justified in placing them within one camp.

Wright highlights God's mighty acts as a departure point for Old Testament theology. These acts, events in history, were for Israel (and hence are for us) disclosures about God. Chief among the events is the Exodus of a people from Egypt, but the list also includes the act of creation, the promise to Abraham, the gift of the land, and the Davidic conquests.[18] The Bible is more than ideas, Wright maintains. It is a record of God's intervention in history.

This emphasis on Salvation History usually includes the belief that Israel, with its stress on history, was unique among ancient Near Eastern peoples. Other peoples, such as the Canaanites, Wright explains, adopted a cyclical interpretation of reality, so that akin to seasons, one marked the death and resurrection of the deity. The notion of a linear or goal-oriented series of events was foreign, Wright claims, to non-Israelite religions. Israel, and by extension Christianity, is differentiated from other religions by the importance attached to history.

Eichrodt with a minimalist attention to history, on the one hand, and von Rad and Wright, with a singularly large focus on history, on the other, illustrate within a three-decade span the ebb and the flow of the category of history within Old Testament theology. The stances of theologians later in the century lie on a continuum within or even beyond these positions.

The Cluster of Four: S. Terrien, W. Kaiser, C. Westermann, and R. Clements

The year 1978 was remarkable in the production of Old Testament theologies, for in that single year, unlike any other year of the century, four books on the subject appeared. One German (C. Westermann), one British (R. E. Clements) and two American scholars (S. Terrien and W. Kaiser) authored books on Old Testament theology. In my sampling of theologians in the twentieth century, these four form a cluster but with divergent ways of incorporating history into Old Testament theology.

Samuel Terrien. Samuel Terrien's theology is a theology of the presence and the absence of God, a theology worked out largely in the con-

---

18. G. E. Wright, *God Who Acts: Biblical Theology as Recital* (London: SCM, 1952).

text of cult, not covenant. In the opening chapter, which touches on methodology and perspective, Terrien has virtually nothing to say about the significance of historical events, nor does he elsewhere discuss the subject.[19] In contrast to Wright, who emphasized events in history as yielding information about God, Terrien asserts that the knowledge of the free and sovereign God "stems from a single factor: the Hebraic theology of presence."[20] The patriarch's sojourn in Palestine and the Exodus are important for Terrien, not as a story charting causes and effects, but traceable, as Israel tells it, to the theophanic appearances of God to Abraham and to Moses. Terrien reaches behind narratives about events to theophanic experiences of God's presence. The history that is reported is dependent on the initial theophany.[21]

Terrien is cautious about the historicity of biblical events. He shares in the "skepticism" about details. "Traditions which are now embedded in the Pentateuch contain a great deal of information about Moses, but they do not constitute the equivalent of historiographic archives."[22] For Terrien, though not for Wright, the historical character of events is of slight importance. When he works through matters relating to the temple, he alludes to earlier stories of the ark but mostly as being in Israel's memory. It is the literary way in which a story is told—patriarchal legend, prophetic confession, or poetry—rather than anything about its history that governs Terrien's theologizing.

What accounts for an approach that fusses so little with the historicity of events or their sequel? A preliminary answer is that the debate about the relationship of history and revelation had, in the words Terrien uses about covenant discussion, "spent its momentum." A further answer is that Terrien eschewed the *Heilsgeschichte* approach; it had centered too much on covenant, which in his opinion surfaces only sporadically. Another, more fundamental reason lies in the appeal held out by newer approaches, such as the literary methods of form criticism, rhetorical criticism, and tradition-history. Earlier in the century the historical-critical method had a particular fascination; at that time history as a category was a formidable factor with which theologians came to terms (*à la* Troeltsch), even if in quite different ways. Terrien's work

---

19. Terrien refers to H. Wheeler Robinson, who in 1946, "laid down the principles for a new Old Testament theology which would adequately discover in the historical traditions of Israel the locus of revelation," but he does not follow Robinson (Samuel Terrien, *The Elusive Presence: Toward a New Biblical Theology* [San Francisco: Harper & Row, 1978], 35–36).

20. Ibid., 28.

21. Ibid., 20–21. Terrien focuses on the literature of the Bible, with its psalms, confessions of the prophets, and poems such as Job, rather than on history (xxvii–xxviii).

22. Ibid., 106; cf. pp. 66, 67, 152 n. 2.

illustrates that appropriating a select set of "criticisms" with which to come to the Scripture clearly affects the outcome theologically. In Terrien's instance the historical dimension has been all but disregarded.[23]

Walter Kaiser.   Though his book also appeared in 1978, Kaiser differs from the other three in that he elevates the category of history to a place of prominence. The word *history* for him means events as they actually or really happened.[24] Kaiser's discussion of methodology is dotted heavily with the word *history.* One finds major headings such as "The Historic Periods of Old Testament Theology" and "The Key Items in each Historic Period." History, together with the significance attached to it in the canon, is Kaiser's starting point.[25]

A basic premise for Kaiser is that history is the medium of revelation. What is known about God emerges out of events. If the events are not to be taken as "real" but are instead the interpretations of some well-meaning Israelite writers, then the resulting theology is hardly reliable. He sets himself deliberately and vigorously against von Rad, for whom the historicity of the events is secondary but for whom the message that emerges from reflection on the events is primary. He joins R. de Vaux, against von Rad and Franz Hesse, in asserting that the "interpretation of history which is offered is true and originates from God, or it is not worthy of Israel's faith or ours."[26]

History is important for Kaiser because for him the center of Old Testament theology is *promise.* Buttressed with words denoting *plan* in the prophets and elsewhere, Kaiser insists that God had a plan that unfolded in history. Its stages of fulfilment can be clearly marked: events become benchmarks for the realization of the plan. Theology is cumulative. Moreover, the sequence of events becomes the grid for a presentation of theology. He outlines theology according to the successive epochs of Israel's history, beginning with Abraham, on to the Exodus, the period of the Judges, the era of the Monarchy, the time of the Exile, and then the post-Exilic period.[27] The category of history is indisputably Kaiser's pre-

23. The disregard for history is not total. Terrien, in the organization of his material, takes a nod toward biblical sequences: epiphanic visions seen by the patriarchs precede the Sinai material, which in turn precedes the temple material.

24. Walter C. Kaiser, Jr., *Toward a Theology of the Old Testament* (Grand Rapids, Mich.: Zondervan, 1978) 26, 43.

25. Ibid., 27, 41, 43, 49.

26. Ibid., 5, 25, 27–28.

27. "In our proposed methodology, biblical theology draws its very structure of approach from the historic progression of the text and its theological selection and conclusions from those found in the canonical focus" (ibid., 12).

occupation. Out of it he fashions his theology, and by it he orders his theology. Kaiser's theologizing is done in the context of cumulative historic experience, and most fundamental of all, the theological center, promise, is wedded to history.

Kaiser's work illustrates the fact that the role one gives to history is definitely influenced by one's conclusion about the center of Old Testament theology. If it is promise, with its concomitant fulfilment, then historical progression will be important. By contrast, Terrien's rubric of presence/absence is dependent on cult and as a result, much less needs to be made of history.

    C. Westermann.   C. Westermann, whose German work appeared in 1978 and was translated four years later under the title *Elements of Old Testament Theology*, might be said to succeed Wright and von Rad, but it must be quickly added that his ideas greatly tempered both of theirs regarding the place of history in theology. Westermann distances himself from the well-worn notion of Salvation History by pointing out its limitations, even though the basic idea is incorporated in his theology. History in the Old Testament is not uniformly a Saving History but is also a history of judging. It must be noted too, he says, that the history is not about a single entity, for sometimes the entity is the nation, sometimes a family or a remnant. Salvation History, by its vocabulary, points to a product, salvation, whereas for Westermann it is important to keep within a verb-structure: God engages in saving activity. Westermann holds, however, that "the *concept of salvation history* . . . coined in the nineteenth century and dependent on that century's understanding of history, cannot, at least not alone, be fully determinative for a theology of the Old Testament."[28]

Still he gives to the category of history a lead position, for the saving event is foundational for Old Testament theology. Events speak loudly about God; fundamentally God is to be understood as Savior. The saving events, whether depicted in the Torah division of the canon, the announcements of God's saving activities in the Prophets or the laments and thanksgivings in the Psalms, unite to provide a characteristic representation of God. Or if one examines the Yahwist or the Deuteronomic History, then one understands that "they serve to show with a particular clarity what theology is in the Old Testament." Westermann's history is not to be confused with the nineteenth-century understanding of history

---

28. C. Westermann, *Elements of Old Testament Theology* (Atlanta: John Knox, 1982) 14–15 [italics his], 45 (German original, *Theologie des Alten Testaments in Grundzügen*).

as objectified event that depends for its verification on documentation. Biblical history is not a political history of a people or nation, in the vein of nineteenth-century thought but includes two other circles, the circle of the individual, as with Abraham, and of humanity at large, as in the primeval history. Within every circle, but especially in the middle circle, that of the nation, God is shown in his saving activity.

Moreover, for Westermann the category of history is one whereby he can order his comments about subthemes, such as prayer or worship, promise and fulfilment, and law. The laws, he says, "demonstrate a strict and unmistakable orientation toward history." Attention to history means that one has a carefully-nuanced understanding of law: it changes with history. It appears differently in the covenant code than in P. "In Israel there was never *the* law as a timeless quantity."[29]

Westermann is middle-of-the-road, compared to Terrien and Kaiser. Much more attuned to the importance of Salvation History than Terrien, he is however not as exclusively preoccupied with history as Kaiser.

Ronald Clements.   The fourth Old Testament theology of 1978 appeared with the title *Old Testament Theology: A Fresh Approach*, written by the British scholar, Ronald E. Clements. The fresh approach consisted of giving attention to the groups that utilize the Old Testament, Jews and Christians, and to the fact that for the first group the Old Testament was primarily law but for the second, primarily promise. One would think that in this approach the category of history surely could not be ignored, especially in the promise column, but surprisingly, for Clements the historical dimension does not have a high profile.

Clements questions the nature of the Old Testament before attempting to elicit a theology from it. He offers a fourfold answer. The Old Testament is a collection of writings: it is literature. Second, it has a historical dimension. Third, the Old Testament has a cultic dimension. Clements observes, "The basic vocabulary of religion in the Old Testament is basically a vocabulary of the cult . . . ."[30] A fourth dimension is intellectual. The Old Testament handles ideas within a language and a culture. Thus the historical dimension is but one of four, and Clements's treatise correspondingly is caught up with matters of history only on occasion. For instance, he devotes only a brief paragraph to the question of what happened in the Exodus. His discussion of the portrait of God is developed, not with

29. Ibid., 14, 20, 61, 154, 176, 184 [italics his], 188, 231–32.
30. Ronald E. Clements, *Old Testament Theology: A Fresh Approach* (Atlanta: John Knox, 1978) 42.

major attention to events or historical sequence, but by means of images, names, cult (as in sanctuary and theophany), and uniqueness.[31] Essentially, Clements mutes the category of history. In an essay that appeared after the publication of his book, Clements stated, "In pursuing a purely historical line of inquiry, we should have abandoned the richly theological quality of the biblical narrative."[32] History for Clements is not in lead position, as it is for Westermann.

On a continuum, then, from minimal to maximum attention to the historical dimensions of the Old Testament, of the 1978 "cluster of four," Terrien would be near the minimalist end of the continuum, followed by Clements, and then Westermann, who already tilts more toward the maximum represented by Kaiser.

Summary

A survey such as this builds in fascination. During the last sixty years, history has been variously rated. Compared to the midcentury position of history in the service of a biblical theology, later positions have all but dismissed history as important for theology. History is for some a fringe element of theology (Terrien); for others it is invoked on occasion (Eichrodt, Clements); for others history is the lead component, supplemented with other elements (Westermann); and for still others it is so decidedly paramount that a biblical theology cannot be conceived without it (von Rad, Wright, and Kaiser). This massive difference in the treatment of historiography within theology calls for analysis, to which I now turn.

TESTING THE TIDE: AN ASSESSMENT
OF THREE APPROACHES

Three distinct classifications can be discerned in the dominance accorded by theologians to the role of history in Old Testament theology. In one approach history is the bedrock of theology; in another, history is tangential to theology; in a third, history is a primary but not exclusive component for theology. A critique of each of these approaches will be helpful in determining how best to link history and faith.

---

31. Ibid., 55, 58–78. Similarly, although set within the framework of Israel's history, Clements's discussion of the "People of God" is along the lines of election, covenant, and institutions, such as kingship, and not in a theologically interpretive history (79–103).

32. Ronald E. Clements, "History and Theology in Biblical Narrative," *HBT* 4/5 (1982–83) 49.

History as the Bedrock of Theology

One group of theologians gives almost exclusive weight to historiography. Among these are von Hoffmann, von Rad, Wright, and Kaiser. History does not function the same way for each, but for each it is determinative: each mines his theology from the mother lode of event. Von Hoffmann and Kaiser develop a theology that follows closely the chronological eras in Israel's history. Wright makes the mighty acts of God the subject matter for the theologian.[33] Von Rad, acknowledging that the Bible is a history book, traces the history of traditions, such as the Patriarchal, Exodus, and Settlement traditions, noting how they were used and reused. For von Rad the events and the expression by Israel of the meaning of the events, particularly the latter, are the subject of theology. Characteristic of the theologians in this group, whatever their differences, is the dominance they give to the historical dimension as foundational and determinative for theology. That is, *Salvation History* is the term, first and last, as well as middle.

The advantages of giving a large place to history are several and can be summarized in checklist fashion. An emphasis on event/tradition takes account of the history within the Old Testament itself. Moreover, the organization of a biblical theology can be guided, as in Kaiser's work, by the biblical historical sequence. Especially in a model such as von Rad's, there is also an incremental nature to the enterprise. The prophets, for example, build on what has preceded, for the prophetic word is informed in part by the tradition to which the prophet is heir.[34] Moreover, given the notion of promise (Kaiser) or the concept of reinterpretation of the promise (von Rad), something of the dynamic of the Old Testament itself is retained in an Old Testament theology. Like the Scripture itself, then, theology tends to lean forward in anticipation. Especially helpful is the bridging between the Old and the New Testaments.[35] The saving acts of God in the Old Testament culminate in God's act in Jesus Christ.

But even though there are many benefits to highlighting history when developing theology, one should not be blind to the problems. One problem is that biblical history is propaganda. History is a human enterprise of chronologically selecting and recording events in time and space and doing so interpretively or with a particular perspective. The requirement that history be objective is an artificial requirement.[36] The his-

---

33. Wright, *God Who Acts*, 11–13.
34. Hasel, "The Problem of History," 26–29.
35. Von Rad, *Old Testament Theology*, 2.382–84.
36. It is questionable whether science is objective. See "Science as Craftsman's Work," in Jerome R. Ravetz, *Scientific Knowledge and Its Social Problems* (New York: Oxford University Press, 1971) 75–108.

torian is as much a part of the process as are the facts and events.[37] In the Old Testament, data and interpretation are intertwined. The events leading to the Exodus are interpreted as divinely purposive. Israel and Egypt are to know: "I am Yahweh" (Exod 6:7, 7:5).[38] Clements rightly says, "It is not difficult to see that the use of historical narrative of this kind [in the Pentateuch] is readily made to serve a theological purpose."[39] This genre of history might be described as a "theological history" or a "faith history."[40] In a sense all the historian can do is to explain the theological-historical perspective of Israel. To the extent that the biblical material identifies events, it is amenable to investigation by the historical-critical method. To the extent that the Bible is theologically interpreted, the historical-critical method is important.

A second problem for theologians for whom biblical history is categorically determinative is the biblical data itself. Is it factual? Is the history authentic, reliable? One could argue, for example, that if the biblical writers depict God's intervention in history, then, given the kind of God they perceived him to be, the writers would have been especially careful to get the facts right. If theology hinges so heavily on event, then the factuality question looms especially large. For example, two views compete for description of Israel's origin. In the Bible the origin of Israel as a people (nation) is tied with the Reed Sea and Sinai, but critical-historical methodology ties Israel's beginning to the time of David.[41] Von Rad's theology is criticized for its double picture of history. As a theologian von Rad operates with the picture of history given in the Bible. As a modern scholar, he accepts the results of modern historical criticism.[42] A tension

37. "History writing is not primarily the accurate reporting of past events. It also considers the reason for recalling the past and the significance given to past events" (John Van Seters, *In Search of History* [New Haven: Yale University Press, 1983], 4–5.

38. Not only is the information given that Uzzah died when he tried to steady the ark of the covenant, but the explanation accompanies the information: "The Lord's anger burned against Uzzah because of his irreverent act; therefore God struck him down" (2 Sam 6:7).

39. Clements, *Old Testament Theology*, 34.

40. Eichrodt, *Theology*, 2.403.

41. See Clements, *Old Testament Theology*, 82–85.

42. The criteria for the historical-critical method were provided by E. Troeltsch: (1) The principle of methodological doubt: the conclusions of historical inquiry are never final since they are subject to revision. (2) The principle of analogy: historical inquiry relies on events being similar in principle and from this it follows that the laws of nature operating in biblical times were the same as those we know. (3) The principle of correlation: there is an interrelationship of cause and effect in the phenomenon of history. This interdependence means that no event can be isolated from the historical flow. Discussion and bibliography can be found in J. J. Collins, "Is a Critical Biblical Theology Possible?" in *The Hebrew Bible and Its Interpreters* (ed. W. H. Propp, B. Halpern, and D. N. Freedman; Biblical and Judaic Studies from the University of California, San Diego 1; Winona Lake: Eisenbrauns, 1990) 1–17; and Walter Kaiser, *Toward Rediscovering the Old Testament* (Grand Rapids, Mich.: Zondervan, 1987) 68ff.

emerges between the "believed history" and the actual or *de facto* history, and the question then becomes, can a theology be trusted which is structured on a history that is not trustworthy?[43]

The response to this double picture of history and the task of integrating it into theology has taken several sharply different forms. One answer to the hiatus created by the biblical version of history and the critical version is to set aside the biblical account and to substitute the critically-restored scenario and develop a corresponding theology. This was the answer of Franz Hesse, an answer that has not been accepted by the scholarly community. But in less radical ways, others have leaned hard on the critically-determined history. Ronald Clements states, "It is absolutely essential, therefore, that an Old Testament theology should evaluate its material and establish its conclusions upon the basis of the results of historical criticism."[44] The assumption is that otherwise an Old Testament theology would not be credible. Similarly, most recently M. Oeming proceeds by developing a biblical theology with heavy reliance on the historical-critical method.[45] J. J. Collins, also a vigorous advocate for the historical-critical method, takes a different position. He questions whether a biblical theology that is grounded in historical criticism is even possible.[46] Hesse, Clements, Oeming, and Collins agree that one answer to the "double version of history" is to let the critical version be the point of departure for theology.

A second answer to the double version of history is to hold to the historical-critical method but to maintain, as R. Rendtorff does, that the traditions about and surrounding the event and transmitted by the faith community are part of God's activity.[47] But this view is problematic, for it claims that the divinely-produced tradition about God's action in event is trustworthy, even though the events to which the tradition bears witness are not trustworthy. Goldingay is right: "If God was really active in the production of this tradition, then surely the events it describes must have happened."[48]

---

43. Discussion of the problem may be found in Eichrodt, *Theology*, 1.512–14; D. G. Spriggs, *Two Old Testament Theologies* (London: SCM/Naperville, Ill.: Allenson, 1971) 49–56; Hasel, "Problem of History," 29–32; Reventlow, *Problems of Old Testament Theology*, 65–71.

44. Clements, *Old Testament Theology*, 12.

45. M. Oeming, *Gesamtbiblische Theologien der Gegenwart: Das Verhältnis von AT und NT in der hermeneutischen Diskussion seit Gerhard von Rad* (Stuttgart: Kohlhammer, 1985).

46. Collins, "Critical Biblical Theology?" 1–17.

47. Rolf Rendtorff, "Geschichte und Überlieferung," *Studien zur Theologie der alttestamentlichen Überlieferungen* (ed. Rolf Rendtorff and Klaus Koch; Neukirchen-Vluyn: Neukirchener, 1961) 81–94, esp. 93–94. See the discussion in Carl E. Braaten, "Heilsgeschichte and the Old Testament," chap. 5 in *New Directions in Theology Today*, vol. 2: *History and Hermeneutics* (Philadelphia: Westminster, 1966) 103–29.

48. Goldingay, "That You May Know," 88.

A third answer is to call into question the validity of the historical-critical method. Von Rad recognizes the limitations of the method. He challenges modern historians whose premise precludes saying anything about God and his history.[49] Similarly, Westermann alleges that the nineteenth-century notion of history alone "cannot be the standard for an Old Testament theology because it *a priori* excludes an act of God as an integral part of history."[50] G. Ladd, who embraces quite another tradition, is blunt: "The simple fact is that the historical-critical method has no room for salvation history." He continues: "The point we are stressing is that the historical-critical method denies the role of transcendence in the history of Jesus as well as in the Bible as a whole, not as a result of scientific study of the evidences, but because of its philosophical presuppositions about the nature of history."[51] The historical-critical method is increasingly coming under attack and its limitations are being recognized.[52] Some argue that the critical method also stands under the judgment of revelation.

By discrediting elements of the historical-critical method, or even the method itself, one has cleared the way for alternatives. Validation of the factuality of bibical history is complex. Goldingay holds that if one cannot "prove" that a reported event such as Sodom and Gomorrah took place, or that a person such as Abraham lived, one may still choose to regard the event as true by reason of the later prophetic witnesses to the event, Christ's validation of the event, or one's personal experience of Christ and the community.[53] He argues that the historical-critical method cannot be the ultimate authority, though it can aid in investigation. One's trust is ultimately in God, a trust that derives from Jesus and his validation of the Old Testament.[54]

---

49. Von Rad holds that the method cannot pontificate on the relationship of history to God (*Old Testament Theology*, 2.viff.). Cf. also G. Hasel, *Old Testament Theology: Basic Issues in the Current Debate* (3d ed.; Grand Rapids, Mich.: Eerdmans, 1982) 171–77.

50. Westermann, *Elements*, 12.

51. George E. Ladd, "The Search for Perspective," *Int* 25 (1971) 49–50. More to the point is the recognition that to determine and delineate the intervention of God in history is simply beyond the competence of the historian and the historical-critical method. Kaiser queries why a text should be considered guilty until proven innocent when the best in jurisprudence works from an opposite principle (*Toward Rediscovering*, 66).

52. G. Maier, *The End of the Historical Critical Method* (St. Louis: Concordia, 1977); Walter Wink, *The Bible in Human Transformation* (Philadelphia: Fortress, 1973); Kaiser, *Toward Rediscovering*, 59–79.

53. John Goldingay, *Approaches to Old Testament Interpretation* (Downers Grove, Ill.: InterVarsity, 1981) 73.

54. "For us, certainty about the historical trustworthiness of the Old Testament historical narratives has to be grounded on the validation they receive from Christ" (Goldingay, "That You May Know," 93).

Among the problems that cluster around the claims made on behalf of Salvation History is yet another. This claim is that the inclusion of history in cult writings was unique to Israel in the ancient Near East.[55] But Bertil Albrektson has shown that interest in history was also found in neighboring cultures. For instance the Weidner Chronicle, written in the late second millennium B.C., tells of the fall of dynasties in the third millennium. Furthermore, like the Deuteronomic Historian, the author attributes the fall to infractions of the cult, in this case the cult of Marduk.[56] Deities in nonbiblical religions were known to have plans for the fulfilment of which they summoned certain kings.[57] Albrektson summarizes: "The Old Testament idea of historical events as divine revelation must be counted among the similarities, not among the distinctive traits: it is part of the common theology of the ancient Near East."[58]

These examples do not mean that there was nothing distinctive about Israel's historiography. In part the difference is the degree to which Israel occupied itself with history. Gnuse states, "Israel affirmed the historical dimension to a greater degree than its contemporaries; for Israel it was the primary arena for divine activity, while for other peoples it remained secondary."[59] Another difference is that intervention by ancient Near Eastern deities was not, as in Israel, on moral grounds. Moreover, these deities championed the status quo, whereas Israel's God urged change.[60] Nonbiblical deities may have had goals, but they were short-range, such as avenging Akkad. In contrast, the God of Israel had a long-range plan that is concerned with human destiny.[61] To draw too stark a contrast between Israel and the ancient Near East is misleading, but to ignore the differences is not responsible. Theological claims for Salvation History must be chastened by means of careful comparison with other histories.

55. Wright, *God Who Acts*, 24–32; see Robert K. Gnuse, "Holy History in the Hebrew Scriptures and the Ancient World: Beyond the Present Debate," *BTB* 18 (1987) 128.

56. Gnuse (ibid.) documents these examples from the work by Eva Osswald and also lists further examples. Historiography comparable to that in Israel may be found, for example, in the second-millennium text "The Curse of Akkad," in which the fall of the Akkadian Empire is explained along theological-political lines (Bertil Albrektson, *History and the Gods: An Essay on the Idea of Historical Events as Divine Manifestations in the Ancient Near East and in Israel* [Lund: CWK Gleerup, 1967], 24). For the Weidner Chronicle, see B. Arnold, "The Weidner Chronicle and the Idea of History in Israel and Mesopotamia," 129–48.

57. Albrektson (*History and the Gods,*" 48) cites the stele containing the text summoning Nebuchadnezzar I (1124–1103 B.C.).

58. Ibid., 114; cf. p. 98.

59. Gnuse, "Holy History," 131.

60. W. G. Lambert, "History and the Gods: A Review Article," *Or* 39 (1970) 170–77.

61. Jacob Licht, "Biblical Historicism," *History, Historiography and Interpretation: Studies in Biblical and Cuneiform Literatures* (ed. H. Tadmor and M. Weinfeld; Jerusalem: Magnes, 1983) 109–11; cited by Gnuse, "Holy History," 130.

A fourth problem for the proponents of Salvation History relates to the claim that events are revelatory. Theodore Vriezen wrote, "One of the most characteristic elements of the Old Testament teaching concerning God is the great stress laid on *God's activity in history*. . . . Israel derives its knowledge of God from His activity in history on behalf of His people, particularly in Egypt and in the desert."[62] This seems simple enough. The Exodus event, for example, disclosed something of the nature of Yahweh. For Vriezen, this disclosure was that God is a living God who is near but who is also holy. But as this connection between event and revelation is probed, blurring sets in. It is clear that revelation was not in the event *per se* but that a word, an interpretation was required. The interface between *word* and *event* became a subject of much discussion.[63] As James Barr notes, part of the problem is that the modern reader is put in touch, not with a biblical event, but with the literary record of an event.[64] To highlight history as yielding theology necessitates clarity of thought regarding the formation of theology out of history.

A fifth problem with talk of Salvation History is ambiguity. In what way is it meaningful today to speak of God's acts? Langdon Gilkey has called attention to the subtle way in which scholars transpose language when moving between an ancient cosmology, such as is in the Bible, in which God spoke and acted, to a modern, quite differently conceived cosmology/ontology, in which speaking and acting are understood quite differently. In the biblical view, to say that God spoke or acted was to use the words as they were used of human beings. If today one uses these words of God, he or she uses them, not univocally, but analogically. It is one thing to speak of God's mighty acts in the Exodus, parroting biblical language. But theologians such as G. E. Wright and B. W. Anderson, because they are moderns, adopt a scientific stance. As an example, Gilkey quotes Anderson's belief that the rescue of the Hebrews at the Exodus "resulted from the East wind blowing over the Reed Sea."[65] Essentially, Gilkey charges, scholars equivocate in their use of language. He presses the question: "To what does one refer when one speaks of the mighty acts of God; how is such theology to be translated for moderns?"[66]

---

62. Theodore Vriezen, *An Outline of Old Testament Theology* (Oxford: Blackwell, 1958) 136 (emphasis his).

63. For a discussion in the nature of a case study on this relationship, see Goldingay, "That You May Know," 67–71; a large bibliography with discussion is given in Reventlow, *Problems of Old Testament Theology*, 71–87; see Goldingay, *Approaches*, 74ff.

64. J. Barr, "The Interpretation of Scripture, II: Revelation through History in the Old Testament and Modern Thought," *Int* 17 (1963) 193–205.

65. L. Gilkey, "Cosmology, Ontology and the Travail of Biblical Language," *JR* 41 (1961) 148.

66. Further criticism of Salvation History as advocated by scholars like G. E. Wright may be found in J. Barr, "Trends and Prospects in Biblical Theology," *JTS* 25 (1974);

Gilkey has been answered in a variety of ways. All history, some say, and not single events, can be viewed as God's activity, just as a person's life is his or her activity. Further, even if the Exodus event were an event explicable by natural forces, the fact that God had promised deliverance means that the event was revelatory. Besides, if God's activity in addition to miracles includes the less mundane, then might not such events as the fall of the Berlin Wall be God in action?[67] The possibility of ambiguity is not sufficient reason to dismiss talk of Salvation History, but it is reason to proceed circumspectly.

A final problem with Salvation History needs only to be mentioned, without elaboration. When a theologian takes his or her cues for theology almost entirely from history, how does he or she make use of legal, poetic, or wisdom literature from the Old Testament? Must one ignore the other genres in Scripture?[68]

The view that history is the bedrock for theology is epitomized by Will Herberg's statement, "Biblical faith is faith enacted as history, or it is nothing at all."[69] The biblical theology movement in the 1940s and 1950s was characterized by the belief that God was revealed in history. Brevard Childs cites reasons that the movement came into crisis, including criticism of Salvation History such as is summarized above.[70] The centerpiece in Wright's theology, namely, the mighty acts of God, for all its gains, collapsed like an overloaded wagon, by its sheer weight. To require history to carry such large theological freight eventually mired down the historical method. Whatever the short-term gains of focusing on history may be, the long-term dividend is problematic.

History as Tangential to Theology

I turn next to examining the theologies in which the historical dimension, while acknowledged, is not central but tangential. Terrien, Clements, and perhaps even Eichrodt (though Eichrodt fits somewhat uneasily here) may be placed in this category. Eichrodt works with concepts, and while he is not oblivious to historical sequence, he is not in his

---

Reventlow, *Problems of Old Testament Theology*, 9; Jesper Høgenhaven, *Problems and Prospects of Old Testament Theology* (The Biblical Seminar 6; Sheffield: JSOT Press, 1988) 59–68.

67. Arguments of this kind are elaborated, with documentation, in Goldingay, *Approaches*, 79–82.

68. Barr, "Interpretation of Scripture," 196–98.

69. Will Herberg, "Biblical Faith as *Heilsgeschichte*," *The Christian Scholar* 29 (1956) 25, cited in B. Childs, *Biblical Theology in Crisis* (Philadelphia: Westminster, 1970) 44.

70. Childs, ibid., 39–44, 61–87.

overall development dependent on it.[71] Clements advocates that the Old Testament be seen in four dimensions: as a body of literature, as a collection dealing with cult, as a set of religious ideas, and also as a narrative of history. It is perhaps an overstatement to say that for Clements history is tangential, since for him the historical dimension is one of four. When compared to Wright, however, Clements clearly must be assigned to another part of the spectrum. Terrien, who is preoccupied with cult, is the one in this group who most sets history matters on the periphery.

Certain advantages accrue to minimizing history as a factor in theology. One avoids the entanglements of choosing between critically reconstructed and biblical history. One can also avoid the question, how does God act in history today? Moreover, one can forthrightly focus on theological constructs directly, as Eichrodt does with covenant, Terrien with the absence-presence motif, and Clements with law and promise. Each of these approaches has an immediate existential relevance. In one way, by concentrating on concepts and freeing themselves from the historical dimension, these theologians are more purely "theological." The approach of these writers, it could be argued, has biblical precedent. The New Testament book of Hebrews theologizes extensively from the Old Testament without resorting to a great extent to the story-line events recorded in the Old Testament.

But the limited attention these theologians give to the historical dimension must be criticized. To cite their shortcomings is in part to defend the use of history in theology, despite the problems listed in the preceding section. I am now turning the argument on its head to show why it is ill-advised to neglect history.

First, the Old Testament itself weaves a connected story. This story is largely told as history, history defined as temporal events, largely but not exclusively in the political arena. The major nodal points are familiar: Israel's Exodus, Conquest, Settlement, Monarchy, Exile, and Restoration. As Westermann puts it, "From beginning to end there is a path; we may say a history [*Geschichte*]."[72] Similarly G. E. Ladd writes, "It is the obvious intent of the Bible to tell a story about God and his acts in history for man's salvation."[73] Paul Hanson speaks of the "deep grounding of Israelite

---

71. Spriggs says of Eichrodt, "Eichrodt can be criticized for giving the impression that ideas are eternal and without historical roots, although he does usually contextualize his major discussions of themes" (Spriggs, *Two Old Testament Theologies*, 62.)

72. C. Westermann, "Aufgabe einer zukünftigen biblischen Theologie," *Erträge der Forschung am Alten Testament: Gesammelte Studien III* (Theologische Bücherei 73; Munich: Chr. Kaiser, 1984) 205, my translation; cf. C. Westermann, "Zur Frage einer biblischen Theologie," *Einheit und Vielfalt biblischer Theologie* (JBTh 1; Neukirchen-Vluyn: Neukirchener Verlag, 1986) 15, 21.

73. Ladd, "Search for Perspective," 48.

faith in historical events."[74] Biblical references to sources, for example
The Book of the Chronicles of the Kings of Judah, attest the interest of
biblical writers in documentation, namely annals. These records presumably were kept in Israel, as they were kept in other nations. Prophetic
messages were referenced via national and international events (e.g., Isa
1:1, Hag 1:1). Moreover, some of these references are verifiable in nonbiblical sources (e.g., Jer 34:7 in the Lachish ostraca; King Jehoiachin's
exile in the Ishtar Gate Tablets; Isa 20:1–3 in the discovery in 1963 by
Moshe Dothan of an inscription of Sargon II at Tell Ashdod).[75] This feature of history is striking when compared to religious literature from
other ancient Middle East or Asian religions. It is too striking not to be
represented in a theological summary of the Old Testament.[76]

Failure to stress the importance of history is to miss the distinctiveness of Israel's faith. W. G. Lambert, who concentrates on Mesopotamian
literature, noted that the Old Testament is distinctive in the far-reaching
plan with which Yahweh is associated.[77] True, earlier emphases on God at
work in history went too far in claiming that other religious writings did
not at all portray their deities as active in history, as Albrektson showed.
But even he notes the remarkable extent to which God's action in human
affairs is depicted in Israel. "It would seem that the idea of historical
events as divine manifestations has marked the Israelite cult in a way that
lacks real parallels among Israel's neighbours."[78]

Attention to history, especially to a comparison with Israel's neighbors, will sharpen the contours of a biblical theology. For example, Daniel

74. Paul Hanson, "Theology, Old Testament," *Harper's Bible Dictionary* (ed. P. J.
Achtemeier; San Francisco: Harper & Row, 1985) 1058.

75. It is true that nonbiblical documentation is not always available, though the extent
to which archaeology has supported many biblical statements is remarkable. Lemke, after
conceding some disparities betweeen the biblical record about the fall of Jericho and the
archaeological conclusion that the city was already in ruins in the thirteenth century,
states, "Today we have no good reason to doubt that there is a significant measure of con-
gruence between the actual events of Israel's history as critically reconstructed and the
way they were remembered in her sacred traditions." The extent to which such verification can be found is less than full, but documentation of some opens the possibility, if not
probability, that what is claimed as historical data might indeed be such and not fabrication or myth (Lemke, "Revelation through History," 45–46). Collins is simply too sweeping when he says, while admitting to some factual data here and there, "The biblical
narratives are imaginative constructs and not necessarily factual" ("Critical Biblical Theology?" 11).

76. Colin Brown, among many others, observes that history is the framework for
revelation ("History and the Believer," *History, Criticism and Faith* (Downers Grove, Ill.:
InterVarsity, 1976) 197. See his *History and Faith: A Personal Exploration* (Grand Rapids,
Mich.: Zondervan, 1987).

77. W. G. Lambert, review of B. Albrektson, *History and the Gods*, in *Or* 39 (1970)
170–77.

78. Albrektson, *History and the Gods*, 115.

Block, in investigating the relationship of deities to nations and comparing Israel and her neighbors, posits that whereas in the ancient Near East the linkage was between a god and a territory, with Israel the linkage was between God and a people.[79] Theological nuances readily emerge from attention to Israel's history.

Another compelling reason for giving priority to the historical dimension when doing Old Testament theology is that Scripture itself does so. Luke's prologue and Paul's discussion about the resurrection are cases in point from the New Testament (Luke 1:1–4, 1 Cor 15:14). The Exodus event, which figures large in theologizing, is referenced by Old Testament writers (cf. Psalms 77, 105, 106; Isaiah 51; Hosea 11). The book of Jeremiah theologizes extensively in the context of political events (e.g., Jer 18:1–12, 29:1–23). Deuteronomy, heavily theological (held by some to be the most theological book), is prefaced by four chapters chronicling history from which theological conclusions are drawn. The significance of the great historical works such as the Deuteronomic History is that "they serve to show with particular clarity what theology is in the Old Testament," namely that God is never abstracted as a concept but is one who is in a "reciprocal occurrence" within a context of "God and world, God and his people, God and a single individual."[80]

A further reason for giving greater attention to history than do Terrien and Clements is that to do so is one means of substantiating theological claims. The claim that God's intent is to form a people for himself is undergirded by the narrative of Israel's origins and subsequent development. As Goldingay notes, "Theological assertions appeal to events for their validation, the former depend upon the historical veracity of the latter, and thus the historical verification of the events will make possible the acceptance of the theological assertions."[81] Goldingay's inductive study from the book of the Kings leads him to formulate the verification principle: "If the history did not happen like this, then my thesis about our situation and about God is unproven."[82] The argument is identical to Paul's argument about Christ: "If Christ be not risen then your faith is in vain" (1 Cor 15:19).[83]

Similarly one might say that if the Exodus, clearly a foundational event, did not occur, then the derivative theological constructs are suspect.

---

79. D. Block, *The Gods of the Nations* (ETS Monograph 3; Jackson, Miss.: Evangelical Theological Society, 1988) 164–65.

80. Westermann, *Elements*, 215.

81. Goldingay, "That You May Know," 64.

82. Ibid., 80.

83. Cf. Kaiser's discussion, leaning for the phrase on G. W. Ramsey, "If Jericho Be Not Razed, Is Our Faith in Vain? (*Toward Rediscovering*, 61–67).

Kaiser puts it bluntly, "Without the Exodus there is nothing to the claim repeated 125 times in the Old Testament, 'I am the Lord God who brought you up out of the land of bondage.'"[84] De Vaux is representative of the traditional emphasis on the importance of history for faith when he says, "If the historical faith of Israel is not in a certain way founded in history, this faith is erroneous and cannot command my assent."[85] Wright was of the conviction that "to refuse to take history seriously as the revelation of the will, purpose and nature of God is the simplest escape from the biblical God and one which leaves us with an idol of our imagining."[86] The enthusiasm for history should be tempered somewhat, but the importance that history has as a substratum for faith needs to be affirmed.

W. G. Dever, however, takes issue with assertions that history is the "primary data of faith." He considers debatable the premise that "faith is dependent on, or at least enhanced by, a demonstration of the historicity of events."[87] True, not every theological claim that is drawn from a historical event is necessarily valid. And while the relationship between faith and history is complex, Paul's argument about the resurrection (cited above) undercuts Dever's assertion.[88]

Zimmerli notes the frequency of the phrase in Ezekiel "and you (they) shall know that I am the Lord." He investigates the premise from which this conclusion follows and finds that it is an act of God, almost always in the political arena. Significantly it is not through speculation, but through an event, that God makes himself known.[89] Theological conclusions, contrary to Dever, are dependent on the historicity of

84. Ibid., 67.

85. Roland de Vaux, "Method in the Study of Early Hebrew History," *The Bible in Modern Scholarship* (ed. J. P. Hyatt; Nashville: Abingdon, 1965) 16; cited in Kaiser, *Toward Rediscovering*, 61.

86. Wright, *God Who Acts*, 58.

87. W. Dever, "Syro-Palestinian and Biblical Archaeology," *The Hebrew Bible and Its Modern Interpreters* (ed. D. A. Knight and G. M. Tucker; Philadelphia: Fortress/Chico, Cal.: Scholars Press, 1985) 58.

88. The authoritative nature of any theology may be argued on grounds other than history, of course. Cf. Ladd's conclusions that his faith is not in history: "In the end I accept the biblical story not because of logical demonstration or historical reasoning [and then quoting Otto Piper] 'but rather on account of an inner quality of the Gospel, namely its truthfulness. The latter so overpowers me that I am rendered willing to stake the rest of my life on the message and to live in accordance with it'" (Ladd, "Search for Perspective," 56).

Clements locates the authoritative nature of theology in the canonization process (*Old Testament Theology*, 15–19). Similarly Hanson enlarges on the community from the earliest times as the legitimator for faith claims ("Theology, Old Testament," 1061–62). Such considerations for validating theological claims have their place, but in the light of the Bible's attention to event and history, they cannot displace the authority which is rooted in actual historical occurrences.

89. W. Zimmerli, *I Am Yahweh* (Atlanta: John Knox, 1982) 89–91.

events. Lemke places Zimmerli's conclusions on a wider platform when he observes that with this emphasis on the historical, the Judeo-Christian faith stands in contrast to other major religious traditions, for at their center may stand a "philosophical metaphysic, a system of ethics, or a written code of conduct."[90] But characteristic of biblical faith is its attention to history. Given this attention to events, Clements' picture is therefore less than adequate when he portrays God with a minimum of attention to historical narrative.[91]

Finally, the practice of theologizing self-consciously within an Old Testament matrix of history can be commended because a ready bridge is thereby provided from the Old Testament to the New Testament. The events described in the Old Testament lean forward in expectation of the New. The New Testament in turn, as in the fulfilment passages in Matthew (e.g., Matt 2:5, 15) or the historical reviews in Acts (e.g., Acts 2:14–36, 7:2–53), reaches back to the Old.[92] A theology of the Old Testament should be a stage in formulating a biblical theology, and for this purpose theologizing should pay major attention to the rubric of history. For all their power, the theologies of Terrien, Clements, and even Eichrodt might have been more compelling still if the dimension of history, for reasons listed, had been brought in from the wings to center stage.

History as the Primary but Not Exclusive Datum for Theology

Between those who place all of their theological eggs in the basket of history and those who marginalize the historical dimension, there are those who give history a lead but not exclusive position. Westermann is in this camp. The format of his book *Elements of Old Testament Theology* is indicative of his position. Following an introductory chapter, "What Does the Old Testament say about God?" he opens with "The Saving God and History." In so doing he places the category of history in strategic position, as the Scriptures themselves do. Westermann is not unduly preoccupied with the category of history, however, since he supplements it with other elements, but he nevertheless weights history heavily.

---

90. Lemke, "Revelation through History," 46.

91. Clements addresses "the Being of God" by discussing anthropomorphic language, sexuality, and morality and then expands on the names of God, the presence of God, and the uniqueness of God (monotheism) (*Old Testament Theology*, 58–78).

92. As J. Bright explained, the two testaments might be considered a two-act play. Act I is clearer in the light of Act II, and Act II apart from Act I would be less than understandable (*The Authority of the Old Testament* [Nashville: Abingdon, 1967] 202–3).

Of the approaches described in this essay, the last is the one most to be commended. An approach like Westermann's takes account of the importance of history (as spelled out in the preceding section) and so avoids marginalizing the historical (as does Terrien). Moreover, an approach like Westermann's is more balanced than Wright's, whose theologizing is exclusively hooked to the historical. To commend Westermann is not necessarily to endorse his view wholesale, but it is to affirm the way in which he goes about incorporating history into a biblical theology.

The argument for the desired balance, in which history is given a primary but not exclusive role in theology, may be made along several lines. First, the widespread cultural fixation on the discipline of history characteristic of the earlier part of the twentieth century needs to be acknowledged. Prior to the middle decades of the twentieth century, an ethos favorable to history dominated the culture. In liberal arts colleges, courses in history (ancient world, European, American, religious, and political) were popular. Attention to the past was said to facilitate an understanding of the present. The academic discipline of history was accorded an honored position. Said J. Reumann, "History is God nowadays."[93] Reventlow quotes E. G. Ebeling, "For modern man everything, the whole of reality, turns to history."[94] This honored position accorded to history was influential in biblical studies. For example, G. Wenham defined biblical theology (crudely, he admitted), as "a theology of history."[95]

This enthusiasm for the historical, however, should be tempered. It is sobering to recognize that in the Hebrew language there is no word clearly equivalent to the English word *history*.[96] Let it be noted that Asian and African biblical theologies have not sensed the need to be as closely wedded to the historical dimension as have the Western. Other social science disciplines have risen to challenge history in importance: sociology,

93. J. Reumann, "*Oikonomia*: Terms in Paul in Comparison with Lucan *Heilsgeschichte*," *NTS* 13 (1966–67) 147–67.

94. E. G. Ebeling, "The World as History," in *Word and Faith* (ed. E. G. Ebeling; Philadelphia, Fortress, 1984) 363. Reventlow also cites von Rad: "If I am right, we are nowadays in serious danger of looking at the theological problems of the Old Testament far too one-sidedly in terms of theology of history" (Reventlow, *Problems of Old Testament Theology*, 111). However, the translation of von Rad by Dicken reads, "If I am right, we are nowadays in serious danger of looking at the theological problems of the Old Testament far too much from the one-sided standpoint of an historically conditioned theology" (G. von Rad, "Some Aspects of the Old Testament World-View" [originally pub. in German in 1964], *The Problem of the Hexateuch and Other Essays* [trans. E. W. Trueman Dicken; London: SCM, 1984] 144).

95. Gordon Wenham, "History and the Old Testament," *History, Criticism and Faith* (Downers Grove, Ill.: InterVarsity, 1976) 21.

96. Barr, "The Interpretation of Scripture," 200.

anthropology, and psychology. The effect on biblical studies, in many ways wholesome, has been the appropriation of insights from these sciences. Theologizing, it becomes clear, does not need to be confined to explications of historical phenomena. For example, John Gammie provides a treatise on holiness, but his ground plan for elaborating on the subject is sociological: nuances provided by the priests, the prophets, the sages, and the apocalypticists.[97] My argument is not that historical investigation should now yield its place totally to anthropology or any other discipline, but that theological constructs are not built solely from biblical history.

One of these bases, in addition to sociology, is literary analysis. Of late a renewed emphasis on story has emerged.[98] Not at all new is the notion that a theological message can be conveyed through story, as in the case of a parable. Truth can also be transmitted through poetic drama, as in Job. The new trend in recent scholarship is to concentrate on the artistry of biblical story and also, for that matter, on artistry in historiography.[99] More recent also are the suggestions that the Bible is history-like and may be treated as story, setting aside questions of factuality.[100] Already in the late 1970s Collins could say, "The discussion of this [history-like] material in recent biblical theology has gradually shifted from an insistence on its historical reliability to an appreciation of its literary form."[101] The suggestion in its baldest form, to substitute *story* for *history*, is clearly to be resisted, for it undercuts the Scripture's witness, which is to a real God in real history.[102] Still the emphasis on the literary dimension of the Bible is helpful in moderating the obsession with history.

97. John G. Gammie, *Holiness in Israel* (Minneapolis: Fortress, 1989).

98. E.g., R. Alter, *The Art of Biblical Narrative* (New York: Basic Books, 1981); Adele Berlin, *Poetics and Interpretation of Biblical Narrative* (Sheffield: Almond, 1983; reprinted, Winona Lake, Ind.: Eisenbrauns, 1994); Meir Sternberg, *The Poetics of Biblical Narrative: Ideological Literature and the Drama of Reading* (Bloomington: Indiana University Press, 1985); Tremper Longman III, *Literary Approaches to Biblical Interpretation* (Grand Rapids, Mich.: Zondervan, 1987).

99. E.g., R. Polzin, *Samuel and the Deuteronomist* (San Francisco: Harper & Row, 1989); V. Philips Long, *The Reign and Rejection of King Saul: A Case for Literary and Theological Coherence* (SBLDS 118; Atlanta: Scholars Press, 1989).

100. The phrase is from Hans Frei, as noted by Swartley. Swartley suggests a preferable term, "narrative-borne history" (W. Swartley, "Beyond the Historical Critical Method," in *Essays in Biblical Interpretation: Anabaptist and Mennonite Perspectives* [Elkhart, Ind.: Institute of Mennonite Studies, 1984], 262).

101. J. J. Collins, "The 'Historical' Character of the Old Testament in Recent Biblical Theology," *CBQ* 41 (1979) 186; cf. p. 194, where he notes that the problems in von Rad's work made it inevitable that biblical theology should move away from the category of history.

102. Willard Swartley puts it graphically: "The God of the Bible does not merely ride in a literary cloud over the blood and guts of historical struggle and eschatological promise" ("Beyond the Historical Critical Method," 257).

In still another way, tempering of history-centered theology is desirable. Not all reported events are equally crucial in building a theology. Goldingay helpfully points out that the theology of the Deuteronomist, as laid out in the book of the Kings, is dependent on the historicity of the Exile. The book of Job is a different case. The event in question in Job did not occur in the public arena of nationhood and politics but in the arena of privacy and family. The function of the book of Job is to select an individual, representative of humankind generally, and by means of a dramatic narrative make a statement about theodicy. The argument in Job, Goldingay points out, appeals to creation, not history. The historical verifiability of the individual Job is not nearly as crucial for theology as is the historicity of the Exodus or the Exile.[103] Is there not some skewing of perspective if for every pericope of the Old Testament, one insists on first processing questions of historicity? If I may compare a commentary on Genesis, in which historical and archaeological considerations are emphasized,[104] with another book that focuses on the literary arrangements of Genesis,[105] the theological insights seem to me to flow more easily from the literary treatment.[106] In other words, the amount of value that theology can derive from historical analysis varies with each biblical text.

Thus a balance may be achieved on the one hand by tempering the intensity of focus on history and on the other hand by focusing on other genres as well as history. Other genres include drama, poetry, and law. Admittedly, biblical theologians who have stressed the salvation dimension of Old Testament theology (people of God, faith, and promise/fulfillment) by following the threads of history have tended to minimize the place of wisdom, cult, and law. James Barr's critique of a history-preoccupied theology must be heeded:[107] a fixation on history results in theological blind spots.

---

103. Goldingay, "That You May Know," 78–81.

104. E.g., H. Stigers, *A Commentary on Genesis* (Grand Rapids, Mich.: Zondervan, 1976), where for example regarding Genesis 14, it is said: "Thus the impact of the archaeological evidence—buildings and artifacts—and written materials is conclusive that Genesis 14 is entirely factual" (p. 148).

105. Thomas Mann, *The Book of the Torah* (Atlanta: John Knox, 1988). Cf. Eugene Roop, *Genesis* (Scottdale, Pa.: Herald, 1987).

106. Similarly Dewey Beegle discusses the ten plagues by trying to "explain" them historically (or apologetically?) (*Moses, the Servant of Yahweh* [Grand Rapids, Mich.: Eerdmans, 1972], 85ff.). In contrast, John I. Durham operates within a literary frame of "tradition" and "form" without an attempt to discuss the historicity questions. "The determination of any exact historical context for events mentioned in the Book of Exodus thus remains impossible" (*Exodus* [WBC 3; Waco Tex.: Word, 1987], xxvi). "Whatever may be the irrecoverable foundation sequence of the proof-of-Presence acts, the sequence of the text at hand is plain" (p. 108).

107. J. Barr, "Story and History in Biblical Theology," *JR* 56 (1976) 72–76. In seeking to curb the enthusiasm for history, however, Barr goes too far when he writes: "I am

One of these blind spots has been identified by Westermann. He notes that in addition to depicting God as saving throughout history (*Heilsgeschichte*), the Bible also depicts God as blessing. Whereas his saving work is punctiliar and interventionist (history category), God's activity of blessing is ongoing (category of providence). In the Pentateuch, Westermann points out, the books of Exodus and Numbers are oriented toward events, whereas in Genesis and Deuteronomy, which bracket the Pentateuch, *blessing* (a nonhistory category) is a dominant theme. By documenting the extent to which *blessing* functions in the Bible, Westermann highlights the nonhistorical elements, such as productivity and fruitfulness in nature, and even the environment generally.[108] A Salvation History–oriented theology has tilted students of the Bible away from a nature-oriented theology, from concerns for creation and stewardship of the earth. The modern agenda, highlighted by the ecological crisis (e.g., ozone layer) and the possibility of nuclear war, receives scant help from a history-dominated theology. In crisis times the prophetic appeal may be to history, as in Hosea, but it may also be to nature and creation, as in Isaiah (chaps. 40–66) or Job. While giving attention to the Exodus experience, theologians must not muffle the message in Genesis or the Psalms on the subject of blessing, a subject that will lead directly to environmental concerns.[109]

The kind of balance Westermann advocates in integrating history with theology is achieved by putting weight on the text, rather than on the event behind the text. If the text deals with an event, it is of considerable interest and is sometimes even crucial that further information about the event itself be supplied. But past events cannot be recreated, and what is available for study is, finally, the text. Moreover, today's reader, because of his or her cultural ethos, may be more fascinated by the text itself than the history behind the text. Fewer uncertainties attach to the text than to the event behind the text. If the reins are pulled in on history, it is in order to forestall a misguided venture caused by devoting excessive energy either to the history of the text or to the verification of

---

simply denying that it [history] can be the principal organizing conceptual bracket with which to view the material as a whole and to identify the common and essential features within its variety" ("Interpretation of Scripture," 198).

108. C. Westermann, *Blessing in the Bible and in the Life of the Church* (Philadelphia: Fortress, 1978) 26–59; and idem, *Elements*, chap. 3.

109. R. Knierim, after lamenting the one-sidedness of the stress on history, remarks that the realm of nature is "one of the most important modes by which Yahweh is manifested" (R. Knierem, "Offenbarung im Alten Testament," in *Probleme biblischer Theologie* [ed. H. W. Wolff; G. von Rad Festschrift; Munich: Chr. Kaiser, 1971] 229). For a compelling statement about the importance of cosmology in the Old Testament relative to history, see R. Knierim, "Cosmos and History in Israel's Theology," *HBT* 3 (1981) 59–123.

events. Polzin's word of caution should not be summarily dismissed. He observes that excessive concern with history may lead to an addiction that diverts effort from, for example, a close analysis of the text.[110] Fascination with historical verification can lead to relying on rationalistic methods, such as the historical-critical method, resulting in a theology subjected mainly to human reason.

Still, historical events are large components in the Old Testament, and so a theology of the Old Testament must give to them primary, though not exclusive, importance. This assertion is directed both to theologians such as G. von Rad, G. E. Wright, and W. Kaiser, who excessively stress salvation history, and to theologians such as S. Terrien and R. E. Clements, who minimize the historical. This position also parts company with theoreticians such as James Barr, who substitute "story" for history.

In short, my appeal is for the kind of balance exhibited in Westermann's approach. In this approach history is neither dismissed nor overplayed. Such a balanced approach will liberate theology from the tight grip that history has had on it in the Western world; will allow exploration of genres other than history, such as wisdom and law; and will afford more attention to historiography in certain pericopes than in others. Finally, a balanced approach will provide for an emphasis on creation, nature, and environment, which are being neglected, not only to the detriment of the globe's current population but at the expense of "rightly dividing the word of truth."

What the African proverb says about authority and governance is applicable to history and theology: holding authority is like holding an egg. If held too tightly authority results in tyranny, and like an egg, shatters. If held too loosely authority, like an egg, slips from the fingers and breaks, resulting in loss of control, anarchy. So also the category of history, when seized single-handedly to shape theology, tyrannizes theology. On the other hand, if history is held too loosely, responsible controls for theology are lost.

110. Polzin, *Samuel and the Deuteronomist*, 11.

Index of Authors

341

Index of Scripture References

350